The 50 Most Dynamic Duos in Sports History

Robert W. Cohen

TAYLOR TRADE PUBLISHING
Lanham • Boulder • New York • London

Published by Taylor Trade Publishing
An imprint of The Rowman & Littlefield Publishing Group, Inc.
4501 Forbes Boulevard, Suite 200, Lanham, Maryland 20706
www.rowman.com

Unit A, Whitacre Mews, 26-34 Stannary Street, London SE11 4AB, United Kingdom

Distributed by NATIONAL BOOK NETWORK

British Library Cataloguing in Publication Information Available

The Library of Congress has cataloged the hardcover edition of this book as follows:

Cohen, Robert W.
  The 50 most dynamic duos in sports history : baseball, basketball, football, and hockey / Robert W. Cohen.
    p. cm.
  Includes bibliographical references and index.
  1. Sports teams—United States—History. I. Title.
  GV583.C62 2013
  796.0922—dc23

[B] 2012030038

ISBN 978-1-63076-049-6 (pbk. : alk. paper)

∞™ The paper used in this publication meets the minimum requirements of American National Standard for Information Sciences—Permanence of Paper for Printed Library Materials, ANSI/NISO Z39.48-1992.

Printed in the United States of America

To Lily and Katie—my own Dynamic Duo:

Lily . . . your love and companionship
mean more to me than you could possibly imagine.

Katie . . . always remember to follow your dreams.

Contents

PART TWO: DYNAMIC FOOTBALL DUOS

PART THREE: DYNAMIC BASKETBALL DUOS

PART FOUR: DYNAMIC HOCKEY DUOS

PART FIVE: OVERALL RANKINGS AND CURRENT DYNAMIC DUOS

Acknowledgments

I would like to express my gratitude to Richard Albersheim of Albersheimsstore.com, Steve of Collectauctions.com, and George Kitrinos, each of whom supplied many of the photos included in this book.

Special thanks go out to the Pittsburgh Steelers, Indianapolis Colts, San Francisco Giants, Boston Bruins, Chicago Blackhawks, and Arizona Diamondbacks, as well as the grandchildren of Leslie Jones, who, through the Trustees of the Boston Public Library, Print Department, supplied several of the photos contained herein.

I also wish to thank Keith Allison, who generously contributed to the photographic content of this work.

Introduction

Inspiration for This Book . . .
and Definition of "Dynamic Duo"

Being an extremely structured and well-organized person (some might even say neurotic), I have always had a tendency to place things in what I perceive to be their proper sequential order. Even as a young boy, I recall assigning a numerical order to just about everything, from my favorite athletes to my favorite movies, songs, and musical artists. Therefore, people who know me well could hardly have been surprised that my first book, *A Team for The Ages: Baseball's All-Time All-Star Team*, represented a ranking of the greatest players in baseball history. Those people closest to me should now feel a similar lack of astonishment when they learn of my latest undertaking—a ranking of the most dynamic duos in sports history.

Yet, surprisingly, it was not my compulsion to assign a numerical standing to practically everything that provided me with the impetus to write this book. Instead, the idea came to me a few years ago after I watched one of the many top-20 countdowns presented on ESPN—this particular one dedicated to sports' most dynamic duos. Although the members of the selection committee made several wise choices, I disagreed with many others, feeling that they revealed a failure to grasp the true meaning of the term *dynamic duo*. Furthermore, I found several tandems missing from the station's list whom I consider to be among the most dynamic in sports history.

My first point of contention with ESPN's ranking centered on its exclusion of some of the greatest athletes who performed together more than 40 or 50 years ago. It seemed that such twosomes received recognition only if their accomplishments were so overwhelming that their names have since remained synonymous with their respective sports. As an example, the combination of Babe Ruth and Lou Gehrig received an appropriately high numerical ranking on ESPN's list of dynamic duos. But completely missing from the list was the tandem of Jimmie Foxx and Al Simmons, which was one that rivaled Ruth and Gehrig during the late 1920s and early 1930s. In fact, Foxx and Simmons provided most of the offensive firepower for a Philadelphia Athletics team that dethroned the Yankees as American League champions from 1929 to 1931.

ESPN's list also failed to mention several combinations that competed more recently than Foxx and Simmons but carved out a place in history greater than that of many of the other tandems that received acknowledgment. Hank Aaron and Eddie Mathews hit more home runs as teammates than any other duo in baseball history, yet they failed to make it into the top 20. ESPN recognized Mickey Mantle and Roger Maris, but another powerful pair of M & M sluggers from the same period—Willie Mays and Willie McCovey—failed to make the cut. ESPN's list also correctly included the basketball duo of Karl Malone and John Stockton. However, the even more potent pairing of Elgin Baylor and Jerry West, which performed some 30 years earlier, failed to receive recognition.

Another problem I had with the selections made by ESPN was the inclusion of several combinations whose contributions extended beyond the playing field. Among the pairings recognized by the station were Bill Russell and Red Auerbach, Branch Rickey and Jackie Robinson, and Muhammad Ali and Howard Cosell. The duo of Auerbach and Russell won nine NBA titles in 10 years as coach and player. But while Auerbach was a brilliant coach and the architect of that Boston Celtics dynasty, he didn't play one minute of any game the Celtics won over the course of those 10 seasons. Therefore, there is no way to measure the contributions he made to the team. In integrating the game of baseball in 1947, Branch Rickey and Jackie Robinson performed a service of incredible social significance to this country. They helped raise the social consciousness of most people in this nation, eliminating some of the barriers that existed and bringing us out of the Dark Ages. By doing so, they made baseball the true "national pastime." But, as with Auerbach, it would be impossible to measure the contributions that Rickey made to the Brooklyn Dodgers on the field, since he didn't play one inning of any game. Furthermore, the feeling here is that the significance of the contributions made by Rickey and Robinson to society as a whole places them in a separate category—one in which they would have to be considered number one on any list. And as for Ali and Cosell . . . they certainly formed quite a unique pairing: a Jewish attorney turned sportscaster who, in spite of his pompous attitude, really did not know a great deal about sports, and a charismatic Muslim prizefighter who arguably became the most recognizable man in the world. Ali and Cosell created magic together, making each other far more famous than they otherwise would have been in the process. But Cosell never stepped in a boxing ring, and the two men, at least in my opinion, represented much more of a form of entertainment than a dynamic sports duo.

While on the subject of Ali, the former three-time heavyweight champion of the world brings to mind my final point of contention with ESPN's ranking, which included a couple of the greatest individual rivalries in sports history. No rivalry was greater than the one between Muhammad Ali and Joe Frazier. Their three matches were among the most exciting in the annals of boxing. Their first contest in particular—held in New York's Madison Square Garden in 1971 and billed as a battle of undefeated champions—transcended the sport in that it was considered to be as much a social event to those in attendance as it was a boxing match. Two other great individual rivalries were waged on the tennis court. The countless matches between Chris Evert and Martina Navratilova helped to popularize women's tennis by generating a tremendous amount of fan interest in the sport. Two of the greatest beneficiaries of this growth in popularity were the Williams sisters, Venus and Serena, who dominated women's tennis for nearly a decade.

However, while individual rivalries of this magnitude in many ways represent the true essence of sports, it is my feeling that they do not form the basis for a "dynamic duo." That particular expression elicits in me thoughts of two extraordinary athletes striving for the same ultimate goal: winning a championship. Since boxing and tennis are among the numerous sports that are individualistic, I felt that their competitors could not be included on any list of dynamic duos. Such a list needed to be reserved for teammates who had the same purpose and who complemented each other in an effort to reach the pinnacle of their sport. Although Venus and Serena Williams occasionally team up with each other in doubles competition, they generally compete as individuals. Therefore, they were among the many outstanding athletes whom I chose to eliminate from consideration during the formulation of my personal rankings.

My interpretation of the term *dynamic duo* also prompted me to exclude great individual rivals who competed against each other within a team venue. Bill Russell and Wilt Chamberlain formed what may have been the greatest individual rivalry in the history of professional team sports. Although they remained friends off the basketball court, Russell and Chamberlain proved to be bitter rivals on it, with their classic confrontations having a tremendous impact on the National Basketball Association's growth in popularity. Larry Bird and Magic Johnson shared a similarly cordial relationship off the court, but they competed against each other with equal fervor some two decades later. Their individual battles and the corresponding rivalry that developed between their two teams— the Boston Celtics and the Los Angeles Lakers—helped to regenerate fan interest in the sport and reenergize the league during the 1980s. Yet, each member of these two duos competed against the other, with the purpose of not only outplaying his rival but also preventing him from achieving his ultimate goal. Therefore, I found it impossible to include either of these pairings on my list.

Also absent from my list are some truly great athletes who dominated their sport as individuals but were not fortunate enough to ever have a teammate that even remotely approached their level of excellence. Jim Brown is generally considered to be not only the greatest running back ever to play in the National Football League but also the greatest player in its history. He dominated the NFL as no other man ever has. But while Brown took the field with some fine players in his nine years in Cleveland, none of them excelled enough to share a spot with Brown in my rankings. Wilt Chamberlain proved to be equally dominant in the NBA, and he too teamed up with some outstanding players. In his first three years in the league, as a member of the Philadelphia Warriors, Chamberlain had Hall of Famer Paul Arizin as a teammate. And Wilt took the court alongside the great Jerry West in his last four full seasons in the league, as a member of the Los Angeles Lakers. But Arizin was in the twilight of his career by the time Wilt joined him in Philadelphia, and Chamberlain's greatest days were behind him by the time he became a teammate of West. As a result, Wilt's name is also conspicuously absent from my list.

The case of Chamberlain actually leads me into my last point regarding my interpretation of the term *dynamic duo*. Through the years, many truly great individual players have competed alongside each other at various stages of their respective careers. However, such pairings have often occurred when one or both players were no longer at their athletic peak. Consider two examples:

FRANK ROBINSON / BROOKS ROBINSON

Frank Robinson and Brooks Robinson served as teammates on the Baltimore Orioles for six years, from 1966 to 1971. Both men performed quite well in most of those seasons, leading the Orioles to four pennants and two World Series victories. They were particularly effective their first year together, leading Baltimore to a four-game sweep of the Dodgers in the World Series. Frank won the American League's Triple Crown that season en route to earning AL MVP honors. Brooks also had a fine season for the Orioles. But 1966 was really the only season in which the two men played together and were at the top of their games. Although Frank proved to be a productive player his five other years in Baltimore, injuries hindered his performance somewhat in 1967 and 1968. Although still extremely effective in 1969 at the age of 33, he never again compiled the same type of numbers he typically posted earlier in his career as a member of the Cincinnati Reds. Brooks remained a solid player well into the 1970s, but he was at his best from 1962 to 1967, and Frank was his teammate in just two of those years.

KAREEM ABDUL-JABBAR / OSCAR ROBERTSON

Kareem Abdul-Jabbar (then known as Lew Alcindor) entered the NBA in 1969. Oscar Robertson joined him on the Milwaukee Bucks the following year, and the two men led their team to the NBA title in their first season together. Jabbar and Robertson spent three more years together as teammates before Oscar retired at the end of the 1973–1974 campaign. Jabbar ended up being the league's dominant player throughout that period. But while Robertson remained an extremely effective player until he decided to call it quits, he was a shell of the man who proved to be the sport's greatest all-around player for much of the 1960s, as a member of the Cincinnati Royals.

Neither of these tandems earned a spot in my rankings, since it is my belief that the members of a dynamic duo should not only be two extraordinary athletes striving for the same goal of winning a championship but also two men who are either at or near the peak of their athletic abilities. Since that was not the case in either of these instances, you will not find either duo on my list. Nor will you be likely to notice any other such combinations in my rankings.

Selection Criteria Used to Determine Rankings

Having formulated my theory regarding the qualities that a true dynamic duo should possess, it became necessary for me to create a set of guidelines so that I might include only the most deserving combinations and then rank the ones that remained. The first matter to consider was the amount of emphasis to place on sustaining a level of excellence versus performing at a dominant level for a relatively brief period. Several pairings have excelled together for one or two seasons, but far fewer have maintained a high level of performance over an extended period. A few examples of duos that dominated their sport for only one or two seasons follow:

ROGERS HORNSBY / HACK WILSON

Rogers Hornsby was the National League's dominant player for much of the 1920s. As a member of the St. Louis Cardinals, he won six consecutive batting titles between 1920 and 1925, hitting over .400 three times and winning two Triple Crowns in the process. After being traded to the Giants at the end of the 1926 campaign, he spent one year in New York and another in Boston before being dealt to the Chicago Cubs prior to the start of the 1929 season. Hornsby hit 39 home runs, knocked in 149 runs, batted .380, and scored a league-leading 156 runs in his first year with the Cubs en route to being named the National

League's Most Valuable Player. That same year, Chicago outfielder Hack Wilson hit 39 home runs, scored 135 runs, batted .345, and led the NL with 159 runs batted in. The following season, Wilson led the league with 56 home runs and established an all-time major-league record by driving in 190 runs. However, Hornsby appeared in only 42 games for the Cubs in 1930 and was never again a full-time player.

CHUCK KLEIN / LEFTY O'DOUL

Philadelphia Phillies outfielders Chuck Klein and Lefty O'Doul were among the National League's best players in 1929 and 1930. In the first of those years, Klein led the league with 43 home runs; he also placed among the leaders with 145 runs batted in, 126 runs scored, and a .356 batting average. Meanwhile, O'Doul, whom the Phillies acquired from the Giants prior to the start of the season, hit 32 homers, drove in 122 runs, scored 152 times, and led the league with 254 hits and a .398 batting average. Klein was even better in 1930, hitting 40 home runs, knocking in 170 runs, batting .386, compiling 250 hits, and topping the circuit with 158 runs scored. O'Doul also had another outstanding year for Philadelphia, hitting 22 homers, driving in 97 runs, scoring 122 others, and batting .383. Klein remained with the Phillies another three years, performing at an extremely high level in each of those campaigns. But O'Doul was traded to Brooklyn prior to the start of the 1931 season, ending the outstanding two-year run of the slugging teammates.

KEVIN MITCHELL / WILL CLARK

After being acquired from the San Diego Padres midway through the 1987 campaign, Kevin Mitchell had a career year for the San Francisco Giants in 1989. In leading his team to the National League pennant and capturing MVP honors along the way, Mitchell topped the circuit with 47 home runs and 125 runs batted in while scoring 100 runs and batting .291. Teammate Will Clark finished second to Mitchell in the MVP voting, hitting 23 homers, driving in 111 runs, scoring a league-leading 104 times, and batting .333. Clark remained an extremely effective player for the Giants the next few years, but Mitchell never came close to duplicating his 1989 performance his final two years with the team.

BILL WALTON / MAURICE LUCAS

The tandem of Bill Walton and Maurice Lucas led the Portland Trailblazers to the NBA championship in 1977. Although Walton missed several games during the 1976–1977 regular season due to injuries, the center averaged 18.6 points in the 65 contests in which he appeared, and he led the NBA with 14.4 rebounds and 3.25 blocked shots per game. Lucas provided the perfect complement to Walton at the power forward position, averaging 20.2 points and 11.4 rebounds per game during the regular season. Lucas also averaged 21.2 points and 9.9 rebounds in Portland's 19 playoff games that year. Meanwhile, Walton posted averages of 18.2 points and 15.2 rebounds per game during the playoffs, earning Finals MVP honors by leading the Trailblazers past the favored Philadelphia 76ers in six games. The following season, Lucas further established himself as arguably the league's top power forward by averaging 16.4 points and just over nine rebounds per contest. Walton was even better, being named league MVP even though he played in only 58 of Portland's 82 regular-season contests because of a left-foot injury. During that 1977–1978 campaign, Walton averaged 18.9 points, 13.2 rebounds, and 2.52 blocks per game. However, while Lucas had one of his finest seasons for Portland in 1978–1979, Walton missed the entire season and then appeared in only 14 games in 1979–1980 before failing to play at all in either of the next two seasons. The big center was never again a full-time player in the NBA.

TOM BRADY / RANDY MOSS

Tom Brady and Randy Moss combined to lead the New England Patriots to a perfect 16–0 record during the 2007 regular season. Forming one of the most prolific passing tandems in NFL history, Brady and Moss established numerous single-season records. Moss caught 98 passes for 1,493 yards. He also recorded an NFL-record 23 touchdown receptions. Moss scored touchdowns in 13 of New England's 16 games, recorded nine 100-yard receiving games, and had six touchdowns of 40 or more yards. Meanwhile, Brady, who restructured his contract to free up space under the salary cap for Moss, led the NFL with 4,806 passing yards and a 68.9 completion percentage. He also broke Peyton Manning's previous single-season record by throwing 50 touchdown passes while tossing only eight interceptions. Both Brady and Moss earned Pro Bowl and First Team All-Pro honors, and the quarterback was also named the league's Most Valuable Player and the AP Offensive Player of the Year. New England subsequently defeated Jacksonville and San Diego in the AFC Playoffs, with Brady completing 92.9 percent of his passes (26 of 28) during the team's first-round victory over the Jaguars—an NFL playoff record. However, the Patriots' quest for a perfect 19–0 season came to an end in the Super Bowl, when the Giants defeated them by a final score of 17–14.

Brady missed virtually all of the ensuing campaign after he suffered a season-ending injury to the anterior cruciate ligament in his left knee midway through the first quarter of the season opener. Nevertheless, Moss continued to post outstanding numbers in Brady's absence, teaming up with backup quarterback Matt Cassel to record 69 receptions for 1,008 yards and 11 touchdowns. Fully healthy again in 2009, Brady returned to the Patriots to once again give them arguably the league's most formidable passing combination. Although Brady, Moss, and the Patriots failed to experience the same level of success they did two years earlier, they all performed extremely well. The team finished 10–6 during the regular season, with Brady completing 65.7 percent of his passes, throwing for 4,398 yards, and tossing 28 touchdown passes. Moss made 83 receptions for 1,264 yards and caught a league-leading 13 touchdown passes. Once again, though, the season ended abruptly for the Patriots when they lost to the Baltimore Ravens in the first round of the playoffs by a score of 33–14.

The loss to the Ravens essentially marked the beginning of the end to Brady and Moss's time together. Tension subsequently developed between the two players, which manifested itself early in 2010, causing the Patriots to part ways with the enigmatic receiver only four games into the campaign. While Brady has continued to thrive in New England, Moss retired in 2011, after splitting the remainder of 2010 between Tennessee and Minnesota, although he made a comeback with San Francisco in 2012.

* * *

Each of these pairings performed at a high level for a brief period, and at least one or two of them would have been included in my rankings had they continued to excel together over a longer period. However, since many other combinations performed at a comparable or even higher level for a greater number of years, it became impossible to seriously consider any of the aforementioned tandems for inclusion on my list.

Nevertheless, there are a few combinations that I included whose period of dominance proved to be relatively brief when compared to some of the other duos in my rankings. In such instances, the players involved generally reached a level of dominance that few others have attained. They may also have had a major impact on both the fortunes of their team and their sport as a whole. But the players likely excelled together for more than just one or two years. Still, in most cases, such pairings received a lower placement in the rankings than those that performed at an extremely high level for a considerably longer period.

While I seriously considered longevity during the selection process, I placed even more importance on the level of dominance that a duo reached during the time they spent together. The degree to which a twosome dominated their sport when performing at optimum proficiency proved to be a key factor in determining my rankings. Statistical compilation certainly played a role in judging the degree to which teammates excelled against their opposition. I placed considerable emphasis on the numbers that a tandem compiled during their time together. Taking this approach proved to be beneficial when comparing players that competed in the same sport. However, I needed to employ a different method when I moved on to the next level of rankings, which involved comparing players that competed in different sports. There is no way to draw a direct correlation between the numbers compiled by a baseball player and the figures posted by a basketball star. As a result, when comparing the statistical achievements of tandems that competed in different sports, I examined the relationship of their numbers to the figures compiled by the other members of their respective sports. Where did the players finish in the all-time statistical rankings of their sport? How many times did they lead their league in a major statistical category? These were the questions that needed to be addressed.

Still, statistics reveal only so much about players, since they invariably tend to present a somewhat one-dimensional picture of them and their accomplishments. Other factors needed to be considered in my attempt to ascertain the true level of dominance that a particular pairing achieved during their time together.

The degree to which the players influenced the fortunes of their team revealed a great deal about their level of dominance. The number of championships they won as teammates ended up being a huge consideration. But even if they failed to win a single title together, the players needed to dramatically improve the performance of their team by turning it into a perennial contender.

The amount of respect that the members of a duo garnered throughout the league also carried a considerable amount of weight. The most accurate way to measure something so seemingly incalculable was to examine the number of times the players were selected to appear on their league's all-star team. Equally important was the amount of recognition the players received in the annual MVP voting. Did either player ever win the award? If not, how often did the members of a tandem finish in the top five in the voting?

Finally, the legacy that the members of a duo created for themselves during their time together needed to be considered. How are they viewed historically? Have their names become almost synonymous with their respective sport? Did they reach a level of greatness together that only a scant few can even approach and to which everyone else can merely aspire?

The last thing that must be mentioned with regard to my rankings is that I elected to exclude known steroid users from my list of dynamic duos. The feeling here is that the legitimate accomplishments of great athletes should not be trivialized by intermingling them with the tainted achievements of men who elected to debase themselves by relying on artificial substances to enhance their performance. As a result, you will not find anywhere in my rankings the names of Jose Canseco and Mark McGwire (aka "the Bash Brothers"). Also absent are Barry Bonds and Jeff Kent, who formed quite a formidable tandem for the San

Francisco Giants from 1997 to 2002. True, Kent's name has never been implicated in connection with steroids, but few people doubt that Bonds would ever have been able to accomplish the things he did for the Giants from 2000 to 2004 without the aid of artificial stimulants.

I have also excluded Manny Ramirez and David Ortiz from my list. This is something I never anticipated doing when I first began formulating my rankings early in the summer of 2009. In fact, Ramirez and Ortiz placed fairly high on my original list. After all, they led the Boston Red Sox to two World Series victories between 2004 and 2007, clearly establishing themselves during that period as baseball's most potent offensive pairing. I even intended to include the two sluggers on my list, albeit at a much lower spot, after Ramirez tested positive for using steroids in 2008. But when it was later announced in 2009 that both men were among the 104 players who tested positive for performance-enhancing drugs in a 2003 survey conducted by Major League Baseball, it became necessary for me to reevaluate my position. Although Ortiz was anything but a dominant hitter in his first six major-league seasons with the Minnesota Twins, from 1997 to 2002, it became quite evident that the prolific numbers he posted for Boston from 2003 to 2007 were directly related to his use of steroids. Therefore, his name and that of Ramirez are nowhere on my list.

The only exception that I made was in the case of Alex Rodriguez, whose name was also on the list of 104 players who tested positive for using perfor-mance-enhancing drugs in 2003. A-Rod later admitted to using steroids from 2001 to 2003 as a member of the Texas Rangers. Yet, he also stated that he didn't use them prior to 2001 and that he hasn't used them since 2003. Ro-driguez's subsequent involvement in the Biogenesis scandal ultimately revealed the fallacy of his claims, exposing the fact that he did indeed continue to use steroids after he joined the Yankees in 2004. Nevertheless, no evidence has yet surfaced that would suggest Rodriguez artificially enhanced his performance in any way during his time in Seattle. That being the case, it was my feeling that he deserved to be on my list because he was a truly great player with the Seattle Mariners from 1996 to 2000, and he teamed up with Ken Griffey Jr. from 1996 to 1999 to give the Mariners one of the most dynamic duos in baseball history. Nevertheless, I found it necessary to drop A-Rod and Griffey somewhat in my rankings due to the former's involvement with steroids.

Now that the ground rules are established, we are ready to begin our evalu-ation of the 50 most dynamic duos in sports history. To create a greater sense of continuity, I elected to place the tandems into four groups, one for each major team sport: baseball, football, basketball, and hockey. However, after ranking the top twosomes in each sport separately, I then created an overall list of the 50 most dynamic duos in the history of professional sports, assigning them each a number from 1 to 50.

Part I

DYNAMIC
BASEBALL DUOS

CHAPTER 1

Babe Ruth / Lou Gehrig

It should not come as much of a surprise to anyone that the number-one tandem on my list of dynamic baseball duos features a pair of New York Yankees named Ruth and Gehrig. The arguments that can be made on their behalf are overwhelming. Babe Ruth and Lou Gehrig were among the greatest sluggers in baseball history. They are generally considered to be among the five or 10 greatest players in the history of the game. Both Ruth and Gehrig are usually ranked as the all-time greatest players at their respective positions. In their 10 full seasons together, Ruth and Gehrig teamed up to form unquestionably the most prolific hitting combination in baseball history. During their seven peak seasons together from 1926 to 1932, the two men led their team to four American League pennants and three world championships. In many of those seasons, they produced numbers in several offensive categories that far exceeded the figures compiled by every other player in the American League. Ruth and Gehrig served as the dominant figures on the 1927 Yankees, the team that most baseball historians still consider to be the greatest ball club ever assembled in the history of the sport. And they attained a level of excellence together to which later generations of players could merely aspire. Ruth and Gehrig accomplished all those things as teammates in spite of their extraordinarily diverse personalities and the extremely dissimilar approaches they took to their chosen profession.

Babe Ruth was already considered to be baseball's greatest player by the time that Lou Gehrig joined him in the New York Yankees starting lineup in 1925. After spending most of his youth in Baltimore's St. Mary's Industrial School for repeatedly running afoul of the law, George Herman Ruth was released by Father Gilbert to pitch for the Baltimore Orioles of the International League. Father Gilbert persuaded Baltimore's owner-manager Jack Dunn to become Ruth's guardian, causing the nickname "Babe" to become affixed to the rambunctious teenager. The Boston Red Sox purchased Ruth's contract in 1914, and the 19-year-old left-handed pitcher made his major-league debut with the team later that year, appearing in four games and winning two of his three decisions. Ruth became a regular member of Boston's starting rotation the following year, compiling a record of 18–8 and an outstanding 2.44 earned run average.

Ruth developed into arguably the best left-handed pitcher in baseball in 1916, helping the Red Sox capture the American League pennant by winning 23 games, completing 23 of his 41 starts, throwing 323 innings, and leading the league with a 1.75 ERA and nine shutouts. He punctuated his great season by contributing to Boston's World Series victory over Brooklyn, holding the National League representatives in the Fall Classic to just one run on six hits in his only series start, a 14-inning, 2–1 complete-game win. Ruth excelled on the mound for Boston again in 1917, concluding the campaign with 24 victories, a 2.01 ERA, and a league-leading 35 complete games. However, the Babe began to demonstrate over the course of that 1917 season that he also excelled at the plate, compiling a .325 batting average in his 123 at bats. Boston subsequently decided to expand Ruth's role as a hitter the following year, reducing his number of mound appearances and placing him in the outfield on those days that he didn't pitch. Ruth responded by excelling in both areas. In addition to winning 13 of his 20 decisions and compiling an outstanding 2.22 ERA, he batted .300 and led the league with 11 home runs, even though he totaled only 317 official plate appearances. Although Ruth continued to pitch sporadically in 1919, he spent most of his time in the outfield, batting .322 and leading the American League with 29 home runs, 114 runs batted in, 103 runs scored, a .456 on-base percentage, and a .657 slugging percentage.

Ruth's exceptional slugging soon made him the most popular player in the game, prompting him to hold out for more money prior to the start of the 1920 season. However, with Red Sox owner Harry Frazee unable and unwilling to meet the Babe's salary demands, Boston ended up selling the star outfielder to the New York Yankees for the unheard of sum of $100,000 in December 1919.

Finding the short right-field porch at New York's Polo Grounds to his liking, Ruth compiled astounding numbers his first year with the Yankees, placing among the AL leaders with a .376 batting average and topping the circuit with 54 home runs, 137 runs batted in, 158 runs scored, a .530 on-base percentage, and an .847 slugging percentage. Reaching a level of dominance never before displayed by any one player, Ruth hit almost three times as many home runs as any other player in the junior circuit. He also compiled a slugging percentage that exceeded the mark posted by the league runner-up in that category by 215 points. Ruth's incredible performance helped the Yankees win 15 more games (95) than they won the previous year en route to finishing a close second in the American League standings, just three games behind the pennant-winning Cleveland Indians.

Ruth followed up his fabulous 1920 campaign with an even better year in 1921, batting .378 and once again distancing himself from every other player in the game by compiling a .512 on-base percentage and an .846 slugging percentage while also establishing new major-league records by hitting 59 home runs, knocking in 171 runs, and scoring 177 others. No other player in either league hit more than 24 homers or compiled a slugging percentage that exceeded .639. Many baseball historians still consider Ruth's 1921 campaign to be the greatest ever turned in by any player. Although the Yankees ended up losing the World Series to the Giants, the team concluded the regular season with a mark of 98–55, capturing in the process its first American League pennant.

After disobeying an edict handed down by baseball commissioner Kenesaw Mountain Landis during the subsequent off-season, Ruth found himself suspended for more than a month of the 1922 campaign. He also missed several games due to various run-ins with umpires. Yet, he still managed to finish among the league leaders with 35 home runs and 99 runs batted in while topping the circuit with a .672 slugging percentage. The Yankees won the AL pennant again, but they were defeated by the Giants in the World Series for the second straight year.

Returning to the Yankees a humbled man in 1923, Ruth ended up appearing in all of New York's 152 games. Calling newly constructed Yankee Stadium home for the first time, the Yankees captured their third consecutive AL pennant, with Ruth earning league MVP honors by batting a career-high .393 and topping the circuit with 41 home runs, 131 runs batted in, 151 runs scored, a .545 on-base percentage, a .764 slugging percentage, and 170 bases on balls—an American League record. The Yankees subsequently won their first world championship when they defeated the Giants in six games in the World Series. Ruth contributed mightily to his team's victory in the Fall Classic by batting .368 and hitting three home runs.

The Yankees failed to repeat as American League champions in 1924, finishing just two games behind the first-place Washington Senators. Yet, Ruth had another great year, driving in 121 runs and leading the league with 46 home runs, 143 runs scored, a .378 batting average, a .513 on-base percentage, and a .739 slugging percentage. Babe was ineligible to win the Most Valuable Player Award since the AL had a rule in place at the time prohibiting any player from winning the award more than once. Otherwise, he likely would have been named AL MVP for the second straight year.

A serious illness caused Ruth to miss two months of the 1925 campaign, limiting him to only 25 home runs, 66 runs batted in, and 61 runs scored—easily his lowest totals since first becoming an everyday player in 1919. Babe's absence from the middle of the lineup for much of the year made a huge impact on the Yankees, who finished seventh in the Junior Circuit, 28.5 games behind the pennant-winning Washington Senators.

As disappointing a year as 1925 ended up being for the Yankees, it continues to hold special historical significance to the team. It was during that 1925 campaign that Lou Gehrig replaced Wally Pipp as New York's starting first baseman, beginning in the process his streak of 2,130 consecutive games played.

Henry Louis Gehrig actually made brief appearances with the Yankees in both 1923 and 1924, but he joined them for good in 1925 after graduating from New York's Columbia University. Playing in the team's final 126 contests, the first baseman hit 20 home runs, drove in 68 runs, scored 73 others, and batted .295. Gehrig appeared in every game for New York for the first of 13 consecutive times the following year, joining Ruth and outfielder Bob Meusel in the middle of the Yankee batting order. In his first full season in pinstripes, Gehrig hit 16 home runs, drove in 112 runs, scored 135 others, and batted .313. Meanwhile, a healthy Ruth returned to top form, batting .372 and leading the league with 47 home runs, 146 runs batted in, and 139 runs scored. The Yankees won 91 games to capture the American League pennant, but the Cardinals subsequently upset them in seven games in the World Series. Gehrig batted .348 and knocked in four runs during the series. Ruth batted .300, drove in five runs, received 11 walks, and hit New York's only four home runs, three of which came in a 10–5 game 4 victory.

Angered by their World Series loss to the Cardinals, the Yankees approached the 1927 campaign as if they had something to prove. They also benefited from the fact that Ruth rededicated himself to his profession during the off-season. Taking note of the outstanding power and overall hitting prowess that Gehrig demonstrated at the plate the previous season, Ruth felt challenged for the first time in his career by another member of his own team. Gehrig was eight years younger than the 32-year-old Ruth, whom many baseball people considered to be past his prime. Not wishing to take a backseat to anyone—least of all, one of his own teammates—the Babe worked harder than ever before during the off-season, reporting to spring training in better condition than at any other time since he first became a member of the club in 1920. The results became apparent shortly after the season got underway, as both Ruth and Gehrig waged an assault on the Babe's single-season record of 59 home runs, which he established six years earlier. A phenomenal month of September enabled Ruth to pull away from his teammate in the home run race, but the individual battle waged between the two men provided much of the impetus for New York's great season. Many other players had outstanding years for the Yankees, including center fielder Earle Combs, second baseman Tony Lazzeri, and pitchers Waite Hoyt, Herb Pennock, and Wilcy Moore. But Ruth and Gehrig served as the central figures on the team throughout the year, dominating the newspaper headlines as much as they dominated American League pitchers. These are the numbers the two men compiled over the course of that 1927 campaign:

Babe Ruth: **60** HRs, 164 RBIs, **158** RUNS, .356 AVG, **.487** OBP, **.772** SLG
   PCT
Lou Gehrig: 47 HRs, **175** RBIs, 149 RUNS, .373 AVG, .474 OBP, .765 SLG
   PCT

Ruth and Gehrig dominated the American League statistical categories, finishing first and second in the league in home runs, runs batted in, runs scored,
walks, slugging percentage, and total bases. They also finished first and third in
on-base percentage. Gehrig led the league in doubles (52), and he placed second
in batting average, hits (218), and triples (18). The performances turned in by
Ruth and Gehrig exceeded those of every other player in the league by such a
wide margin that no one else hit more than 18 home runs or knocked in more
than 120 runs. With Ruth still not eligible to be named the league's Most Valuable Player a second time, Gehrig ran away with the vote. Both men were named
to the *Sporting News* All-Star Team.

The Yankees proved to be equally dominant, compiling a regular-season
record of 110–44 en route to finishing 19 games ahead of the second-place
Philadelphia Athletics. They continued their dominance during the postseason,
sweeping the Pittsburgh Pirates in four games in the World Series while outscoring them by a combined 23–10 margin. Gehrig batted .308 and knocked in four
runs in the four contests, while Ruth batted an even .400, drove in seven runs,
and hit the only two home runs struck by either team during the series. Although
members of the Pirates continued to maintain years later that any such accusa-
tions were false, legend has it that the Pittsburgh players were essentially beaten
before they even took the field for Game 1. The story goes that they watched
in awe as Ruth and Gehrig repeatedly drove balls into the outfield seats during
batting practice before the opening contest. Feeling that they had little chance
to prevail, the Pirates put up little resistance as the Yankees quickly disposed
of their National League counterparts. The veracity of such a story is certainly
open to debate. Nevertheless, the fact remains that the Pirates lost the series
in overwhelming fashion and that Ruth and Gehrig knocked in more runs by
themselves than did the entire Pittsburgh team during the Fall Classic.

The Yankees repeated as American League champions in 1928, but this
time they received far more competition along the way, finishing only 2.5 games
ahead of the second-place Athletics. Ruth and Gehrig were again the league's
premier players, posting the following numbers during the regular season:

Babe Ruth: **54** HRs, 142 RBIs, **163** RUNS, .323 AVG, .461 OBP, **.709** SLG
   PCT
Lou Gehrig: 27 HRs, **142** RBIs, 139 RUNS, .374 AVG, **.467** OBP, .648 SLG
   PCT

Ruth and Gehrig again finished first and second in the league in home runs, runs batted in, runs scored, on-base percentage, and slugging percentage. Ruth led the league in walks and total bases, while Gehrig placed among the leaders in both categories as well. The first baseman also led the league in doubles (47), placed second in hits (210), and finished third in batting average. Since neither Ruth nor Gehrig was eligible to win the MVP award, the honor instead went to Philadelphia's Mickey Cochrane, who hit only 10 home runs, knocked in just 57 runs, and batted only .293. There is little doubt, though, that the two Yankee sluggers were the league's most valuable players. Both men were named to the *Sporting News* All-Star Team for the second straight year.

The Yankees once again vanquished their World Series opponents, gaining revenge on the Cardinals by sweeping them in four straight games. Ruth batted .635 during the series, drove in four runs, and duplicated his 1926 feat by hitting three home runs in one World Series game—New York's championship-clinching game 4 victory. Gehrig was even more productive, batting .545, homering four times, and knocking in nine runs—only one fewer than the Cardinals scored the entire series. Between them, Ruth and Gehrig hit seven of New York's nine home runs. They also drove in 13 of the team's 27 runs.

The combination of a superb Philadelphia Athletics team and an aging and substandard pitching staff in New York prevented the Yankees from winning the American League pennant in 1929, 1930, and 1931. The Yankees finished well behind the first-place A's all three years, even though they possessed the best offense in baseball in both 1930 and 1931. New York scored a major league-leading 1,062 runs in the first of those years, then followed that up by tallying an all-time record 1,067 runs in 1931. Ruth and Gehrig were at the heart of New York's attack throughout the period, compiling the following numbers:

1929
Babe Ruth: **46** HRs, 154 RBIs, 121 RUNS, .345 AVG, .430 OBP, **.697** SLG
    PCT
Lou Gehrig: 35 HRs, 126 RBIs, 127 RUNS, .300 AVG, .431 OBP, .584 SLG
    PCT
1930
Babe Ruth: **49** HRs, 153 RBIs, 150 RUNS, .359AVG, **.493** OBP, **.732** SLG
    PCT
Lou Gehrig: 41 HRs, **174** RBIs, 143 RUNS, .379 AVG, .473 OBP, .721 SLG
    PCT
1931
Babe Ruth: **46** HRs, 163 RBIs, 149 RUNS, .373AVG, **.495** OBP, **.700** SLG
    PCT

Lou Gehrig: **46** HRs, **184** RBIs, **163** RUNS, .341 AVG, .446 OBP, .662 SLG PCT

In addition to leading the league in home runs and slugging percentage all three years, Ruth finished among the leaders in runs batted in, runs scored, batting average, on-base percentage, and total bases each season.

After finishing second to Ruth in the home run race in both 1929 and 1930, Gehrig finally tied his teammate for the league lead in that category in 1931. The first baseman also placed among the leaders in runs batted in, runs scored, on-base percentage, and slugging percentage all three years. Gehrig led the league with 419 total bases in 1930 while finishing second in batting average and hits (220) and placing third in triples (17). Gehrig's 184 runs batted in the following year established an American League record that still stands. He also topped the circuit in runs scored, hits (211), and total bases (410) while finishing second in triples (15).

Ruth and Gehrig were at their very best together during that 1931 campaign, finishing first and second in the league in home runs, runs batted in, runs scored, slugging percentage, and total bases. The two men also finished first and third in hits, walks, and on-base percentage while placing second and fifth in batting average. After Ruth earned *Sporting News* All-Star honors by himself in 1929 and 1930, Gehrig joined him on the squad in 1931. With the rules governing the MVP elections having been altered to allow players to win the award multiple times, Gehrig placed second in the voting, while Ruth finished fifth.

Although the numbers that Gehrig compiled each year were comparable to those posted by Ruth, the former continued to perform in the Babe's shadow throughout the entire period. Gehrig's quiet, reserved, and dignified manner made him the polar opposite of the loud and rambunctious Ruth. Writers sought out the Babe for quotes, glorifying his every accomplishment with flowery rhetoric while overlooking his many vices, which included overindulging in food, liquor, and women. Meanwhile, Gehrig, a devoted son and husband, was largely ignored by the media—something he didn't mind in the least. Asked about playing in Ruth's shadow, Gehrig responded, "It's a pretty big shadow. It gives me lots of room to spread myself."[1]

However, Gehrig surpassed Ruth as New York's most potent offensive weapon in 1932. Although the 37-year-old Babe had another outstanding season, Gehrig posted better numbers in most offensive categories:

Babe Ruth: 41 HRs, 137 RBIs, 120 RUNS, .341 AVG, **.489** OBP, .661 SLG PCT
Lou Gehrig: 34 HRs, 151 RBIs, 138 RUNS, .349 AVG, .451 OBP, .621 SLG PCT

Ruth led the league in on-base percentage, and he finished second in home runs and slugging percentage. But Gehrig posted better numbers in every other category. He finished second in the league in batting average and total bases; he also placed among the leaders in home runs, runs batted in, runs scored, hits (208), on-base percentage, and slugging percentage. The Yankees won the American League pennant, finishing 13 games ahead of the second-place Athletics. Gehrig placed second to Philadelphia's Jimmie Foxx in the league MVP voting, while Ruth finished a distant seventh. On June 3 of that year, Gehrig became the only player in Yankees history to hit four home runs in one game. Yet, Ruth once again grabbed the spotlight away from his teammate in the World Series when he hit his famous "called shot" during New York's 7–5 game 3 victory over the Chicago Cubs. Ruth's home run proved to be easily the most memorable moment from New York's four-game sweep of the Cubs, and it was not the Babe's only contribution to his team during the series. He batted .333, with two home runs and six runs batted in. But Gehrig was the star of the series, batting .529, with three homers, eight runs batted in, and nine runs scored.

Gehrig clearly established himself as the Yankees' best player in 1933, posting significantly better numbers than Ruth in virtually every offensive category. Still, the Babe had an extremely productive year—the last in which he was among the better players in the game. Here are the numbers the two men compiled during the 1933 campaign:

Babe Ruth: 34 HRs, 103 RBIs, 97 RUNS, .301 AVG, .442 OBP, .582 SLG PCT

Lou Gehrig: 32 HRs, 139 RBIs, **138** RUNS, .334 AVG, .424 OBP, .605 SLG PCT

Ruth finished among the league leaders in home runs, on-base percentage, and slugging percentage. Meanwhile, Gehrig placed among the leaders in most offensive categories, topping the circuit in runs scored, and finishing second in runs batted in, slugging percentage, and total bases. The Yankees, though, finished in second place, seven games behind the pennant-winning Senators, enabling Gehrig to compile just the fourth-highest vote total in the league MVP balloting.

Merely a shell of his former self by 1934, Ruth hit only 22 home runs, knocked in just 84 runs, and batted only .288 in his final season in New York. Released by the Yankees at the end of the year, he ended his career with the National League's Boston Braves in 1935, appearing in only 28 games and batting just .181 in his 72 official plate appearances. Upon his retirement, Ruth was the major leagues' all-time leader in home runs (714) and runs batted in (2,213). He scored 2,174 runs, batted .342, amassed 2,873 hits, and compiled a .474 on-base percentage. Ruth's .690 career slugging percentage is the highest in baseball history. He surpassed 50 homers four times, leading the league in that category on 12 occasions. He also topped the circuit in slugging percentage 12 times, on-base percentage 10 times, runs scored eight times, runs batted in six times, and batting average once, surpassing the .370 mark on six occasions.

Long after Ruth retired from the game, his legendary feats continued to be recounted by those who had witnessed them. Hall of Fame pitcher Dizzy Dean stated, "No one hit home runs the way Babe did. They were something special. They were like homing pigeons. The ball would leave the bat, pause briefly, suddenly gain its bearings, then take off for the stands."[2]

Leo Durocher, who gained most of his notoriety for his managerial ability after his playing career ended, served as a backup infielder on the Yankees in 1928 and 1929. Commenting on his onetime teammate, Durocher later stated, "There's no question about it, Babe Ruth was the greatest instinctive baseball player who ever lived. He was a great hitter, and he would have been a great pitcher."[3]

Meanwhile, Tommy Holmes spent much of his career as a sportswriter marveling at Ruth's accomplishments. Holmes said admiringly on the day of Ruth's funeral, "Some 20 years ago I stopped talking about the Babe for the simple reason that I realized that those who had never seen him didn't believe me."[4]

Ruth's last year in New York was one of Gehrig's finest. The Yankee first baseman captured the American League's Triple Crown in 1934, leading the league with 49 home runs, 165 runs batted in, and a .363 batting average while topping the circuit with a .465 on-base percentage and a .706 slugging percentage. Gehrig also placed among the leaders with 128 runs scored and 210 hits. His outstanding season enabled the Yankees to finish second in the league, seven games behind the first-place Tigers. Yet the baseball writers somehow placed Gehrig fifth in the MVP voting, awarding the honor instead to Detroit catcher Mickey Cochrane, who batted .320 but hit only two home runs, drove in just 76 runs, and scored only 74 others.

Gehrig had three more exceptional years for the Yankees, performing particularly well in 1936 and 1937. He won his second MVP award in 1936 for leading his team to the first of four consecutive world championships. Gehrig led the league with 49 home runs and 167 runs scored that year, while driving in 152 runs and batting .354. He hit 37 homers the following year, while knocking in 159 runs, scoring 138 others, and batting .351.

Although Gehrig put up solid numbers again in 1938, his offensive production decreased dramatically. He hit 29 home runs, drove in 114 runs, scored another 115 times, and batted only .295. It later surfaced that Gehrig's declining performance stemmed from the fact that he suffered from amyotrophic lateral sclerosis, a disease that attacks the central nervous system. The fatal illness gradually sapped Gehrig of his strength, causing him to take himself out of the lineup for the first time in almost 14 years, on May 2, 1939, after playing in 2,130 consecutive games.

Two months later, on July 4, 1939, the Yankee captain made the most famous speech in sports history. Looking frail and weak as he stepped to the microphones in front of an emotional crowd at Yankee Stadium, the man known to fans everywhere as the Iron Horse told a packed house, "I may have been given a bad break, but, with all this, I have a lot to live for. I consider myself the luckiest man on the face of the earth."[5]

Both Gehrig's speech and the tragic manner in which his career ended have contributed greatly to his legend, often obscuring his greatness as a ballplayer. The Iron Horse ended his career with 493 home runs, 1,995 runs batted in, 1,888 runs scored, 2,721 hits, a .340 batting average, a .447 on-base percentage, and a .632 slugging percentage. He led the league in home runs three times, runs batted in and on-base percentage five times each, runs scored four times, doubles and slugging percentage two times each, and batting average and triples once each. Gehrig surpassed 40 homers five times, 150 runs batted in seven times, and 130 runs scored nine times, and he batted over .350 on six occasions. A tremendous clutch performer, Gehrig batted .361, hit 10 home runs, and drove in 34 runs in 34 World Series games. He holds the major-league record of 23 career grand slams. In addition to his two Most Valuable Player Awards, Gehrig finished in the top five in the voting six other times. He played on seven pennant winners and six world-championship teams during his career.

Yet, sportswriter John Kieran once wrote in the *New York Times*, "His greatest record doesn't show in the book. It was the absolute reliability of Henry Louis Gehrig. He could be counted upon. He was there every day at the ballpark bending his back and ready to break his neck to win for his side. He was there day after day and year after year. He never sulked or whined or went into a pout or a huff. He was the answer to a manager's dream."[6]

In their 10 full seasons as teammates, Babe Ruth and Lou Gehrig combined for 771 home runs, 2,748 runs batted in, and 2,569 runs scored. The two men were at their respective peaks from 1926 to 1932, averaging:

Babe Ruth: 49 HRs, 151 RBIs, 143 RUNS, .353 AVG
Lou Gehrig: 35 HRs, 152 RBIs, 142 RUNS, .347 AVG

Either Ruth or Gehrig led the American League in home runs in six of those seven seasons. One or the other also topped the league in runs batted in five times, runs scored four times, and on-base and slugging percentage six times each. Ruth and Gehrig finished first and second in the league in one of those five offensive categories a total of 18 times. The Yankees won four pennants and three world championships, and they failed to lose a single game in any of the three World Series they won. There has never been a more dominant tandem in the history of professional sports.

Notes

Numbers printed in bold indicate that the player led his league in a statistical category.

1. Fred Lieb, *Baseball As I Have Known It* (Lincoln: University of Nebraska Press, 1996), 169–84.

2. Dizzy Dean, http://www.baseball-almanac.com/quotes/quoruth.shtml.

3. Leo Durocher, http://www.baseball-almanac.com/quotes/quoruth.shtml.

4. Tommy Holmes, http://www.baseball-almanac.com/quotes/quoruth.shtml.

5. Lou Gehrig, "Lou Gehrig Appreciation Day at Yankee Stadium," July 4, 1939, http://www.baseball-almanac.com/quotes/quogehr.shtml.

6. John Kieran, *New York Times*, 1939, http://www.baseball-almanac.com/quotes/quogehr.shtml.

CHAPTER 2

Jimmie Foxx / Al Simmons

During their time together on the Philadelphia Athletics, Jimmie Foxx and Al Simmons didn't receive nearly as much media attention as their New York counterparts, Babe Ruth and Lou Gehrig. However, Foxx and Simmons were both among the greatest hitters of all time, rivaling Ruth and Gehrig as the most productive offensive tandem in baseball from 1929 to 1932. The two Philadelphia sluggers served as the primary offensive threats for a truly great Athletics team that captured three consecutive American League pennants and two world championships between 1929 and 1931, ending in the process years of frustration for Philadelphia fans.

Philadelphia A's owner and manager Connie Mack created something of a dynasty in the city of Philadelphia during the second decade of the 20th century. After capturing the American League pennant in both 1902 and 1905, Mack's Athletics won four more pennants and three world championships between 1910 and 1914. However, Mack decided to part ways with most of his best players after the team surprisingly lost the 1914 World Series to the light-hitting Boston Braves. Star pitchers Eddie Plank and Chief Bender were allowed to sign with the newly formed Federal League. Hall of Fame third baseman Frank "Home Run" Baker sat out the 1915 season over a contract dispute, before eventually being sold to the Yankees. The penurious Mack continued to break up his "hundred-thousand-dollar infield" when he sold 1914 AL MVP Eddie Collins to the Chicago White Sox.

Mack's frugal ways turned a once-proud franchise into the laughingstock of the American League. Philadelphia finished last in the AL standings each year from 1915 to 1921, failing to win more than 55 games in any of those seasons and compiling fewer than 40 victories on two occasions. The A's improved slightly in 1922, winning 65 games and finishing seventh in the eight-team league. They ascended to sixth place the following season, posting a total of 69 victories. But it was mostly the horrible play of the Boston Red Sox and the Chicago White Sox that enabled Philadelphia to climb out of the AL cellar. The sale of Babe Ruth to the Yankees and the subsequent distribution of most of their other top players to contending teams completely decimated the Red Sox. Meanwhile, it took the White Sox years to recover after many of their best players were banished from baseball for life for throwing the 1919 World Series to Cincinnati.

Entering into Philadelphia's sad situation in 1924 was Aloysius Szymanski, the Milwaukee-born son of Polish immigrants. After taking the name Simmons from a newspaper ad, Al Simmons first broke into professional ball with the Milwaukee Brewers in 1922. Mack purchased the right-handed hitting outfielder from Milwaukee at the conclusion of the 1923 campaign, and Simmons made his major-league debut in Philadelphia the following season. Simmons had an outstanding rookie year, batting .308 and driving in 102 runs, to help the A's post 71 victories and finish fifth in the American League—their best showing since their last pennant-winning season of 1914.

Fellow future Hall of Famers Mickey Cochrane and Lefty Grove joined Simmons in Philadelphia in 1925, making the Athletics a contending team for the first time in more than a decade. The A's ended up winning 88 games en route to finishing second in the league, 8.5 games behind the pennant-winning Washington Senators. Simmons had as good a year as anyone in the junior circuit, finishing among the league leaders with 24 home runs, 129 runs batted in, 122 runs scored, 43 doubles, and a .387 batting average and leading the loop with 253 hits, a .599 slugging percentage, and 392 total bases. For his efforts, the left fielder earned a second-place finish in the league MVP voting.

Simmons had another outstanding year in 1926, hitting 19 homers, driving in 109 runs, scoring 90 others, and batting .341. Philadelphia finished third in the American League, only six games behind the first-place Yankees, and Simmons placed seventh in the MVP balloting.

Various physical ailments limited Simmons to just 106 games and 406 official at bats in 1927, but he still managed to knock in 108 runs and bat a career-high .392. Despite winning 91 games, the Athletics finished second, 19 games behind the pennant-winning Yankees, who compiled one of the greatest seasons in baseball history. Nevertheless, Simmons placed fourth in the league MVP voting.

Simmons missed a considerable amount of playing time again in 1928, but he drove in 107 runs and batted .351, to help lead the A's to 98 victories and a close second-place finish to the Yankees. The Philadelphia effort was aided by a young slugger named Jimmie Foxx, who became a starter on the team for the first time that year.

Foxx first came up with the A's as a 17-year-old catcher in 1925. He garnered very little playing time his first three seasons, appearing in a total of only

97 games between 1925 and 1927. However, splitting his time between first and third base, Foxx played in 118 games for the Athletics in 1928, batting .327, driving in 79 runs, and scoring 85 others, in just 400 official plate appearances.

The following season, Simmons and the 21-year-old Foxx began a string of seasons together that ranked among the most productive in baseball history for two teammates. Foxx established himself as the Athletics' full-time first baseman and as one of the American League's most feared batsmen. Simmons, fully healthy again for the first time since 1926, continued to build on his reputation as one of the game's great sluggers. These are the numbers the two men posted from 1929 to 1932:

1929

Jimmie Foxx: 33 HRs, 118 RBIs, 123 RUNS, .354 AVG, **.463** OBP, .625 SLG PCT

Al Simmons: 34 HRs, **157** RBIs, 114 RUNS, .365 AVG, .398 OBP, .642 SLG PCT

1930

Jimmie Foxx: 37 HRs, 156 RBIs, 127 RUNS, .335 AVG, .429 OBP, .637 SLG PCT

Al Simmons: 36 HRs, 165 RBIs, **152** RUNS, **.381** AVG, .423 OBP, .708 SLG PCT

1931

Jimmie Foxx: 30 HRs, 120 RBIs, 93 RUNS, .291 AVG, .380 OBP, .567 SLG PCT

Al Simmons: 22 HRs, 128 RBIs, 105 RUNS, **.390** AVG, .444 OBP, .641 SLG PCT

1932

Jimmie Foxx: **58** HRs, **169** RBIs, **151** RUNS, **.364** AVG, .469 OBP, **.749** SLG PCT

Al Simmons: 35 HRs, 151 RBIs, 144 RUNS, .322 AVG, .368 OBP, .548 SLG PCT

Foxx and Simmons both finished among the league leaders in home runs, runs batted in, and slugging percentage all four years. In addition to leading the league in batting average in both 1930 and 1931, Simmons finished a close second in the 1929 batting race. He also placed among the league leaders in hits and total bases all four years, topping the circuit with 216 safeties in 1932. Simmons finished near the top of the league rankings in runs scored in three of the four years as well. Although the American League did not present an official MVP Award in either 1929 or 1930, an "unofficial" poll taken in 1929 named Simmons the league's Most Valuable Player. He also finished third and ninth, respectively, in the official MVP voting conducted at the conclusion of the 1931 and 1932 campaigns.

Foxx placed among the league leaders in batting average, on-base percentage, and runs scored in three of the four years. The first baseman established himself as baseball's dominant hitter in 1932, when he led the American League in six offensive categories en route to winning the Triple Crown and earning his first MVP award. Foxx and Simmons were at their best that season, finishing first and second in the league in runs batted in and runs scored while placing first and third in the rankings in home runs and total bases. The two sluggers were almost as dominant in 1930, when they finished in the top five in home runs, runs batted in, slugging percentage, and total bases. Simmons also topped the circuit in runs scored and batting average that year.

The A's became baseball's dominant team during that period, capturing the American League pennant in 1929, 1930, and 1931 and winning the World Series in both 1929 and 1930. Philadelphia ended New York's three-year reign as AL champions in 1929 by posting 104 victories to finish 18 games ahead of the second-place Yankees. The A's subsequently defeated the Chicago Cubs in five games in the World Series, outscoring their opponents by a 26–17 margin. Foxx batted .350, hit two home runs, knocked in five runs, and scored five others in the Fall Classic. Simmons batted .300, hit two homers, scored six runs, and drove home another five runs, four of which came in Philadelphia's 9–3 victory in game 2.

The Athletics repeated as American League champions in 1930, finishing the regular season with a 102–52 record, eight games ahead of the second-place Washington Senators. Although Foxx and Simmons were the team's two greatest players, they received ample support from Mickey Cochrane and Lefty Grove. Cochrane batted .357 and scored 110 runs. Grove led the league with 28 victories and a 2.54 ERA. Philadelphia defeated St. Louis in six games in the World Series, with Foxx and Simmons proving to be the hitting stars of the Fall Classic for the second straight year. Foxx batted .333 and won game 5 with a two-run homer in the ninth inning. Simmons homered twice, drove in four runs, and batted .364.

The Athletics captured their third consecutive AL pennant in 1931, compiling a franchise-best 107–45 record during the regular season to finish 13.5 games ahead of the second-place Yankees. Both Foxx and Simmons had outstanding seasons, with the latter leading the league with a .390 batting average. But Grove was the team's most dominant player, posting a record of 31–4 and a league-leading 2.06 ERA en route to earning AL MVP honors. Although the A's lost the World Series to the Cardinals in seven games, Foxx and Simmons once again carried the team's offense, hitting the only three home runs that the Athletics struck during the series and driving in half the runs they scored. Foxx batted .348, hit one homer, and knocked in three runs. Simmons batted .333, hit two homers, and drove in eight runs.

Even though the A's won 94 games and received phenomenal seasons from both Foxx and Simmons in 1932, they failed to win their fourth consecutive pennant. The Yankees put an end to Philadelphia's mini-dynasty by winning 107 games and finishing 13 games ahead of the second-place Athletics.

In addition to providing the Athletics with a superb one-two punch in the middle of their batting order during that four-year period, Foxx and Simmons absolutely terrified opposing pitchers. Despite possessing different batting styles, the two men had as much power as just about anyone, rivaling Babe Ruth and Lou Gehrig as the era's two greatest sluggers. In fact, Foxx was often compared to Ruth, while Simmons was frequently likened to Gehrig as a hitter.

Although Simmons stood just under six feet tall, he had unusually long arms, which provided him exceptional plate coverage, enabling him to drive the ball with power to all fields. The right-handed slugger hardly had a classic batting stance, often stepping toward third base before unleashing his powerful swing. The left fielder's awkward style of hitting earned him the nickname "Bucketfoot" over the course of his career, since he frequently appeared to be stepping in a bucket with his left foot just before swinging at the pitcher's offering. Ranked number 14 by Ted Williams on his list of baseball's all-time greatest hitters, the 210-pound Simmons was predominantly a line-drive hitter, but he also had outstanding home run power. Williams discussed Simmons in his book *Ted Williams' Hit List*: "Al Simmons had as much raw power at the plate as anyone who ever played the game. . . . When I looked at Simmons he reminded me of Gargantua. Of all the hitters that I saw with a bat, he looked the most menacing. Not big and heavy, just BIG! Big arms, big hands—a big, strong, burly guy. He had a bat as long as a barge pole and he'd stride up to the plate with that thing and scare you to death."[1]

Foxx was comparable to Simmons in stature, coming in at about 5'11" tall. He had a somewhat smaller frame, though, weighing approximately 190 pounds. But with his massive forearms, biceps, and chest, Foxx was perhaps the most muscular player of his era, possessing incredible power at the plate, which prompted others to frequently refer to him as "the Beast." Known for his tape measure home runs, Foxx was more of a pull hitter than Simmons, although he had the ability to drive the ball out of any part of the ballpark.

Ted Williams ranked Foxx number three on his all-time list, behind only Babe Ruth and Lou Gehrig (he excluded himself from his rankings). Williams described Foxx in his book: "When you talk about power, you start with Foxx and Ruth. . . . If anyone was ever capable of actually tearing the cover off the ball, it would be Double-X."[2]

Williams went on to say:

It sounded like cherry bombs going off when Foxx hit them. Hank Greenberg hit them pretty near as far, but they didn't sound that same way. They sounded like firecrackers when Mantle and Foxx hit them—and I never heard anyone say that about Ruth's or Greenberg's home runs. Foxx and Mantle were two guys from different eras, but I saw quite a bit of them both. I never saw another right-handed hitter, except Mantle and Foxx, really crush the ball—I mean crush it—when he hit it like those guys did.[3]

New York Yankees Hall of Fame catcher Bill Dickey corroborated the Splendid Splinter's assessment of Foxx, saying, "If I were catching blindfolded, I'd always know when it was Foxx who connected. He hit the ball harder than anyone else."[4]

Although Foxx hit many mammoth home runs, perhaps his most famous one came against Lefty Gomez at New York's Yankee Stadium. Foxx hit a long line drive that eventually struck a seat in the deepest part of the upper deck in left center field. Estimates revealed that the ball would have traveled well over 500 feet had its flight not been interrupted by the shattered seat. A stunned Gomez later commented, "I've developed a deep-rooted hatred for Foxx. He hit two of the longest home runs I've ever seen—and they were both off me."[5]

On one particular occasion, Gomez faced Foxx in a crucial situation at Yankee Stadium. As Yankee catcher Bill Dickey flashed his signs to Gomez from behind home plate, the left-hander continued to shake off his receiver. Finally, Dickey approached Gomez on the mound in an attempt to find out what pitch he wished to throw to Foxx. Gomez responded by saying, "Nothing. I figure if I wait awhile, maybe he'll get a phone call."[6]

A look at the numbers compiled by Foxx and Simmons during their peak seasons together reveals that any comparisons made between them and the tandem of Ruth and Gehrig were well justified. These are the figures that the two sets of sluggers posted from 1929 to 1932:

Jimmie Foxx / Al Simmons: 285 HRs, 1,164 RBIs, .350 AVG, 1,009 RUNS
Babe Ruth / Lou Gehrig: 338 HRs, 1,242 RBIs, .348 AVG, 1,111 RUNS

Although Ruth and Gehrig produced at a slightly higher rate, the disparity wasn't nearly as great as most people would probably tend to think.

Unfortunately, the pairing of Foxx and Simmons ended at the conclusion of the 1932 campaign. After failing to win the pennant for the first time in four years, Connie Mack elected to break up his team, much as he did almost two decades earlier. Simmons was the first to go, being dispatched to the Chicago White Sox. Lefty Grove and Mickey Cochrane were the next two stars that Mack peddled to other teams, with Grove being sold to Boston and Cochrane to

Detroit at the end of the 1933 season. Foxx remained the last link to Philadelphia's three championship teams until Mack finally sold him to Boston prior to the start of the 1936 campaign. The Athletics remained competitive in 1933, but they subsequently found themselves mired in last place much of the time from 1935 to 1946.

Simmons spent three years in Chicago, making the All-Star Team each season, and batting well over .300 while driving in more than 100 runs in each of the first two campaigns. He then moved on to Detroit, where he had an outstanding season for the Tigers in 1936. At the end of the year, Simmons was dealt to the Senators, with whom he spent his final two seasons as a regular. He split his final five years among the Braves, Reds, Red Sox, and Athletics, ending his career in 1944 with the team he came up with 20 years earlier. Simmons retired from the game with 307 home runs, 1,827 runs batted in, 1,507 runs scored, 2,927 hits, a .334 lifetime batting average, a career on-base percentage of .380, and a lifetime slugging percentage of .535. He led the league in batting average and hits two times each, and he topped the circuit in runs batted in, runs scored, and slugging one time each. Simmons surpassed 30 homers three times, 40 doubles four times, 200 hits six times, and 100 runs scored on six occasions. He drove in more than 100 runs and batted over .300 in 11 straight seasons from 1924 to 1934, surpassing 150 runs batted in three times and batting over .350 in six different seasons.

Foxx continued his onslaught on American League pitching for several more years. He captured his second consecutive MVP award in 1933, becoming in the process the only player in baseball history to win two straight Triple Crowns by leading the American League with 48 home runs, 163 runs batted in, and a .356 batting average. Foxx had two more extremely productive years with the A's before he moved on to Boston in 1936. As a member of the Red Sox in 1938, Foxx became the first player to win three Most Valuable Player Awards and surpass 50 home runs with two teams. In addition to hitting 50 homers and scoring 139 runs, Foxx led the American League with 175 runs batted in, 119 walks, a .349 batting average, a .462 on-base percentage, and a .704 slugging percentage. Foxx also performed extremely well in each of the next three seasons, before his skills finally began to erode in 1942. He spent his final three years as a part-time player with the Red Sox, Cubs, and Phillies, retiring at the conclusion of the 1945 campaign.

Foxx ended his career as the second-leading home run hitter in baseball history, trailing only Babe Ruth, with 534 round-trippers. He also compiled 1,922 runs batted in, 1,751 runs scored, 2,646 hits, and a .325 batting average. In addition to winning three Most Valuable Player Awards, Foxx finished in the top 10 in the balloting three other times, placing second to New York's Joe DiMaggio in 1939. He led the American League in home runs four times; runs batted in, batting average, and on-base percentage three times each; runs scored once; and slugging percentage five times. Foxx surpassed 40 homers five times, 150 runs batted in five times, and 120 runs scored eight times. He also batted over .350 on four occasions. Foxx hit more than 30 homers and knocked in more than 100 runs in 12 straight seasons, from 1929 to 1940. Alex Rodriguez is the only other player in baseball history to accomplish that feat.

Jimmie Foxx and Al Simmons were both full-time players on the Athletics for five seasons. In their four peak years together, they averaged 71 home runs, 291 runs batted in, and 252 runs scored between them. They also led their team to three pennants and two world championships. Had they spent more time together, the two sluggers likely would have mounted a serious challenge to Babe Ruth and Lou Gehrig as the most formidable twosome in baseball history.

Notes

Numbers printed in bold indicate that the player led his league in a statistical category.

1. Ted Williams, with Jim Prime, *Ted Williams' Hit List* (Indianapolis, IN: Masters Press, 1996), 119–20.

2. Williams, *Ted Williams' Hit List*, 67.

3. Williams, *Ted Williams' Hit List*, 67.

4. Harold Kaese, "Foxx in Many Halls," *Baseball Digest* (April 1951): 37–38.

5. Lefty Gomez, http://www.baseball-almanac.com/quotes/quofoxx.shtml.

6. Williams, *Ted Williams' Hit List*, 70.

CHAPTER 3

Hank Aaron / Eddie Mathews

Perhaps Hank Aaron and Eddie Mathews went mostly unnoticed during their time together because they didn't perform in a major media market. Maybe they didn't receive the recognition they deserved because they were both quiet and dignified men who played the game without much fanfare and lacked the charisma of some of their contemporaries. Aaron possessed neither the coy boyish smile nor the massive forearms of Mickey Mantle, and his home runs didn't travel nearly as far as the Mick's. Willie Mays, his cap flying from his head, ran the bases and tracked down fly balls with far more flair than Aaron. And Mathews didn't have Brooks Robinson's magical gold glove at third base. Nevertheless, Aaron and Mathews were their generation's most productive players at their respective positions, forming one of the most prolific offensive tandems in baseball history.

The only man to play for the Braves in Boston, Milwaukee, and Atlanta, Eddie Mathews made his major-league debut with the team at the tender age of 20 in 1952. Even before he joined the Braves, though, the left-handed-hitting third baseman drew praise from none other than Ty Cobb, who noted in the fall of 1951, "I've seen three or four perfect swings in my time. This lad has one of them."[1] Mathews batted only .242 for the Braves in their last year in Boston, but he hit 25 home runs and scored 80 runs. He had his breakout year when the team moved to Milwaukee the following season, leading the National League with 47 home runs; scoring 110 runs; batting .302; placing among the league leaders with 135 runs batted in, 99 walks, a .406 on-base percentage, and a .627 slugging percentage; and making the All-Star Team for the first time. The 21-year-old third baseman's outstanding performance helped the Braves improve their record 28 games over the mark they posted the previous season, enabling them to finish second in the National League to the Brooklyn Dodgers.

The writers acknowledged Mathews's contributions to his team by placing him second to Dodger catcher Roy Campanella in the MVP balloting.

Mathews had another outstanding year in 1954, hitting 40 home runs, driving in 103 runs, scoring another 96, batting .290, and once again finishing among the league leaders in walks, on-base percentage, and slugging percentage. Yet, even though the Braves won 89 games and finished third in the National League—only eight games behind the pennant-winning Giants—Mathews failed to place in the top 10 in the MVP voting.

A shy 20-year-old from Mobile, Alabama, named Henry Aaron joined Mathews in the Milwaukee lineup during that 1954 campaign. Originally a second baseman, the right-handed-hitting outfielder played mostly left field in his first big-league season, hitting 13 home runs, driving in 69 runs, and batting .280. Aaron moved to right field in 1955, and although he played all three outfield positions at different times in future seasons, he remained primarily a right fielder the rest of his career. Aaron had a big year in 1955, hitting 27 home runs, knocking in 106 runs, scoring 105 others, batting .314, and leading the league with 37 doubles. Mathews turned in an equally productive campaign, hitting 41 home runs, driving in 101 runs, scoring another 108, batting .289, leading the league with 109 bases on balls, and finishing among the leaders in both on-base and slugging percentage for the third straight year. Both men earned a spot on the NL All-Star Team for the first of eight consecutive times. Aaron also placed ninth in the league MVP balloting.

Both Aaron and Mathews had outstanding seasons again in 1956. Mathews hit 37 home runs, knocked in 95 runs, scored 103 others, and batted .272. Aaron was just as effective, hitting 26 homers, driving in 92 runs, scoring another 106, and leading the league with 200 hits, 34 doubles, and a .328 batting average. The Braves finished only one game behind the pennant-winning Dodgers, and Aaron placed third in the MVP voting.

Aaron supplanted Mathews as Milwaukee's best player the following year, establishing himself in the process as perhaps the National League's finest all-around player. Mathews had a solid season, hitting 32 home runs, driving in 94 runs, scoring 109 others, and batting .292. He finished eighth in the MVP balloting. But Aaron was the league's best player, batting .322 and topping the circuit with 44 home runs, 132 runs batted in, 118 runs scored, and 369 total bases en route to winning NL MVP honors. He also finished among the leaders with 198 hits and a .600 slugging percentage. The Braves captured the National League pennant and then defeated the Yankees in seven games in the World Series to win their only world championship in Milwaukee. Both Aaron and Mathews contributed greatly to the Braves' World Series triumph. Aaron batted .393, with 11 hits, three home runs, seven runs batted in, and five runs scored. Although Mathews batted just .227, he walked eight times, won game 4 with a

10th-inning homer, scored the only run in game 5, and doubled in the first two runs of game 7.

The Braves repeated as National League champions in 1958, finishing eight games ahead of second-place Pittsburgh. Mathews had a slightly subpar season, batting only .251 and driving in just 77 runs, despite hitting 31 home runs and scoring 97 runs. Aaron had another outstanding season, hitting 30 homers, knocking in 95 runs, and placing among the league leaders with 109 runs scored, 196 hits, 34 doubles, a .326 batting average, and a .546 slugging percentage. He finished third in the MVP voting and won the first of three consecutive Gold Gloves for his outstanding play in the outfield. Although Milwaukee lost the World Series to the Yankees in seven games, Aaron batted .333, with nine hits in his 27 at bats.

The Braves failed to win the National League pennant in any of Aaron's and Mathews's remaining years with the team, but they contended for the league championship each season from 1959 to 1961, losing a tie-breaking play-off to the Dodgers in 1959. They placed second in the standings again the following year, before slipping to fourth in 1961. Those three seasons were among the most productive in the careers of both Aaron and Mathews. Here are the numbers they posted in each of those years:

1959
Hank Aaron: 39 HRs, 123 RBIs, 116 RUNS, **.355** AVG, .406 OBP, **.636** SLG PCT
Eddie Mathews: **46** HRs, 114 RBIs, 118 RUNS, .306 AVG, .391 OBP, .593 SLG PCT
1960
Hank Aaron: 40 HRs, **126** RBIs, 102 RUNS, .292 AVG, .359 OBP, .566 SLG PCT
Eddie Mathews: 39 HRs, 124 RBIs, 108 RUNS, .277 AVG, .401 OBP, .551 SLG PCT
1961
Hank Aaron: 34 HRs, 120 RBIs, 115 RUNS, .327 AVG, .386 OBP, .594 SLG PCT
Eddie Mathews: 32 HRs, 91 RBIs, 103 RUNS, .306 AVG, .405 OBP, .535 SLG PCT

Both men finished among the league leaders in home runs and runs scored all three years. Aaron also finished near the top of the league rankings in RBIs each season, and he ranked among the leaders in hits, doubles, and batting average twice. Mathews also placed among the leaders in on-base percentage all three seasons, and he ranked near the top in RBIs and slugging percentage twice. The two sluggers were particularly effective in 1959 and 1960. In the first of those years, they both placed in the league's top five in home runs, runs batted in, runs scored, on-base percentage, slugging percentage, and total bases. Aaron also topped the circuit in batting average and base hits. Mathews placed second in the MVP balloting, while Aaron came in third. In 1960, they finished first and second in the league in runs batted in; they also placed second and third in home runs. Furthermore, both men finished in the league's top five in runs scored. Mathews finished 10th in the MVP voting, while Aaron came in 11th.

Although the Braves posted a winning record in each of the five remaining seasons that Mathews spent with the team, they mounted only one serious challenge for the National League pennant, in 1964, when they finished in fifth place, just five games behind the first-place Cardinals. Mathews remained a productive player throughout much of the period, surpassing 20 homers four times, driving in and scoring 80 runs three times each, and leading the league in walks twice and on-base percentage once. But after hitting only 16 home runs and knocking in just 53 runs in 1966, the third baseman was traded to the Houston Astros, with whom he spent the 1967 campaign. He then served as a backup on the 1968 world champion Detroit Tigers, before retiring at the end of the year. Mathews ended his career with 512 home runs, 1,453 runs batted in, 1,509 runs scored, a .271 batting average, and an excellent .378 on-base percentage. In addition to being a two-time home run champion, Mathews led the National League in walks four times and on-base percentage once. He topped the 30-homer mark a total of 10 times, hitting at least 30 round-trippers each year from 1953 to 1961. Mathews surpassed 40 homers on four occasions. He also drove in more than 100 runs five times, scored more than 100 runs eight times, and batted over .300 in three seasons. He appeared in a total of nine All-Star Games.

Shortstop Johnny Logan, who spent 10 years playing alongside Mathews on the left side of the Braves infield, said of his former teammate, "I think he was one of the greatest third basemen of all time. He had one of the sweetest swings I ever saw."[2]

As the career of Mathews began to wind down, Aaron continued to display the remarkable consistency that defined him as a player, compiling the numbers shown in table 3.1 in some of his best seasons between 1962 and 1971.

In addition to leading the league in home runs and slugging percentage three times each during that 10-year span and topping the circuit in runs batted in and runs scored twice each, Aaron led the league in doubles once and collected more than 200 hits in a season for the third time in his career. He also displayed his base-running skills by stealing more than 20 bases five times. Aaron became a member of the elite 30–30 club in 1963 by hitting 44 home runs and swiping 31 bases.

Yet, in spite of his brilliant all-around play, Aaron was not generally regarded as baseball's greatest player throughout much of his career. That distinction

Table 3.1. Hank Aaron: 1962–1971

Year	HR	RBIs	AVG	RUNS	OBP	SLG PCT
1962	45	128	.323	127	.393	.618
1963	**44**	**130**	.319	**121**	.394	**.586**
1966	**44**	**127**	.279	117	.360	.539
1967	**39**	109	.307	**113**	.373	**.573**
1969	44	97	.300	100	.398	.607
1970	38	118	.298	103	.389	.574
1971	47	118	.327	95	.414	**.669**

invariably was reserved for Willie Mays. And Mickey Mantle was usually ranked ahead of Aaron as well, until injuries began to catch up with the Mick his last several seasons. But in truth, Aaron took a backseat to no one in terms of his all-around playing ability. He didn't have Mantle's awesome power, and he lacked Mays's charisma. However, Aaron played the outfield exceptionally well, excelled on the base paths, and produced at the plate more consistently than either Mantle or Mays, hitting for just as high a batting average while typically driving in more runs.

While the other two sluggers generated much of their power with their arms and shoulders, Aaron's extraordinarily quick wrists enabled him to create tremendous bat speed through the hitting zone. Longtime Braves first baseman Joe Adcock once said of his teammate, "Trying to sneak a pitch past Hank Aaron is like trying to sneak the sunrise past a rooster."[3] Meanwhile, Dodger great Sandy Koufax nicknamed Hank "Bad Henry" because of the difficulties he encountered whenever he faced the Braves outfielder.

Mickey Mantle acknowledged Aaron's greatness when he said, "As far as I'm concerned, Aaron is the best ballplayer of my era. He is to baseball of the last 15 years what Joe DiMaggio was before him. He never received the credit he's due."[4]

It wasn't until Aaron began to approach Babe Ruth's career home run record that most people came to realize how great a player Bad Henry truly was. As Aaron drew closer to 714 home runs during the early 1970s, he gained the recognition that eluded him for most of his career. But fame has its price, and Aaron discovered that last fact when he began receiving insulting letters and death threats from hateful people who simply weren't prepared to have the most cherished record in all of American sports broken by a black man. The abuse that Aaron endured left a bitter taste in his mouth when he finally hit his 715th home run in April 1974. Instead of experiencing exultation over his tremendous accomplishment, Henry felt relieved, afterward telling the assembled mass, "I'm glad it's all over."

Aaron remained with the Braves until the end of that 1974 season, when he left Atlanta to return to the city of Milwaukee. He spent his final two years playing for the Brewers, finally retiring after the 1976 campaign. Aaron finished his career with 755 home runs, 2,297 runs batted in, 2,174 runs scored, and 3,771 hits. He is the all-time leader in RBIs, and he ranks in the top five all-time in each of the other three categories. Aaron compiled a lifetime .305 batting average. He led the National League in home runs, runs batted in, doubles, and slugging percentage four times each; runs scored three times; and batting average and hits twice each. Aaron hit more than 40 homers eight times, knocked in more than 100 runs 11 times, scored more than 100 runs 15 times, and batted over .300 on 14 occasions. He placed in the top five in the league MVP voting a total of eight times. Aaron was selected to 21 straight All-Star Teams.

Hank Aaron and Eddie Mathews compiled the following numbers in their 13 years as teammates on the Braves:

Hank Aaron: 442 HRs, 1,432 RBIs, 1,406 RUNS
Eddie Mathews: 421 HRs, 1,195 RBIs, 1,262 RUNS

Their total of 863 home runs is an all-time record for two teammates. In their 13 seasons together, Aaron and Mathews averaged 66 home runs, 202 runs batted in, and 205 runs scored between them. They combined to lead the league in home runs and runs batted in four times each, runs scored and slugging percentage twice each, and on-base percentage once. Aaron also led the league in doubles four times, and he topped the circuit in hits and batting average twice each during his and Mathews' time together. Aaron and Mathews combined for 13 top-10 finishes in the league MVP voting. One or the other placed in the top five in the balloting on six occasions. They also combined for 20 All-Star Game appearances as teammates. The Braves won two pennants and one World Series between 1954 and 1966, finished second in the National League four times, and compiled a winning record each season, finishing in the bottom half of the league standings just once.

Aaron later suggested, "We weren't jealous of each other at all. That's one reason we were so successful."[5]

Notes

Numbers printed in bold indicate that the player led his league in a statistical category.

1. Ty Cobb, http://www.baseball-almanac.com/quotes/quomths.shtml.
2. Johnny Logan, http://www.baseball-almanac.com/quotes/quomths.shtml.
3. Joe Adcock, http://www.baseball-almanac.com/quotes/quoaar.shtml.
4. Mickey Mantle, http://www.baseball-almanac.com/quotes/quoaar.shtml.
5. Hank Aaron, http://www.baseball-almanac.com/quotes/quomths.shtml.

CHAPTER 4

Willie Mays / Willie McCovey

Nicknamed the "M & M Boys" by members of the New York press corps, Mickey Mantle and Roger Maris received a tremendous amount of media coverage during their time together on the Yankees. However, another pair of M & M Boys proved to be equally productive over a longer period for the San Francisco Giants. Willie Mays and Willie McCovey established themselves as the National League's most dynamic offensive tandem for much of the 1960s, combining to lead the Giants to one pennant and five second-place finishes between 1962 and 1969. Mays gained widespread acclaim as the greatest all-around player in the game, while McCovey instilled fear in opposing pitchers more than perhaps any other hitter in the sport.

Already a legend in New York by the time the Giants moved to San Francisco in 1958, Willie Mays made key contributions to the Giants during their miraculous comeback that earned them the 1951 National League pennant. Appearing in a Giants uniform for the first time that year, the 20-year-old Mays struggled mightily with his self-confidence early in the season as he attempted to justify the faith that New York manager Leo Durocher placed in him. Things got so bad for the rookie during the early stages of the campaign that he frequently turned to roommate Monte Irvin for consolation, crying himself to sleep at night in the arms of the veteran outfielder and former Negro League star. However, Mays eventually righted himself, finishing the year with 20 home runs, 68 runs batted in, and a .274 batting average. His contributions during the season's second half helped the Giants overcome a 13.5-game deficit to the Dodgers, thereby forcing a three-game playoff between the bitter rivals that resulted in a Giants victory.

Mays spent most of the next two years in the military, appearing in only 34 games in 1952 and missing the entire 1953 campaign. Returning to the Giants in 1954, Mays led his team to the pennant and world championship, establishing himself in the process as one of the game's great players. Mays hit 41 home runs, drove in 110 runs, scored 119 others, and led the league with a .345 batting average en route to earning NL MVP honors. He punctuated his great season by making one of the most famous catches in World Series history during New York's four-game sweep of the Indians—a spectacular over-the-shoulder grab of a ball hit some 450 feet by Cleveland slugger Vic Wertz.

Mays had another superb year in 1955, leading the league with 51 home runs, driving in 127 runs, scoring another 123, batting .319, and finishing fourth in the MVP balloting. The center fielder also performed quite well in each of the next two seasons, surpassing 30 homers and 100 runs scored both years, batting .333, and leading the league with 20 triples in 1957. However, the Giants finished well out of contention both times, placing sixth in the final standings in each of those years.

With attendance falling off dramatically at New York's Polo Grounds and the West Coast beckoning, team owner Horace Stoneham decided to relocate the Giants to the city of San Francisco at the conclusion of the 1957 campaign. The move left Mays feeling disconsolate and dejected, since New York had become his adopted home. Possessing the enthusiasm of a young boy and an unmatched love of the game, Mays often played stickball on the streets of New York with the neighborhood children when he returned home at the end of the day. Heartbroken as he was, Mays joined his teammates when they journeyed west at the start of the 1958 season.

Even though Mays continued to play exceptionally well after the Giants moved to San Francisco, the hometown fans treated him somewhat indifferently his first few years there, since they considered him to be very much a New Yorker. They also resented the favorable comparisons being made of Mays to Bay Area legend Joe DiMaggio. The Yankee Clipper reached icon-like status while playing for the San Francisco Seals of the Pacific Coast League before he joined the Yankees in 1936. Local fans scoffed at the notion that anyone could be as good as DiMaggio, and they correspondingly reacted unfavorably to Mays. However, they immediately adopted 1958 NL Rookie of the Year Orlando Cepeda as one of their own, choosing to welcome him with open arms while simultaneously displaying little in the way of affection toward Mays. Nevertheless, Willie remained one of the finest all-around players in the game, having superb years in both 1958 and 1959. In the first of those seasons, Mays hit 29 home runs, knocked in 96 runs, scored a league-leading 121 times, and placed second in the batting race with a career-high .347 batting average. He hit 34 homers and drove in 104 runs in 1959 while scoring 125 runs and batting .313.

The Giants spent their first two years in San Francisco playing in old Seals Stadium, the same ballpark in which Joe DiMaggio made a name for himself some 25 years earlier. In 1960, they moved to Candlestick Park, which remained the team's home until well after Willie retired. With its cold, swirling winds, Candlestick Park presented a new challenge to Mays. Not only did he have to learn to perform under extremely adverse conditions, but he also needed to adapt his swing to accommodate his new surroundings. The gusty winds at Candlestick generally tended to blow in from left field and out toward right. The right-handed-hitting Mays soon discovered that it behooved him to become less of a pull hitter and to drive the ball more to the opposite field. Hitting the ball to right field was something Willie did with great regularity in subsequent seasons, slugging a significant number of home runs over Candlestick's right-field fence.

By 1960, Orlando Cepeda wasn't the only Giants player with whom Mays needed to compete for the affection of the fans. Big Willie McCovey won the NL Rookie of the Year Award one year earlier, even though he appeared in only 52 games for San Francisco. The 6'4", 230-pound McCovey hit 13 home runs, drove in 38 runs, and batted .354 in only 192 official at bats in 1959, enabling him to become an instant favorite of the fans. Yet, it wasn't until 1963 that the left-handed slugger earned a full-time starting job in the Giants lineup. Splitting his time between first base and the outfield from 1960 to 1962, McCovey often found himself sitting on San Francisco's bench against opposing left-handers, giving way to outstanding right-handed batters, such as first baseman Cepeda and outfielder Felipe Alou. When his name was entered on the lineup card, McCovey produced more often than not; however, he failed to appear in more than 106 games or compile more than 328 official at bats in any of those seasons. He was most productive during San Francisco's 1962 pennant-winning campaign, batting .293, hitting 20 home runs, and driving in 54 runs in only 229 official plate appearances. Meanwhile, Mays had some of his finest seasons during that period, posting the following numbers:

1960: 29 HRs, 103 RBIs, .319 AVG, 107 RUNS, **190** HITS
1961: 40 HRs, 123 RBIs, .308 AVG, **129** RUNS, 176 HITS
1962: **49** HRs, 141 RBIs, .304 AVG, 130 RUNS, 189 HITS

Mays finished among the league leaders in home runs, runs batted in, and runs scored all three years. His league-leading 49 homers and career-best 141 RBIs in 1962 helped lead the Giants to the National League pennant, earning him in the process a close second-place finish to the Dodgers' Maury Wills in the MVP voting.

McCovey joined Mays as a full-time starter on the Giants the following year, continuing to split his time between first base and the outfield the next two seasons until finally supplanting Cepeda as the team's regular first baseman in 1965. The two sluggers combined to give the Giants the league's most formidable one-two punch the next few years, compiling the numbers shown in table 4.1 from 1963 to 1966.

Table 4.1. Willie Mays and Willie McCovey: 1963-1966

Player	Year	HR	RBIs	AVG	RUNS	OBP	SLG PCT
Mays	1963	38	103	.314	115	.384	.582
	1964	**47**	111	.296	121	.384	.607
	1965	**52**	112	.317	118	**.399**	**.645**
	1966	37	103	.288	99	.370	.556
McCovey	1963	**44**	102	.280	103	.350	.566
	1965	39	92	.276	93	.383	.539
	1966	36	96	.295	85	.394	.586

Mays finished among the league leaders in home runs, runs batted in, runs scored, and slugging percentage all four years. He also placed near the top of the league rankings in on-base percentage three times and batting average once. Willie won his second Most Valuable Player Award in 1965, and he finished no lower than sixth in the voting the other three years.

McCovey had a subpar 1964 campaign, but he was among the league's most productive hitters in each of the other three seasons, placing among the leaders in both home runs and slugging percentage all three years.

Mays and McCovey were particularly dominant in 1963, both finishing among the league leaders in home runs, runs batted in, runs scored, and slugging percentage. They also finished first and second in the league in home runs in 1965. The Giants finished third in the NL in 1963, 11 games behind the pennant-winning Dodgers. They finished a close fourth the following year, only three games behind the first-place Cardinals. San Francisco then battled Los Angeles right down to the wire in both 1965 and 1966, finishing second both years by a combined margin of only 3.5 games.

The 1966 season turned out to be the last great year for Mays. Father Time finally started to catch up to Willie in 1967, and he never again posted huge offensive numbers. Still, Mays remained a productive player the next five years, averaging 21 homers, 70 runs batted in, and 81 runs scored from 1967 to 1971 while batting over .280 in three of those seasons. He was most productive in 1970, hitting 28 home runs, driving in 83 runs, scoring 94 others, and batting .291. Willie followed that up by stealing 23 bases in 1971 while also leading the league in walks (112) and on-base percentage (.429).

Strictly a part-time player by 1972, Mays was traded to the New York Mets early that season. He spent his final two years in New York, ending his magnificent career in the city in which it began some 22 years earlier. Mays retired from the game with 660 home runs, 1,903 runs batted in, 2,062 runs scored, 3,283 hits, 338 stolen bases, a .302 career batting average, a .384 on-base percentage, and a .557 slugging percentage. He surpassed 40 homers six times, topping the 50-mark on two occasions. He also knocked in more than 100 runs 10 times, scored more than 100 runs 12 times, batted over .300 on 10 occasions, and stole more than 30 bases three times. Mays led the National League in home runs and stolen bases four times each, slugging percentage five times, triples three times, runs scored and on-base percentage two times each, and hits and batting average one time each. Considered to be one of the greatest defensive center fielders in baseball history, Mays won 12 Gold Gloves over the course of his career. In addition to winning the Most Valuable Player Award twice, Willie placed in the top five in the voting seven other times. He earned a total of 20 selections to the All-Star Team.

As the career of Mays began to wind down in 1967, McCovey's reached its zenith. After hitting 31 home runs and driving in 91 runs in 1967, the big first baseman established himself in 1968 as the National League's most feared and intimidating hitter. McCovey topped the circuit in home runs and RBIs in each of the next two seasons, compiling the following numbers from 1968 to 1970:

1968: **36** HRs, **105** RBIs, .293 AVG, 81 RUNS, .383 OBP, **.545** SLG PCT
1969: **45** HRs, **126** RBIs, .320 AVG, 101 RUNS, **.458** OBP, **.656** SLG PCT
1970: 39 HRs, 126 RBIs, .289 AVG, 98 RUNS, .446 OBP, **.612** SLG PCT

McCovey earned NL MVP honors in 1969 when he established career highs in home runs, runs batted in, batting average, on-base percentage, and slugging percentage. He also finished third in the voting the previous year. In addition to leading the league with a .612 slugging percentage in 1970, McCovey topped the circuit with 137 walks. Opposing pitchers simply had no desire to pitch to the powerfully built slugger, whose mere presence in the batter's box caused their knees to weaken. Although the mark was later surpassed, McCovey established a new major-league record in 1970 by receiving 42 intentional walks. Manager Gene Mauch said of McCovey, "He's the most awesome hitter I've ever seen."[1]

Although McCovey remained a productive hitter several more seasons, he began experiencing knee problems in 1971 that severely limited his playing time the remainder of his career. After appearing in fewer than 105 games for the Giants in two of the previous three seasons, McCovey was traded to the San Diego Padres at the end of 1973. He spent three years in San Diego before returning to the Giants in 1977. McCovey remained with the Giants four more years, finally retiring at the end of the 1980 campaign. He ended his career with 521 home runs, 1,555 runs batted in, 1,229 runs scored, a .270 batting average, a .374 on-base percentage, and a .515 slugging percentage. McCovey hit more than 30 homers seven times, knocked in more than 100 runs four times, scored more than 100 runs twice, batted over .300 twice, and collected more than 100 bases on balls three times. In addition to winning the NL MVP award in 1969, McCovey finished in the top 10 in the voting three other times. He was named to the All-Star Team on six occasions.

Willie Mays and Willie McCovey were teammates on the Giants from 1959 to 1971. Over the course of those 13 seasons, they combined for 814 home runs and 2,344 runs batted in. Mays and McCovey were both full-time players from 1963 to 1970. The two men hit a total of 548 home runs during that time, drove in 1,511 runs, and scored another 1,467 times for an average of 69 homers, 189 RBIs, and 183 runs scored per season. They were most effective together in 1963, 1965, and 1966, posting the following totals between them in those three seasons:

1963: 82 HRs, 205 RBIs, 218 RUNS
1965: 91 HRs, 204 RBIs, 211 RUNS
1966: 73 HRs, 199 RBIs, 184 RUNS

Either Mays or McCovey led the National League in home runs six times between 1962 and 1970, with one of them topping the circuit each year from 1962 to 1965. In their eight full seasons together, they also led the league in slugging percentage five times and runs batted in and on-base percentage two times each. Each man won a Most Valuable Player Award during that time, with the two sluggers also combining for 12 selections to the All-Star Team. The Giants finished second in five of those seasons, winning at least 86 games each year and surpassing 90 victories on five occasions.

Note

Numbers printed in bold indicate that the player led his league in a statistical category.

1. Tony DeMarco, *The Sporting News Selects 50 Greatest Sluggers* (St. Louis, MO: Times Mirror Magazines, 2000), 32.

CHAPTER 5

Mickey Mantle / Roger Maris

Although Mickey Mantle and Roger Maris served as teammates on the New York Yankees from 1960 to 1966, they both remained healthy enough to assume a regular spot in the team's starting lineup in only four of those seven seasons. Injuries greatly reduced the offensive productivity of both men in 1963, 1965, and 1966. However, when healthy, Mantle and Maris formed as potent a pairing as any twosome in the American League. The two sluggers helped lead the Yankees to five straight pennants and two world championships, with either Maris or Mantle earning league MVP honors from 1960 to 1962. Nevertheless, both men heard the taunts of Yankee fans at different times during their years in New York.

As a shy 19-year-old, Mickey Mantle had huge expectations thrust upon him as soon as he arrived in New York in 1951. Considered by most people to be the heir apparent to the aging Joe DiMaggio in center field, the Oklahoma native found himself being built up by Yankee manager Casey Stengel as someone who would eventually become DiMaggio, Babe Ruth, and Lou Gehrig all rolled into one. Stengel observed the switch-hitting outfielder's blinding speed and awesome power from both sides of the plate, and he began singing the youngster's praises to the New York media. Adding to the pressures placed on Mantle was the uneasiness that the insecure country boy felt over being in the big city for the first time in his life.

Unable to live up to his advance billing early in his rookie season, Mantle found himself striking out frequently and often being booed by Yankee fans, who believed everything they had read and heard about the talented youngster. Before long, the struggling outfielder was sent down to the minor leagues, where he eventually righted himself. Returning to New York later in the year, Mantle ended up posting respectable numbers in his first big-league season, batting .267 and collecting 13 home runs and 65 RBIs in only 341 official at bats. However, an injury that Mantle suffered during the World Series proved to be a portent of things to come for the star-crossed slugger, who spent most of his career playing in pain, at less than 100-percent capacity.

In the only meeting of three of the greatest center fielders in baseball history, Mantle opened up the 1951 Fall Classic at Yankee Stadium playing right field alongside Joe DiMaggio, who retired at the end of the year. Meanwhile, Willie Mays manned center field for the New York Giants—the Yankees' opponents in the series. During the latter stages of game 2, Mays hit a fly ball to right center field that Mantle seemed to have well within his grasp. However, DiMaggio called off his young teammate at the last moment, causing Mantle to stop abruptly to avoid a collision. In so doing, Mantle caught his right foot in an outfield drainage ditch, seriously injuring his leg and causing him to be carried off the field on a stretcher.

Although Mantle never again played without experiencing some sort of pain, his incredible natural ability enabled him to become a truly great player. Even after losing some of his great running speed, he remained one of the fastest players in the game. Mantle's thick and extremely muscular 5'11", 200-pound frame also gave him a tremendous amount of raw power, enabling him to drive the ball more than 500 feet from either side of the plate.

With DiMaggio having announced his retirement during the off-season, Mantle took over the starting center-field job when he returned to the Yankees in 1952. Despite striking out 111 times, Mantle put up very good numbers his second year in the league, hitting 23 home runs, knocking in 87 runs, scoring 94 others, batting .311, and earning the first of 11 consecutive All-Star nominations. He continued to establish himself as one of the American League's best players over the course of the next three seasons, averaging 28 home runs, 98 runs batted in, and 118 runs scored from 1953 to 1955 while posting a batting average in excess of .300 in two of those years. Particularly effective in 1954 and 1955, Mantle topped the junior circuit with 129 runs scored in the first of those seasons, before leading the league with 37 homers, a .433 on-base percentage, and a .611 slugging percentage the following campaign. Nevertheless, Yankee fans continued to find fault with his frequent strikeouts and inability to attain the same level of greatness that his predecessor in center field, Joe DiMaggio, reached during his time in New York.

Mantle finally won over the fans in 1956, when he had a season of historic proportions. In addition to capturing the American League Triple Crown by leading the league with 52 home runs, 130 runs batted in, and a .353 batting average, he topped the circuit with 132 runs scored and a .705 slugging percentage. Mantle's fabulous performance earned him AL MVP honors for the first of three times and recognition as the top professional athlete of the year. He followed that up with another great year in 1957, when he hit 34 home runs, drove in 94 runs, and batted a career-high .365 en route to winning his second straight league MVP trophy and leading the Yankees to their sixth pennant in his first seven seasons with the club. Yet, when Mantle's numbers fell off a bit the next two years, the fans once again took to booing him regularly. All that changed, though, shortly after a disappointing third-place finish in 1959 prompted the Yankees to make a major deal during the subsequent offseason.

The Yankees actually had their eyes on Roger Maris for quite some time before finally acquiring him prior to the start of the 1960 campaign. They took note of the outfielder's compact yet powerful left-handed swing and believed that it would be a perfect fit for Yankee Stadium's short right-field porch. Approaching Kansas City with a package of four players—which included veterans Don Larsen and Hank Bauer along with promising youngster Norm Siebern—the Yankees added Maris's powerful bat to the middle of their lineup during the offseason, hoping that it might help restore them to prominence in the junior circuit.

A product of the Cleveland Indians farm system, Roger Maris was a small-town boy who grew up in Fargo, North Dakota. After spending 1957 with the Indians, Maris was traded to the Kansas City Athletics early in 1958. Happy in the Midwestern town, the quiet and shy Maris played well for his new team, hitting 28 home runs, knocking in 80 runs, and scoring 87 others his first year in Kansas City. He followed that up by earning All-Star honors for the first time in his career in 1959.

Fully expecting to spend the remainder of his career with the Athletics, Maris felt stunned when he learned of the trade that sent him to New York. Extremely honest and forthright, Maris made his first mistake when he informed the New York media upon his arrival in the big city that he would have preferred to remain in Kansas City.

Nevertheless, the Yankees benefited greatly from the trade, since their new right fielder provided excellent protection for Mantle in the middle of their batting order. These are the numbers the two men posted in their first season together:

Mickey Mantle: **40** HRs, 94 RBIs, **119** RUNS, .275 AVG, .402 OBP, .558 SLG PCT

Roger Maris: 39 HRs, **112** RBIs, 98 RUNS, .283 AVG, .374 OBP, **.581** SLG PCT

Mantle led the league in home runs, runs scored, and total bases. Maris finished second in all three categories. Maris topped the circuit in runs batted in and slugging percentage. Mantle finished second to his teammate in the last category. The two sluggers also finished first and second in the league MVP voting, with Maris edging out Mantle by just three points. Maris also won a Gold

Glove for his outstanding play in right field. Although the Yankees were upset by the Pittsburgh Pirates in the World Series, they won their first of five straight AL pennants, beating out the second-place Baltimore Orioles by eight games in the final standings.

In spite of the tremendous contributions that Maris made to the success of the team over the course of the campaign, Yankee fans began to resent him somewhat as he continued to challenge Mantle for the league lead in home runs as the season wore on. Since they considered Mickey to be a "true" Yankee, fans of the team rooted for the center fielder to win the home run crown and correspondingly rooted against Maris whenever he stepped to the plate. Mantle subsequently became their hero, something he remained the rest of his career, while they begrudgingly accepted Maris as a necessary evil.

The 1960 home run race between Mantle and Maris merely served as a precursor to the epic battle that the two men waged the following year, when they spent the entire campaign chasing Babe Ruth's 34-year-old single-season mark. Since a Yankee held the existing record, fans of the team felt that Mantle should be the one to break it. They correspondingly cheered him wildly every time he stepped to the plate while displaying total indifference toward Maris, which they revealed on the season's final day when fewer than 15,000 fans showed up at Yankee Stadium to witness the slugger establish a new single-season record. Yet, Maris once again proved to be invaluable to the Yankees over the course of the season, teaming up with Mantle to give New York the league's two best players for the second consecutive season. These are the numbers they compiled over the course of that 1961 campaign:

Mickey Mantle: 54 HRs, 128 RBIs, **132** RUNS, .317 AVG, .452 OBP, **.687** SLG PCT

Roger Maris: **61** HRs, **142** RBIs, **132** RUNS, .269 AVG, .376 OBP, .620 SLG PCT

Mantle and Maris finished tied for the league lead in runs scored and finished first and second in the circuit in home runs for the second straight year. Both men also placed in the top five in runs batted in, slugging percentage, and total bases; Mantle also finished among the leaders in batting average and on-base percentage. The Yankees won the pennant by eight games over the second-place Detroit Tigers, after which they defeated the Cincinnati Reds in five games in the World Series. Maris and Mantle again finished first and second in the MVP balloting, with Maris edging out his teammate in the voting for the second straight year, this time by only four points.

The Yankees repeated as world champions in 1962, barely defeating the Giants in a closely contested seven-game World Series. Mantle and Maris were both among the American League's best players once more during the regular season, compiling the following numbers:

Mickey Mantle: 30 HRs, 89 RBIs, 96 RUNS, .321 AVG, **.488** OBP, **.605** SLG PCT

Roger Maris: 33 HRs, 100 RBIs, 92 RUNS, .256 AVG, .357 OBP, .485 SLG PCT

Mantle posted those numbers despite missing almost 40 games and compiling only 377 official at bats. In addition to leading the league in on-base and slugging percentage, he finished first in walks and second in batting average. Mantle earned AL MVP honors for the third and final time in his career.

Although Maris placed among the league leaders in home runs and runs batted in, his overall numbers weren't nearly as good as they were in either of his two MVP seasons. As a result, most fans of the team viewed his 1961 record-setting performance as a fluke, and they took to booing him more vociferously than ever. Adding to the furor surrounding Maris was the negative image that the New York media created of him in the local newspapers. Never comfortable in the spotlight, the shy and uncharismatic Maris often came across to reporters as being sullen and moody since he tended to respond to their questions in an extremely succinct manner. Furthermore, he always remembered if a member of the press corps twisted his words to present him in an inaccurate light. In such instances, Maris invariably chose to stop dealing with the writer. However, after he snubbed powerful sportswriter Jimmy Cannon on one particular occasion, Cannon wrote a scathing article on the right fielder that painted a particularly poor picture of him to the general public.

As the New York media grew increasingly hostile toward Maris, its members became overtly affectionate toward Mantle. Far more gregarious than he was earlier in his career, Mantle spoke quite freely to the members of the press, fully understanding the types of answers they appreciated and taking every opportunity to oblige them. Reporters began portraying him as a hero of sorts, writing stories that praised him for the courage he displayed every time he took the field in pain. As a result, Mantle eventually reached a level of popularity that few athletes have ever experienced.

One of Mantle's most serious injuries occurred in Baltimore in 1963, when he ran into a wire fence in the outfield, breaking his left foot and tearing the cartilage in his left knee. Mantle appeared in only 65 games for the Yankees that year, hitting 15 home runs, driving in 35 runs, and batting .314 in just 172 official at-bats. He underwent surgery to remove cartilage from the knee at the end of the season. Maris also missed a good portion of the campaign, playing in only 90 games, hitting 23 home runs, knocking in 53 runs, and batting .269.

Mantle and Maris returned to the team's everyday starting lineup the following year to help lead the Yankees to their fifth consecutive pennant. Despite playing in constant pain and limping noticeably, Mantle managed to finish near the top of the league rankings with 35 home runs, 111 runs batted in, a .303 batting average, and a .591 slugging percentage while topping the circuit with a .426 on-base percentage. He ended up placing second to Baltimore's Brooks Robinson in the AL MVP balloting. After struggling during the season's first half, Maris came on in the final three months to hit 26 home runs, drive in 71 runs, score 86 others, and bat .281. Although the Yankees came up just a bit short in the World Series, losing to the Cardinals in seven games, Mantle batted .333, drove in eight runs, and hit the final three of his record 18 World Series home runs.

The Yankee dynasty ended at the conclusion of the 1964 campaign, and Mantle and Maris never again played a full season together. Injuries forced both men to sit out huge portions of each of the next two seasons, with a broken hand sidelining Maris for much of 1965. Although later tests revealed a small bone fracture, an initial set of X-rays failed to detect the break. As a result, fans and the already-antagonistic media grew increasingly hostile toward Maris, questioning the severity of his injury as he sat on New York's bench, unable to play.

The Yankees finally put an end to Maris's misery by trading him to the St. Louis Cardinals at the end of the 1966 season. The right fielder played two more years in St. Louis, helping the Cardinals win two pennants and one world championship. In the Cardinals' seven-game victory over the Boston Red Sox in the 1967 World Series, Maris batted .385, with 10 hits and seven runs batted in. He retired at the conclusion of the 1968 campaign with career totals of 275 home runs, 851 runs batted in, 826 runs scored, and a .260 batting average.

Perhaps the most misunderstood and misrepresented athlete of his time, Roger Maris was very much appreciated by the people who knew him best.

Bobby Richardson, Yankees second baseman during Maris's seven years with the team, said of his former teammate, "He was the most reserved, quiet individual I think I ever knew, so the press' portrayal of him was not the real Roger Maris."[1]

Third baseman Clete Boyer, whom the Yankees also traded away at the end of the 1966 season, said of Maris, "The guy was a great player. They like to say that 1961 was a fluke, but Roger hit 39 homers and was the American League MVP in 1960. Not too many stiffs become back-to-back MVPs."[2]

Whitey Ford stated in his book *Few and Chosen*, "He was fast, and he was a great base-runner with excellent instincts when it came to taking the extra base. And he was as good as I've seen at breaking up the double play."[3]

Yankee first baseman Moose Skowron said of Maris, "He could run, he could throw, he could hit . . . great defensive outfielder. He did the little things to win a ballgame . . . and the writers crucified him . . . no way!"[4]

In speaking of Maris, Mickey Mantle said, "When people think of Roger, they think of the 61 home runs, but Roger Maris was one of the best all-around players I ever saw. He was as good a fielder as I ever saw, he had a great arm, he was a great base-runner—I never saw him make a mistake on the bases—and he was a great teammate. Everybody liked him."[5]

While Roger Maris spent his final days in New York being burned in effigy, Mickey Mantle spent his remaining years as arguably the most beloved sports figure in New York history. Playing in great pain until he finally retired at the conclusion of the 1968 campaign, Mantle represented merely a shell of his former self the last four years of his career. Yet he remained arguably New York's best player in most of those years, which represented the beginning of one of the darkest eras in franchise history. Mantle ended his career third on the all-time home run list, with 536 to his credit. He also knocked in 1,509 runs, scored 1,677 others, amassed 2,415 hits, compiled a lifetime batting average of .298, and posted a .423 on-base percentage and a .557 slugging percentage. Mantle led the league in home runs four times, reaching the 50-homer plateau on two separate occasions. He also topped the circuit in runs scored six times; walks five times; slugging percentage four times; on-base percentage three times; and runs batted in, triples, and batting average one time each. Mantle scored more than 100 runs in nine consecutive seasons, from 1953 to 1961. He batted over .300 ten times, earned a spot on the All-Star Team in 16 of his 18 seasons, and won a Gold Glove. In addition to being named American League MVP three times, Mantle earned a top-five finish in the balloting six other times.

Beloved by fans and teammates alike, Mantle drew high praise from those who knew him best. In his book *Few and Chosen*, former teammate and close friend Whitey Ford refers to Mickey as "a superstar who never acted like one. He was a humble man who was kind and friendly to all his teammates, even the rawest rookie. He was idolized by all the other players."[6]

Ford also says, "Often he played hurt, his knees aching so much he could hardly walk. But he never complained, and he would somehow manage to drag himself onto the field, ignore the pain, and do something spectacular."[7]

Clete Boyer once expressed his admiration for his teammate by saying, "He is the only baseball player I know who is a bigger hero to his teammates than he is to the fans."[8]

The Yankees won five straight pennants and two world championships in the seven seasons that Mickey Mantle and Roger Maris played alongside each other in the team's outfield. In the four years that the two players both appeared in a majority of the team's games, Mantle and Maris combined to average 80 home runs, 212 runs batted in, and 212 runs scored. One or the other led the league in home runs, runs batted in, runs scored, and on-base percentage two times each, and either Mantle or Maris topped the circuit in slugging percentage in three of those years. Mantle and Maris finished first and second in the league in home runs and runs scored two times each and total bases and slugging percentage one time each. They also finished first and second in the MVP voting twice, winning the award each year from 1960 to 1962. Mantle and Maris combined to hit 419 home runs in their seven years as teammates, for an average of 60 per season. They hit 257 of those homers between 1960 and 1962, averaging 86 round-trippers per season between them during that three-year stretch. Both men made the All-Star Team in each of those years. The total of 115 home runs that the two sluggers hit in 1961 still stands as the single-season record for two teammates.

Notes

Numbers printed in bold indicate that the player led his league in a statistical category.

1. *Pinstripe Power: The Story of the 1961 New York Yankees*, VHS tape (New York: Major League Baseball Productions, 1987).

2. *Pinstripe Power.*

3. Whitey Ford, with Phil Pepe, *Few and Chosen: Defining Yankee Greatness across the Eras* (Chicago: Triumph Books, 2001), 131.

4. *Pinstripe Power.*

5. *Pinstripe Power.*

6. Ford, *Few and Chosen*, 112.

7. Ford, *Few and Chosen*, 113.

8. Clete Boyer, http://www.baseball-almanac.com/quotes/quomant.shtml.

CHAPTER 6

Ken Griffey Jr. / Alex Rodriguez

Alex Rodriguez's involvement with steroids as a member of the Texas Rangers and New York Yankees has done irreparable damage to his reputation and greatly diminished his place in baseball history. Once considered to be one of the greatest players in the history of the sport, Rodriguez is now widely viewed as a cheater and a fraud whose statistical accomplishments bear little significance. As a result, I felt compelled to drop the tandem of Rodriguez and Ken Griffey Jr. one or two notches in these rankings, for fear that some of the things they accomplished together as teammates on the Seattle Mariners from 1996 to 1999 might be tainted. Nevertheless, I found it impossible to completely exclude A-Rod and Junior from my list, since they unquestionably formed one of the greatest offensive combinations in baseball history during their relatively brief time together.

After first entering the American League as an expansion team in 1977, the Seattle Mariners won more than 74 games just once in their first 10 seasons, finishing the 1982 campaign with a record of 78–84. Although first baseman Alvin Davis and pitcher Mark Langston began to establish themselves as solid players during the mid-1980s, Seattle had little in the way of talent most of those years. Nevertheless, finishing a major league–worst 67–95 in 1986 greatly benefited the Mariners, since their poor showing enabled them to select 17-year-old outfielder Ken Griffey Jr. with the first overall pick of the 1987 amateur baseball draft.

Griffey spent two years honing his skills in the minor leagues, while Seattle continued to struggle at the major-league level, compiling records of 78–84 in 1987 and 68–93 in 1988. The 19-year-old outfielder impressed Seattle management so much in spring training of 1989 that he began the year as the team's starting center fielder. Displaying tremendous all-around ability, Griffey did a superb job in the outfield and at the plate during the season's first half, hitting

13 home runs, driving in 45 runs, and batting .287, before a broken bone in his left hand forced him out of the Mariner lineup for six weeks. Griffey struggled upon his return, concluding the campaign with only 16 home runs, 61 runs batted in, and a .264 batting average. Seattle ended the year with a record of 73–89.

Healthy again in 1990, Junior quickly developed into Seattle's best all-around player, hitting 22 home runs, knocking in 80 runs, scoring 91 others, batting .300, and winning his first of 10 consecutive Gold Gloves. He also earned the first of his 11 straight selections to the AL All-Star Team. Still, the Mariners posted a losing record for the 14th consecutive season, finishing in fifth place in the AL West with a record of 77–85.

Both Griffey and the Mariners made major strides in 1991. The 21-year-old centerfielder clearly established himself as one of the American League's top players by hitting 22 homers, driving in 100 runs, and placing among the league leaders with a .327 batting average. Though still evolving as a player, Griffey displayed his vast array of skills for all to see. A five-tool player, he drove the ball with power to all fields while hitting for a high batting average; he ran the bases well; and he did a superb job in the outfield, making several spectacular catches while throwing out opposing base runners who dared to challenge his arm. Junior's exceptional play helped the Mariners post an 83–79 record—their first winning mark in franchise history.

Although Seattle took a step backward in 1992, finishing last in the AL West with a 64–98 record, Griffey had another outstanding year, hitting 27 home runs, knocking in 103 runs, and batting .308. He developed into a truly dominant player the following year, finishing second in the American League with 45 home runs and a .617 slugging percentage, knocking in 109 runs, scoring 113 others, batting .309, and topping the circuit with 359 total bases. Griffey's superb play helped the Mariners improve their record to 82–80, earning him a fifth-place finish in the league MVP voting.

The strike-shortened 1994 campaign turned out to be a disappointing one for the Mariners, who returned to their losing ways by compiling a record of only 49–63. Nevertheless, Griffey had another fabulous all-around year, topping the junior circuit with 40 home runs and placing among the league leaders with 90 runs batted in, 94 runs scored, a .323 batting average, and a .674 slugging percentage en route to earning a second-place finish in the AL MVP balloting.

A broken wrist forced Griffey to miss more than half of the 1995 season, but he returned in time to join Randy Johnson, Edgar Martinez, Jay Buhner, and the rest of the young Mariners in their first pennant race. Junior hit 17 home runs in only 72 games to help lead Seattle to the Western Division title. He subsequently hit five home runs, batted .391, knocked in seven runs, and scored nine others, including the series clincher during the Mariners' five-game victory over the Yankees in the AL Division Series. Although Seattle lost the American League Championship Series to the Indians in six games, Griffey batted .333, with one homer and two RBIs.

Receiving his first significant playing time with the Mariners over the course of that 1995 campaign was 20-year-old shortstop Alex Rodriguez. Originally selected by Seattle with the first overall pick of the 1993 amateur draft, Rodriguez actually made his major-league debut with the team in 1994, batting .204 in his 59 plate appearances. Called up from the minor leagues for the 1995 pennant drive, Rodriguez played in 48 games over the season's final two months, hitting five home runs, driving in 19 runs, and batting .232. A tremendously gifted athlete, Rodriguez was considered to be the team's shortstop of the future, prompting the Mariners to trade the slick-fielding Omar Vizquel to the Cleveland Indians at the conclusion of the 1993 season.

Rodriguez became Seattle's starting shortstop in 1996, combining with Griffey, Edgar Martinez, and Jay Buhner to give the Mariners one of baseball's most potent offenses. Junior and A-Rod were particularly outstanding, forming the American League's most prolific tandem. These are the numbers the two men posted in their first full season together:

Ken Griffey Jr.: 49 HRs, 140 RBIs, 125 RUNS, .303 AVG, .392 OBP, .628 SLG PCT

Alex Rodriguez: 36 HRs, 123 RBIs, **141** RUNS, **.358** AVG, .414 OBP, .631 SLG PCT

By placing among the league leaders in home runs, runs batted in, and runs scored, Griffey earned a fourth-place finish in the league MVP voting.

Rodriguez finished second to Texas outfielder Juan Gonzalez in the MVP balloting. In addition to leading the league in batting average and runs scored, A-Rod topped the circuit with 54 doubles and 379 total bases. He also placed among the leaders with 215 hits. Rodriguez earned his first of three straight nominations to the All-Star Team; he also earned *Sporting News* Major League Player of the Year honors.

However, with injuries limiting Randy Johnson to only 14 appearances, Seattle's pitching struggled all year. As a result, the team failed to make the playoffs, finishing the season with a record of 85–77, 4.5 games behind the first-place Texas Rangers in the AL West.

Rodriguez wasn't nearly as productive in 1997, hitting only 23 home runs, driving in just 84 runs, and scoring only 100 others. But he batted .300 and continued to develop his all-around game, stealing 29 bases, almost twice as many as he swiped the previous season. Seattle also received a lift from Randy Johnson, who returned to the team's starting rotation to win 20 games. The team's dominant player, though, was Ken Griffey Jr., who had another sensational year. Junior earned league MVP honors by batting .304 and topping the circuit with 56 home runs, 147 runs batted in, 125 runs scored, and a .646 slugging percentage. He also was named the *Sporting News* Major League Player of the Year. Although the Baltimore Orioles quickly disposed of the Mariners in the first round of the playoffs, Seattle captured the Western Division title for the second time in three years, winning 90 games for the first time in franchise history.

Poor pitching prevented the Mariners from advancing to the playoffs in either 1998 or 1999. Nevertheless, Griffey and Rodriguez proved to be two of the game's very best players both years, compiling the following numbers:

1998
Ken Griffey Jr.: **56** HRs, 146 RBIs, 120 RUNS, .284 AVG, .365 OBP, .611 SLG PCT
Alex Rodriguez: 42 HRs, 124 RBIs, 123 RUNS, .310 AVG, .360 OBP, .560 SLG PCT
1999
Ken Griffey Jr.: **48** HRs, 134 RBIs, 123 RUNS, .285 AVG, .384 OBP, .576 SLG PCT
Alex Rodriguez: 42 HRs, 111 RBIs, 110 RUNS, .285 AVG, .357 OBP, .586 SLG PCT

In addition to leading the league in home runs both years, Junior placed among the leaders in runs batted in, runs scored, slugging percentage, and total bases both times. He finished fourth in the MVP balloting in 1998, and he came in 10th the following year.

Rodriguez finished ninth in the MVP voting in 1998, when he led the league with 213 hits and placed among the leaders in home runs, runs batted in, runs scored, total bases, and stolen bases. His 42 home runs and 46 thefts that year enabled him to become only the third player in baseball history to surpass 40 homers and 40 steals in the same season. An injury forced Rodriguez to miss almost a month of the 1999 campaign, but he still managed to hit 42 homers, knock in 111 runs, and score 110 others.

The 1999 season turned out to be the last one that Griffey and Rodriguez spent as teammates. With free agency looming for Junior at the end of 2000, the Mariners elected to trade their star center fielder to the Cincinnati Reds for four players prior to the start of the season. Returning to his hometown, Griffey had one big year for the Reds before injuries significantly reduced his playing time and offensive productivity the next several seasons. After hitting 40 home runs, driving in 118 runs, scoring 100 others, and batting .271 for Cincinnati in 2000, Junior found himself limited to only 317 games and 63 homers the next four years, essentially ending his pursuit of the all-time career home run record. Although Griffey had a nice comeback year in 2005, hitting 35 home runs, driving in 92 runs, and batting .301, he never again reached the level of dominance he attained earlier in his career. After two more solid seasons in Cincinnati, he split the 2008 campaign between the Reds and White Sox. Griffey returned to Seattle in 2009, ending his career the following season in the city where it began some 21 years earlier. He announced his retirement on June 2, 2010, with totals of 630 home runs, 1,836 runs batted in, 1,662 runs scored, and 2,781 hits, a .284 lifetime batting average, a .370 career on-base percentage, and a .538 career slugging percentage. Griffey surpassed 40 homers seven times, 100 RBIs eight times, and 100 runs scored on six occasions. He also batted over .300 eight times. In addition to winning the Most Valuable Player Award once, he finished in the top five in the voting four other times. Griffey appeared in 13 All-Star Games.

Rodriguez remained in Seattle one more year, hitting 41 home runs, driving in 131 runs, scoring 134 others, and batting .316 in 2000. He signed a huge free agent contract with the Texas Rangers at the end of the season, becoming the highest-paid player in baseball history. Rodriguez spent three years in Texas, later admitting to using performance-enhancing drugs throughout the period. In attempting to explain his actions, A-Rod stated, "When I arrived in Texas in 2001, I felt an enormous amount of pressure. I felt like I had all the weight of the world on top of me and I needed to perform, and perform at a high level every day."[1]

Rodriguez's three years with the Rangers were among the most productive of his career. He led the American League in home runs all three years, surpassing 50 homers twice. He also led the league in runs batted in once and runs scored twice. Rodriguez earned *Sporting News* Major League Player of the Year honors for the second of three times in 2002, when he led the AL with 57 home runs and 142 runs batted in, scored 125 runs, batted .300, and won the first of two consecutive Gold Gloves for his outstanding play at shortstop. He won the first of his three Most Valuable Player Awards the following year, when he topped the circuit with 47 home runs and 124 runs scored while knocking in 118 runs and batting .298.

Despite Rodriguez's exceptional individual play, the Rangers experienced little in the way of success those three seasons. As a result, team ownership elected to trade him to the Yankees prior to the start of the 2004 campaign. A-Rod shifted to third base upon his arrival in New York, in deference to Yankee captain and shortstop Derek Jeter. Rodriguez subsequently put together seven outstanding seasons for the Yankee before injuries began to adversely affect his performance, capturing league MVP honors in 2005 and 2007. In his first MVP season with the team, A-Rod led the league with 48 home runs and 124 runs scored, drove in 130 runs, and batted .321. He had perhaps his finest all-around year in 2007, batting .314 and leading the league with 54 homers, 156 runs batted in, and 143 runs scored.

Yet, even as Rodriguez posted exceptional numbers year after year in New York, he continued to be perceived by most people as a selfish player who tended to wilt under pressure. A-Rod's critics steadfastly maintained that he was not likely to ever play for a championship team. Rodriguez put to rest any such claims in 2009 when he helped lead the Yankees to their first world championship since 2000. Performing magnificently throughout the postseason, A-Rod exorcised any old demons by coming up with one clutch hit after another. He batted .455, with two home runs and six RBIs during New York's three-game sweep of Minnesota in the American League Division Series. He continued his superlative play against the Angels in the American League Championship Series, batting .429 with three more homers and six RBIs. Rodriguez capped off his outstanding postseason by hitting one home run and driving in six runs during New York's six-game World Series victory over the Phillies.

Rodriguez followed up his memorable 2009 postseason with another solid year, hitting 30 homers, driving in 125 runs, and batting .270 in 2010, before missing a significant amount of playing time in each of the next three seasons due to injury. During that time, it also surfaced that A-Rod reportedly received HGH from Biogenesis of America, an anti-aging clinic in Coral Gables, Florida. Subsequently suspended by Major League Baseball from August 8, 2013 through the end of the 2014 campaign, Rodriguez will enter the 2015 season having appeared in a total of only 44 games in the last two years. Since he will turn 40 years old in July of 2015, Rodriguez does not figure to add significantly to the numbers he has compiled over the course of his career, if he does return to the playing field at all. He enters the campaign with 654 home runs, 1,969 RBIs, 1,919 runs scored, 2,939 hits, and a .299 lifetime batting average. Rodriguez has led the league in home runs and runs scored five times each; slugging percentage and total bases four times each; runs batted in twice; and batting average, hits, and doubles once each. He has surpassed 40 homers eight times, topping the 50-mark on three occasions. He has also driven in more than 100 runs 14 times, scored more than 100 runs 13 times, and batted over .300 on nine occasions. In addition to earning A.L. MVP honors three times, Rodriguez has been named to the All-Star Team a total of 14 times.

Ken Griffey Jr. and Alex Rodriguez played only four full seasons together. The Mariners advanced to the postseason just once over that four-year stretch. Nevertheless, Junior and A-Rod were unquestionably baseball's most prolific offensive tandem during that period. They combined to lead the league in home runs three times, and they topped the circuit in runs scored and total bases two times each and runs batted in, batting average, slugging percentage, doubles, and hits once each. Griffey averaged 52 home runs, 142 runs batted in, and 123 runs scored from 1996 to 1999. Meanwhile, Rodriguez averaged 36 homers, 111 RBIs, and 119 runs scored over that same period. Between them, they posted averages of 88 home runs, 253 runs batted in, and 242 runs scored per season. The two men were at their very best in 1996 and 1998. In the first of those years, they combined to hit 85 home runs, drive in 263 runs, and score 266 others. In 1998, they combined for 98 homers, 270 RBIs, and 243 runs scored. Rodriguez placed second in the MVP voting in 1996, while Griffey finished fourth. Junior won the award in 1997, and he finished fourth in the balloting again in 1998. Griffey and Rodriguez combined for seven All-Star Game appearances during their time together. Further validating their status as one of the most dynamic duos in sports history is the fact that both men are generally considered to be among the handful of greatest players at their respective positions in baseball history.

Note

Numbers printed in bold indicate that the player led his league in a statistical category.

1. From an interview conducted by ESPN's Peter Gammons on February 9, 2009.

CHAPTER 7

Ty Cobb / Sam Crawford

The Detroit Tigers' outfield combination of Ty Cobb and Sam Crawford served as baseball's most prolific offensive tandem for much of the first two decades of the 20th century. Cobb was the dominant player and greatest hitter of the period, winning 10 batting titles between 1907 and 1919, while Crawford was one of the era's foremost sluggers and run producers. The two men played alongside one another in the Tigers outfield for 12 seasons, leading the team to three straight American League pennants at one point and dominating the circuit's offensive statistical categories during their time together.

Sam Crawford made his major-league debut with the National League's Cincinnati Reds in 1899, batting .307 in 31 games and 127 at bats. After serving the team as a part-time player the following year, Crawford became the Reds starting right fielder in 1901, leading the Senior Circuit with 16 home runs while batting .330 and driving in 104 runs. Crawford then batted .333 in his second full season while amassing a league-leading 22 triples. Prior to the start of the 1903 campaign, though, Crawford elected to jump to the Detroit Tigers of the rival American League, which had its inaugural season in 1901. Detroit's new right fielder had an outstanding year in 1903, driving in 89 runs, placing second in the league with a .335 batting average, and topping the circuit with 25 triples. However, Crawford's performance slipped somewhat the next three seasons, with the slugger failing to bat over .300, knock in more than 75 runs, or compile more than 16 triples in any of those campaigns. The Tigers also struggled during that period, winning more games than they lost just once between 1904 and 1906.

It was during the second of those seasons that a pugnacious 18-year-old named Tyrus Raymond Cobb joined Crawford in the Detroit outfield. The combative youngster made his first appearance in a Tigers uniform in 1905, batting just .240 in 41 games over the second half of the season. Cobb never again failed to bat over .300 in any of his 23 remaining seasons in the big leagues. The young centerfielder hit .316 over the first four months of the 1906 campaign, before the personal demons that drove him throughout his career forced him to spend the final six weeks of the season in a sanitarium.

As the 18-year-old Cobb struggled to adjust to life in the major leagues during the latter stages of his first campaign, he received a telegram informing him that his mother had shot and killed his father in what she claimed to be a case of mistaken identity. Home alone late one evening, Cobb's mother contended that she heard strange noises emanating from the porch of her private home. Rushing to the window, she shot the intruder once in the stomach and again in the face. The victim of the shooting turned out to be Cobb's father, who intended to surprise his wife since he suspected her of infidelity. The weight of his father's death and the subsequent murder trial of his mother exacted a major toll on the youngster as the 1906 season progressed. Adding to the pressures placed on the 19-year-old was the brutal hazing he received at the hands of his Detroit teammates, who resented his arrogant and boastful nature. Driven by the memory of his demanding father, who opposed Cobb's pursuit of a career in baseball, the outfielder considered it essential to become the best at his chosen profession, and he let everyone around him know that he believed himself to be the most talented player in the game. He also considered anyone who disagreed with him to be his adversary—be it opponent or teammate. As a result, Cobb played his entire career as if he were possessed by demons, displaying an anger and contentiousness on the ball field never manifested by any other player, either before or since.

Cobb described the warlike attitude he brought with him to the baseball diamond when he said, "Baseball is a red-blooded sport for red-blooded men. It's no pink tea, and mollycoddles had better stay out. It's a struggle for supremacy, a survival of the fittest." He added, "I had to fight all my life to survive. They were all against me, but I beat the bastards and left them in the ditch."[1]

Even though they resented their young teammate, the other members of the Tigers benefited greatly from the passion with which Cobb played the game when he returned to the team in 1907. Capturing the first of three consecutive batting titles, Cobb led the league with a .350 batting average. He also finished first in the junior circuit with 119 runs batted in, 212 hits, 49 stolen bases, and a .468 slugging percentage, in leading Detroit to the first of three straight American League pennants. Cobb's numbers slipped somewhat in 1908, but he still led the league with a .324 batting average, 108 runs batted in, 20 triples, 36 doubles, and 188 hits. If there remained a doubt in anyone's mind who the game's greatest player was, Cobb removed it in 1909 by leading the league in virtually every major statistical category. In addition to capturing the Triple Crown by finishing first in home runs (9), runs batted in (107), and batting average

(.377), Cobb topped the circuit with 116 runs scored, 216 hits, 76 stolen bases, a .431 on-base percentage, and a .517 slugging percentage.

Meanwhile, as Cobb established himself as the sport's greatest player, Crawford continued to build on his reputation as one of the game's great sluggers. During the dead-ball era, the measure of a player's slugging ability was not so much in the number of home runs he hit but rather in the number of triples he compiled. Crawford amassed a total of 47 triples between 1907 and 1909 en route to tallying an all-time major-league record 309 three-baggers over the course of his career. When Crawford led the AL with seven home runs in 1908, he became one of the few players in baseball history to lead each league in four-baggers. Although Crawford found himself overshadowed by Cobb during each of Detroit's pennant-winning seasons, the right fielder had a prominent role in the success of the team. He led the league with 102 runs scored in 1907 while placing second to his teammate in batting average (.323) and slugging percentage (.460). In addition to leading the league in home runs in 1908, Crawford finished second with 80 runs batted in, 102 runs scored, 184 hits, a .311 batting average, and a .457 slugging percentage. He also placed second to Cobb with 97 runs batted in and a .452 slugging percentage in 1909. Although the Tigers lost the World Series all three years, the combination of Cobb and Crawford enabled them to win three very close American League pennant races in 1907, 1908, and 1909.

Detroit failed to win another pennant in the six remaining seasons that Cobb and Crawford spent together as full-time players on the team. Nevertheless, the two men continued to excel throughout the period. Table 7.1 presents the numbers they compiled from 1910 to 1915.

Table 7.1. Ty Cobb and Sam Crawford: 1910–1915

Player	Year	AVG	RUNS	RBIs	HITS	SB	OBP	SLG PCT	TRIPLES
Cobb	1910	.383	**106**	91	194	65	**.456**	**.551**	13
	1911	**.420**	**147**	**127**	**248**	**83**	.467	**.621**	24[a]
	1912	**.409**	120	83	**226**	61	.456	**.584**	23
	1913	**.390**	70	67	167	51	**.467**	.535	16
	1914	.368	69	57	127	35	.466	.513	11
	1915	**.369**	**144**	99	**208**	**96**	**.486**	.487	13
Crawford	1910	.289	83	**120**	170	20	.332	.423	**19**
	1911	.378	109	115	217	37	.438	.526	14
	1912	.325	81	109	189	42	.373	.470	21
	1913	.317	78	83	193	13	.371	.489	23[b]
	1914	.314	74	**104**	183	25	.388	.483	**26**
	1915	.299	81	**112**	183	24	.367	.431	**19**

a. Doubles: 47.

b. Home runs: 9.

Cobb won the batting title in four of the six years, finishing second by less than 1 percentage point another time. He compiled the league's highest batting average in 1914 as well, but he failed to accumulate enough official at bats to qualify for the batting championship. Cobb finished among the league's top five in stolen bases, on-base percentage, and slugging percentage in five of the six seasons; he also placed among the leaders in runs scored and hits four times each and in doubles, triples, and runs batted in three times each. Cobb was named the league's Most Valuable Player in 1911, when he topped the circuit in eight statistical categories and posted a career-high .420 batting average. His 96 stolen bases in 1915 stood as the major-league single-season record for 47 years, until finally eclipsed by Maury Wills of the Dodgers in 1962.

Although Crawford continued to play in Cobb's shadow throughout much of the period, he led the league in runs batted in and triples three times each, and he finished among the leaders in both categories two other times during that six-year stretch. He also finished in the top five in hits five times, slugging percentage four times, and batting average twice. Crawford led the American League with 298 total bases in 1913, and his nine home runs and 193 hits that year placed him second in the league rankings. Crawford finished second in the MVP balloting in 1914, when he topped the circuit with 104 runs batted in and 26 triples.

The 1915 campaign was Crawford's last as a full-time player. He assumed a part-time role in his final two years with the Tigers before retiring at the conclusion of the 1917 season. Crawford ended his career with a .309 batting average, 1,525 runs batted in, 1,391 runs scored, 2,961 hits, and an all-time record 309 triples. He surpassed 20 triples five times in his career, leading the league in that category a total of six times. Crawford also knocked in more than 100 runs and batted over .325 six times each.

Cobb continued to terrorize American League pitchers for another decade, winning three more batting titles before finally retiring in 1928 at the age of 42. He was particularly effective in 1916, 1917, and 1922. In the first of those years, Cobb batted .371, compiled 201 hits, and led the league with 113 runs scored and 68 stolen bases. He topped the circuit with a .383 batting average, 225 hits, 24 triples, 44 doubles, 55 stolen bases, and a .570 slugging percentage the following year. Cobb then batted .401 in 1922 at the age of 36. He also collected 211 hits, 16 triples, and 42 doubles that year.

Upon his retirement in 1928, Cobb ranked first on the all-time list with 1,937 runs batted in, 2,246 runs scored, and 4,189 hits. He also ranked near the top with 891 stolen bases, 295 triples, and 724 doubles. Cobb still possesses the highest lifetime batting average in baseball history, with a mark of .367. He batted over .400 three times during his career, surpassed 200 hits nine times, scored more than 100 runs 11 times, drove in more than 100 runs on seven occasions, topped 60 stolen bases six times, and surpassed 20 triples and 40 doubles four times each. Cobb led the league in batting 10 times, hits and slugging percentage eight times each, stolen bases and on-base percentage six times each, runs scored five times, runs batted in and triples four times each, and doubles three times.

Shirley Povich, longtime sports columnist and reporter for the *Washington Post*, stated emphatically during a 1990s television interview, "If Babe Ruth isn't the greatest baseball player who ever lived, then Ty Cobb is, by far!"[2]

Ruth himself once praised his bitter rival for his playing ability when he said, "Cobb is a prick. But he sure can hit. God Almighty, that man can hit."[3]

Hall of Fame outfielder Tris Speaker, who competed against both Ruth and Cobb, had this to say: "The Babe was a great ballplayer, sure, but Cobb was even greater. Babe could knock your brains out, but Cobb would drive you crazy."[4]

Casey Stengel paid Cobb the ultimate tribute, saying, "I never saw anyone like Ty Cobb. No one even close to him. He was the greatest all time ballplayer. That guy was superhuman, amazing."[5]

George Sisler spent most of his career playing against Cobb as a member of the St. Louis Browns. The Hall of Fame first baseman said, "The greatness of Ty Cobb was something that had to be seen, and to see him was to remember him forever."[6]

Ty Cobb and Sam Crawford were teammates on the Detroit Tigers from 1905 to 1917. During that time, they combined for 4,500 hits. They were both full-time players from 1907 to 1915. Over that stretch of time, Cobb won seven batting titles, and either he or Crawford led the league in home runs twice, runs batted in seven times, runs scored five times, hits six times, and triples six times. The two men finished first and second in the league in runs batted in on four occasions, batting average and base hits twice each, slugging percentage three different times, and total bases four times. They had perhaps their greatest season together in 1911. Cobb was at his very best that year, leading the league in eight statistical categories, including batting average (.420), runs batted in (127), runs scored (147), hits (248), and slugging percentage (.621). Crawford finished among the league leaders in several offensive categories as well, placing second to Cobb with 115 runs batted in; third in batting average (.378), hits (217), and slugging percentage (.526); fourth in on-base percentage (.438); and fifth in runs scored (109). Although the Tigers failed to win a world championship during the time that Cobb and Crawford spent together, they won three pennants and finished second another two times.

Yet, in spite of the considerable amount of success that Cobb and Crawford experienced as teammates, the two men disliked each other a great deal. When Cleveland's Napoleon Lajoie edged out Cobb for the American League batting title on the final day of the 1910 season, Crawford displayed the disdain he felt toward his teammate by sending Lajoie a congratulatory telegram.

Reflecting back on his former teammate years later, Crawford stated, "[Cobb] didn't outhit and he didn't outrun them, he out-thought them."[7]

Crawford provided further insight into the psyche of the Georgia native when he suggested, "He was still fighting the Civil War, and as far as he was concerned, we were all damn Yankees. But who knows, if he hadn't had that terrible persecution complex, he never would have been about the best ballplayer who ever lived."[8]

Notes

Numbers printed in bold indicate that the player led his league in a statistical category.

1. Ty Cobb, http://www.baseball-almanac.com/quotes/quocobb.shtml.
2. *SportsCentury: Fifty Greatest Athletes—Ty Cobb*, television program (ESPN, 1999).
3. Babe Ruth, http://www.baseball-almanac.com/quotes/quocobb.shtml.
4. Tris Speaker, http://www.baseball-almanac.com/quotes/quocobb.shtml.
5. Casey Stengel, http://www.baseball-almanac.com/quotes/quocobb.shtml.
6. George Sisler, http://www.baseball-almanac.com/quotes/quocobb.shtml.
7. Sam Crawford, http://www.baseball-almanac.com/quotes/quocobb.shtml.
8. Sam Crawford, http://www.baseball-almanac.com/quotes/quocobb.shtml.

CHAPTER 8

Hank Greenberg / Charlie Gehringer

One of the most productive offensive tandems in baseball history manned the right side of the Detroit Tigers infield for much of the 1930s. First baseman Hank Greenberg and second sacker Charlie Gehringer teamed up from 1933 to 1940 to help make Detroit the most serious threat to Joe McCarthy's great New York Yankees teams for supremacy in the American League. Greenberg rivaled New York's Lou Gehrig as the period's top RBI man, while Gehringer was an outstanding run producer and excelled in every other aspect of the game as well.

Charlie Gehringer appeared briefly with the Tigers in 1924 and 1925 before winning the team's starting second-base job in 1926. After a rather mediocre rookie season, the lefty-swinging Gehringer had a strong sophomore campaign, batting .317 and scoring 110 runs for the fourth-place Tigers. Detroit slipped to sixth in the American League standings in 1928, but Gehringer had another solid year, batting .320, driving in 74 runs, and scoring 108 others. The Tigers remained in sixth place in 1929, even though Gehringer established himself that year as one of the best all-around players in the game. The 26-year-old second baseman batted .339; knocked in 106 runs; and led the league with 131 runs scored, 215 hits, 19 triples, 45 doubles, and 27 stolen bases. He also compiled the highest fielding percentage among all AL second basemen.

Gehringer continued to perform at an extremely high level the next four seasons, batting well over .300 and scoring in excess of 100 runs three times each while surpassing 100 runs batted in and 200 hits twice each. He finished among the league leaders with 144 runs scored, 47 doubles, and 19 stolen bases in 1930, then placed near the top of the league rankings with 42 doubles and a .325 batting average in 1933. Gehringer performed so consistently that he soon became known as the "Mechanical Man." He seemed to do everything so effortlessly and with so little flair that it eventually became quite easy to take him for granted. Former teammate Mickey Cochrane once said of Gehringer, "He says hello on Opening Day and goodbye on Closing Day, and in between all he does is hit .350."[1]

The style and grace that Gehringer exhibited in the field and on the base paths stood in stark contrast to the awkwardness displayed by a young first baseman who joined him on the right side of the Tigers infield in 1933. The mannerisms of 6'4", 220-pound Hank Greenberg could hardly be described as elegant. The ponderous first baseman appeared somewhat clumsy in the field, and he lumbered from side to side when running the bases. Soon after the 22-year-old slugger took over at first base for the Tigers in 1933, he and Gehringer agreed to let the second baseman field whatever was within his reach. But while Greenberg had to put forth a great deal of effort to gradually turn himself into a decent fielder, he excelled as a hitter from the very beginning. In only 117 games as a rookie in 1933, Greenberg knocked in 87 runs and batted .301.

Heading into the 1934 campaign, Detroit had not won the American League pennant in more than two decades. Although the Tigers occasionally contended for the American League title, they had failed to finish atop the league standings since they captured three consecutive pennants from 1907 to 1909. They were particularly unimpressive in the few preceding seasons, finishing well below .500 each year from 1928 to 1932 and failing to seriously contend for the AL flag since 1924.

However, with Greenberg and Gehringer leading the way, the Tigers won 101 games in 1934 to finish seven games ahead of the second-place Yankees in the American League standings. The numbers posted by the two men clearly illustrate the impact they had on the fortunes of their team that year:

Hank Greenberg: 26 HRs, 139 RBIs, 118 RUNS, .339 AVG, 201 HITS, **63** DOUBLES

Charlie Gehringer: 11 HRs, 127 RBIs, 134 RUNS, .356 AVG, 214 HITS, 50 DOUBLES

Greenberg and Gehringer both placed among the league leaders in batting average, hits, runs batted in, and runs scored, and they finished first and second in the circuit in doubles. The Tiger infield ended up knocking in more runs that year (462) than any other in baseball history. The baseball writers named teammate Mickey Cochrane AL MVP even though the catcher posted relatively modest numbers (2 HR, 76 RBIs, 74 RUNS, .320 AVG). But truth be told, either Greenberg or Gehringer would have made a better choice. Gehringer finished runner-up in the balloting, while Greenberg came in sixth.

Detroit ended up losing the 1934 World Series to St. Louis in seven games. Nevertheless, both Gehringer and Greenberg excelled during the hotly contested series. The second baseman batted .379, collected 11 hits, and scored five runs.

Greenberg batted .321, accumulated nine hits, homered once, and drove in seven runs.

The Tigers captured their second consecutive AL pennant the following year, this time beating out the runner-up Yankees by only three games. Greenberg and Gehringer again served as the focal points of Detroit's offense, compiling the following numbers during the regular season:

Hank Greenberg: **36** HRs, **170** RBIs, 121 RUNS, .328 AVG, 203 HITS, 46
   DOUBLES
Charlie Gehringer: 19 HRs, 108 RBIs, 123 RUNS, .330 AVG, 201 HITS, 32
   DOUBLES

Both men finished among the league leaders in batting average, hits, and runs scored. In addition to leading the league in home runs and runs batted in, Greenberg topped the circuit in total bases and placed near the top of the league rankings in doubles, triples (16), and slugging percentage (.628). Greenberg earned AL MVP honors, while Gehringer finished sixth in the voting.

The Tigers fared much better in the 1935 World Series than they did in the previous year's Fall Classic, defeating the Chicago Cubs in six games. Yet, in spite of the Detroit victory, Greenberg failed to derive much pleasure out of the series. The AL MVP badly injured his wrist in the second contest, forcing him to sit out the four remaining games. Greenberg's injury put an exclamation point on a trouble-filled series for the slugging first baseman, who had to endure an endless stream of verbal taunts from the Chicago players over the course of the first two contests. The Cubs repeatedly made derisive remarks about Greenberg's Jewish heritage, hurling ethnic slurs at him as he stood at first base and in the batter's box. As the slugger stood at home plate on one particular occasion waiting for the opposing pitcher to deliver his next offering, one Chicago player yelled, "Throw him a pork-chop . . . he can't hit that!" The abuse eventually got so bad that home plate umpire George Moriarty stopped the game and instructed the Cubs to tone down their remarks.

Such shabby treatment of Greenberg was not at all unusual, especially early in his career. Anti-Semitism ran rampant throughout the United States at the time, with Detroit serving as one of the nation's least-tolerant places. Henry Ford, one of the city's leading citizens, harbored deep resentment toward people of the Jewish faith, publishing *The International Jew* during the 1920s, a work that blamed a Jewish conspiracy for both communism and a capitalistic plot designed to destroy Christian civilization. And Father Charles Coughlin expressed pro-Nazi sentiments while denouncing Jews and blacks during his weekly radio shows that were broadcast throughout the city and the nation.

Things being as they were during Greenberg's playing days, he often had to endure verbal abuse from fans and opposing players alike. The big first baseman was not the first Jewish man to play in the major leagues. But he was one of a select few who elected not to conceal his heritage by changing his name, and he was certainly the first truly great Jewish player to don a big-league uniform. As a result, Greenberg became a symbol of success for many Jewish Americans as much as he became a target of abuse for those hateful-minded people who resented him merely because of his faith. Greenberg usually chose to ignore the many ignorant comments that were directed toward him, but he sometimes elected to retaliate when his adversary pushed him too far.

One such instance occurred during a game against the Chicago White Sox. With Greenberg holding on Chicago base runner Joe Kuhel at first base, the White Sox first baseman attempted to spike his counterpart as he slid back to the bag on an attempted pickoff. Greenberg responded by slapping Kuhel, but the confrontation was quickly broken up before it was allowed to escalate. After the game, though, Greenberg followed the White Sox players into their clubhouse and proceeded to berate Kuhel in front of the entire team. No one on the White Sox moved a muscle as the hulking Greenberg continued to convey his anger to Kuhel, who sat quietly throughout the diatribe. Detroit pitcher Eldon Auker followed his teammate into the Chicago clubhouse and observed the entire episode. Auker later recalled that the Chicago player's submissive attitude during the reproach "was probably a good thing because Hank was real tough."[2]

Following Detroit's World Series victory in 1935, Greenberg reinjured his wrist early in 1936, causing him to miss virtually the entire year. Gehringer did all he could to keep the Tigers in the pennant race, driving in 116 runs, scoring 144 others, batting .354, compiling 227 hits, and leading the league with 60 doubles. But Greenberg's absence proved to be too much for the Tigers to overcome. They ended up finishing a distant second to the Yankees in the standings, 19.5 games behind the AL champions.

The Yankees won their second of four consecutive world championships in 1937, but the Tigers closed the gap on them somewhat, finishing second again, this time 13 games back. Both Greenberg and Gehringer had fabulous seasons:

Hank Greenberg: 40 HRs, **183** RBIs, 137 RUNS, .337 AVG, 200 HITS, 49 DOUBLES

Charlie Gehringer: 14 HRs, 96 RBIs, 133 RUNS, **.371** AVG, 209 HITS, 40 DOUBLES

Both men finished among the league leaders in hits, doubles, runs scored, and on-base percentage. Gehringer won the first batting title of his career at age 34. Greenberg finished second in the league in home runs, doubles, slugging percentage, walks, and total bases, and his 183 runs batted in left him just one short of Lou Gehrig's American League record of 184. Gehringer was named the league's Most Valuable Player, and Greenberg finished third in the voting.

The Tigers slipped to fourth in the AL standings in 1938, even though Greenberg and Gehringer again had outstanding seasons:

Hank Greenberg: **58** HRs, 146 RBIs, **144** RUNS, .315 AVG
Charlie Gehringer: 20 HRs, 107 RBIs, 133 RUNS, .306 AVG

Greenberg and Gehringer finished first and third in the league in runs scored. Greenberg placed second in the league in runs batted in, and his league-leading 58 home runs left him just two short of tying Babe Ruth's cherished single-season home run record of 60, which stood for another 23 years. Although Greenberg continued to reject the notion years later, some of his Tiger teammates believed that opposing pitchers refused to pitch to the slugger during the season's final days because they didn't want a person of Jewish heritage to break the Babe's record. (Greenberg had 58 home runs with 5 games remaining, and he ended up leading the league with 119 walks.) The Detroit first baseman finished third in the MVP voting, behind Boston's Jimmie Foxx and New York's Bill Dickey.

The Tigers finished a disappointing fifth in 1939 as Gehringer's skills began to diminish ever so slightly. The second baseman batted .325, but he appeared in only 118 games, driving in just 86 runs and scoring only another 86 times. Meanwhile, Greenberg had another very solid year, hitting 33 home runs, knocking in 112 runs, scoring 112 others, and batting .312.

Detroit broke New York's stranglehold on the American League pennant in 1940, finishing just one game ahead of the runner-up Indians and two games in front of the third-place Yankees. Gehringer had his last productive season, hitting .313, knocking in 81 runs, and scoring another 108. Greenberg had one of his best years after moving to left field to make room at first base for slugging youngster Rudy York. Playing the outfield for the first time in his career, Greenberg batted .340, scored 129 runs, and led the league with 41 home runs, 150 runs batted in, 50 doubles, and a .670 slugging percentage. The baseball writers named Greenberg AL MVP for the second time, making him the first player to earn the honor at two positions. Although the Tigers lost the World Series to the Reds in seven games, Greenberg batted .357, with 10 hits, one home run, six runs batted in, and five runs scored.

Gehringer and Greenberg never again played a full season together. The second baseman batted only .220 in 127 games the following year, and he served the Tigers primarily as a pinch hitter in 1942, his final year with the team. Gehringer retired with a career batting average of .320, 1,427 runs batted in, 1,774 runs scored, and 2,839 hits. He trails only Eddie Collins in runs scored among second basemen, and his 574 doubles place him behind only Napoleon Lajoie among players at the position. He batted over .300 on 13 occasions, knocked in more than 100 runs seven times, scored more than 100 runs 12 times, and compiled more than 200 hits, 40 doubles, and 10 triples seven times each. Gehringer served as the American League's starting second baseman in each of the first six All-Star Games.

As Gehringer approached the end of his career in 1941, Greenberg's strong anti-Nazi sentiments prompted him to become the first major-league player to enlist in the U.S. military at the beginning of the Second World War. The reigning AL MVP appeared in only 19 games in 1941. He spent the next 4.5 years away from the game, finally returning to the Tigers midway through the 1945 campaign. Greenberg helped lead Detroit to the AL pennant that year, driving in 60 runs in only 78 games. He subsequently hit two home runs and knocked in seven runs against the Cubs in the World Series, leading the Tigers to a seven-game victory.

Greenberg spent only one more year in Detroit, leading the American League with 44 home runs and 127 RBIs in 1946. He was traded to the Pirates at the end of the season, after which he spent his final year in Pittsburgh mentoring future Hall of Famer Ralph Kiner. Greenberg ended his career with a .313 batting average, 331 home runs, and 1,276 RBIs in only 1,394 games. He surpassed 40 homers on four occasions, knocked in more than 100 runs seven times, scored more than 100 runs six times, collected more than 40 doubles five times, and amassed more than 200 hits three times. Greenberg led the AL in home runs and runs batted in four times each; he also topped the circuit in runs scored once and doubles and walks twice each. He was selected to appear in the All-Star Game each year from 1937 to 1940.

Hank Greenberg and Charlie Gehringer were both full-time regulars on the Tigers for six seasons between 1934 and 1940 (Greenberg missed most of the 1936 campaign with an injury). Greenberg averaged 39 home runs, 150 runs batted in, and 127 runs scored during that period, and he batted well over .300 each year. Gehringer averaged 103 runs batted in and 123 runs scored; he also batted well over .300 each season, surpassing the .350 mark on three separate occasions. Between them, Greenberg and Gehringer averaged 253 RBIs and 250 runs scored during that time. Greenberg won three of his four home-run and RBI titles during that period; the two men also combined to lead the league in doubles three times, runs scored twice, and batting average, hits, and slugging percentage once each. They won three MVP awards, and they finished in the top 10 in the voting seven other times. Greenberg and Gehringer combined for nine All-Star Game appearances as teammates.

Notes

Numbers printed in bold indicate that the player led his league in a statistical category.

1. Mickey Cochrane, http://www.baseball-almanac.com/recbooks/rb_2bdp.shtml.
2. *The Life and Times of Hank Greenberg*, documentary (Twentieth Century Fox, 2001).

CHAPTER 9

Pete Rose / Joe Morgan

Cincinnati's "Big Red Machine" dominated the National League for much of the 1970s, terrorizing NL pitchers while doing so. The Reds captured five divisional titles, four pennants, and two world championships between 1970 and 1976, with Cincinnati batsmen winning six Most Valuable Player Awards over an eight-year stretch at one point. The Reds generally possessed decent starting pitching and a solid bullpen throughout much of the period, but they truly separated themselves from their opposition with their powerful offense. Serving as the Reds' offensive catalysts during the greatest period in franchise history were Pete Rose and Joe Morgan, who manned two of the top three spots in Cincinnati's batting order for most of the decade. Rose and Morgan constantly reached base, enabling them to consistently place among the NL leaders in runs scored. Rose also regularly placed among the leaders in base hits and batting average, while Morgan typically finished near the top of the league rankings in stolen bases, walks, and on-base percentage. Between them, Rose and Morgan made the jobs of Johnny Bench, Tony Perez, and the other members of Cincinnati's powerful lineup much easier since they provided their teammates with numerous opportunities to drive in runs and forced opposing pitchers to give them better pitches to hit. It could be argued that no other team ever had two such outstanding table setters at the top of its batting order.

Pete Rose first came up with the Cincinnati Reds in 1963 as a second baseman. Appearing in 157 of the team's 162 games in his first big-league season, Rose batted .273 and scored 101 runs to earn NL Rookie of the Year honors. After a subpar sophomore campaign, Rose began in 1965 a string of nine consecutive seasons in which he batted over .300. He earned NL All-Star honors in seven of those years, making the squad as both a second baseman and an outfielder. Rose earned his first All-Star selection in 1965 by knocking in 81 runs, scoring 117 others, batting .312, and leading the league with 209 hits.

After moving to the outfield to accommodate young second baseman Tommy Helms, Rose made the first of five consecutive All-Star Game appearances as an outfielder in 1967. Splitting his time between left field and right field before moving in to play third base later in his career, Rose put together some of his finest seasons. He led the National League in batting in 1968 and 1969, with averages of .335 and .348, respectively. He also topped the circuit with 210 hits in 1968. Rose may have had his finest all-around season in 1969, though. In addition to leading the league in hitting, he established career highs with 16 home runs and 82 runs batted in, collected 218 hits, and led the NL with 120 runs scored. Rose scored another 120 runs the following season, batted .316, and topped the circuit with 205 base hits. Although he batted over .300 again in 1971, Rose had a less productive year, driving in only 44 runs and crossing the plate only 86 times himself.

The Reds won the pennant in 1970, but they finished well out of contention in the NL West the following year, prompting the team to make a major move at the conclusion of the 1971 campaign that set up the Reds as the National League's dominant team for the next several seasons. Cincinnati traded Helms and slugging first baseman Lee May to Houston for center fielder Cesar Geronimo, third baseman Denis Menke, and second baseman Joe Morgan. The acquisition of Menke enabled Cincinnati to move Tony Perez back to his more natural position of first base, and Geronimo gave the team an outstanding defensive center fielder. Morgan, who quickly developed into one of the best all-around players in the game, proved to be even more important to the ultimate success of the ball club. Speedy, intelligent, and extremely talented, the second baseman barely scratched the surface of his abilities during his time in Houston.

Joe Morgan appeared briefly with the Astros in 1963 and 1964 before earning the team's starting second-base job in 1965. Morgan batted .271, scored 100 runs, and led the NL with 97 bases on balls in his first full season. After putting together two more solid years, the 5'7", 165-pound second-sacker missed virtually all of 1968 with an injury. Returning to the Houston lineup in 1969, Morgan failed to bat any higher than .268 in any of the next three seasons. However, his diminutive stature and keen batting eye enabled him to compile more than 100 walks in two of those years, thereby posting an extremely effective on-base percentage in the process. Morgan made the National League All-Star Team for the first time in 1970, when he scored 102 runs. He also developed into one of the league's top base stealers with the Astros, surpassing 40 thefts in each of his final three seasons with the club.

After Morgan joined Cincinnati prior to the start of the 1972 campaign, Reds manager Sparky Anderson quickly recognized the many unique talents that his new second baseman possessed. Morgan not only had solid fielding and exceptional base-running skills but possessed tremendous patience at the plate and outstanding baseball instincts. Anderson elected to turn loose the reins on Morgan, giving him complete freedom both at the plate and on the base paths. Before long, the second baseman realized he also had untapped power at the plate that allowed him to develop into one of the team's better RBI men. Over the next six seasons, Morgan and Rose led a Cincinnati offense generally considered to be one of the best in baseball history. Table 9.1 presents the numbers that the two men posted from 1972 to 1977.

Rose led the National League in runs scored, doubles, and base hits three times each during that period. He earned NL MVP honors in 1973, when he helped lead Cincinnati to the Western Division title by topping the circuit with 230 hits and a .338 batting average while finishing third in the league with 115 runs scored. Rose also placed in the top five in the MVP balloting in both 1975 and 1976.

Morgan finished among the league leaders in runs scored, stolen bases, walks, and on-base percentage all six years, topping the circuit in the last category on four occasions. He also placed near the top of the league rankings in batting average in both 1975 and 1976, winning the MVP award both years. In the first of those campaigns, Morgan finished in the league's top five in five offensive categories while capturing the third of his five consecutive Gold Gloves and leading the Reds to the pennant and world championship for the first of two straight times. He posted even better numbers in 1976, leading the league in on-base and slugging percentage and finishing second in four other offensive categories. In addition to winning the MVP award in 1975 and 1976, Morgan placed in the top five in the voting in 1972 and 1973.

Morgan's offensive productivity began to decline in 1978, and he spent two more years in Cincinnati before rejoining the Astros in 1980. He helped Houston win the Western Division title that year, then split his final four seasons among San Francisco, Philadelphia, and Oakland before deciding to call it quits at the conclusion of the 1984 campaign. Morgan ended his career with 268 home runs, 1,133 runs batted in, 1,650 runs scored, 2,517 hits, 689 stolen bases, a .271 batting average, and a superb .395 on-base percentage. Morgan's 1,650 runs scored are the third most ever tallied by a second baseman. He scored more than 100 runs and compiled more than 100 walks in a season eight times each, and he stole more than 40 bases on nine separate occasions.

Rose spent only one more year with the Reds before signing on as a free agent with the Phillies at the end of the 1978 season. In his last year in Cincinnati, Rose batted .302, scored 103 runs, led the league with 51 doubles, and put together a National League record 44-game hitting streak. He spent five seasons in Philadelphia, playing first base throughout his tenure there. Rose's first two years with the Phillies proved to be his most productive. He batted .331, amassed 208 hits, and scored 90 runs in 1979. He followed that up by help-

Table 9.1. Pete Rose and Joe Morgan: 1972–1977

Player	Year	RUNS	AVG	HITS	DOUBLES	HR	RBIs	SB	BB	OBP
Rose	1972	107	.307	**198**	31					
	1973	115	**.338**	**230**	36					
	1974	**110**	.284	185	**45**					
	1975	**112**	.317	210	**47**					
	1976	**130**	.323	**215**	**42**					
	1977	95	.311	204	38					
Morgan	1972	**122**	.292			16	73	58	**115**	**.419**
	1973	116	.290			26	82	67	111	.408
	1974	107	.293			22	67	58	120	**.430**
	1975	107	.327			17	94	67	**132**	**.471**
	1976	113	.320			27	111	60	114	**.453**[a]
	1977	113	.288			22	78	49	117	.420

a. SLG PCT: .576.

ing the Phillies capture their first-ever world championship in 1980 by batting .282, scoring 95 runs, and leading the league with 42 doubles. Rose eventually returned to Cincinnati, where he served as player/manager for his final two seasons, before finally retiring at the end of 1986. He ended his career with a .303 batting average, 2,165 runs scored, and an all-time record 4,256 hits and 14,053 at bats. In addition to being a three-time batting champion, Rose led the league in hits seven times, runs scored four times, and doubles five times. He batted over .300 on 15 occasions, compiled more than 200 hits and 100 runs scored 10 times each, and earned 17 All-Star selections. Yet, in spite of his impressive list of accomplishments, Rose remains suspended from baseball and ineligible for induction into the Hall of Fame due to the fact that he bet on the sport that made him famous while managing in Cincinnati.

Pete Rose and Joe Morgan spent six seasons as teammates in Cincinnati. From 1972 to 1977, they combined to score a total of 1,347 runs, for an average of just under 225 per season. Either Rose or Morgan led the National League in runs scored and on-base percentage four times each during that period, and Rose topped the circuit in hits and doubles three times each. Both men placed in the top five in runs scored five times, on-base percentage twice, and batting average once. In their six years together, Rose and Morgan combined for a total of 11 appearances on the National League All-Star Team (Rose failed to make the squad in 1972). Rose won the MVP award in 1973. Morgan captured the honor in 1975 and 1976. The two men placed in the top five in the balloting on three occasions. The Reds finished first in the NL West in four of those six seasons, winning the pennant three times and capturing back-to-back world championships in 1975 and 1976. It could be argued that no other member of the Cincinnati ball club played a more integral role in the success of the team throughout that period than Morgan and Rose.

Note

Numbers printed in bold indicate that the player led his league in a statistical category.

CHAPTER 10

Greg Maddux / Tom Glavine

The Atlanta Braves were the National League's dominant team throughout virtually all of the 1990s, capturing eight division titles, five pennants, and one world championship between 1991 and 1999. Atlanta had one of the league's better lineups in most of those years, featuring solid hitters such as David Justice, Fred McGriff, Ron Gant, Chipper Jones, and Andruw Jones at various times. Nevertheless, outstanding starting pitching continued to define the Braves throughout the decade, with hurlers such as Steve Avery, Denny Neagle, and Kevin Millwood all excelling for the team at different times. John Smoltz proved to be one of the league's top pitchers for several seasons, even serving as the ace of Atlanta's pitching staff for one or two years. However, the team's two best pitchers in most of those seasons were Greg Maddux and Tom Glavine, who were also two of the finest hurlers of their generation.

Tom Glavine first joined the Atlanta Braves when they were in the midst of an extremely unsuccessful run during the latter half of the 1980s. The Braves failed to win more than 72 games in any season from 1985 to 1990, finishing last in their division in four of those six years. After posting a record of only 69–92 in 1987 (Glavine's first year with the team), they subsequently failed to win more than 65 games in any of the next three seasons. Glavine struggled along with the rest of the team, compiling a 33–41 record over his first four seasons and losing a league-high 17 games in 1988. However, with the development of young outfielders David Justice and Ron Gant, the blossoming of starters Steve Avery and John Smoltz, and the acquisition from St. Louis of league MVP Terry Pendleton, the Braves finished first in the NL West in 1991 with a record of 94–68. They then defeated the Pirates in the National League Championship Series to capture their first pennant since 1958. As important as anyone to the success of the team that year was the 25-year-old Glavine, who had his breakout season. Depending more on outstanding control and the ability to successfully spot his pitches to the corners of the plate than on exceptional velocity, the left-hander finished 20–11 to lead all NL hurlers in victories. He also topped the circuit with nine complete games and placed among the league leaders with a 2.55 ERA and 192 strikeouts. Glavine's exceptional performance earned him the NL Cy Young Award and his first appearance on the NL All-Star Team.

Glavine continued to perform exceptionally well in each of the next two seasons, posting records of 20–8 in 1992 and 22–6 in 1993 en route to leading the league in wins both years. He also compiled an outstanding 2.76 ERA and a league-leading five shutouts for the pennant-winning Braves in the first of those years to earn a second-place finish in the Cy Young voting. Glavine placed third in the balloting in 1993.

Beating out Glavine for Cy Young honors both years was Greg Maddux, who became a member of Atlanta's starting rotation in the second of those two seasons. After capturing his first Cy Young Award as a member of the Chicago Cubs in 1992, Maddux signed on with the Braves as a free agent prior to the start of the ensuing campaign. The right-hander subsequently won his second consecutive trophy in his first year with his new team. But as was the case with Glavine, Maddux did not experience immediate success at the major-league level.

After first coming up with the Cubs in 1986, Maddux suffered through two horrific seasons before he found himself in 1988. Maddux posted a combined record of 8–18 his first two years while compiling an ERA in excess of 5.50 each season. However, the 22-year-old right-hander finally mastered control of his pitches his third year in the league. Not only did Maddux learn how to spot his pitches to the corners, but he also mastered the art of breaking his fastball back toward the plate after initially releasing it toward the batter's waist.

Hall of Fame outfielder Tony Gwynn discussed the strategy that Maddux used to baffle opposing hitters: "He's like a meticulous surgeon out there. He puts the ball where he wants to. You see a pitch inside and wonder, 'Is it the fastball or the cutter?' That's where he's got you."[1]

His new technique perfected, Maddux won 37 games for the Cubs over the next two seasons before having his greatest year for them in 1992. Maddux finished 20–11 to tie Glavine for the league lead in victories. He also topped the circuit with 268 innings pitched, and he placed among the leaders with a 2.18 earned run average. Maddux continued to excel after he signed on with Atlanta at the end of the year, compiling a record of 20–10 in his first year with his new team and leading the league with a 2.36 ERA, 267 innings pitched, and eight complete games en route to winning his second straight Cy Young Award.

Fellow Braves right-hander John Smoltz was among those whom Maddux impressed with his cerebral approach to pitching. Smoltz noted, "Every pitch has a purpose. Sometimes [Maddux] knows what he's going to throw two pitches ahead. I swear, he makes it look like guys are swinging foam bats against him."[2]

The Braves failed to win the pennant in 1993, and the 1994 campaign ended prematurely due to a players' strike. Nevertheless, Maddux captured his third straight Cy Young Award in 1994 after going 16–6 with a league-leading 10 complete games and 1.56 ERA during the abbreviated season. He became the first pitcher to win the award four consecutive times the following year, when he helped lead Atlanta to the NL pennant by topping all league hurlers in every major statistical category. Maddux finished the 1995 season with a 19–2 record, a 1.63 ERA, 210 innings pitched, 10 complete games, and three shutouts. His extraordinary performance earned him a third-place finish in the league MVP voting. Glavine also pitched quite well for Atlanta that year, going 16–7 with a 3.08 ERA during the regular season. The left-hander then defeated Cleveland twice in the World Series, compiling an ERA of 1.29 and allowing only four hits in 14 innings of work against the Tribe. The Braves defeated the Indians in the Fall Classic to capture their first world championship in 38 years, with Glavine copping World Series MVP honors.

Both Maddux and Glavine had solid seasons for the Braves in 1996 and 1997, helping them win another two division titles and another NL pennant in the first of those years. Maddux pitched particularly well in 1997, going 19–4 with a 2.20 ERA in his 233 innings of work en route to earning a second-place finish in the Cy Young balloting. The two hurlers subsequently had two of their finest seasons together in 1998 and 2000:

1998
Maddux: 18 wins, 9 losses; **2.22** ERA, 251 IP, 9 CG
Glavine: **20** wins, 6 losses; 2.47 ERA, 229 IP, 4 CG
2000
Maddux: 19 wins, 9 losses; 3.00 ERA, 249 IP, 6 CG
Glavine: 21 wins, 9 losses; 3.40 ERA, 241 IP, 4 CG

In addition to leading the league in ERA in 1998, Maddux finished near the top of the league rankings in wins, innings pitched, and complete games. Glavine topped the circuit in wins both years, capturing his second Cy Young Award in 1998. He also finished runner-up in the balloting in 2000, a year in which the *Sporting News* selected him as its Pitcher of the Year. The Braves finished first in the NL East both years; they also captured the division title in 1999, when they won their fifth pennant of the decade.

Glavine had his last big year for Atlanta in 2002, finishing 18–11 with a 2.96 ERA, before signing on as a free agent with the rival New York Mets at the end of the season. He spent the next five years in New York, never again experiencing the same level of success. Glavine returned to the Braves in 2008, but he was unceremoniously released by the team early in 2009 after going only

2–4 with a 5.54 ERA in his 13 starts the previous season. He ended his career with a record of 305–203 and an ERA of 3.54.

Maddux pitched extremely well for Atlanta in both 2001 and 2002, before his performance began to slip somewhat the following year. He signed with the Chicago Cubs as a free agent prior to the start of the 2004 campaign, spending the better part of the next three seasons with the team he originally came up with, before joining the Dodgers toward the latter portion of 2006. Maddux split his last two seasons between Los Angeles and San Diego, finally retiring at the end of the 2008 season with a career record of 355–227 and an ERA of 3.16. His 355 victories are the most wins compiled by any pitcher whose career began after 1950.

Although Maddux was well past his prime by the time he began his second tenure with the Cubs in 2004, the right-hander continued to impress his teammates with his intellectual approach to his craft. Cubs right-hander Ryan Dempster commented, "Any pitcher on this team should have the pleasure of parking their butt next to him on the bench during games and learning whatever you can from him and then watching him when he is pitching."[3]

Chicago outfielder Juan Pierre said of Maddux, "He's the definition of pitching. He's not overpowering, he doesn't have tremendous stuff, but he gets it done every day, day in and day out. It's good that I can tell my grandkids that I had the chance to play behind Greg Maddux, the Hall of Famer."[4]

Greg Maddux and Tom Glavine were teammates on the Atlanta Braves from 1993 to 2002. In their 10 years together, the Braves won nine division titles, three NL pennants, and one World Series. During that time, the two pitchers combined to win four Cy Young Awards, placing in the top five in the voting a total of 11 times between them. They made 12 All-Star Game appearances, and Maddux won 10 Gold Gloves. Either Maddux or Glavine led the league in wins, innings pitched, and shutouts five times each; earned run average four times; and complete games three times. One or the other posted an ERA under 3.00 a total of 11 times, won at least 20 games four times, and surpassed 18 victories another six times. They compiled a combined record of 347–160.

Notes

Numbers printed in bold indicate that the player led his league in a statistical category.

1. Tony Gwynn, http://www.baseball-almanac.com/quotes/greg_maddux_quotesshtml.

2. John Smoltz, http://www.baseball-almanac.com/quotes/greg_maddux_quotes.shtml.

3. Ryan Dempster, http://www.baseball-almanac.com/quotes/greg_maddux_quotes.shtml.

4. Juan Pierre, http://www.baseball-almanac.com/quotes/greg_maddux_quotes.shtml.

CHAPTER 11

Sam Thompson / Billy Hamilton

One would think that putting two of the greatest run producers in baseball history in the same starting lineup would result in a considerable amount of run production. That theory was proven true when Sam Thompson and Billy Hamilton teamed up for six seasons on the National League's Philadelphia Quakers during the last decade of the 19th century. Thompson was the period's greatest slugger and RBI man, while Hamilton was the era's top leadoff hitter, base stealer, and run scorer.

"Big Sam" Thompson began his professional baseball career with the National League's Detroit Wolverines in 1885. After becoming a regular member of the Detroit outfield in his second season, the 6'2", 207-pound Thompson helped lead the Wolverines to the league championship in 1887 when he established a 19th-century record by driving in 166 runs in only 127 games. The right fielder also hit 11 home runs, scored 118 runs, and led the league with 23 triples, 203 hits, a .372 batting average, and a .571 slugging percentage. Known for his powerful throwing arm, Thompson excelled in the outfield as well. Said to be the originator of the one-hop throw to the plate, Thompson often used that technique to throw out opposing base runners when they attempted to score on either base hits or fly balls to him in the outfield.

After being sidelined for much of the 1888 season with a sore arm, Thompson was sold to the Philadelphia Quakers (who eventually became the Phillies) at the end of the year. Big Sam responded by knocking in 111 runs, scoring another 103, batting .296, and hitting a 19th-century record 20 home runs in 1889.

Thompson was joined in Philadelphia the following season by speedy center fielder Billy Hamilton, who spent the previous two years with Kansas City of the American Association. Known for his daring base running and head-first slides, the 5'6", 165-pound Hamilton stole 111 bases and scored 144 runs in only 137 games with Kansas City in 1889. In addition to being an exceptional base runner and stealer of bases, the diminutive outfielder was an outstanding hitter who used his size, or lack thereof, to his advantage. Not only did Hamilton consistently bat well over .300, but his propensity for drawing bases on balls also enabled him to post a career on-base percentage of .455, which places him fourth on the all-time list, behind only Ted Williams, Babe Ruth, and John McGraw.

Paired up with each other in Philadelphia, Hamilton and Thompson began a string of highly successful seasons together in 1890. Over the next three years, Thompson batted over .300 and surpassed 100 runs batted in twice each, scored more than 100 runs each season, and led the league in base hits and doubles once each. Serving as the team's leadoff hitter, the left-handed-swinging Hamilton batted well over .300 and scored well in excess of 100 runs all three seasons, leading the league in both departments in 1891. He also topped the circuit in walks, base hits, and stolen bases that year, leading the league with more than 100 thefts for the second consecutive time.

After the powers that be moved the pitcher's mound back to 60 feet, 6 inches at the end of the 1892 season, offensive numbers began to soar throughout all of baseball. The figures posted by Hamilton and Thompson were no exception. The two players had their three best years together from 1893 to 1895, compiling the statistics shown in tables 11.1 and 11.2.

Hamilton and Thompson joined fellow Philadelphia outfielder Ed Delahanty in 1894 to form the only all-.400 hitting outfield in baseball history. Hamilton's total of 192 runs scored that year still stands as the major-league record. Hamilton and Thompson subsequently combined to lead the league in six offensive categories in 1895, when the latter came within one RBI of matching his own 19th-century mark.

Thompson played one more full season in Philadelphia, knocking in 100 runs and scoring 103 others in 1896. He then appeared in a total of only 17 games over the course of the next two years before retiring at the end of the 1898 campaign. Thompson ended his career with a .331 batting average, 127 home runs, 160 triples, 1,299 runs batted in, and 1,256 runs scored in only 1,407 games. His ratio of .923 RBIs to games played places him first on the all-time list, slightly ahead of Lou Gehrig and Hank Greenberg. Thompson's 127 home runs represent the second-highest total compiled by any 19th-century player (Roger Connor hit 138). He knocked in more than 100 runs eight times, scored more than 100 runs 10 times, and batted over .370 four times.

Table 11.1. Billy Hamilton: 1893–1895

Year	RUNS	AVG	OBP	SB	HITS	WALKS
1893	110	**.380**	**.490**	43	135	63
1894	**192**	.404	**.523**	**98**	220	**126**
1895	**166**	.389	.490	**97**	201	**96**

Table 11.2. Sam Thompson: 1893–1895

Year	RUNS	AVG	HR	RBIs	HITS	DOUBLES	TRIPLES	SLG PCT
1893	130	.370	11	126	**222**	**37**	13	.530
1894	108	.407	13	141	187	32	27	.686
1895	131	.392	**18**	**165**	211	45	21	.654

While Thompson played his last full season in 1896, Hamilton remained an extremely effective player after he joined the Boston Beaneaters that very same year. He led the National League in on-base percentage and bases on balls two more times, and he topped the circuit in runs scored once more, crossing the plate 152 times for Boston in 1896 and 1897. Hamilton finally retired from the game at the conclusion of the 1901 season, ending his career with a .344 batting average, a .455 on-base percentage, 912 stolen bases, 2,158 hits, and 1,690 runs scored in only 1,591 games. His ratio of runs scored to games played is the highest in baseball history. Hamilton's 912 stolen bases also stood as the major-league record until Lou Brock surpassed that figure some 75 years later. However, it should be noted that a player was credited with a stolen base prior to 1892 if he tagged up on a fly ball, advanced from first to third on a single, or moved up on a ground ball to the right side.

The two most prolific run producers of the 19th century spent six full seasons together in Philadelphia. Sam Thompson averaged 121 runs batted in, 117 runs scored, and 15 triples over those six years. Hamilton averaged 140 runs scored and 85 stolen bases. Thompson led the league in home runs, RBIs, hits, and slugging percentage once each. Hamilton topped the circuit in stolen bases four times, runs scored and on-base percentage three times each, batting average twice, and hits once. Philadelphia failed to capture the National League pennant in any of those seasons. However, after barely finishing over the .500 mark in both 1888 and 1889, the team compiled one of the league's best records in five of the next six years, with Thompson and Hamilton starting alongside one another in the outfield.

Note

Numbers printed in bold indicate that the player led his league in a statistical category.

CHAPTER 12

Sandy Koufax / Don Drysdale

The pitching-dominated 1960s featured several outstanding pitching tandems whose members excelled together for a period: Jim Bunning and Chris Short combined to win 112 games for the Philadelphia Phillies from 1964 to 1966. Denny McLain and Mickey Lolich won a total of 187 games for the Detroit Tigers from 1965 to 1969. Juan Marichal and Gaylord Perry combined to average 39 wins per season for the San Francisco Giants from 1966 to 1969. And Tom Seaver and Jerry Koosman combined to win a total of 77 games for the New York Mets in 1968 and 1969, leading the team to a miraculous World Series victory in the second of those seasons. However, the Los Angeles Dodgers' combination of Sandy Koufax and Don Drysdale formed the decade's most dominant pitching duo, leading their team to three pennants and two world championships between 1963 and 1966.

Don Drysdale first came up with the Dodgers in 1956, compiling a record of 5–5 and an ERA of 2.64 while serving the team as both a starter and a reliever. The 6'6", 225-pound right-hander had his first big year for the Dodgers the following season, finishing 17–9 with a 2.69 ERA and 221 innings pitched in the team's last year in Brooklyn. The California native pitched less effectively after the club moved out west in 1958, going just 12–13 with a 4.17 earned run average in his first year in Los Angeles. Drysdale rebounded in 1959, though, finishing the year with a record of 17–13, an ERA of 3.46, 270 innings pitched, and a league-leading 242 strikeouts for the world champion Dodgers. Drysdale's strong performance earned him his first NL All-Star selection and established him as the workhorse of the Los Angeles pitching staff. The big right-hander also began to develop a reputation for being one of the sport's nastiest and most intimidating pitchers. Not only did Drysdale's size make him an extremely imposing figure on the mound, but he also did not hesitate in the least to claim the inside part of the plate for himself by throwing at opposing batters. On one particular occasion, Dodger manager Walter Alston instructed him to intentionally walk Frank Robinson. Drysdale responded by knocking down Robinson with four consecutive pitches, the last of which hit the Cincinnati slugger squarely in the ribs.

Drysdale's mean streak reflected the attitude he carried with him to the mound before each start. The hard-throwing right-hander once proclaimed, "I hate all hitters. I start a game mad and I stay that way until it's over."[1]

Drysdale also had two rules that he always followed. He explained the first by saying, "My own little rule was two for one. If one of my teammates got knocked down, then I knocked down two on the other team."[2]

Drysdale expounded on his principle of pitching inside: "When the ball is over the middle of the plate, the batter is hitting it with the sweet part of the bat. When it's inside, he's hitting it with the part of the bat from the handle to the trademark. When it's outside, he's hitting it with the end of the bat. You've got to keep the ball away from the sweet part of the bat. To do that, the pitcher has to move the hitter off the plate."[3]

Opposing batters became all too familiar with Drysdale's aggressive approach to pitching. Orlando Cepeda suggested, "The trick against Drysdale is to hit him before he hits you."[4]

Dick Groat, who faced Drysdale as a member of the Pirates, Cardinals, and Phillies, quipped, "Batting against Don Drysdale is the same as making a date with a dentist."[5]

Mickey Mantle faced Drysdale in the 1963 World Series and in numerous All-Star Games. The New York Yankee great commented, "I hated to bat against Drysdale. After he hit you he'd come around, look at the bruise on your arm, and say, 'Do you want me to sign it?'"[6]

Drysdale's size, nasty temperament, and talent made him one of the league's most difficult pitchers for opposing batters to face. He continued to establish himself as one of baseball's top hurlers in 1960, compiling a record of 15–14 with a 2.84 ERA, 269 innings pitched, and a league-leading 246 strikeouts. The big right-hander was somewhat less effective the following year, though, going 13–10 with a 3.69 ERA and only 182 strikeouts in 244 innings of work.

The 1961 campaign proved to be the breakout year for another Dodger hurler who previously experienced little in the way of success in his tenure with the team. Brooklyn-born left-hander Sandy Koufax originally joined the Dodgers as a promising 19-year-old in 1955. It became apparent from the outset that Koufax had great velocity on his fastball but had yet to master either his curveball or his control over any of his other pitches.

Hall of Fame outfielder Duke Snider was with the Dodgers when Koufax first joined them. Snider later recalled, "When [Koufax] first came up he couldn't throw a ball inside the batting cage."[7]

Pitching mostly out of the Dodgers bullpen during the team's final three years in Brooklyn, Koufax posted a combined record of only 9–10, with an ERA well over 3.00 each season. In 203 total innings of work, the struggling southpaw struck out 182 batters, but he also walked another 108. Koufax was equally ineffective after the team moved to Los Angeles, compiling a record of 27–30 between 1958 and 1960 while pitching to an ERA near or above 4.00 in each of those three seasons. Koufax averaged slightly more than a strikeout an inning during that time, but he also allowed more than one walk every two innings.

Koufax eventually became so frustrated with his lack of success that he seriously considered leaving the game before he turned 25 years of age. But everything began to turn around for the left-hander during spring training in 1961, when Dodger catcher Norm Sherry taught him to grip the ball less tightly on the mound and to relax his body before releasing the ball. Koufax later noted, "I became a good pitcher when I stopped trying to make them miss the ball and started trying to make them hit it."[8]

The results were immediate and startling. Koufax finished the 1961 campaign with a record of 18–13, an earned run average of 3.52, 255 innings pitched, a league-leading 269 strikeouts, only 96 bases on balls, and his first selection to the NL All-Star Team.

Koufax continued his progression during the 1962 season, going 14–7, leading the league with a 2.54 earned run average, and striking out 216 batters in only 26 starts and 184 innings. Drysdale was even better, finishing 25–9 to lead the league in victories. He also placed among the league leaders with a 2.83 ERA and 19 complete games while topping the circuit with 232 strikeouts and 314 innings pitched. Drysdale's outstanding performance earned him the major-league Cy Young Award (only one award was presented to the best pitcher in both leagues combined until 1967) and helped the Dodgers to a close second-place finish behind the San Francisco Giants in the NL pennant race. In fact, it took a three-game playoff between the two teams to decide the league champion.

After playing second fiddle to Drysdale the previous year, Koufax established himself as the ace of the Dodger pitching staff in 1963. In fact, Sandy was the best pitcher in the game over the next four seasons and quite possibly the greatest ever. With an arsenal of pitches that included an explosive fastball and the sharpest-breaking curveball in the sport, Koufax was practically unhittable.

Hall of Fame outfielder Richie Ashburn stated, "Either he throws the fastest ball I've ever seen, or I'm going blind."[9]

Philadelphia Phillies manager Gene Mauch commented, "[Koufax] throws a 'radio ball,' a pitch you hear, but you don't see."[10]

Willie Stargell expressed his admiration for the left-hander by saying, "Trying to hit Koufax was like trying to drink coffee with a fork."[11]

John Roseboro served as the Dodgers' primary receiver during Koufax's peak seasons. He recalled, "Catching [Koufax] was like, 'Well, we're gonna kick someone's ass tonight.'"[12]

Duke Snider, who saw Koufax close up during the various stages of the left-hander's career, said of his former teammate, "He was a fantastic pitcher . . . the best I've seen."[13]

The numbers that Koufax posted from 1963 to 1966 were certainly quite impressive—see table 12.1. In addition to leading the league in earned run average all four years, Koufax topped all NL pitchers in wins and strikeouts three times each and in shutouts, innings pitched, and complete games twice each. Koufax earned Cy Young honors in 1963, 1965, and 1966. He also won the NL MVP award in 1963, and he finished second in the balloting in 1965 and 1966. Koufax compiled an amazing 97–27 record over that four-year stretch.

The figures that Drysdale posted during that same period weren't too shabby either—see table 12.2. Drysdale finished among the league leaders in innings pitched all four years, leading all NL hurlers in that category in 1964. He also placed near the top of the league rankings in wins once, strikeouts twice, and complete games three times.

The Dodgers won the National League pennant in 1963, 1965, and 1966, and they captured the world championship in both 1963 and 1965. In the first of those years, Los Angeles swept the Yankees in the World Series, limiting New York's offense to only four runs in the four contests. Koufax set the tone for the

Table 12.1. Sandy Koufax: 1963–1966

Year	Wins	Losses	ERA	Strikeouts	Innings Pitched	Shutouts	Complete Games
1963	**25**	5	**1.88**	**306**	311	**11**	20
1964	19	5	**1.74**	223	223	**7**	15
1965	**26**	8	**2.04**	**382**	**335**	8	**27**
1966	**27**	9	**1.73**	**317**	**323**	5	**27**

Table 12.2. Don Drysdale: 1963–1966

Year	Wins	Losses	ERA	Strikeouts	Innings Pitched	Complete Games
1963	19	17	2.63	251	315	17
1964	18	16	2.18	237	**321**	21
1965	23	12	2.77	210	308	20
1966	13	16	3.42	177	273	11

Note: Drysdale had seven shutouts in 1965.

entire series in game 1, striking out a record-setting 15 New York batters during the Dodgers' 5–2 victory. After Los Angeles won game 2, Drysdale allowed the Yankees only three hits in game 3, outdueling New York starter Jim Bouton, 1–0. Koufax returned in game 4 to clinch the series for the Dodgers by striking out another eight Yankee batters during his team's 2–1 victory.

After Koufax's victory in the Series finale, Yankee player/coach Yogi Berra commented, "I can see how [Koufax] won 25 games. What I don't understand is how he lost five."[14]

The combined stat line for Koufax and Drysdale in the Fall Classic reveals the degree to which the two hurlers dominated New York's lineup:

Koufax and Drysdale: 3 wins, 0 losses; 1.00 ERA, 3 complete games, 27 innings pitched, 15 hits allowed, 32 strikeouts, 4 walks

The Dodgers returned to the World Series in 1965, and their two staff aces once again carried them to the world championship. Los Angeles appeared flat in the first two contests, played against the Twins in Minnesota. Koufax refused to pitch game 1 since the contest happened to coincide with Yom Kippur, the holiest of all Jewish holidays. Although he wasn't a particularly religious man, Koufax believed that he needed to set an example for all the young Jewish children who looked up to him. Drysdale started the game for the Dodgers instead, and he pitched ineffectively, lasting only into the third inning of Minnesota's 8–2 victory. Although Koufax pitched quite well in game 2, allowing only one earned run in his six innings of work, the Twins came out on top again, this time by a score of 5–1. After Dodger pitcher Claude Osteen halted Minnesota's momentum after the teams traveled to Los Angeles for game 3 by throwing a five-hit shutout, Drysdale and Koufax proceeded to take over the series. The former allowed only five hits during a 7–2 complete-game victory in game 4. Koufax followed that up with a four-hit shutout in game 5 before the Twins defeated Osteen in game 6 back in Minnesota. Although Los Angeles manager Walter Alston had Drysdale ready to work on full rest, he elected instead to pitch Koufax on only two days' rest in the decisive seventh game of the series. Koufax rewarded the faith that his manager placed in him by going the distance and allowing the Twins only three hits during the Dodgers' 2–0 win. The left-hander ended up posting a 2–1 record and a 0.38 ERA during the series while throwing two complete-game shutouts and allowing only one earned run and 13 hits in 24 innings of work. He also amassed 29 strikeouts.

The incredible success that Koufax and Drysdale experienced together over the course of the 1965 campaign (they combined to post 49 of their team's 97 victories during the regular season) prompted them to conduct a joint holdout at the end of the season. Although they ended up settling for less than the original amount they demanded from the Dodgers, the two pitchers did quite well for themselves that off-season. Koufax eventually signed for $120,000, while Drysdale's deal for 1966 netted him $105,000.

The Dodgers made it back to the World Series for the third time in four years in 1966, but the outcome proved to be far less favorable for them this time. Baltimore swept Los Angeles in four games, with neither Koufax nor Drysdale faring particularly well. Koufax pitched well in his lone start, allowing the Orioles only one earned run on six hits in his six innings of work. But, betrayed by his defense, he ended up losing a 6–0 decision. Drysdale wasn't nearly as effective, going 0–2 with a 4.50 ERA in his two starts.

The 1966 season proved to be the last that Koufax and Drysdale spent as teammates. Koufax decided to retire after the World Series while still at the top of his game, due to the constant pain he experienced in his pitching arm after every start. The left-hander first began experiencing arthritis in his throwing shoulder during the 1964 campaign, causing him to spend the final two years of his career pitching in great discomfort.

Upon announcing his retirement, the 30-year-old Koufax explained to the assembled media, "I've been getting cortisone shots pretty regularly, and I don't want to take a chance on completely disabling myself. . . . I've got a lot of years to live after baseball and I would like to live them with the complete use of my body."[15]

Koufax's swan song to Major League Baseball was the greatest ever. He led major-league pitchers in virtually every major statistical category in 1966, finishing the year with 27 wins, a 1.73 ERA, 317 strikeouts, 323 innings pitched, and 27 complete games. Koufax ended his career with a record of 165–87, an ERA of 2.76, and 2,396 strikeouts in 2,324 innings pitched. He also allowed only 1,754 hits and threw four no-hitters, including one perfect game.

Koufax's importance to the success of the Dodgers became fully evident in 1967, when the team finished eighth in the National League, with only 73 victories. They finished eighth the following year as well, although Drysdale pitched effectively for Los Angeles in each of those seasons. Although he finished just 13–16 in 1967, Drysdale compiled a very respectable 2.74 ERA. He posted a 14–12 record the following year, placing among the league leaders with an outstanding 2.15 earned run average. Drysdale finished second among National League pitchers with eight shutouts, and he established a new major-league record for throwing consecutive scoreless innings—58^2/$_3$ at one point during the season (a mark later broken by Orel Hershiser). However, arm problems forced Drysdale into retirement at the end of the 1969 campaign, after he finished only 5–4 with a 4.45 ERA in his 12 starts that year. The right-hander ended his career with a record of 209–166 and a 2.95 ERA.

Sandy Koufax and Don Drysdale were teammates on the Dodgers for 11 seasons. Both men were regular members of the team's starting rotation from

1961 to 1966. During that six-year period, they combined to win a total of 240 games, for an average of 40 per year. Between them, Koufax and Drysdale led the league in wins four times, strikeouts five times, innings pitched four times, shutouts three times, and complete games twice. Koufax led all NL pitchers in earned run average in five of those years as well. Either Koufax or Drysdale threw at least 300 innings in a season seven times, and one or the other compiled more than 200 strikeouts in a season on 10 occasions. Koufax and Drysdale won four of the six Cy Young Awards presented between 1961 and 1966, and they were named to the All-Star Team 11 times during that six-year period. Their greatest season together was 1965, a year in which Koufax led the league in wins, ERA, strikeouts, complete games, and innings pitched. He also finished second in shutouts. Drysdale finished third in the league in wins, complete games, and shutouts, and he placed second in innings pitched. Koufax finished second in the league MVP balloting that year, while Drysdale came in fifth. And in the Dodgers' World Series triumphs of 1963 and 1965, Koufax and Drysdale combined to post six of the team's eight victories, allowing just nine earned runs in almost 63 innings of work for a combined ERA of only 1.28.

Notes

Numbers printed in bold indicate that the player led his league in a statistical category.

1. Don Drysdale, http://www.baseball-almanac.com/quotes/quodrys.shtml.
2. Don Drysdale, http://www.baseball-almanac.com/quotes/quodrys.shtml.
3. Don Drysdale, http://www.baseball-almanac.com/quotes/quodrys.shtml.
4. Orlando Cepeda, http://www.baseball-almanac.com/quotes/quodrys.shtml.
5. Dick Groat, http://www.baseball-almanac.com/quotes/quodrys.shtml.
6. Mickey Mantle, http://www.baseball-almanac.com/quotes/quodrys.shtml.
7. *SportsCentury: Fifty Greatest Athletes—Sandy Koufax*, television program (ESPN, 1999).
8. *Fifty Greatest Athletes—Sandy Koufax*.
9. *Fifty Greatest Athletes—Sandy Koufax*.
10. *Fifty Greatest Athletes—Sandy Koufax*.
11. *Fifty Greatest Athletes—Sandy Koufax*.
12. *Fifty Greatest Athletes—Sandy Koufax*.
13. *Fifty Greatest Athletes—Sandy Koufax*.
14. *Fifty Greatest Athletes—Sandy Koufax*.
15. *Fifty Greatest Athletes—Sandy Koufax*.

CHAPTER 13

Ted Williams / Bobby Doerr

Ted Williams and Bobby Doerr won only one American League pennant in their 10 full seasons as teammates on the Boston Red Sox. However, they helped transform the Red Sox into perennial contenders during that time, making Boston the most serious challengers to the Yankees for supremacy in the Junior Circuit and providing much of the initial spark for a rivalry that eventually became the most intense in all of professional team sports.

The Boston Red Sox were one of baseball's best teams throughout the second decade of the 20th century, winning four world championships during that 10-year period. However, after selling Babe Ruth to the Yankees at the end of the 1919 season and subsequently trading away most of their best players to other American League clubs, the Red Sox spent the better part of the next two decades as one of baseball's least-successful franchises. Boston posted a losing record in 15 consecutive seasons at one point, finishing last in the AL nine times between 1920 and 1933. Only after free-spending Tom Yawkey took over ownership of the team did the Red Sox become competitive once more during the second half of the 1930s. Yawkey began restructuring Boston's roster at the conclusion of the 1933 campaign when he purchased Hall of Fame pitcher Lefty Grove from the Philadelphia Athletics. He acquired fellow Hall of Famers Joe Cronin and Jimmie Foxx from Washington and Philadelphia, respectively, the next two seasons, enabling the Red Sox to post 80 victories in 1937—their highest win total in 20 years.

Yawkey also helped rebuild Boston's farm system, which soon began producing talented players at a rapid rate. The first outstanding young player to come up to the Red Sox from the minor leagues during this period was second baseman Bobby Doerr, who appeared in his first 55 games with the team in 1937. The smooth-fielding Doerr won the starting second base job the following year, driving in 80 runs, batting .289, and displaying the defensive skills that quickly established him as one of baseball's top players at the position. Boston finished second to New York in the American League standings in 1938, compiling a record of 88–61.

The Red Sox finished runner-up to the Yankees again the following year, with Doerr having another solid season by batting .318 and knocking in 73 runs in only 127 games. But Boston fans eventually came to remember 1939 mostly as the year that Ted Williams appeared in a Red Sox uniform for the first time. The cocky 20-year-old had a brilliant rookie season, hitting 31 home runs, scoring 131 runs, batting .327, leading the league with 145 runs batted in and 344 total bases, and finishing fourth in the AL MVP voting. Williams had so much confidence in his ability to hit a baseball that he even surprised some of his own teammates with the temerity that he often displayed. As the rookie prepared for his first batting practice session with the big club, one of his teammates said to him, "Wait until you see Foxx hit!" Unimpressed, Williams responded, "Wait until Foxx sees me hit!"[1]

Foxx and Williams gave the Red Sox the American League's most formidable one-two punch from 1939 to 1941, leading the team to another second-place finish in the last of those three years. After sharing the spotlight with Foxx his first two seasons, Williams became Boston's leading man in 1941, knocking in 120 runs and leading the league with 37 home runs, 135 runs scored, a .406 batting average, a .551 on-base percentage, and a .735 slugging percentage. No man has batted .400 since. Still, Williams finished second to New York's Joe DiMaggio in the league MVP voting (DiMaggio hit in 56 consecutive games that year and led his team to the AL pennant).

When Foxx's productivity began to decline the following year, Boston traded away the slugging first baseman, leaving Doerr the team's number-two offensive threat. The second baseman, who also performed quite well in each of the previous two seasons, responded with 102 runs batted in and a .290 batting average. Meanwhile, Williams captured the AL Triple Crown, leading the league with 36 home runs, 137 RBIs, and a .356 batting average and topping the circuit with 141 runs scored, a .499 on-base percentage, and a .648 slugging percentage. Yet, even though the Red Sox finished a very respectable second to the Yankees in the American League standings, Williams again failed to win the MVP award. The honor instead went to New York second baseman Joe Gordon.

There is little doubt that Williams failed at times to receive as much support as he should have from the baseball writers when they cast their MVP ballots due to the contentious relationship that he shared with them throughout his career. The slugger was moody, hot-tempered, impatient, and somewhat temperamental, especially in his early years in the league. As a result, Williams had numerous confrontations with various members of the press early in his career that jaded their opinion of him throughout the remainder of his playing days. Williams was extremely honest and forthright in his responses to their questions, and he didn't particularly care how they might react to his answers. The writers often misinterpreted Williams's self-confidence as arrogance, and they conveyed their feelings toward him to the Boston faithful in their newspaper articles. Before long, Red Sox fans turned against Williams as well, finding particularly objectionable his habit of practicing his swing in the outfield during the opposing team's at bats. Boston fans believed that the sport's greatest hitter didn't pay as much attention to the other aspects of the game as he should have, and they soon took to booing him at every opportunity. Williams responded by refusing to ever again tip his cap to them when they cheered him after hitting a home run.

Following his Triple Crown performance, Williams missed the 1943–1945 seasons, spending those three years serving his country in the U.S. military during World War II. However, Doerr missed only the 1945 campaign, having one of his finest seasons in 1944. With many of the game's greatest players absent, Doerr appeared in 125 games before joining the war effort himself. In those 125 contests, he drove in 81 runs, scored 95 others, finished second in the league with a career-high .325 batting average, and led the AL with a .528 slugging percentage.

Both Williams and Doerr returned to Boston in 1946, leading the team to its first pennant since 1918. Doerr hit 18 home runs, knocked in 116 runs, scored 95 others, and batted .271. He finished third in the MVP voting. Williams finally won the award by placing among the league leaders with 38 home runs, 123 runs batted in, and a .342 batting average and topping the circuit with 142 runs scored, 156 walks, a .497 on-base percentage, a .667 slugging average, and 343 total bases. The Red Sox, though, ended up losing the World Series to the Cardinals in seven games.

Boston slipped to third in the American League standings in 1947, even though the team received outstanding performances from both Doerr and Williams. The second baseman had another solid season, hitting 17 home runs and driving in 95 runs. Williams was again the league's best player, capturing his second Triple Crown by topping the circuit with 32 home runs, 114 RBIs, and a .343 batting average. He also finished first in runs scored, walks, on-base percentage, slugging average, and total bases. Yet Williams again found himself the victim of voter bias, finishing just one point behind Joe DiMaggio in the AL MVP voting when a Boston sportswriter who didn't get along well with the Red Sox slugger left him completely off his ballot.

The Red Sox narrowly missed capturing the American League pennant in each of the next three seasons, losing a one-game playoff to the Indians in 1948, finishing only one game behind the Yankees in 1949, and losing out to New

York by four games in 1950. Williams and Doerr had some of their best years together during that time, posting the following numbers:

1948
Bobby Doerr: 27 HRs, 111 RBIs, .285 AVG, 94 RUNS
Ted Williams: 25 HRs, 127 RBIs, **.369** AVG, 124 RUNS
1949
Bobby Doerr: 18 HRs, 109 RBIs, .309 AVG, 91 RUNS
Ted Williams: **43** HRs, **159** RBIs, .343 AVG, **150** RUNS
1950
Bobby Doerr: 27 HRs, 120 RBIs, .294 AVG, 103 RUNS
Ted Williams: 28 HRs, 97 RBIs, .317 AVG, 82 RUNS

Doerr earned a spot on the AL All-Star Team in 1948 and 1950. Williams appeared on the squad all three years and finished third in the MVP balloting in 1948. He won the award for the second time the following year, when he came within a few percentage points of capturing his third Triple Crown. Although Williams compiled solid numbers again in 1950, they would have been much better had he not been forced to sit out more than 60 games with an injury.

Doerr played his final year with the Red Sox in 1951, batting .289 and knocking in 73 runs in 106 games. He retired with 223 home runs, 1,247 runs batted in, 1,094 runs scored, and a .288 career batting average. Doerr earned nine selections to the American League All-Star Team during his career, and he finished in the top 10 in the MVP voting twice.

Williams had another outstanding season for Boston in 1951, hitting 30 home runs, driving in 126 runs, scoring 109 others, and batting .318. He then missed virtually all of the next two seasons serving as a pilot in the U.S. Air Force during the Korean War. Following his return to the game as a 35-year-old in 1954, Williams appeared in as many as 130 games in only two of his seven remaining seasons, never again compiling more than 420 official at bats in any single campaign. Yet, he remained a great hitter to the very end, winning three more batting titles and leading the league with a mark of .388 in 1957 at the age of 38. Williams homered in the final at bat of his career in front of a sparse turnout at Boston's Fenway Park on a cool, dreary, late-September afternoon. Knowing that Williams intended to retire after the game, the Fenway faithful gave him a standing ovation. Always true to himself, Williams refused to tip his cap to the hometown fans, later recalling, "I thought about tipping my cap to them for one brief moment. But I just couldn't bring myself to do it."[2]

Williams left the sport at the end of that 1960 season with 521 career home runs, 1,839 runs batted in, 1,798 runs scored, 2,654 hits, a .344 batting average, a .634 slugging average, an all-time best .483 on-base percentage, and as arguably the greatest hitter in baseball history. In addition to his seven batting titles, Williams led the league in home runs and runs batted in four times each, runs scored six times, walks eight times, slugging average nine times, and on-base percentage 12 times. He finished in the top five in the league MVP voting a total of nine times, winning the award twice and coming in second four other times.

Stan Musial expressed his admiration for Williams when he stated, "Ted was the greatest hitter of our era. He won seven batting titles and served his country for five years, so he would have won more. He loved talking about hitting and was a great student of hitting and pitchers."[3]

Carl Yastrzemski, who claimed the starting left-field job in Boston after Williams retired from the game, commented, "They can talk about Babe Ruth and Ty Cobb and Rogers Hornsby and Lou Gehrig and Joe DiMaggio and Stan Musial and all the rest, but I'm sure not one of them could hold cards and spades to Williams in his sheer knowledge of hitting. He studied hitting the way a broker studies the stock market, and could spot at a glance mistakes that others couldn't see in a week."[4]

Ted Williams, arguably the greatest hitter in baseball history, and Bobby Doerr served as teammates on the Boston Red Sox for 10 full seasons. During their time together, the Red Sox won one pennant, finished second five times, and came in third on three other occasions. Williams and Doerr averaged 51 home runs and 236 runs batted in between them in their 10 years together. They combined for a total of 16 appearances on the All-Star Team, as well as a total of eight top-five finishes in the league MVP balloting.

Notes

Numbers printed in bold indicate that the player led his league in a statistical category.

1. Quote taken from http://www.aagpbl.org/index.cfm/articles/foxx-jimmie/44.

2. *SportsCentury: Fifty Greatest Athletes—Ted Williams,* television program (ESPN, 1999).

3. Stan Musial, http://www.baseball-almanac.com/quotes/quowilt.shtml.

4. Carl Yastrzemski, http://www.baseball-almanac.com/quotes/quowilt.shtml.

CHAPTER 14

Roberto Clemente / Willie Stargell

Roberto Clemente and Willie Stargell did more than just turn the Pittsburgh Pirates into perennial contenders in the National League during their time together. They also helped to completely alter the losing mind-set instilled in the franchise from years of failure while raising the social consciousness of an entire city.

The Pittsburgh Pirates team that Roberto Clemente joined as a 20-year-old in 1955 was one of the National League's least successful franchises. The Pirates won their last pennant in 1927, challenging for the NL flag just once since 1938. The National League's dominant team the first few years of the 20th century and a strong contender throughout most of the 1920s and 1930s, Pittsburgh posted a winning record only one time between 1946 and 1954, finishing either last or next to last in the league each year from 1950 to 1954. In fact, the Pirates' 53 victories in 1954 represented their highest win total in four years.

Not much changed in Pittsburgh during Clemente's first few years with the team. Although the Pirates won a few more games, they continued to flounder near the bottom of the National League standings. Making life even more difficult for the Puerto Rican–born Clemente was the fact that he needed to adjust to a completely foreign culture that often treated him quite unfairly. While dark-skinned players always had a difficult time being accepted into the world of white baseball during that period, things were particularly hard on Clemente. As the first truly great Latino ballplayer, not only did he have to deal with the prejudices that were bound to come his way because of the color of his skin, but he also had to learn a new culture and a new language. However, neither the members of the media nor most of Clemente's own teammates made his transition an easy one. The newspaper columnists and broadcasters of the day seemed unwilling to fully accept his Latin heritage. The writers openly mocked Clemente's speech in their newspaper articles, and broadcasters attempted to Americanize his name by referring to him as either "Bob" or "Bobby" instead of "Roberto," which was the name that he wished to be called by. Even most of Clemente's teammates, with whom he rarely socialized, failed to call him by his proper name. They also often questioned his motivation and desire, since Roberto typically missed a significant number of games each season due to the various physical ailments that plagued him throughout much of his career. Members of the media, as well as many of Clemente's teammates, considered him to be a hypochondriac because he frequently complained of body aches and pains. However, they failed to realize that much of the source of Clemente's discomfort stemmed from a partially damaged spinal column he suffered from as the result of an automobile accident he was involved in as a young man.

Clemente's injuries cut into his playing time significantly his first few seasons, limiting him to fewer than 125 games in three of his first five years in Pittsburgh. He found his offensive productivity further curtailed by the many cultural problems he faced during his period of adjustment. As a result, Clemente failed to hit more than seven home runs, drive in more than 60 runs, or score more than 69 runs in any of his first five seasons. He also batted over .300 just once, compiling an average of .311 in 1956.

Nevertheless, with young players such as Dick Groat and Bill Mazeroski, the Pirates began to show signs of improvement by the end of the decade, posting a winning record in both 1958 and 1959. Pittsburgh finally made it all the way back in 1960, winning 95 games during the regular season to capture the National League pennant and subsequently upsetting the heavily favored Yankees in the World Series. Clemente had his finest season to date, establishing new career highs with 16 home runs, 94 runs batted in, 89 runs scored, and a .314 batting average. Yet he could do no better than eighth in the MVP balloting, finishing well behind teammates Dick Groat and Don Hoak, who finished first and second in the voting. Groat was generally considered to be the leader of the Pirates, and as a shortstop, he played one of the most demanding defensive positions on the diamond. Furthermore, Groat led the league with a .325 batting average. But he also hit just two home runs, drove in only 50 runs, scored just 85 others, and had limited range in the field. Third baseman Hoak compiled better overall numbers than Groat, hitting 16 home runs, knocking in 79 runs, scoring another 97, and batting a solid .285. But Hoak's numbers were certainly no better than Clemente's, and the right fielder was clearly a better all-around player than either of his teammates. Clemente had outstanding speed, exceptional base-running skills, and superb range and a powerful throwing arm in the outfield. In fact, he won the first of his 12 consecutive Gold Gloves the very next year. Unfortunately, the members of the media that selected the league's Most Valuable Player simply didn't appear ready to acknowledge Clemente as one of the sport's finest all-around players. In later years, Roberto commented that he did not have a particularly strong objection to not winning the award that year. However, he remained very much disturbed by his eighth-place showing, since he felt that he deserved to finish higher in the balloting.

Clemente demonstrated any objections that he may have had with his brilliant all-around play in subsequent seasons. Running the bases with a fury rarely seen, patrolling right field with unmatched grace and elegance, and playing the game with great passion, Clemente established himself as one of baseball's greatest players. He was particularly outstanding from 1961 to 1967, a period during which he won four National League batting titles. Table 14.1 presents the numbers that Clemente posted over that seven-year stretch.

Clemente earned NL MVP honors in 1966, when he established career highs in home runs, runs batted in, and runs scored. He also finished third in the voting in 1967, and he placed fourth in the 1961 balloting.

One of the things that made Clemente such a difficult hitter for opposing pitchers to face was his ability to hit bad pitches. San Francisco Giants Hall of Fame right-hander Juan Marichal once noted, "The big thing about Clemente is that he can hit any pitch. I don't mean only strikes. He can hit a ball off his ankles or off his ear."[1]

Pittsburgh pitcher Steve Blass spoke about the respect that other players around the league had for Clemente when he said, "[Clemente] was the one player that players on other teams didn't want to miss. They'd run out of the clubhouse to watch him take batting practice. He could make a 10-year veteran act like a 10-year-old kid."[2]

As outstanding as Clemente was at the plate, he may have been even better in the field. The owner of baseball's strongest throwing arm among right fielders, Roberto completely intimidated opposing runners on the base paths. Longtime Dodgers broadcaster Vin Scully once commented, "Clemente could field the ball in New York and throw out a guy in Pennsylvania."[3]

In spite of Clemente's brilliant all-around play, the Pirates seriously contended for the National League flag just once between 1961 and 1964, finishing over .500 only in 1962, when they compiled a record of 93–68 to finish

Table 14.1. Roberto Clemente: 1961–1967

Year	HR	RBIs	AVG	RUNS	HITS
1961	23	89	**.351**	100	201
1962	10	74	.312	95	168
1963	17	76	.320	77	192
1964	12	87	**.339**	95	**211**
1965	10	65	**.329**	91	194
1966	29	119	.317	105	202
1967	23	110	**.357**	103	**209**

eight games out of first. It wasn't until 1965 that the Pirates became consistent winners when a young, power-hitting outfielder named Wilver Stargell joined Clemente in Pittsburgh's everyday starting lineup.

Willie Stargell made his major-league debut with the Pirates late in 1962, appearing in 10 games and hitting .290 in 31 official at bats. The powerful left-handed batter assumed a part-time role with the team the next two seasons, hitting 21 home runs and knocking in 78 runs in only 117 games in 1964 en route to earning a spot on the National League All-Star Team for the first time. Stargell became a full-time player for Pittsburgh in 1965, quickly establishing himself as one of the league's most feared hitters. Possessing awesome power at the plate, the 6'3", 230-pound Stargell had the ability to hit a ball as far as anyone in the game. One-time Pirates manager Harry Walker stated, "I never have seen a batter who hits the ball any harder. For sheer crash of bat meeting ball, Stargell simply is the best."[4]

Stargell joined his teammate Clemente on the National League All-Star Team in both 1965 and 1966, hitting 27 home runs, driving in 107 runs, and batting .272 in the first of those years. While Clemente earned league MVP honors in 1966 by hitting 29 home runs, knocking in 119 runs, and batting .317, Stargell posted numbers almost as impressive. The Pittsburgh left fielder hit 33 homers, drove in 102 runs, and batted .315. The Pirates surpassed 90 victories in both 1965 and 1966, finishing third in the league both years.

Pittsburgh finished well out of contention in each of the next two seasons, though, posting a record right around the .500 mark and placing sixth in the league standings both times. Clemente performed exceptionally well in 1967, leading the NL with 209 hits and a .357 batting average. He also had a solid season the following year, hitting 18 home runs and batting .291. But Stargell slumped badly both years, particularly in 1968, when he drove in only 67 runs and batted just .237.

After the major leagues realigned to four divisions in 1969, the Pirates contended for the NL East title in each of the next four seasons. Pittsburgh won 88 games in 1969 to finish third in the division and then captured three consecutive division crowns with win totals of 89, 97, and 96. The Cincinnati Reds defeated the Pirates in the National League Championship Series in both 1970 and 1972, but Pittsburgh won the World Series in 1971, edging out Baltimore in seven games. Clemente and Stargell had some of their best years together during that four-year period, compiling the following numbers shown in table 14.2.

Clemente finished a close second to Pete Rose in the 1969 National League batting race. He also placed among the league leaders the other three years, although he didn't qualify for the batting title in either 1970 or 1972 due to a lack of sufficient plate appearances. Clemente finished eighth in the MVP balloting in 1969; he also placed fifth in the 1971 voting. He was named to the All-Star

Table 14.2.   Roberto Clemente and Willie Stargell: 1969–1972

Player	Year	HR	RBIs	AVG	RUNS
Clemente	1969	19	91	.345	87
	1970	14	60	.352	65
	1971	13	86	.341	82
	1972	10	60	.312	68
Stargell	1969	29	92	.307	89
	1970	31	85	.264	70
	1971	**48**	125	.295	104
	1972	33	112	.293	75

Team all four years. The highlight of Clemente's career took place in the 1971 World Series, when he had an opportunity to display his considerable talents before a national television audience. Clemente not only captivated the nation with his extraordinary play in right field but also dominated the vaunted Baltimore Orioles pitching staff, hitting two home runs and batting .414 en route to winning series MVP honors. Baltimore first baseman Boog Powell later said, "No one hit our pitchers like that. Some players might have had the number of one or two of our starters, but no other player dominated our entire staff that way."[5]

Meanwhile, Stargell not only led the league with 48 home runs in 1971 but finished second in runs batted in and slugging percentage while placing third in runs scored and total bases. Stargell's exceptional performance earned him a second-place finish to Joe Torre in the MVP balloting. He also finished third in the 1972 voting. Stargell appeared in the All-Star Game in both 1971 and 1972.

It was during the early 1970s that Stargell established himself as the National League's most dangerous hitter. Dodger right-hander Don Sutton said, "I never saw anything like it. [Stargell] doesn't just hit pitchers, he takes away their dignity."[6]

Pirates manager Chuck Tanner commented, "Having Willie Stargell on your ball club is like having a diamond ring on your finger."[7]

It was also during this period that Clemente and Stargell helped to change the climate both in the Pittsburgh clubhouse and in the city as a whole. The Pirates were predominantly white when Roberto first joined them in 1955, and they remained that way throughout the first half of his career. Many members of the organization tended to frown upon black and Latino players, who found themselves being viewed suspiciously by the media and the general public. But the team became increasingly integrated during the 1960s, with black players such as Stargell, Donn Clendenon, and Al Oliver coming aboard, along with several Latino players, such as Matty Alou, Manny Mota, Manny Sanguillen, and Jose Pagan. Clemente's comfort level began to grow as other players who spoke his native language joined him on the Pirates roster, allowing him to become much more of a team leader than he had been earlier in his career. Roberto not only took the other Latin players under his wing but served as mentor to the other young players on the club, such as Stargell. Clemente taught Stargell how to play the game properly and how to carry himself with dignity and class off the field. Stargell, in turn, passed that knowledge on to the next generation of Pirates players. Toward the end of his career, Clemente commented, "My greatest satisfaction comes from helping to erase the old opinion about Latin Americans and blacks."[8]

Clemente stroked the 3,000th hit of his career in his final at bat of the 1972 season. Unfortunately, that turned out to be his last hit. Clemente was tragically killed in a plane crash just off the coast of San Juan, Puerto Rico, on December 31, 1972, while taking supplies to Nicaraguan earthquake victims. Some 40 years later, Roberto Clemente remains a legendary figure, particularly among members of the Latino community. Major League Baseball presents an annual Roberto Clemente Award to "the player who best exemplifies the game of baseball, sportsmanship, community involvement and the individual's contribution to his team." And as Puerto Rican journalist Luis Mayoral said, "Clemente was our Jackie Robinson. He was on a crusade to show the American public what an Hispanic man, a black Hispanic man, was capable of."[9]

Former Pirates general manager Joe L. Brown expressed his admiration for Clemente by saying, "He's a shining star to many, many people. He grows and grows over time. He doesn't diminish. . . . The sad part is that there are not enough TV pictures of him. He made so many great plays that people can only talk about. You could never capture the magnificence of the man."[10]

Former baseball commissioner Bowie Kuhn stated in his 1973 eulogy to Clemente, "He gave the term 'complete' a new meaning. He made the word 'superstar' seem inadequate. He had about him the touch of royalty."[11]

In addition to amassing 3,000 hits, Roberto Clemente compiled 240 home runs, 1,305 runs batted in, 1,416 runs scored, and a .317 batting average over his 18 big-league seasons. His .328 batting average during the 1960s was the highest figure posted by any player who competed during the decade. In winning four batting titles, Clemente topped the .350 mark three times, and he surpassed .340 on two other occasions. He was named to 12 All-Star Teams during his career.

Following the passing of Clemente, the Pirates slumped to third in the NL East in 1973, finishing the regular season with a record of just 80–82. However, Stargell had perhaps his finest all-around season, batting .299, scoring 106 runs, and leading the National League with 44 home runs, 119 runs batted in, 43 doubles, and a .646 slugging percentage. He finished a close second to Pete Rose in the league MVP voting.

Stargell had one more outstanding season for the Pirates before injuries began to cut into his playing time and offensive productivity in 1975. After hitting

25 home runs, driving in 96 runs, scoring 90 others, batting .301, and leading the Pirates to their fourth division title in five years in 1974, Stargell missed a total of 182 games over the next three seasons. Pittsburgh advanced to the play-offs in only one of those years (1975, a season in which Stargell batted .295 and drove in 90 runs despite appearing in only 124 games).

Yet Stargell continued to assume an increasingly larger role as Pittsburgh's team leader as the decade progressed. The Pirates' elder statesman by the late 1970s, Stargell was admired and respected by every other member of the team. Stargell's younger teammates looked to him for advice and guidance, both on and off the field, with his wisdom and calm demeanor giving him an exalted position within the Pittsburgh clubhouse.

Teammate Al Oliver once stated, "If Willie Stargell asked us to jump off the Fort Pitt Bridge, we would ask him what kind of dive he wanted. That's how much respect we have for the man."[12]

By 1979, a family-type atmosphere existed on the Pirates, with Stargell considered to be the patriarch of that family. The closeness that existed on the team helped carry Pittsburgh to the division title during the regular season and then to victories over both Cincinnati in the National League Championship Series and Baltimore in the World Series. Stargell appeared in only 126 games during the regular season, hitting 32 home runs, knocking in 82 runs, and batting .281. But the baseball writers recognized his leadership skills and other intangible qualities by splitting their MVP votes between him and St. Louis first baseman Keith Hernandez, awarding them each a share of the trophy.

The 1979 campaign ended up being Stargell's last big year. Injuries and advancing age severely limited his playing time the next few years, finally forcing him into retirement at the end of the 1982 season. Stargell ended his career with 475 home runs, 1,540 runs batted in, 1,195 runs scored, and a .282 batting average. He appeared in a total of seven All-Star Games and finished in the top 10 in the MVP balloting a total of seven times, winning the award once and making it into the top five on three other occasions.

Roberto Clemente and Willie Stargell were teammates on the Pirates for parts of 11 seasons. They were both regular members of the Pittsburgh lineup from 1964 to 1972. They combined for a total of 14 All-Star Game appearances during that period—nine for Clemente and five for Stargell. They were most productive together from 1965 to 1969, combining for 232 home runs and 953 RBIs over that five-year period for an average of 47 homers and 191 RBIs per year. Stargell knocked in more than 100 runs and batted over .300 in two of those seasons. Clemente drove in more than 100 runs twice, batted over .300 four times, twice surpassing the .340 mark, and won two of his four batting titles. More important, the Pirates won at least 88 games in seven of their nine full seasons together, capturing three division titles and one World Series championship.

Notes

Numbers printed in bold indicate that the player led his league in a statistical category.

1. Juan Marichal, http://www.baseball-almanac.com/quotes/roberto_clemente_quotes. shtml.

2. Steve Blass, http://www.baseball-almanac.com/quotes/roberto_clemente_quotes .shtml.

3. Vin Scully, http://www.baseball-almanac.com/quotes/roberto_clemente_quotes .shtml.

4. Tony DeMarco, *The Sporting News Selects 50 Greatest Sluggers* (St. Louis, MO: Times Mirror Magazines, 2000), 55.

5. *SportsCentury—Roberto Clemente*, television program (ESPN, 2003).

6. Don Sutton, http://www.baseball-almanac.com/quotes/quostar.shtml.

7. Chuck Tanner, http://www.baseball-almanac.com/quotes/quostar.shtml.

8. *SportsCentury—Roberto Clemente*.

9. *SportsCentury—Roberto Clemente*.

10. Joe L. Brown, http://www.baseball-almanac.com/quotes/roberto_clemente_quotes .shtml.

11. Bowie Kuhn, http://www.baseball-almanac.com/quotes/roberto_clemente_quotes .shtml.

12. Al Oliver, http://www.baseball-almanac.com/quotes/quostar.shtml.

CHAPTER 15

Johnny Bench / Tony Perez

I earlier examined the roles that Pete Rose and Joe Morgan played in the success of the Cincinnati Reds during the 1970s. Batting at the top of Cincinnati's powerful lineup, Rose and Morgan served as offensive catalysts for the "Big Red Machine" for much of the decade. However, immediately following the sport's top two table setters in Cincinnati's batting order were sluggers Johnny Bench and Tony Perez, who served as the team's primary power threats and top RBI men throughout the first half of the decade.

Tony Perez first came up with Cincinnati in 1964, making a brief 12-game appearance with the team and hitting only .080 in 25 official at bats. He joined the Reds for good the following season, experiencing a moderate amount of success platooning at first base with the left-handed hitting Gordy Coleman. Perez claimed the starting third base job from Deron Johnson in 1967, earning a spot on the National League All-Star Team by hitting 26 home runs, driving in 102 runs, and batting .290. The right-handed hitting slugger had another solid season in 1968, hitting 18 homers, knocking in 92 runs, scoring 93 others, batting .282, and again being named to the All-Star Team. Perez continued to establish himself as one of baseball's most consistent RBI men in subsequent seasons, driving in more than 100 runs a total of seven times and knocking in at least 90 runs in 11 consecutive seasons at one point.

Johnny Bench joined Perez in the Cincinnati starting lineup in 1968. After appearing briefly with the team the previous year, Bench won NL Rookie of the Year honors by hitting 15 home runs, driving in 82 runs, batting .275, and making the first of 13 straight All-Star Game appearances at catcher for the National League. The receiver's hitting had a great deal to do with him being named NL Rookie of the Year. However, even more impressive was his tremendous defensive ability, which earned him the first of his 10 consecutive Gold Gloves. Stating confidently, "I can throw out any man alive,"[1] Bench intimidated opposing base runners with his cannon-like throwing arm. Longtime general manager Harry Dalton expressed his admiration for the young catcher's throwing ability when he commented, "Every time Bench throws, everybody in baseball drools."[2] Bench also possessed great quickness behind the plate, and he did an exceptional job of handling Cincinnati's pitching staff. Veteran right-hander Jim Maloney once noted about Bench, "He'll come out on the mound and treat me like a two-year-old, but so help me, I like it."[3]

Perez and Bench both enjoyed their best seasons to date in 1969, being named to the All-Star Team for the second of three straight times. Bench hit 26 home runs, drove in 90 runs, scored 83 others, and batted .293. Perez posted even better numbers, batting .294 and establishing new career highs with 37 home runs, 122 runs batted in, and 103 runs scored en route to earning a 10th-place finish in the league MVP voting. The outstanding performances turned in by the two men enabled the Reds to post 89 victories—their highest total since 1965—and finish a close third in the NL West. Bench and Perez had their greatest season together the following year, leading Cincinnati to the Western Division title and the National League pennant. These are the numbers the two men posted during the Reds' 102-win 1970 campaign:

Tony Perez: 40 HRs, 129 RBIs, .317 AVG, 107 RUNS, .589 SLG PCT, 346
     TOTAL BASES
Johnny Bench: **45** HRs, **148** RBIs, .293 AVG, 97 RUNS, .587 SLG PCT, 355
     TOTAL BASES

In addition to leading the league in home runs and runs batted in, Bench finished second in total bases and third in slugging percentage. Perez finished third in home runs, RBIs, and total bases and placed second in slugging percentage. Bench earned NL MVP honors, with Perez finishing third in the balloting.

Both Bench and Perez had subpar seasons in 1971, relegating Cincinnati to a fourth-place finish in the NL West. But the sluggers rebounded the following year, beginning an extremely productive four-year run together. These are the numbers they posted during that period:

Bench
1972: **40** HRs, **125** RBIs, .270 AVG, 87 RUNS
1973: 25 HRs, 104 RBIs, .253 AVG, 83 RUNS
1974: 33 HRs, **129** RBIs, .280 AVG, 108 RUNS
1975: 28 HRs, 110 RBIs, .283 AVG, 83 RUNS
Perez
1972: 21 HRs, 90 RBIs, .283 AVG
1973: 27 HRs, 101 RBIs, .314 AVG

1974: 28 HRs, 101 RBIs, .265 AVG
1975: 20 HRs, 109 RBIs, .282 AVG

Bench won his second National League MVP award in 1972, leading the Reds to their second division title and NL pennant in three seasons. He also finished fourth in the voting in both 1974 and 1975 and placed 10th in the 1973 balloting—three places behind Perez.

It was during this period that the Reds established themselves as a National League powerhouse and as baseball's most potent offensive ball club. In addition to Bench, Perez, Rose, and Morgan, young players such as Ken Griffey, George Foster, and Dave Concepcion gradually developed into stars in Cincinnati's starting lineup. After losing the 1972 World Series to Oakland and the 1973 National League Championship Series to the underdog Mets, the Reds finally reached the zenith of their sport in 1975, defeating the Red Sox in a classic seven-game World Series.

Cincinnati proved to be baseball's dominant team again in 1976, winning 102 games during the regular season, before sweeping both the Phillies in the National League Championship Series and the Yankees in the World Series. Perez had another productive year, hitting 19 home runs and driving in 91 runs, but Bench was injured much of the time, forcing him to suffer through the worst year of his career. Still, the receiver rose to the occasion during the postseason, batting .333 against Philadelphia in the playoffs and capturing World Series MVP honors by hitting .533 against New York, with two home runs and six runs batted in.

The Reds subsequently made an error in judgment at the end of the season when they traded Perez to Montreal to make room at first base for promising youngster Dan Driessen. Although Driessen posted solid numbers for the Reds over the course of the next few seasons, he never came close to replacing the leadership that Perez brought to his Cincinnati teammates. Long considered to be the number-one leader in the Reds' clubhouse, Perez was sorely missed by his old team, which failed to make it back to the playoffs in either of the next two seasons.

Perez continued to perform well in his three years with the Expos, hitting 19 homers, driving in 91 runs, and batting .283 in his first season with his new club. He then spent three years in Boston, hitting 25 homers and driving in 105 runs in 1980, before becoming a part-time player his final two years with the team. From Boston, Perez moved on to Philadelphia, where he spent one season before he returned to Cincinnati in 1984. He spent his final three years as a part-time player with the Reds, finally retiring from the game at the conclusion of the 1986 campaign. Perez ended his career with 379 home runs, 1,652 runs batted in, and a .279 batting average.

Rebounding from his injury-marred 1976 campaign, Bench had his last big year for the Reds in 1977, hitting 31 home runs, driving in 109 runs, and batting .275. His playing time reduced in subsequent seasons due to injury, Bench failed to produce numbers the remainder of his career that even approached his 1977 figures. Splitting time between catcher, first base, and third base, he continued to play through 1983, when he decided to announce his retirement. Bench concluded his career with 389 home runs, 1,376 runs batted in, and a .267 batting average.

Johnny Bench and Tony Perez were both full-time players in Cincinnati from 1968 to 1976. In their nine years together, they combined to average 54 home runs and 205 runs batted in per season. They made 15 All-Star Game appearances as teammates, won two Most Valuable Player Awards, and finished in the top 10 in the balloting on six other occasions. The Reds surpassed 100 victories three times during that period, won at least 95 games three other times, and finished with a losing record just once.

Notes

Numbers printed in bold indicate that the player led his league in a statistical category.

1. Johnny Bench, http://www.baseball-almanac.com/quotes/quobnch.shtml.
2. Harry Dalton, http://www.baseball-almanac.com/quotes/quobnch.shtml.
3. Jim Maloney, http://www.baseball-almanac.com/quotes/quobnch.shtml.

CHAPTER 16

Jeff Bagwell / Craig Biggio

Playing during an era when free agency prompted players to change teams with great regularity, Jeff Bagwell and Craig Biggio remained unique in that they both spent their entire major-league careers with the same team. Lining up alongside each other on the right side of the Houston Astros infield for more than a decade, Bagwell and Biggio formed quite a formidable duo, establishing themselves as arguably the most productive tandem in baseball during their time together.

Craig Biggio originally came up to the Astros as a catcher in 1988. After struggling at the plate as a rookie, he became a major contributor on offense in his second season, one in which he was named the team's starting catcher. He manned that position two more years, earning his first All-Star nomination in 1991, when he batted .295 and scored 75 runs. Biggio moved to second base prior to the start of the 1992 campaign, after which he quickly developed into one of the National League's top second-sackers. With his outstanding speed, good range, and soft hands making him a natural for the position, Biggio made the All-Star Team in his first season at second. He had his first big offensive season the following year, hitting 21 home runs, driving in 64 runs, scoring 98 others, and batting .287.

Biggio was joined in Houston in 1991 by first baseman Jeff Bagwell. Originally signed by Boston, Bagwell made his major-league debut with the Astros that year, hitting 15 home runs, driving in 82 runs, and batting .294 en route to winning NL Rookie of the Year honors. He continued to develop into a solid offensive performer over the next two seasons, batting as high as .320 in 1993 and averaging 18 home runs and 89 runs batted in over his first three years.

Bagwell and Biggio subsequently began, during the strike-shortened 1994 campaign, a 10-year run in which they functioned as baseball's most productive offensive tandem much of the time. Table 16.1 shows the figures that the two men posted in some of their best years together during that period.

Table 16.1. Jeff Bagwell and Craig Biggio: 1994-2001

Player	Year	HR	RBIs	AVG	RUNS	SB
Bagwell	1994	39	**116**	.368	**104**	15
	1996	31	120	.315	111	21
	1997	43	135	.286	109	31
	1998	34	111	.304	124	19
	1999	42	126	.304	**143**	30
	2000	47	132	.310	**152**	9
	2001	39	130	.288	126	11
Biggio	1995	22	77	.302	**123**	33
	1996	15	75	.288	113	25
	1997	22	81	.309	**146**	47
	1998	20	88	.325	123	50
	1999	16	73	.294	123	28

Bagwell earned National League MVP honors in 1994 when, in addition to leading the league in runs batted in and runs scored, he placed second in home runs and batting average. The slugging first baseman finished runner-up in the balloting in 1999; he also placed third in the voting in 1997, when he finished second in the league in home runs and runs batted in. Biggio finished fourth in the MVP balloting in 1997.

The keen batting eyes of Bagwell and Biggio enabled both men to regularly place among the league leaders in walks, on-base percentage, and runs scored. In the seven seasons between 1994 and 2000, either Bagwell or Biggio led the National League in runs scored a total of five times. One or the other placed in the league's top five in that category on six other occasions during their time together. The two men combined to lead the league in doubles four times as well. Bagwell, who usually batted third in the Houston lineup, also finished in the top five in home runs and runs batted in four times each. Biggio, who typically batted either first or second, placed in the top five in doubles five times and in hits and stolen bases three times each.

After hitting 27 home runs, driving in 89 runs, and scoring 104 others in 2004, Bagwell missed most of 2005 with a severely injured shoulder that eventually forced him to retire at the end of the year. He ended his career with 449 home runs, 1,529 runs batted in, 1,517 runs scored, a .297 batting average, and an outstanding .408 on-base percentage. He appeared in four All-Star games and won a Gold Glove for his outstanding defensive work at first base.

Meanwhile, Biggio remained a productive player for the Astros until he finally retired at the conclusion of the 2007 campaign with 3,060 hits to his credit. He also compiled 291 home runs, 1,175 runs batted in, 1,844 runs scored, and a .281 batting average.

Jeff Bagwell and Craig Biggio were teammates for 15 seasons. During their time together, they combined for 689 home runs, 2,485 runs batted in, and 3,083 runs scored. They appeared in a total of 11 All-Star Games as teammates; they also placed in the top 10 in the league MVP voting a total of nine times. From 1994 to 2003, their 10 peak seasons together, Bagwell and Biggio made a total of nine appearances on the All-Star Team, placed in the top five in the MVP balloting a total of five times, and won five Gold Gloves between them. During that period, Bagwell surpassed 40 home runs three times, drove in more than 100 runs eight times, scored in excess of 100 runs eight times, batted over .300 on five occasions, and compiled more than 100 walks seven times. Biggio topped 20 homers and 75 runs batted in four times each, scored more than 100 runs seven times, and batted over .300 four times. The two men averaged a combined 226 runs scored per year between them over that 10-year span. Of even greater significance is the fact that Bagwell and Biggio helped the Astros advance to the postseason six times, making two appearances in the National League Championship Series and winning one NL pennant.

Note

Numbers printed in bold indicate that the player led his league in a statistical category.

CHAPTER 17

Randy Johnson / Curt Schilling

Randy Johnson and Curt Schilling served as members of the same pitching staff for only two full seasons and for parts of two others. Nevertheless, the dominance they displayed during the two full seasons they spent together in Arizona earned them a place in these rankings. Indeed, Johnson and Schilling formed as dominant a pitching duo during their relatively brief time together as any other tandem of hurlers in baseball history. They carried the Diamondbacks on their backs to the world championship in 2001, leading all National League pitchers in virtually every major statistical category over the course of the campaign. Although the Diamondbacks failed to return to the World Series the following year, Johnson and Schilling repeated their virtuoso performance, once again dominating the statistical categories for NL hurlers. Yet, by the time the two pitchers joined forces in Arizona, they were both wily veterans who were approaching the latter stages of their respective careers.

Randy Johnson made his major-league debut with the Montreal Expos late in 1988, going 3–0 and compiling a 2.42 ERA in his four starts. He remained with the team for the first two months of the 1989 campaign, before Montreal elected to trade him to Seattle for left-hander Mark Langston. Johnson showed glimpses of brilliance over the next four seasons, averaging about a strikeout an inning and leading all AL pitchers with 241 strikeouts in 1992. But Johnson's lack of control prevented him from being an elite pitcher, since he also led the league in walks in three of those seasons while posting a combined record of 46–44.

Johnson finally learned to control his blazing fastball and sharp-breaking slider in 1993, enabling him to evolve into one of baseball's most dominant hurlers. Johnson finished 19–8 with a 3.24 ERA and a league-leading 308 strikeouts that year, earning in the process a spot on the All-Star Team for the first time. The combination of Johnson's 6'10" frame, the tremendous velocity on his fastball, and the movement on his breaking ball made the southpaw virtually impossible for left-handed batters to hit. And right-handers struggled as well with his sharp-breaking slider. Rapidly developing into the league's most intimidating pitcher, the "Big Unit" won 13 games and led the AL with 204 strikeouts during the strike-shortened 1994 campaign. He subsequently reached new heights in 1995, compiling a record of 18–2, leading the league with 294 strikeouts and a 2.48 ERA and capturing his first Cy Young Award while helping the Mariners reach the playoffs for the first time in history. Johnson missed most of the 1996 season with an injury, but he returned the following year to post a record of 20–4, along with 291 strikeouts and an ERA of 2.28.

With free agency looming at the end of 1998, Johnson was traded by Seattle to Houston midway through the season. He went 10–1 with the Astros, finishing the year with a combined record of 19–11, an ERA of 3.28, and 329 strikeouts. After becoming a free agent at season's end, Johnson signed on with the Arizona Diamondbacks, with whom he began a string of four consecutive Cy Young Award campaigns in 1999. These are the numbers that the left-hander posted in his first two years with his new team:

1999: 17 wins, 9 losses; **2.48** ERA, **364** SO, **271** IP, **12** CG
2000: 19 wins, 7 losses; 2.64 ERA, **347** SO, 249 IP, **8** CG, **3** shutouts

The Diamondbacks failed to make the playoffs those two seasons, but Johnson helped make them respectable for the first time in their brief history. Arizona's fortunes improved even more in 2001, when Curt Schilling teamed up with Johnson to give the Diamondbacks baseball's most formidable one-two pitching combination.

As was the case with his future teammate, Schilling made his major-league debut in 1988, joining the Baltimore Orioles for the first time late that year. Also like Johnson, the right-handed-throwing Schilling struggled early in his career. Pitching almost exclusively in relief, Schilling went a combined 1–6 in his three years in Baltimore, posting an ERA well in excess of 6.00 in two of those seasons. Schilling improved only slightly after he was traded to Houston at the end of the 1990 campaign, going just 3–5, with a 3.81 ERA and eight saves in his 56 relief appearances. However, Schilling rededicated himself to his sport after Texas native Roger Clemens chastised him that off-season for wasting his considerable talent. Clemens, who Schilling idolized, accused the 25-year-old hurler of failing to take the game seriously and of not taking full advantage of his physical gifts and wide assortment of pitches, which included an overpowering fastball.

Fully motivated for the first time in his young career, Schilling had his breakout season for the Philadelphia Phillies in 1992 after being traded to the team just prior to the start of the campaign. Becoming a regular member of Philadelphia's starting rotation during the season's first half, Schilling finished

14–11 with an outstanding 2.35 earned run average. Although his ERA jumped to 4.02 the following year, Schilling compiled a record of 16–7 while helping the Phillies win the 1993 National League pennant. Arm problems forced Schilling to miss large portions of the next three campaigns, but he returned to full health in 1997 to have his best year to date, finishing the campaign with a record of 17–11, a 2.97 ERA, and a league-leading 319 strikeouts. He followed that up with two more outstanding seasons for a mediocre Philadelphia team. Schilling finished 15–14 in 1998 with a 3.25 ERA and a league-leading 300 strikeouts, 15 complete games, and 268 innings pitched. He went 15–6 the following year, with a 3.54 ERA and 152 strikeouts in only 180 innings of work.

After winning six of 12 decisions for the Phillies over the first half of the 2000 campaign, Schilling was traded to the Diamondbacks for four players at midseason. He went only 5–6 for Arizona during the season's second half, posting a rather pedestrian 3.69 ERA in his 13 remaining starts. However, Schilling experienced something of a renaissance the following year, pitching at a level that he failed to reach even in his best years in Philadelphia. In fact, Schilling vied with his new teammate Randy Johnson for supremacy among National League hurlers in each of the next two seasons. These are the numbers the two men posted in 2001 and 2002:

2001
Randy Johnson: 21 wins, 6 losses; **2.49** ERA, **372** SO, 250 IP
Curt Schilling: **22** wins, 6 losses; 2.98 ERA, 293 SO, **257** IP
2002
Randy Johnson: **24** wins, 5 losses; **2.32** ERA, **334** SO, **260** IP
Curt Schilling: 23 wins, 7 losses; 3.23 ERA, 316 SO, 259 IP

Johnson and Schilling were the National League's dominant pitchers both years, finishing first and second in virtually every statistical category. Schilling led the league in wins and innings pitched in 2001. Johnson finished right behind him in both categories. The Big Unit topped the circuit in ERA and strikeouts; Schilling finished second in both departments. Johnson led all NL hurlers in every major statistical category in 2002, winning the pitcher's version of the Triple Crown in the process. Schilling placed second to his teammate in wins, strikeouts, and innings pitched. Johnson was named the league's Cy Young Award winner both years, with Schilling finishing second in the balloting. Meanwhile, the *Sporting News* selected Schilling as its Pitcher of the Year at the end of both seasons.

It was during the 2001 postseason that the entire nation witnessed the dominance of the two hurlers. Schilling compiled a record of 3–0 with a 0.67 ERA and three complete games during the National League playoffs. Johnson went 2–1 with an ERA just under 2.00 in his three starts. The two men then practically defeated the heavily favored New York Yankees in the World Series by themselves, posting all four Arizona victories. Schilling went 1–0 in his three starts, compiling an ERA of 1.69 and striking out 26 batters in 21 innings of work while allowing only 12 base hits. Starting two games and entering another in relief, Johnson went 3–0 with a 1.04 ERA, striking out 19 batters in 17 innings while allowing the Yankees just nine hits. The two aces were named co-winners of the World Series MVP Award.

The shared brilliance of Johnson and Schilling came to an end in 2003 when the latter's arm problems limited him to only 24 appearances. Schilling finished just 8–9 with a 2.95 ERA, prompting Arizona to trade him to Boston at the end of the year. Healthy again in 2004, Schilling went 21–6 with a 3.26 ERA and 203 strikeouts for Boston. More important, he helped lead the Red Sox to their first world championship in 86 years by going 3–1 during the postseason. Perhaps the finest big-game pitcher of his generation, Schilling posted a career record of 11–2 in postseason play, along with an outstanding 2.23 earned run average. The 2004 season turned out to be Schilling's last big year, though, since arm problems cut into his playing time significantly and greatly limited his effectiveness the next few seasons. After missing the entire 2008 campaign, Schilling finally retired, ending his career with a record of 216–146, an ERA of 3.46, and 3,116 strikeouts in 3,261 innings of work. He led his league in wins, innings pitched, and strikeouts two times each and in complete games a total of four times. Schilling finished in the top five in the Cy Young voting four times, placing second in the balloting on three occasions. He also appeared in six All-Star Games.

Johnson remained in Arizona two more years, posting a combined record of 22–22 in 2003 and 2004. He then spent two seasons in New York after signing a free agent contract with the Yankees prior to the start of the 2005 campaign. After experiencing only a moderate amount of success back in the American League, Johnson returned to the Diamondbacks, with whom he spent the 2007 and 2008 campaigns. He then signed on with the Giants as a free agent, spending 2009 pitching on the West Coast, where he won only eight games. Nevertheless, Johnson reached the 300-win plateau with one of those victories. He ended 2009 with a career record of 303–166 and a 3.29 ERA. Johnson subsequently elected to retire during the off-season, leaving him second only to Nolan Ryan on the all-time strikeout list, with a total of 4,875 to his credit. The Big Unit led his league in strikeouts a total of nine times, surpassing the 300 mark on six separate occasions. He also finished first in ERA and complete games four times each, innings pitched twice, and wins once. In addition to winning the Cy Young Award five times, Johnson finished second in the balloting three other times. He appeared in a total of 10 All-Star Games.

Randy Johnson and Curt Schilling spent only two full seasons together. But their combined record in those two seasons was an astounding 90–24. They finished first and second in the Cy Young voting both years, made the All-Star Team together both seasons, and finished first and second in the league in a major statistical category a total of six times. They also went a combined 9–1 during the 2001 postseason, leading the Diamondbacks to their only world championship in the process.

Note

Numbers printed in bold indicate that the player led his league in a statistical category.

CHAPTER 18

Warren Spahn / Johnny Sain

The Boston Braves were not a very good baseball club for most of the first half of the 20th century, posting a winning record only 10 times between 1900 and 1945. The Braves failed to win more than 68 games in any of the seven seasons from 1939 to 1945. However, Boston's fortunes began to change in 1946, due primarily to an outstanding pair of hurlers that dominated the National League's statistical categories for pitchers as much as they dominated NL hitters over the course of the next five seasons. In fact, Warren Spahn and Johnny Sain pitched so effectively while the remainder of Boston's pitching staff performed so erratically that fans of the team coined the phrase "Spahn and Sain and pray for rain."

Both Warren Spahn and Johnny Sain made their major-league debuts with the Braves in 1942. The 21-year-old left-handed throwing Spahn appeared in only four games, failing to post a won-lost record. The right-handed Sain, who was three years older than Spahn, pitched mostly in relief his first season, making 40 appearances and compiling a record of 4–7. Both men missed all of the next three seasons, serving their country during World War II.

Spahn pitched quite effectively when he returned to the Braves in 1946 at age 25, going 8–5 in his 16 starts and finishing the year with a 2.94 earned run average. Meanwhile, Sain quickly established himself as the ace of Boston's pitching staff, compiling a record of 20–14 and a 2.21 ERA and throwing a league-leading 24 complete games. The efforts of the two men enabled the Braves to finish fourth in the National League standings with a record of 81–72.

The Braves won 86 games the following year and came in third—their best finish since 1916. Along with NL MVP Bob Elliott, Spahn and Sain carried the team most of the year, combining for 42 of the team's 86 victories. Sain finished 21–12 with a 3.52 ERA, 22 complete games, 266 innings pitched, and three shutouts. With a record of 21–10, Spahn tied his teammate for second in the league in victories. The left-hander also tied Sain for second in the circuit with 22 complete games, and he led all National League hurlers with a 2.33 ERA, 289 innings pitched, and seven shutouts. Both men earned spots on the NL All-Star Team.

Spahn pitched less effectively in 1948, going 15–12 with a 3.71 earned run average, 16 complete games, and 257 innings pitched. But Sain was absolutely brilliant, compiling an ERA of 2.60 and a record of 24–15 to lead the league in wins. He also topped the circuit with 28 complete games and 314 innings pitched. Sain's exceptional performance helped the Braves capture the National League pennant—their first since 1914. The right-handed curveball artist occasionally pitched on only two days' rest during the pennant drive, tossing nine complete games over a 29-day stretch at one point and coming out on top in seven of those contests. He suffered his only two losses over that stretch of time by scores of 2–1 and 1–0. Sain's extraordinary efforts over the course of the campaign earned him his second straight All-Star selection and a second-place finish to Stan Musial in the league MVP voting. He capped off his outstanding season by defeating the Cleveland Indians' Bob Feller in game 1 of the World Series by a score of 1–0 in one of the greatest pitching duels in the history of the Fall Classic.

Boston slipped to fourth place in 1949, largely because of Sain's poor season. He followed up his greatest year with arguably his worst, going just 10–17 while pitching to a 4.81 earned run average. Spahn, though, returned to top form, compiling a record of 21–14 to lead the league in victories while posting an ERA of 3.07. In addition to leading the NL in wins, Spahn topped the circuit with 25 complete games and 302 innings pitched. He earned his second All-Star selection and finished seventh in the league MVP balloting.

The Braves finished fourth again in 1950—the last full season that Spahn and Sain spent together. In combining for 41 victories, the two men accounted for virtually half of their team's 83 wins. Spahn finished 21–17 to lead the league in wins. He also compiled a 3.16 ERA, led all NL hurlers with 191 strikeouts, and placed among the leaders with 25 complete games and 293 innings pitched en route to earning his third selection to the All-Star Team. Sain went 20–13 to finish second to Spahn in victories. He also pitched to a 3.94 earned run average and placed among the league leaders with 25 complete games and 278 innings pitched.

After hurting his shoulder early in 1951, Sain was traded to the Yankees for Lew Burdette later in the year. The right-hander subsequently spent the better part of the next five years in New York before finishing his career with the Kansas City Athletics in 1955. He retired from the game with a record of 139–116 and an ERA of 3.49. Following his playing days, Sain became one of the most successful pitching coaches in baseball.

Meanwhile, Spahn's career was just beginning. He remained with the Braves after they moved to Milwaukee in 1953, continuing to pitch for them through

1964. He split his final season between the Mets and the Giants, finally retiring from the game in 1965 at the age of 44. Spahn ended his career with a record of 363–245 and an ERA of 3.09. His 363 victories are the most by any left-handed pitcher in baseball history, and they represent the highest total compiled by any pitcher whose career began after 1920 (the end of the dead-ball era). Spahn was a 20-game winner a total of 13 times, and he led all National League pitchers in victories on eight occasions. He also finished first in the Senior Circuit in earned run average three times, complete games nine times, and innings pitched, strike-outs, and shutouts four times each. Spahn won the Cy Young Award in 1957, the same year the Braves won their only world championship in Milwaukee. He played for three pennant winners during his career.

One of baseball's most respected players, Spahn drew praise from his team-mates and opponents alike. Fred Haney, manager of the Braves from 1956 to 1959, had this to say about his star left-hander: "The things he can remember about pitching just amaze me. Spahnie studies. He can pitch to a certain hitter in a certain way and get him out. Another pitcher can't. The thing that impresses me most about him, though, is his spirit. He's the oldest guy on the club, but he works the hardest. He's my 'go-to-sleep' pitcher. I know when he's due to pitch the next day, I can get a good night's sleep the night before."[1]

New York Yankees Hall of Fame pitcher Whitey Ford stated, "If anyone asks me who my favorite pitcher of all-time is, I say Warren Spahn."[2]

Discussing Spahn's incredible durability, Stan Musial commented, "I don't think Spahn will ever get into the Hall of Fame. He'll never stop pitching."[3]

Warren Spahn and Johnny Sain spent four full seasons together between 1947 and 1950. During that time, they combined for 153 (or 46 percent) of their team's 335 victories. Between them, they averaged 38 wins per year. Either Spahn or Sain led the National League in wins and innings pitched in three of those four seasons. One or the other also led the league in complete games and strikeouts in two of those years. They combined for five appearances on the All-Star Team during their brief time together.

Notes

1. Gary Caruso, *Braves Encyclopedia* (Philadelphia: Temple University Press, 1995).

2. Thad Mumau, *An Indian Summer: The 1957 Milwaukee Braves, Champions of Baseball* (Jefferson, NC: McFarland, 2007).

3. Stan Musial, http://www.baseball-almanac.com/quotes/quosphn.shtml.

CHAPTER 19

Bill Terry / Mel Ott

The New York Giants' Bill Terry and Mel Ott found themselves being over-shadowed much of the time by another pair of New York sluggers named Ruth and Gehrig, who played their home games just a few miles away from the Polo Grounds at Yankee Stadium. Nevertheless, over a seven-year period beginning in 1929 and ending in 1935, Terry and Ott easily proved to be the National League's most prolific offensive tandem, making their team perennial contenders in the Senior Circuit.

Bill Terry appeared briefly with the Giants in both 1923 and 1924 before joining the team for good in 1925. The lefty-swinging first baseman played in 133 games his first full season, batting .319, driving in 70 runs, and scoring 75 others. With future Hall of Famer George Kelly serving as New York's regular first baseman in 1926, Terry assumed a part-time role, splitting his time between first base and the outfield. Terry finally supplanted Kelly as the team's everyday first baseman the following year, maintaining a stranglehold on the position for the next nine seasons.

Terry gave the Giants outstanding production from his number-three spot in the batting order in 1927 and 1928, surpassing 100 runs batted in and 100 runs scored both seasons while compiling a .326 batting average each year. He also used his soft hands and silky moves around the bag to quickly establish himself as the Senior Circuit's top-fielding first baseman.

As Terry rapidly developed into the National League's premier first sacker, a diminutive outfielder on the Giants began to emerge as one of the league's top sluggers. Standing 5'9" and weighing only 170 pounds, Mel Ott first came up to New York at the age of 17 in 1926. Used sparingly his first two seasons, Ott became a regular member of New York's lineup in 1928, hitting 18 home runs, driving in 77 runs, and batting .322 in 124 games. Ott had the most productive year of his career the following season (1929), placing among the league leaders in six offensive categories:

1929: 42 HRs, 151 RBIs, .328 AVG, 138 RUNS, .635 SLG PCT, .449 OBP

Ott finished second in the NL in home runs and runs batted in; placed third in runs scored, on-base percentage, and slugging percentage; and led the league with 113 walks. Employing an unusual batting style that included a high leg kick, the lefty-swinging Ott learned how to take full advantage of the Polo Grounds short right-field porch, frequently pulling the ball into the stands over the 257-foot sign. Meanwhile, Terry sprayed the ball all over the park, hitting only 14 home runs that year but driving in 117 runs, scoring another 103, batting .372, and accumulating 226 hits.

Terry and Ott continued to perform at an extremely high level the next three years, posting the following numbers:

Terry
1930: 23 HRs, 129 RBIs, **.401** AVG, 139 RUNS, **254** HITS
1931: 9 HRs, 112 RBIs, .349 AVG, **121** RUNS, 213 HITS
1932: 28 HRs, 117 RBIs, .350 AVG, 124 RUNS, 225 HITS
Ott
1930: 25 HRs, 119 RBIs, .349 AVG, 122 RUNS, **.458** OBP
1931: 29 HRs, 115 RBIs, .292 AVG, 104 RUNS, .392 OBP
1932: **38** HRs, 123 RBIs, .318 AVG, 119 RUNS, **.424** OBP

In addition to establishing a National League record that still stands by collecting 254 hits in 1930, Terry became the last player in the Senior Circuit to bat over .400. He also finished second in the batting race in each of the next two years, failing to win the batting title in 1931 by mere percentage points. Terry topped the circuit that year with 20 triples.

Ott led the National League in on-base percentage in both 1930 and 1932, and he tied for the league lead with 38 home runs in the second of those two years. Yet the Giants finished seventh in the NL in 1932—the only time they finished lower than third while Terry and Ott served as regular members of their starting lineup.

Terry remained the team's starting first baseman another three years, batting well over .300 each season and representing the National League as its starter at the position in each of the first three All-Star games. He served as a part-time player/manager in his final season, retiring from the game at the end of the 1936 campaign with a lifetime batting average of .341. Terry batted over .350 four times during his career, compiled more than 200 hits six times, drove in more than 100 runs six times, and scored more than 100 runs on seven separate occasions.

As Terry's career drew to a close, Ott's blossomed. After a solid 1933 season, the diminutive slugger posted exceptional numbers from 1934 to 1938:

1934: **35** HRs, **135** RBIs, .326 AVG, 119 RUNS, .415 OBP
1935: 31 HRs, 114 RBIs, .322 AVG, 113 RUNS, .407 OBP
1936: **33** HRs, 135 RBIs, .328 AVG, 120 RUNS, .448 OBP
1937: **31** HRs, 95 RBIs, .294 AVG, 99 RUNS, .408 OBP
1938: **36** HRs, 116 RBIs, .311 AVG, **116** RUNS, **.442** OBP

The Giants captured the National League pennant in both 1936 and 1937, finishing no lower than third in any of the other three years as well. Ott remained a starting outfielder for the team through 1945, following in Terry's footsteps as player/manager during the latter stages of his career. He finally retired in 1947 with 511 home runs, 1,860 runs batted in, 1,859 runs scored, and a .304 batting average. At the time of his retirement, Ott held National League records for most home runs, runs batted in, runs scored, and bases on balls. Over the course of his career, Ott surpassed 30 home runs eight times, knocked in more than 100 runs nine times, scored more than 100 runs nine times, and batted over .300 on 10 occasions. He led the league in home runs six times, runs batted in and slugging percentage once each, runs scored twice, and on-base percentage four times. Ott earned 12 selections to the NL All-Star Team.

Bill Terry and Mel Ott spent seven seasons together as everyday players on the Giants, from 1929 to 1935. Terry batted over .300 each of those years, surpassing .350 on four separate occasions. He also drove in more than 100 runs four times during that period, and he scored more than 100 runs five times. Ott surpassed 100 runs batted in each of those years, topped 30 homers four times, scored more than 100 runs six times, and batted over .300 five times. From 1929 to 1932, Terry and Ott combined to average 246 runs batted in and 243 runs scored per season. They were at their best together in 1931 and 1932. In the first of those years, Terry led the league with 121 runs scored and 20 triples; he also placed in the top five in six other offensive categories. Ott led the league in walks and finished in the top five in four other categories. In 1932, Ott topped the circuit in home runs, walks, and on-base percentage, and he finished in the top five in another four categories. Terry placed second in batting average, runs scored, hits, and total bases, and he finished third in home runs and slugging percentage.

Both Terry and Ott were named to the National League All-Star Team for each of the first three contests. They also helped lead the Giants to the 1933 world championship, to the 1936 National League pennant, and to second-place finishes in 1928, 1931, and 1934.

Note

Numbers printed in bold indicate that the player led his league in a statistical category.

CHAPTER 20

Derek Jeter / Bernie Williams

In 2000, the New York Yankees became the first team since the 1972–1974 Oakland Athletics to win three consecutive World Series. They also joined the 1936–1939 Yankees and the 1949–1953 Yankees on an extremely exclusive list of teams to capture as many as four world championships over a five-year period. Several players made major contributions to each of the Yankees' four championships during their latest dynasty. First baseman Tino Martinez and right fielder Paul O'Neill brought leadership and intensity to the locker room, as well as power and run production to the middle of the batting order. Left-hander Andy Pettitte and right-hander David Cone anchored the starting rotation from 1996 to 2000. Perhaps New York's most indispensable player was closer Mariano Rivera, who practically guaranteed his team victory any time he received the ball with a lead. The two best all-around players on the Yankees, though, were center fielder Bernie Williams and shortstop Derek Jeter, both of whom provided the team with outstanding hitting and run production, exceptional speed, and solid defense up the middle. Although the Yankees were a "team" in the truest sense of the word, Williams and Jeter were, with the possible exception of Rivera, New York's two most important players during their amazing championship run.

After first signing with the Yankees in 1985 as a 17-year-old amateur free agent out of San Juan, Puerto Rico, Bernie Williams spent five long years working his way up through New York's minor league system. Generally considered to be the jewel of the Yankee farm system throughout that period, Williams disappointed team brass after he finally joined the big club in 1991, failing to display much in the way of offensive production over the course of his first two major-league seasons. Furthermore, some members of the Yankee hierarchy considered Williams too shy and timid to succeed on the world's grandest stage, prompting them to seriously consider including him in a trade for a more established player. However, with the patient Gene Michael essentially running the Yankees during George Steinbrenner's two-year suspension from baseball, the front office never consummated such a deal, allowing the switch-hitting outfielder to remain with the organization.

After becoming the team's starting center fielder in 1993, Williams posted solid numbers in each of the next two seasons, combining for a total of 24 home runs, 125 runs batted in, and 147 runs scored while compiling batting averages of .268 and .289. Nevertheless, the Yankees remained somewhat disappointed in the lack of power and run production that Williams continued to display at the plate. They also grew increasingly frustrated with the lack of baseball instincts he demonstrated from time to time, particularly on the base paths, where he stole only 25 bases over the course of his first two full seasons in spite of his outstanding running speed.

The 26-year-old Williams finally began to fulfill his great promise in 1995, when he helped the Yankees advance to the postseason for the first time in 14 years by hitting 18 home runs, knocking in 82 runs, scoring 93 others, and batting .307. He established himself as one of the league's better players the following year, when he hit 29 homers, drove in 102 runs, scored another 108 times, and batted .305 en route to helping the Yankees win the AL East title. He punctuated his breakout season with an exceptional postseason, during which he led New York into the World Series by belaboring the pitching staffs of both the Texas Rangers and the Baltimore Orioles. After torching the Rangers for three home runs, five runs batted in, and a .467 batting average in the AL Division Series, Williams captured AL Championship Series MVP honors by hitting two homers, driving in six runs, and batting .474 during New York's five-game victory over the Orioles. The Yankees subsequently won their first world championship since 1978 when they defeated Atlanta in the World Series.

That 1996 campaign was the first full season in New York for another extremely talented product of the Yankee farm system. After appearing briefly with the Yankees the previous year, 21-year-old Derek Jeter earned the team's starting shortstop job during spring training of 1996. Displaying the quiet confidence that is such an intricate part of his persona, Jeter seemed overwhelmed neither by the New York spotlight nor by the thought of playing shortstop for baseball's most famous franchise. After homering on opening day, Jeter went on to win AL Rookie of the Year honors by hitting 10 home runs, driving in 78 runs, scoring 104 others, and batting .314. He continued to exhibit the poise of a veteran during the playoffs and World Series, batting .361 in New York's 15 postseason contests.

Although the Yankees failed to repeat as American League champions in 1997, both Williams and Jeter had outstanding seasons. The former hit 21 homers, knocked in 100 runs, scored 107 others, and batted .328. Williams earned the first of his five consecutive selections to the American League All-Star Team;

he also received the first of four straight Gold Gloves. Jeter hit 10 homers, drove in 70 runs, batted .291, stole 23 bases, and finished among the league leaders with 116 runs scored.

The Yankees won the World Series in each of the next three seasons, with Williams and Jeter serving as key contributors to each of those championship teams. These are the numbers the two men posted from 1998 to 2000:

1998
Bernie Williams: 26 HRs, 97 RBIs, 101 RUNS, **.339** AVG, 169 HITS
Derek Jeter: 19 HRs, 84 RBIs, **127** RUNS, .324 AVG, 203 HITS
1999
Bernie Williams: 25 HRs, 115 RBIs, 116 RUNS, .342 AVG, 202 HITS
Derek Jeter: 24 HRs, 102 RBIs, 134 RUNS, .349 AVG, **219** HITS
2000
Bernie Williams: 30 HRs, 121 RBIs, 108 RUNS, .307 AVG, 165 HITS
Derek Jeter: 15 HRs, 73 RBIs, 119 RUNS, .339 AVG, 201 HITS

In addition to leading the league with a .339 batting average in 1998, Williams finished second with a .422 on-base percentage. He placed among the leaders in both categories the following year as well while finishing third in the league in hits. Williams established career highs in home runs and RBIs in 2000.

In addition to leading the league with 127 runs scored in 1998, Jeter placed among the leaders in both hits and batting average. The Yankee shortstop had perhaps his finest season in 1999, establishing career highs in home runs, runs batted in, runs scored, hits, batting average, on-base percentage (.438), and slugging percentage (.552). Jeter led the league with 219 hits; placed second in batting average, runs scored, and triples (9); and finished third in on-base percentage. He again finished among the league leaders in runs scored, hits, and batting average in 2000. Jeter joined Williams on the American League All-Star Team all three years. He also finished in the top 10 in the MVP balloting each year, placing as high as third in the 1998 voting. Jeter was named Most Valuable Player of both the All-Star Game and the World Series in 2000.

The Yankees established a new American League record by winning 114 games during the 1998 regular season, before defeating Texas, Cleveland, and San Diego in the postseason. After struggling at the plate throughout the AL playoffs, Jeter collected six hits in 17 official trips to the plate against the Padres in the World Series en route to compiling a batting average of .353. He had a phenomenal postseason the following year, hitting a combined .375 against Texas, Boston, and Atlanta in helping the Yankees capture the 1999 world championship. Jeter subsequently batted .409 with two home runs against the Mets when he captured World Series MVP honors the following year. The

Yankees lost only one game in their three World Series appearances, sweeping both the Padres and the Braves, before defeating the Mets in five games in 2000.

In addition to being two of the American League's best players, Williams and Jeter were among the circuit's most versatile performers throughout the period. Williams, who usually batted fourth in New York's lineup, was not a prototypical cleanup hitter in that he possessed outstanding running speed, hit for a high batting average, and didn't strike out that frequently. Meanwhile, Jeter excelled in virtually every aspect of the game. Though not a home run hitter, he had good power at the plate, possessing an ability to hit the ball exceptionally well to the opposite field, which made him the perfect second-place hitter in the Yankee batting order. Jeter also ran the bases extremely well, and he was among the league's better defensive shortstops. Furthermore, he possessed several intangible qualities that simply do not show up in the box scores. An extremely intelligent and instinctive player, Jeter always seemed to be in the right place at the right time. He also had a knack for rising to the occasion—something he did with great regularity during the Yankees' championship run.

Discussing Jeter's ability to perform well under pressure, Reggie Jackson (also known as "Mr. October" for his ability to excel during the postseason) said, "In big games, the action slows down for him where it speeds up for others. I've told him, 'I'll trade my past for your future.'"[1]

Former Yankees teammate Charlie Hayes noted, "The thing that sets Derek apart is that he's not afraid to fail."[2]

Discussing his shortstop, former Yankees manager Joe Torre once stated, "This kid, right now, the tougher the situation, the more fire he gets in his eyes. You don't teach that."[3]

Jeter even drew praise from Michael Jordan, who certainly knows something about winning. The greatest player in NBA history had this to say about the Yankees shortstop: "I love his work ethic. He has a great attitude. He has the qualities that separate superstars from everyday people, and a lot of it is attributable to his great family background."[4]

Although the Yankees failed to repeat as world champions in either 2001 or 2002, they captured the AL East title both years, with Williams and Jeter having two of their finest seasons together:

2001
Bernie Williams: 26 HRs, 94 RBIs, 102 RUNS, .307 AVG, 166 HITS
Derek Jeter: 21 HRs, 74 RBIs, 110 RUNS, .311 AVG, 191 HITS
2002
Bernie Williams: 19 HRs, 102 RBIs, 102 RUNS, .333 AVG, 204 HITS
Derek Jeter: 18 HRs, 75 RBIs, 124 RUNS, .297 AVG, 191 HITS

Jeter made the All-Star Team and finished among the league leaders in runs scored both years. Meanwhile, Williams continued his string of seven consecutive seasons in which he batted over .300 and scored more than 100 runs. He also topped 20 homers six times during that period while knocking in more than 100 runs on five separate occasions.

Yankees manager Joe Torre expressed his admiration for Williams when he said, "He's got a calm about him that I trust, and he's electric at times. . . . I expect big things from him because he doesn't panic. For me, he's in the upper echelon among switch-hitters all-time."[5]

Nevertheless, the 2002 campaign turned out to be the Yankee center fielder's last big year. After turning 34 late in the season, Williams never again posted numbers that approached the figures he typically compiled during his peak seasons. He hit as many as 20 home runs and scored as many as 100 runs just one time each over the course of the next four years, while failing to knock in more than 70 runs or bat any higher than .281 during that same period. His advancing age and decreased offensive production prompted the Yankees to choose not to offer him a new contract when he became a free agent at the end of 2006. Electing not to peddle his services to other teams, Williams subsequently entered into involuntary retirement. He ended his career with 287 home runs, 1,257 runs batted in, 1,366 runs scored, and a .297 batting average. Williams posted a .275 career batting average in postseason play, hit 22 home runs, and knocked in a record 80 runs during the playoffs and World Series.

Even as Williams became less of a factor in New York's offense, Jeter remained one of the team's top threats. The shortstop finished third in the league with a .324 batting average in 2003, then placed second in the batting race in 2006 with a mark of .343. He also drove in 97 runs and scored another 118 times in the second of those campaigns to earn a second-place finish in the league MVP voting. Jeter placed among the league leaders in runs scored each year from 2004 to 2006, tallying well over 100 runs all three seasons. He also earned a Gold Glove at the end of each of those seasons for his solid play at shortstop.

Jeter continued to perform well after Williams left the Yankees at the end of 2006, batting over .300 in each of the next two seasons. Yet, his production appeared to be on the decline after he hit just 11 home runs, scored only 88 runs, and compiled only 179 hits in 2008. Jeter returned to top form, though, in 2009, hitting 18 homers and placing among the league leaders with a .334 batting average, 212 hits, 107 runs scored, and a .406 on-base percentage. Jeter's outstanding season earned him his 10th appearance on the All-Star Team, his fourth Gold Glove, and a third-place finish in the league MVP balloting. More important, it helped the Yankees win their first world championship since 2000 and their fifth with Jeter as their starting shortstop.

Although Jeter never again reached such heights, he remained an integral part of New York's offense the next three seasons, before his skills finally began to erode. After surpassing Lou Gehrig as the team's all-time hits leader in 2009, Jeter became the 28th member of the 3,000-hit club on July 9, 2011, joining the select group by homering off Tampa Bay left-hander David Price at Yankee Stadium. Following an injury-marred 2013 season in which he appeared in only 17 games, Jeter announced that the ensuing campaign would be his last. He retired at season's end with 260 career home runs, 1,311 runs batted in, 1,923 runs scored, a .310 batting average, and Yankee franchise records for most hits (3,465), doubles (544), and stolen bases (358). Jeter batted over .300 on 12 occasions, scored more than 100 runs 13 times, amassed more than 200 hits eight times, stole more than 30 bases four times, hit more than 20 homers three times, and knocked in more than 90 runs twice. In addition to winning five Gold Gloves and five Silver Sluggers, Jeter finished in the top 10 in the league MVP balloting eight times, placing in the top three of the voting on three separate occasions. Of even greater significance is the fact that the Yankees advanced to the playoffs in 16 of his 18 full seasons, winning 13 A.L. East titles, seven American League pennants, and five world championships.

Bernie Williams and Derek Jeter were teammates on the Yankees for 11 full seasons. During their time together, they combined for 12 appearances on the All-Star Team and eight top-10 finishes in the league MVP voting. Williams won four Gold Gloves, while Jeter captured three. Either Williams or Jeter placed in the league's top five in batting average nine times, hits eight times, and runs scored seven times. One or the other scored more than 100 runs 18 times, batted over .300 15 times, and topped 200 hits on seven occasions. Between 1996 and 2006, Williams and Jeter combined to score 2,316 runs and amass a total of 3,882 hits. During that same period, they helped lead New York to nine AL East titles, six American League pennants, and four world championships.

Notes

Numbers printed in bold indicate that the player led his league in a statistical category.

1. Reggie Jackson, http://www.baseball-almanac.com/quotes/derek_jeter_quotes .shtml.

2. Charlie Hayes, http://www.baseball-almanac.com/quotes/derek_jeter_quotes .shtml.

3. Joe Torre, http://www.baseball-almanac.com/quotes/derek_jeter_quotes.shtml.

4. Michael Jordan, http://www.baseball-almanac.com/quotes/derek_jeter_quotes .shtml.

5. Joe Torre, http://www.baseball-almanac.com/quotes/bernie_williams_quotes .shtml.

CHAPTER 21

Duke Snider / Roy Campanella

Duke Snider and Roy Campanella helped form the nucleus of a legendary Brooklyn Dodgers team that dominated the National League from 1949 to 1956. The Dodgers surpassed 90 victories in seven of those eight years, never finishing any lower than second in the Senior Circuit while capturing five NL pennants and one world championship. Although Brooklyn's impressive lineup included standout performers such as Gil Hodges, Pee Wee Reese, and Jackie Robinson throughout that period, it could be argued that no other members of the squad contributed as much to the success of the team as Snider and Campanella.

After spending time in the armed forces during World War II, Duke Snider first came up to the Brooklyn Dodgers in the pennant-winning season of 1947. He played sparingly his first two years with the club, hitting only five home runs and driving in just 26 runs in 243 total at bats over the course of the 1947 and 1948 campaigns. Snider finally claimed the starting center-field job for Brooklyn in 1949—a position he held for the next nine years.

Catcher Roy Campanella also became a member of Brooklyn's starting lineup in 1949, just one year after he debuted with the club by hitting nine home runs and knocking in 45 runs in 279 at bats. Prior to that, though, Campanella spent several years in the Negro Leagues, where only Josh Gibson established a greater reputation among Negro League receivers.

In their first year together as everyday players in Brooklyn, Snider and Campanella teamed up with National League MVP Jackie Robinson to lead the Dodgers to the pennant. Snider hit 23 home runs, drove in 92 runs, scored another 100, and batted .292. Campanella hit 22 long balls, knocked in 82 runs, batted .287, and earned his first selection to the NL All-Star Team. Unfortunately for the Dodgers, the Yankees defeated them in five games in the World

Series—a scenario that became all too familiar to the Dodgers and their fans in subsequent seasons.

The following year, Snider and Campanella began a string of seven consecutive seasons in which they both received nominations to the National League All-Star Team. Although the Dodgers failed to repeat as league champions in 1950, placing just two games behind the first-place Phillies in the final standings, Snider and Campanella had outstanding seasons for Brooklyn. Campanella hit 31 home runs, drove in 89 runs, and batted .281. Snider also hit 31 homers, knocked in 107 runs, placed among the league leaders with 109 runs scored and a .321 batting average, and topped the circuit with 199 hits and 343 total bases.

Campanella won the first of his three Most Valuable Player Awards the following year, even though Bobby Thomson's "shot heard 'round the world" enabled the arch-rival Giants to defeat the Dodgers in a three-game playoff for the National League pennant. Campanella edged out Stan Musial for league MVP honors by scoring 90 runs and placing among the circuit leaders with 33 home runs, 108 runs batted in, and a .325 batting average. Snider also posted impressive numbers, hitting 29 homers, driving in 101 runs, scoring 96 others, and batting .277.

Snider and Campanella subsequently enjoyed some of their finest seasons together, as the Dodgers captured the NL pennant in four of the next five seasons. Although injuries hampered Campanella's performance in both 1954 and 1956, the Brooklyn receiver compiled outstanding numbers the other three years:

1952: 22 HRs, 97 RBIs, .269 AVG, 73 RUNS
1953: 41 HRs, **142** RBIs, .312 AVG, 103 RUNS
1955: 32 HRs, 107 RBIs, .318 AVG, 81 RUNS

The baseball writers named Campanella NL MVP in both 1953 and 1955, enabling him to join Stan Musial at the time as the only league players to be so honored on three occasions. The cornerstone of the Dodgers throughout the period, Campanella not only wielded a potent bat in the middle of the team's batting order but also excelled behind the plate and did a tremendous job of handling Brooklyn's pitching staff. Those are the qualities that helped him earn three MVP trophies.

Meanwhile, the 1952–1956 seasons were among the best of Snider's career—see table 21.1 for the figures he compiled those five years. Snider placed in the top 10 in the league MVP balloting in each of those years, placing third to Campanella in 1953 and finishing a close second to his teammate in 1955. The center fielder replaced Jackie Robinson as the team's best all-around player during the period. Robinson held that distinction prior to 1953. However, advancing age caused his skills to gradually diminish his last few years in Brooklyn. With Robinson no longer as much of a factor as he was earlier in his career, Snider became the focal point of the team's offense and the squad's most complete player. Although the Dodger center fielder received far more notoriety for his hitting, he did an excellent job of patrolling the outfield. Hall of Famer Ralph Kiner once noted, "I'd say Duke covers more ground, wastes less motion, and is more consistent than anyone since DiMaggio."[1]

Snider had one more outstanding year in 1957, hitting 40 homers, knocking in 92 runs, and scoring 91 others, before age began to catch up with him in 1958. Ironically, the Dodgers left Brooklyn and moved to Los Angeles prior to the start of that 1958 season. Snider became a part-time player for the Dodgers that year, a role he maintained his last five years with the team. He returned to New York in 1963 to play for the Mets, then spent his final season back in California with the Giants. Snider retired at the end of 1964 with 407 career home runs, 1,333 runs batted in, 1,259 runs scored, and a .295 batting average. He appeared in eight All-Star Games.

While Snider continued to play several more years after the Dodgers left Brooklyn, Campanella was not as fortunate. After hitting only 13 home runs and driving in just 62 runs during an injury-plagued 1957 campaign, the catcher was expected to be far more productive once he returned to full health in 1958. However, Campanella was involved in a tragic automobile accident during the off-season that ended his playing career. Driving back to his Long Island home late one rainy evening after doing a double shift at his Harlem liquor store, Campanella fell asleep behind the wheel of his car. Skidding along the road's slick surface, his vehicle crashed into a pole and flipped over onto its side, leaving Campanella paralyzed from the chest down. He spent the remainder of his life confined to a wheelchair, retaining only limited use of his arms. Yet, after initially suffering through a period of deep depression, Campanella eventually resigned himself to his condition and became an inspiration for millions of Americans, giving motivational speeches to youngsters around the nation.

Over the course of 10 major-league seasons, Campanella compiled 242 home runs, 856 runs batted in, 627 runs scored, and a .276 batting average. He appeared in a total of eight All-Star Games.

Table 21.1. Duke Snider: 1952–1956

Year	HR	RBIs	AVG	RUNS	SLG PCT	OBP
1952	21	92	.303	80	.494	.368
1953	42	126	.336	**132**	**.627**	.419
1954	40	130	.341	**120**	.647	.427
1955	42	**136**	.309	**126**	.628	.421
1956	**43**	101	.292	112	**.598**	**.402**

Duke Snider and Roy Campanella spent nine seasons together as regulars in the Dodgers starting lineup. Over those nine seasons, Campanella won three Most Valuable Player Awards, and Snider finished in the top five in the voting on three separate occasions. They made 15 total appearances on the National League All-Star Team between them during that period. Campanella led the league in home runs once. Snider topped the circuit in runs scored three times; runs batted in and slugging percentage twice; and home runs, hits, and on-base percentage one time each. Between them, they topped the 40-homer mark six times and surpassed the 30-homer plateau another four times. They also drove in more than 100 runs a total of nine times, scored at least 100 runs seven times, and topped the .300 mark in batting on eight separate occasions. Snider and Campanella were at their best together in 1953 and 1955. In the first of those seasons, they combined to hit 83 home runs, drive in 268 runs, and score 235 others. In 1955, they totaled 74 home runs and 243 runs batted in between them. More important, that was the year they led the Dodgers to the only world championship they ever won in Brooklyn.

Note

Numbers printed in bold indicate that the player led his league in a statistical category.

1. Ralph Kiner, http://www.baseball-almanac.com/quotes/quosnid.shtml.

CHAPTER 22

Ron Santo / Billy Williams

Ron Santo and Billy Williams never won a pennant together. In fact, after each major league expanded to two divisions in 1969, Santo and Williams never even led their team to a divisional title. But in 1967, their seventh full season together as everyday players on the Chicago Cubs, Santo and Williams helped elevate the Cubs out of the National League's second division for the first time in two decades. The Cubs posted a winning record just once between 1947 and 1966. But with Santo and Williams leading the way, Chicago compiled a record of 87–74 in 1967 en route to finishing third in the Senior Circuit. The Cubs' 87 victories represented their highest win total since they captured the National League pennant in 1945. They also posted a winning mark in each of the next five seasons, compiling as many as 92 victories in 1969. In teaming up with Ernie Banks and Ferguson Jenkins to turn the Cubs into one of the National League's stronger clubs during the latter portion of the 1960s, Santo and Williams gave Chicago one of the league's best one-two punches for more than a decade.

Sweet-swinging Billy Williams began his major-league career by making brief appearances with the Chicago Cubs at the end of the 1959 and 1960 seasons. He came up to stay in 1961, claiming the team's left-field job—a position he manned for the next 14 years. Williams hit 25 home runs, knocked in 86 runs, and batted .278 in his first full season, earning NL Rookie of the Year honors in the process. Over the next three years, Williams demonstrated the consistency that eventually became his trademark, averaging 27 home runs, 95 runs batted in, and 94 runs scored from 1962 to 1964 while posting batting averages of .298, .286, and .312. Williams took his game to the next level in 1965, placing among the league leaders with 34 home runs, 108 runs batted in, 115 runs scored, 203 hits, 39 doubles, 356 total bases, a .315 batting average, and a .552 slugging percentage.

As Williams gradually developed into one of the National League's top offensive performers, Ron Santo evolved into the league's best all-around third baseman and one of its top run producers. After first coming up to the Cubs in 1960, Santo became the team's regular third-sacker the following season, hitting 23 homers, driving in 83 runs, scoring 84 others, and batting .284 in his first full year in the majors. After a subpar 1962 campaign, Santo bounced back in 1963 with 25 home runs, 99 RBIs, and a .297 batting average. He began to challenge St. Louis third baseman Ken Boyer for league supremacy at the position the following year by hitting 30 home runs, knocking in 114 runs, scoring another 94, batting .313, and topping the circuit with 13 triples and a .401 on-base percentage, all while playing a stellar third base. Although Boyer captured NL MVP honors by leading the Cardinals to the 1964 pennant, Santo posted comparable offensive numbers and won the first of his five consecutive Gold Gloves.

In discussing Santo's ability to play the hot corner, Billy Williams stated, "Was Brooks Robinson a better fielder than Ron Santo? I played left field behind Santo in Chicago all those years and I'm telling you that sucker was quick. I saw him make plays that nobody else could have made. He was out there every day, hurt or not, he had marvelous instincts and he could hit."[1]

Santo clearly established himself as the National League's top third baseman in 1965, a year in which he hammered 33 home runs, drove in 101 runs, scored 88 others, and batted .285.

Williams and Santo were both among the league's most consistent performers the next few seasons. Williams averaged 27 home runs, 92 RBIs, and 97 runs scored from 1966 to 1969, batting over .275 in each of those years. Meanwhile, Santo averaged 29 homers, 96 runs batted in, and 95 runs scored from 1966 to 1968, also batting over .300 in two of those three seasons. He had the most productive year of his career in 1969, hitting 29 homers, driving in a career-best 123 runs, scoring 97 others, and batting .289 en route to earning a fifth-place finish in the league MVP balloting. The third baseman also performed quite well in 1970, hitting 26 home runs and driving in 114 runs, before his production began to fall off somewhat the following season. Santo spent three more years with the Cubs before moving across town to join the White Sox for his final season in 1974. He retired at the end of the year with 342 home runs, 1,331 runs batted in, 1,138 runs scored, and a .277 career batting average. In addition to his five Gold Gloves, Santo appeared in nine All-Star Games and placed in the top five in the league MVP voting twice.

As Santo's career began to wane, that of Williams flourished. The Chicago left fielder had arguably his greatest season in 1970, establishing career highs with 42 home runs, 129 runs batted in, and a league-leading 137 runs scored. Williams also topped the circuit with 205 hits and placed among the leaders with a .322 batting average and a .586 slugging percentage. He finished second to Johnny Bench in the league MVP voting at the end of the year. After a solid 1971 campaign, Williams had another great year in 1972, finishing among the league leaders with 37 home runs, 122 runs batted in, and a .403 on-base percentage and topping the circuit with a .333 batting average and a .606 slugging percentage. Williams once again finished second to Bench in the MVP balloting. After putting up good numbers for the Cubs in each of the next two campaigns, Williams was traded to the Oakland A's, with whom he spent his final two seasons serving as a designated hitter. He retired at the end of 1976 with 426 home runs, 1,475 runs batted in, 1,410 runs scored, 2,711 hits, a .290 career batting average, and a plaque waiting for him at Cooperstown. In addition to finishing runner-up in the MVP balloting on two separate occasions, Williams was named to the National League All-Star Team a total of six times.

Williams and Santo played 14 years together, from 1960 to 1973. During that time, they combined for 725 home runs, 2,641 runs batted in, 2,385 runs scored, 4,563 hits, and 15 appearances on the All-Star Team. In their 13 seasons together as regulars in the Chicago lineup, they combined to average 55 home runs, 194 runs batted in, and 178 runs scored per campaign. Santo and Williams were also among the most durable players of their era, missing a total of only 20 games between them from 1962 to 1969. Williams appeared in every game for the Cubs for six consecutive seasons at one point, while Santo missed only 23 of a possible 1,595 starts from 1961 to 1970.

The third baseman took the field almost every day despite playing his entire career with diabetes. Santo begged those who knew about his illness not to reveal his condition to others, preventing it from becoming common knowledge until his playing days were over.

Santo later said, "I was always careful not to give myself a shot of insulin in the locker room in front of anybody. I always did it in private." He also revealed that the disease drove him on the field: "It was one reason I played so hard. I kept thinking my career could end any day. I never really wanted out of the lineup. The diabetes thing was hanging over my head."[2]

Notes

1. Mike Shalin and Neil Shalin, *Out by a Step: The 100 Best Players Not in the Baseball Hall of Fame* (South Bend, IN: Diamond Communications, 2002), 22.

2. Shalin and Shalin, *Out by a Step*, 24.

Part II

DYNAMIC FOOTBALL DUOS

CHAPTER 23

Joe Montana / Jerry Rice

That Jerry Rice is the only player who is included in two separate places in these rankings really should not come as much of a surprise to anyone. The greatest wide receiver in NFL history combined with Joe Montana and Steve Young at different times to form the league's most prolific passing combination. In the six years he played with Montana, Rice earned five First Team All-Pro selections and one AP Offensive Player of the Year nomination. In his eight years with Young, Rice made First Team All-Pro five times and was named the AP Offensive Player of the Year once.

The only thing that might surprise some people is that Rice actually compiled significantly better numbers playing with Young than he did during Montana's years with the 49ers. The following is a breakdown of the totals amassed by the wide receiver during the time he spent with each quarterback:

With Montana: 446 receptions, 7,866 yards, 83 touchdowns
With Young: 693 receptions, 9,746 yards, 84 touchdowns

The two extra years that Rice played with Young were largely responsible for the discrepancy in the numbers. Nevertheless, Jerry Rice caught more passes and compiled more receiving yards with Steve Young than he did with any other quarterback, including Joe Montana. Still, I feel compelled to award a higher place in these rankings to the combination of Montana and Rice. The twosome won two Super Bowls and appeared in three NFC Championship games in their six seasons together. Young and Rice played in four NFC title games as teammates, but they won only one Super Bowl over eight seasons. Furthermore, in spite of the outstanding numbers that Young compiled over the course of his career, his name rarely is mentioned during discussions involving the NFL's best quarterbacks of all time. Montana, though, is considered by many people to be perhaps the greatest quarterback ever to play the game.

Since the tandem of Young and Rice appears later in these rankings, this chapter focuses primarily on the time that Montana and Rice spent together on the 49ers from 1985 to 1990. It also examines the overall accomplishments of arguably the greatest quarterback in NFL history and the man widely considered to be the greatest wide receiver in the history of the league.

The San Francisco 49ers were one of the National Football League's worst teams from 1977 to 1979, winning only nine games. In fact, after capturing three consecutive NFC West titles from 1970 and 1972, the 49ers posted a winning record just once in the next seven seasons. The team's unsettled quarterback situation proved to be one of its biggest shortcomings throughout that period. Following the retirement of John Brodie in 1973, the position very much resembled a revolving door, with players such as Steve Spurrier, Jim Plunkett, and Steve DeBerg all failing in their attempts to establish themselves as the team's long-term starter at the position.

The 49ers finally found a leader for their offense in 1980, in second-year quarterback Joe Montana. San Francisco selected the former Notre Dame QB in the third round of the 1979 NFL draft with the 82nd overall pick. Montana spent most of his rookie season sitting on the San Francisco bench, watching DeBerg lead the team through a horrible 2–14 campaign. Montana took over as the team's starting quarterback midway through his sophomore season, winning only two of his seven starts but leading the league with a 64.5 completion percentage. The 49ers finished the year just 6–10 under second-year coach Bill Walsh, but they played better during the latter stages of the campaign, winning three of their final five games. San Francisco's week 14 victory made NFL history, as Montana led his team to an amazing 38–35 come-from-behind home win over the New Orleans Saints, after the 49ers trailed 35–7 at halftime. In addition to marking the greatest comeback in NFL history, the extraordinary effort demonstrated to the 49ers that they had the ability to overcome almost any deficit, as long as Montana was calling the signals behind center.

Montana developed into one of the league's top quarterbacks in his first full season as a starter the following year, leading the 49ers to a 13–3 record and the NFC West title in 1981. Rookie starters Eric Wright, Carlton Williamson, and Ronnie Lott helped bolster San Francisco's defensive secondary. Nevertheless, Montana was the team's most important player, establishing himself as the leader of the offense and giving the 49ers someone they could trust in pressure situations. The quarterback completed a league-leading 63.7 percent of his passes during the regular season, for a total of 3,565 yards, 19 touchdowns, and only 12 interceptions en route to earning the first of his eight Pro Bowl selections. It was during the playoffs, though, that Montana began to build his reputation as one of the greatest clutch performers in NFL history.

Trailing the Dallas Cowboys by a score of 27–21 with only minutes remaining in the NFC title game, the 49ers gained possession of the ball on their own 11-yard line. Demonstrating the poise and confidence for which he eventually became noted, Montana calmly drove his team down the field. With less than a minute left on the clock, the 49ers found themselves in a third-down-and-goal situation on the Dallas six-yard line. Flushed out of the pocket by three Cowboy defenders, Montana lured Dallas defensive lineman Ed "Too Tall" Jones into leaving his feet by faking a pass. With Jones no longer in his line of vision, Montana tossed the ball toward the back of the end zone in the direction of his favorite wide receiver, Dwight Clark. Leaping high in the air, Clark made the grab that has become known simply as "The Catch." The play enabled the 49ers to defeat the Cowboys by a final score of 28–27, thereby claiming their first NFC championship. San Francisco subsequently went on to defeat Cincinnati 26–21 in Super Bowl XVI, earning the first of their four NFL titles during the 1980s. Montana was named Super Bowl MVP for the first of three times.

San Francisco subsequently suffered through a disappointing 1982 campaign, finishing just 3–6 in the strike-shortened season. Yet Montana performed extremely well, passing for 2,613 yards in his nine starts and throwing for more than 300 yards in five consecutive games at one point.

The 49ers returned to the top of the NFC West the following year, finishing the 1983 season with a 10–6 record. However, they had their hopes of advancing to the Super Bowl for the second time in three years dashed by the defending champion Washington Redskins, who edged them out in the NFC title game by a final score of 24–21. Montana once again demonstrated his ability to rally his team from far behind by hurling three fourth-quarter touchdown passes that allowed the 49ers to overcome a 21–0 deficit. Washington prevailed in the end, though, when Mark Mosley kicked a game-winning field goal with only 40 seconds remaining in the contest.

Montana and the 49ers were at their best the following year, finishing the 1984 campaign with a record of 15–1. The quarterback completed just under 65 percent of his passes while throwing for 3,630 yards, 28 touchdowns, and only 10 interceptions. San Francisco swept through the NFC playoffs, defeating New York and Chicago by a combined score of 44–10 and shutting out the Bears in the NFC title game. The 49ers then dominated Dan Marino and the Miami Dolphins in Super Bowl XIX, winning the contest by a final score of 38–16. Montana threw for 331 yards and four touchdowns to earn Super Bowl MVP honors for the second time.

As good as Montana was, he benefited greatly from playing in Coach Bill Walsh's "West Coast Offense," a system designed to take advantage of the quarterback's mobility by using the short-passing game very much like the running game. Montana did not possess a powerful throwing arm, but he was an extremely accurate passer who excelled at delivering the ball to his receivers on routes that were of the short and intermediate variety. He also had an exceptionally quick release, outstanding pocket presence, and excellent mobility, with the capability of throwing the ball well on the run. All those qualities made Montana a perfect fit for the system Walsh installed in San Francisco.

Still, Montana's greatest gift was the poise he always exhibited under the most stressful of situations. Ronnie Lott, who played with Montana for 10 seasons in San Francisco, discussed his teammate's ability to perform well under pressure: "He's like Indiana Jones. He can go up against odds, and he just believes in himself. He believes nothing can stop him. . . . Joe finds a way to come out on top."[1] The master of late-game heroics, Montana led his team to 31 fourth-quarter come-from-behind victories over the course of his career.

San Francisco's extraordinary 1984 campaign did not prevent the team from bolstering its roster the following year. The 49ers selected Mississippi Valley State wide receiver Jerry Rice in the first round of the 1985 NFL draft with the 16th overall pick. The rookie wide receiver made an immediate impact making 49 receptions for 927 yards and four touchdowns after becoming a starter at midseason. The highlight of Rice's year ended up being a 10-catch, 241-yard performance against the Rams in December. At the end of the year, Rice was named the NFC Offensive Rookie of the Year.

Rice's presence in San Francisco's offense gave Montana another weapon, helping him earn Pro Bowl honors for the third consecutive year. The San Francisco quarterback led the NFL in completion percentage for the third time, posting a mark of 61.3 percent for the season. He also threw for 3,653 yards, 27 touchdowns, and only 13 interceptions. The 49ers advanced to the playoffs for the third straight year, but the New York Giants ended up eliminating them in the first round.

Montana missed the first half of the 1986 campaign with an injured back. Appearing somewhat frail after he rejoined the 49ers at midseason, the quarterback nevertheless led his team into the playoffs by compiling a 6–2 record in his eight starts. San Francisco's season ended in the first round of the postseason tournament, though, with a 49–3 thrashing at the hands of the Giants. A vicious hit by New York nose tackle Jim Burt knocked Montana out of the game in the closing moments of the first half. The lopsided contest obscured to some degree the 49ers' strong finish to the season and the exceptional year turned in by Jerry Rice. The second-year wide receiver made 86 receptions, led the NFL with 1,570 receiving yards, and caught 16 touchdown passes en route to earning Pro Bowl honors for the first of 11 consecutive times, and for the first of 13 total times in his career. He also earned First Team All-Pro honors for the first of 10 times.

Rice possessed many outstanding qualities that enabled him to excel at the NFL level. Although he was neither the strongest nor the fastest wide receiver in the league, the 6'2", 200-pound wideout had good size and speed. Rice also possessed outstanding hands and a unique ability to create separation between himself and the defensive back. A superb route runner, Rice was called "the best route-runner I've ever seen" by former NFL head coach Dennis Green. And even though other players in the league might have posted faster times in the 40-yard dash, Rice never seemed to get caught from behind once he broke into the open.

Joe Montana discussed the wide receiver's running ability in the open field: "Jerry has the ability to turn a short pass into a long gain very easily. He has great 'going from zero to full speed' speed. You don't see him being caught from behind by guys who are faster than him."[2]

Perhaps Rice's most special qualities, though, were his tremendous desire, determination, dedication, and focus. Known for his grueling workout regimen, the wide receiver was an incredibly well-conditioned athlete who possessed a will to excel that was second to none.

Rice described the attitude that he brought with him to the playing field: "So many receivers, once they catch the football they just fall down. But, with me, once I catch the football I feel that excitement is just starting. So, somehow, I'm gonna try to keep my balance and try to get into the end zone."[3]

Rice's determination and extraordinary conditioning enabled him to start every game for 10 straight seasons at one point. He appeared in all of his team's games in 19 of his 20 NFL seasons.

Following their disappointing loss to the Giants in the 1986 playoffs, the 49ers earned a postseason berth for the fifth consecutive time in the strike year of 1987. San Francisco posted a record of 10–1 in Montana's 11 starts, with the quarterback compiling a league-leading 66.8 completion percentage and 31 touchdown passes. Montana also topped 3,000 yards passing for the fifth time in his career and threw only 13 interceptions en route to earning First Team All-Pro honors for the first of three times.

Of Montana's 31 touchdown passes, 22 went to Rice, who established a new single-season NFL record for TD pass receptions (later broken by Randy Moss in 2007), despite appearing in only 12 games for the 49ers. The wide receiver scored a league-leading 23 touchdowns and made 65 receptions to earn AP Offensive Player of the Year honors for the first of two times. However, San Francisco fell short in the playoffs again, this time losing to Minnesota in the divisional playoffs by a score of 36–24.

With Montana and Rice leading the way, the 49ers established themselves as the NFL's dominant team once again in 1988, winning the first of two consecutive Super Bowls and compiling the league's best record over the next three seasons combined. These are the numbers the two men posted from 1988 to 1990:

Montana
1988: 59.9 COMP %, 2,981 PASSING YDS, 18 TD PASSES, 10 INTS

1989: **70.2** COMP %, 3,521 PASSING YDS, 26 TD PASSES, 8 INTS
1990: 61.7 COMP %, 3,944 PASSING YDS, 26 TD PASSES, 16 INTS
Rice
1988: 64 RECEPTIONS, 1,306 YDS, 10 TDS
1989: 82 RECEPTIONS, **1,483** YDS, **17** TDS
1990: **100** RECEPTIONS, **1,502** YDS, **13** TDS

Rice averaged a career-high 20.4 yards per reception in 1988, then capped off his season by making 11 catches for 215 yards and one touchdown during the 49ers' 20–16 Super Bowl win over the Cincinnati Bengals. Rice's Super Bowl–record 11 catches and 215 receiving yards earned him the game's Most Valuable Player Award. The wide receiver led the NFL in receiving yardage and touchdown receptions for the first of two consecutive times the following year, before torching the Denver Broncos' defensive secondary for seven catches, 148 yards, and three touchdowns during San Francisco's lopsided 55–10 victory in Super Bowl XXIV. Rice captured the Triple Crown for wide receivers in 1990, leading all NFL wideouts in receptions, receiving yardage, and touchdown catches. The highlight of Rice's season came in week 6 against the Falcons, when he recorded five touchdown receptions. Rice earned First Team All-Pro honors all three seasons.

Montana's 1988 numbers were compromised somewhat by the fact that he started only 13 games for the 49ers. Nevertheless, he led his team to a 10–6 record during the regular season and then to one-sided victories over Minnesota and Chicago in the NFC playoffs. Montana subsequently completed 23 of 36 passes for 357 yards and two touchdowns during San Francisco's 20–16 win over Cincinnati in Super Bowl XXIII. He again demonstrated his ability to perform under extreme pressure in the closing moments of that contest by leading the 49ers on a 92-yard touchdown drive that ended with a touchdown pass to John Taylor with only 39 seconds remaining on the clock.

Montana earned NFL MVP and AP Offensive Player of the Year honors the following year by leading the 49ers to a 14–2 record under new head coach George Seifert. The quarterback then completed his trifecta by capturing Super Bowl MVP honors for the third time by throwing five touchdown passes against the Broncos during San Francisco's 55–10 victory in Super Bowl XXIV.

The Giants ended the 49ers hopes for a "threepeat" in 1990 by upsetting the two-time defending champions in the NFC title game, 15–13, on a last-second field goal. Still, Montana had one of his finest campaigns, throwing for just under 4,000 yards, leading his team to an NFL-best 14–2 record during the regular season, capturing league MVP honors for the second straight year, and being named First Team All-Pro for the third and final time in his career.

The 49ers' loss to New York in the championship game proved to be devastating since it cost them Montana's services for the entire 1991 season and much of 1992 as well. Injured midway through the fourth quarter of that contest on a hit from behind by Giants defensive end Leonard Marshall, Montana required off-season surgery on his throwing arm. By the time he returned to the 49ers midway through the 1992 campaign, Montana had been replaced as the team's starting quarterback by Steve Young. Unhappy with his situation in San Francisco, Montana made a trade request at the end of the year that ultimately dealt him to the Kansas City Chiefs, with whom he spent his final two seasons. The quarterback led the Chiefs into the playoffs each year, helping them advance as far as the AFC title game in 1993. Montana was named to the Pro Bowl for the eighth and final time that year, before retiring at the conclusion of the following season.

Montana ended his career in 1994 with a record of 117–47 as a starter. He threw for a total of 40,551 yards, completed 273 touchdown passes, threw only 139 interceptions, and completed 63.2 percent of his passes. Montana's 3,409 completions, 273 touchdown passes, 40,551 passing yards, and 92.3 passer rating all place him in the top 10 all-time. He led the NFL in completion percentage five times, and he topped the league in touchdown passes twice. In addition to passing for more than 400 yards in a game seven times during the regular season, Montana threw for more than 300 yards in the playoffs an NFL-record six times. He holds career playoff records for completions, touchdown passes, and total passing yardage. Montana led his team into the playoffs in 11 of his 12 years as a full-time starter. His teams won nine divisional titles and four Super Bowls, and he is the only player to be named Super Bowl MVP on three occasions. In 2006, *Sports Illustrated* rated him the number-one clutch quarterback of all time.

Jerry Rice's career continued to flourish after Steve Young took over as starting quarterback in San Francisco in 1991. The wide receiver earned First Team All-Pro honors five more times; he also earned a spot in the Pro Bowl eight more times. Rice was named the AP Offensive Player of the Year for the second time in 1993, led the NFL in receptions for the second time in 1996, and topped all receivers in reception yardage and touchdown receptions three more times each. After signing with the Oakland Raiders at the end of the 2000 season, Rice was named to the Pro Bowl for the 13th and final time in 2002. The Raiders made it to the Super Bowl that year, and even though they lost the game 48–21, Rice's 48-yard TD catch in the fourth quarter enabled him to become the first player ever to catch a touchdown pass in four Super Bowls.

Upon his retirement at the conclusion of the 2004 campaign, Rice held numerous NFL records, including

Most receptions: 1,549
Most receiving yards: 22,895
Most total all-purpose yards: 23,546

Most receiving touchdowns: 197
Most total touchdowns: 208

Rice's 1,549 receptions are 447 more than the 1,102 catches that runner-up Marvin Harrison made during his career. Rice's 22,895 receiving yards place him almost 7,000 yards ahead of Terrell Owens, who is second on the all-time list. Rice's 197 touchdown receptions place him some 44 ahead of Owens, who is also second on that list. And his 208 total touchdowns are 33 more than the 175 that Emmitt Smith tallied during his career. Those are the figures that prompted Ronnie Lott to say, "Without a doubt—hands down—Jerry Rice is the best receiver to play in the National Football League."[4]

Lott is not the only one who feels that way. Rice was named to the NFL All-Decade Teams for both the 1980s and the 1990s. He was also picked for the NFL's 75th Anniversary All-Time Team. And in 1999, he was ranked second to Jim Brown on the *Sporting News* list of the 100 greatest football players.

Montana joined his former teammate on both the 1980s All-Decade Team and the NFL's 75th Anniversary All-Time Team. He also finished third to Brown and Rice on the *Sporting News* list of 100 greatest football players.

In the six years in which they were both starters on the San Francisco offense, Joe Montana and Jerry Rice combined for nine appearances in the Pro Bowl, eight First Team All-Pro selections, two AP Offensive Player of the Year Awards, and two NFL MVP awards. Rice was named MVP of Super Bowl XXIII, and Montana received the honor the following year. Montana led the NFL in passing twice, while Rice led the league in receptions once, receiving yards three times, and touchdown receptions on four occasions. The 49ers advanced to the playoffs each year, appeared in three NFC title games, and won two Super Bowls.

Notes

Numbers printed in bold indicate that the player led his league in a statistical category.

1. *Greatest Ever: NFL Dream Team* (Polygram Video, 1996).
2. *Greatest Ever: NFL Dream Team.*
3. *Greatest Ever: NFL Dream Team.*
4. *Greatest Ever: NFL Dream Team.*

CHAPTER 24

Peyton Manning / Marvin Harrison

In spite of the greatness that Joe Montana and Jerry Rice displayed during their time together in San Francisco, they did not form the most prolific passing combination in NFL history. Instead, Peyton Manning and Marvin Harrison of the Indianapolis Colts composed the most productive passing duo in league history. Over a period of 11 seasons, Manning and Harrison hooked up for more pass completions, total yardage, and touchdowns than any other quarterback–wide receiver pairing in the history of the National Football League. In the process, they helped make the Colts perennial contenders for the AFC title during their time together.

The glory years of Johnny Unitas and Raymond Berry were just a distant memory by the time that the Colts left Baltimore for the city of Indianapolis in 1984. After winning consecutive NFL titles in 1958 and 1959, the Colts contended for the league championship throughout most of the 1960s, finally capturing a third title in 1970 when they defeated the Dallas Cowboys in Super Bowl V. However, the Colts spent most of their remaining years in Baltimore playing subpar football, posting a winning record only four times between 1971 and 1983.

The Colts fared no better after they moved to Indianapolis, compiling a winning mark in just four of their first 12 seasons in their new home and failing to win more than nine games in any single season between 1984 and 1995. The fortunes of the Colts appeared to be on the upswing in 1996, though, after they advanced to the AFC playoffs as a wild-card entry, despite finishing just 9–7 during the regular season. Even a 42–14 thrashing at the hands of the Pittsburgh Steelers in the first round of the postseason tournament failed to dull the hopes of Indianapolis fans, who saw their team's future as quite promising.

One of the reasons that Colts' fans felt good about their team was the outstanding play of rookie wide receiver Marvin Harrison. Indianapolis selected

Harrison in the first round of the 1996 NFL draft with the 19th overall pick, after he spent his collegiate career catching passes from Donovan McNabb at Syracuse University. In an outstanding wide-receiver draft class that also included Keyshawn Johnson, Terry Glenn, Eric Moulds, Terrell Owens, and Amani Toomer, the Colts obtained the pick they eventually used on Harrison by trading former number-one draft pick Jeff George (quarterback) to the Atlanta Falcons. At 6'0" and 185 pounds, Harrison lacked the size of Johnson, Owens, and Toomer. He also didn't possess the exceptional running speed of Glenn. However, Harrison's outstanding moves, precise route running, and extraordinary hands eventually enabled him to establish himself as the best of that year's wide-receiver corps. The Syracuse product exhibited as a rookie that he had a bright future, catching 64 passes for 836 yards and eight touchdowns.

Although Harrison performed well in his second year in the league, making 73 receptions for 866 yards and six touchdowns, the Colts finished a horrendous 3–13, causing the organization and its fans to realize that the team was much further away from contending for a title than they initially believed.

The Colts' dismal showing in 1997 enabled them to select Tennessee quarterback Peyton Manning with the first overall pick of the 1998 NFL draft. After winning 39 of 45 games as a starter in college, Manning found himself being projected by most NFL scouts as a franchise-type quarterback. At 6'5" and 230 pounds, he certainly had the size to become an elite quarterback at the NFL level; he also possessed outstanding strength, a powerful throwing arm, superior intelligence, and exceptional leadership skills. Another quality that Manning possessed was a willingness to work hard.

Jim Mora, who coached Manning when he first entered the league in 1998, said, "You really don't know a guy until you coach him, and the first thing you see is he has a tremendous work ethic. He is always well prepared."[1]

Tony Dungy coached Manning in Indianapolis from 2002 to 2007. The coach said of his quarterback, "He's probably the hardest-working guy I've been around who has great ability. Overachievers work hard because they have to. Peyton has rare talent, but chooses to push himself like he doesn't."[2]

Dungy added, ""I've never seen a guy with so much ability and the dedication to match."[3]

Adam Meadows, a teammate of Manning when he first joined the Colts, commented, "From the first day, it was [Manning's] huddle. Anyone who works as hard as he does gets respect."[4]

Manning took over as the Colts' starting quarterback at the start of his rookie season, showing a great deal of promise by throwing for 3,739 yards and 26 touchdowns en route to earning a spot on the All-NFL Rookie First Team. Still, Manning frequently exhibited his lack of experience, throwing a league-leading 28 interceptions. With Manning experiencing the inevitable growing

Table 25.1.   Peyton Manning: 1999–2006

Year	COMP %	Passing YDS	TD Passes	INTS
1999	62.1	4,135	26	15
2000	62.5	**4,413**	**33**	15
2001	62.7	4,131	26	23
2002	66.3	4,200	27	19
2003	**67.0**	**4,267**	29	10
2004	67.6	4,557	**49**	10
2005	67.3	3,747	28	10
2006	65.0	4,397	**31**	9

pains of any first-year signal caller, the Colts suffered through another dreadful 3–13 campaign. Since Marvin Harrison also needed to adjust to playing with a rookie quarterback, he posted slightly subpar numbers, finishing the campaign with 59 receptions for 776 yards and seven touchdowns.

Everything came together for Manning, Harrison, and the Colts the following season, though. Manning and Harrison developed a rapport that few passing combinations have ever shared, helping their team begin an extremely successful run during which they advanced to the playoffs in seven of the next eight seasons. Tables 25.1 and 25.2 present the numbers that Manning and Harrison compiled over that eight-year stretch.

Manning finished among the NFL's top three quarterbacks in passing yardage in seven of the eight years, posting the league's highest passer rating three straight times, from 2004 to 2006. In addition to leading the league in touchdown passes three times, he finished second on three other occasions. Manning's 49 touchdown passes in 2004 established a new NFL record (later surpassed by Tom Brady in 2007). Manning was named the NFL's Most Valuable Player in both 2003 and 2004; he also earned AP Offensive Player of the Year honors in the second of those two seasons. Manning appeared in the Pro Bowl in all but

Table 25.2.   Marvin Harrison: 1999–2006

Year	Receptions	YDS	TD Receptions
1999	115	**1,663**	12
2000	**102**	1,413	14
2001	109	1,524	15
2002	**143**	**1,722**	11
2003	94	1,272	10
2004	86	1,113	15
2005	82	1,146	12
2006	95	1,366	12

the 2001 season, and he received First Team All-Pro honors in 2003, 2004, and 2005.

In addition to leading the NFL with 12 touchdown receptions in 2005, Harrison finished second in the league five other times during the period. He also finished either first or second in receiving yardage on four occasions. Harrison's 143 receptions in 2002 broke Herman Moore's existing single-season record by 20 catches; the Indianapolis wide receiver also led the NFL with 1,722 receiving yards. He became the first receiver in league history that year to surpass 100 receptions four consecutive seasons. In December of 2006, Harrison became just the fourth player in NFL history to record 1,000 career receptions, joining Jerry Rice, Cris Carter, and Tim Brown on an exclusive list. He later surpassed both Carter and Brown, leaving him second to Rice on the all-time list. Harrison was named to the Pro Bowl all eight seasons, earning First Team All-Pro honors in 1999, 2002, and 2006.

Reflecting on his first seven seasons with Manning at the conclusion of the 2004 campaign, Harrison commented, "We went through the bumps and bruises that first year or two. . . . But we've developed a rapport where we can do things without speaking. Of the 83 touchdowns we've had, I can't tell you how many we've come up with on the fly."[5]

The Colts were one of the National Football League's most successful franchises during that eight-year period, making the playoffs each season, with the exception of 2001. Nevertheless, Manning's ability to play well in big games often came into question since both he and the team invariably faltered in the postseason.

After finishing 13–3 in 1999, Indianapolis lost to the Tennessee Titans by a score of 19–16 in the first round of the playoffs. Following a regular season in which he threw for over 4,000 yards, Manning found himself unable to lead the Colts to a single point during the second half of the contest.

Indianapolis finished 10–6 in 2000 to earn a spot in the playoffs as a wild card. The team again came up short in the first round of the postseason, though, failing to protect a 14-point third quarter lead against the Miami Dolphins, who eventually defeated the Colts 23–17 in overtime.

Tony Dungy assumed head-coaching responsibilities in Indianapolis after Jim Mora was fired at the conclusion of a disappointing 2001 campaign. The defensive-minded Dungy led the Colts to a 10–6 record and a wild-card playoff berth in 2002. However, Indianapolis once again made an early exit from the postseason, losing a 41–0 road game to the New York Jets.

The Colts improved their record to 12–4 in 2003, with Manning sharing league MVP honors with Titans quarterback Steve McNair. The Indianapolis QB began to silence the critics who claimed that he could not perform well during the postseason when he led the Colts to consecutive playoff victories over the

Denver Broncos and Kansas City Chiefs. Manning threw for 377 yards and five touchdowns in a 41–10 win against Denver. He followed that up by passing for another 304 yards and three touchdowns during the Colts' 38–31 victory over the Chiefs. Manning, though, came up short against the New England Patriots in the AFC Championship Game, throwing four interceptions during a 24–14 loss at snowy Foxboro.

The Colts finished 12–4 again in 2004, with Manning earning league MVP honors for his record-setting performance. The quarterback continued his exceptional play in the first round of the playoffs, passing for 457 yards and four touchdowns during a 49–24 thrashing of the Denver Broncos. However, Manning again struggled against the Patriots in snowy Foxboro, this time failing to lead the Colts into the New England end zone during a 20–3 loss in the Divisional Playoff contest.

After Manning and Harrison broke Steve Young's and Jerry Rice's record of 86 touchdown connections early in 2005, the Colts exorcised their demons by mauling the Patriots 40–21 in a midseason showdown at Foxboro. Manning threw for 321 yards and three touchdowns during the lopsided contest. The Colts went on to compile a record of 14–2 after starting the season a perfect 13–0. However, they failed to make it past the first round of the playoffs, losing a heartbreaking 21–18 home affair to the Pittsburgh Steelers.

The Colts compiled a 12–4 record for the third time in four seasons in 2006 en route to capturing their fourth consecutive AFC South title. They subsequently overcame three Peyton Manning interceptions to defeat the Kansas City Chiefs 23–8 in the first round of the playoffs. The Indianapolis quarterback struggled again the following week against Baltimore, but the Colts managed to edge out the Ravens by a score of 15–6. Manning then led his team to a stunning comeback against the Patriots in the AFC Championship Game, directing the Colts to four second-half touchdowns that enabled them to overcome a 21–6 halftime deficit. The Colts took the lead for good when they scored a touchdown with just over a minute remaining on the clock, advancing to the Super Bowl with a 38–34 victory over the Patriots. Manning then won Super Bowl MVP honors by throwing for 247 yards and one touchdown during the Colts' 29–14 victory over the Chicago Bears.

Although the Colts compiled an outstanding 13–3 record in 2007, winning their fifth consecutive division title in the process, they lost Marvin Harrison to a knee injury for all but five games, bringing to an end the extraordinarily successful run that the receiver and Manning experienced. However, Harrison returned in 2008 to catch 60 passes for 636 yards and five touchdowns. Nevertheless, Harrison was unhappy with his somewhat reduced role in the team's offense and asked for his release at the end of the season. He subsequently went unclaimed by every NFL team, ostensibly ending his playing career. In his 13 years in the league, Harrison caught 1,102 passes for 14,580 yards and 128 touchdowns. In addition to being second all-time in pass receptions, he is fourth in receiving yards and fifth in touchdown receptions. Among Harrison's numerous accomplishments is the fact that he is the only player in NFL history to

Have 50 or more receptions in his first 11 seasons
Make at least 100 receptions in four consecutive seasons
Compile at least 1,400 receiving yards in four consecutive seasons

Manning and the Colts continued to excel as Harrison's career drew to a close and even after it eventually ended. Although the Colts failed to advance beyond the first round of the playoffs in either 2007 or 2008, they posted regular-season records of 13–3 and 12–4, respectively. Manning earned Pro Bowl honors each year, and in 2008 he earned First Team All-Pro honors for the fourth time and NFL MVP honors for the third time. In 2009, he became the first quarterback in NFL history to pass for more than 40,000 yards in any single decade. In leading Indianapolis to an AFC-best 14–2 regular-season record, Manning also became the first player to win four MVP trophies. The Colts eventually lost to the New Orleans Saints in the Super Bowl, but Manning passed for more than 300 yards twice during the AFC Playoffs, establishing a new NFL postseason record by surpassing the 300-yard mark a total of eight times during his career.

Indianapolis had another solid season in 2010, concluding the campaign with a record of 10–6. Manning led all NFL quarterbacks in completions (450) for the third time in his career, and his 4,700 passing yards gave him a record 11 seasons with more than 4,000 yards passing. With the Colts trailing the New York Jets by a score of 14–13 late in the fourth quarter of the AFC wild-card game, Manning led a 48-yard drive that ended in an apparent game-winning 50-yard field goal by Adam Vinatieri with only 53 seconds left on the clock. However, the Jets ultimately kicked a field goal as time expired, giving them a 17–16 victory and bringing the Colts' season to an end.

The Colts subsequently placed their franchise tag on Manning during the off-season, eventually signing him to a five-year $90 million contract. But, after undergoing neck surgery on May 23, 2011, Manning experienced a setback in his recovery that forced him to miss the entire season, ending in the process his consecutive starts streak of 208 games. Manning had another surgery performed on September 8, 2011, putting into further question his ability to return from an injury that very much placed the remainder of his career in doubt. Released by the Colts following the conclusion of the 2011 campaign, Manning elected to sign on with the Broncos as a free agent. The 36-year-old quarterback returned to top form in Denver, earning Pro Bowl, First-Team All-Pro, and AP

NFL Comeback Player of the Year honors his first year in the Mile-High City by passing for 4,659 yards and 37 touchdowns, while also finishing first in the league with a career-high 68.6 completion percentage. Manning followed that up with a season for the ages in 2013, leading the Broncos into the playoffs for the second straight time and winning his fifth MVP trophy by completing 68.3 percent of his passes and establishing new league marks for most passing yardage (5,477) and most TD passes (55).

Although Manning's critics continue to point to the fact that he has won just one Super Bowl over the course of his illustrious career, many people consider him to be the greatest quarterback in NFL history. He holds the second-highest career passer rating (97.2) in the history of the league, and his career average of 270.7 passing yards per game places him third all-time. Manning also ranks second all-time in pass completions (5,532), total passing yardage (64,964), and touchdown passes completed (491). In 2009, *The Sporting News* listed Manning as the NFL's top player, and Fox Sports named him player of the decade. Meanwhile, the NFL's top 100 show identified him as the eighth best player in league history in 2010.

With all his physical talent, Manning's intelligence and toughness have contributed greatly toward making him the legend he has become. Teammate Brandon Stokley stated emphatically, "He's the best that's ever played this game as far as quarterbacks are concerned. When he's retired, they'll compare everybody to Peyton Manning, without a doubt."[6]

Brian Urlacher of the Chicago Bears attempted to match wits with Manning at the line of scrimmage in Super Bowl XLI by calling his team's defensive signals. The middle linebacker later suggested, "You're not going to fool Peyton Manning. He knows where he's going with the football before the snap."[7]

Pro Bowl quarterback Tom Brady of the Patriots expressed his admiration for Manning by saying, "He's incredible to watch."[8]

Rams coach Scott Linehan suggested, "I guarantee you, if Peyton Manning was on the Pats, he would have won a minimum of three Super Bowls."[9]

Former NFL head coach Dick Vermeil noted, "The thing about him is he doesn't throw an inaccurate ball. Every time a receiver has to make a catch, it's right there in any type of throw. He's been doing that for a long time."[10]

In their 10 full seasons as teammates in Indianapolis, Peyton Manning and Marvin Harrison combined for 16 appearances in the Pro Bowl and seven First Team All-Pro selections. They hold the record for most completions between a quarterback and a wide receiver, connecting on a total of 965 passes. Manning and Harrison also hold the record for most touchdown passes between a quarterback and a wide receiver, with a total of 114. The two men helped lead the Colts to nine playoff appearances, six division titles, and one Super Bowl championship.

Notes

Numbers printed in bold indicate that the player led his league in a statistical category.

1. Jim Mora, http://www.jockbio.com/Bios/Manning/Manning_they-say.html.
2. Tony Dungy, http://www.jockbio.com/Bios/Manning/Manning_they-say.html.
3. Tony Dungy, http://www.jockbio.com/Bios/Manning/Manning_they-say.html.
4. Adam Meadows, http://www.jockbio.com/Bios/Manning/Manning_they-say .html.
5. Marvin Harrison, http://www.jockbio.com/Bios/Manning/Manning_they-say .html.
6. Brandon Stokley, http://www.jockbio.com/Bios/Manning/Manning_they-say .html.
7. Brian Urlacher, http://www.jockbio.com/Bios/Manning/Manning_they-say .html.
8. Tom Brady, http://www.jockbio.com/Bios/Manning/Manning_they-say.html.
9. Scott Linehan, http://www.jockbio.com/Bios/Manning/Manning_they-say.html.
10. Dick Vermeil, http://www.jockbio.com/Bios/Manning/Manning_they-say.html.

CHAPTER 25

Steve Young / Jerry Rice

We earlier examined the success that Jerry Rice experienced during the six years he played alongside Joe Montana on the San Francisco 49ers offense. However, the wide receiver actually had some of his greatest seasons after Steve Young assumed the role of starting quarterback in San Francisco prior to the start of the 1991 campaign. Rice made some 250 more pass receptions and accumulated almost 2,000 more reception yards with Young behind center than with Montana calling the signals. San Francisco's offense as a whole also continued to function at optimum proficiency with Young at the helm, enabling the 49ers to advance to four NFC title games and one Super Bowl.

Steve Young spent the first two years of his professional career playing in the ill-fated USFL. After the league folded in 1984, the former All-American quarterback out of Brigham Young University was selected by the Tampa Bay Buccaneers with the first overall pick of the 1984 NFL supplemental draft. Mired in a losing situation in Tampa Bay, Young compiled a 3–16 record in his 19 starts with the team in 1985 and 1986. In his two seasons with the Buccaneers, the left-handed-throwing QB completed just 53 percent of his passes, throwing 11 touchdown passes and only two interceptions.

Convinced that Young was not the quarterback who could lead them out of their doldrums, the Buccaneers traded their former number-one pick to the San Francisco 49ers prior to the start of the 1987 campaign. Young saw limited playing time over the next four seasons, serving primarily as Joe Montana's backup and starting a total of only 10 games. Yet, Young impressed San Francisco's coaching staff whenever he got an opportunity to play, compiling a record of 7–3 in his 10 starts and throwing 23 touchdown passes and only six interceptions.

Young finally became the 49ers' starting quarterback in 1991, when off-season surgery on Montana's throwing arm forced him to sit out the entire year. Young played so well in Montana's absence that it became difficult to remove him from the starting unit when Montana returned to the team midway through the following campaign. A quarterback controversy soon developed in San Francisco, causing friction between the two men and finally prompting Montana to request a trade to another team.

The fact that Young was five years younger than Montana certainly made the 49ers' decision to part with their disgruntled quarterback much easier than it otherwise would have been. But Young also possessed a great deal of talent, and he had certain physical gifts that the team's former quarterback lacked. At 6'2" and 215 pounds, Young was bigger and stronger than the somewhat slight-of-build 6'2", 195-pound Montana. He also ran the ball better than Montana. The latter moved around in the pocket quite well, and he excelled at avoiding the opposing team's pass rush. But Young was a talented runner who often used his legs to pick up huge chunks of yardage. He also was an exceptionally accurate thrower and a perfect fit for the 49ers' "West Coast Offense," which Montana previously executed so well.

Young displayed his ability to run the San Francisco offense in his first year as a starter, completing 64.5 percent of his passes, throwing for 17 touchdowns and only eight interceptions, and rushing for 415 yards and four touchdowns, despite missing five games with a knee injury. Nevertheless, the 49ers missed the playoffs for the first time since 1982, even though they finished the season with a record of 10–6.

Starting all 16 games in 1992, Young led the 49ers to a 14–2 record in his second year as a starter. He completed 66.7 percent of his passes, threw for 3,465 yards and a league-leading 25 touchdowns, tossed only seven interceptions, and rushed for 537 yards and four touchdowns en route to earning AP Offensive Player of the Year and NFL MVP honors. He also earned the first of three consecutive First Team All-Pro nominations.

Also earning First Team All-Pro honors was Young's favorite wide receiver, Jerry Rice, who was named to the team for the sixth time in his first eight years in the league. Rice failed to make the team the previous year for the first time since his rookie season, despite making 80 receptions for 1,206 yards and 14 touchdowns. He compiled virtually the same numbers in 1992, totaling 84 receptions for 1,201 yards and 11 touchdowns. Yet in spite of Young and Rice's outstanding individual performances, the season ended in utter disappointment for them both when the 49ers lost the NFC title game to the Cowboys by a score of 30–20.

Dallas again defeated San Francisco in the NFC championship game in 1993, a season that marked the first of four straight years in which Young and Rice were clearly the National Football League's top passing combination. Tables 26.1 and 26.2 show the figures they posted in each of those seasons.

In addition to leading the NFL with 1,503 receiving yards in 1993, Rice led the league with 15 touchdown receptions, earning in the process AP Offensive

Table 26.1. Steve Young: 1993–1996

Year	COMP %	Passing YDS	Rushing YDS	TD Passes	INTS	Rushing TDS
1993	68.0	4,023	407	**29**	16	2
1994	**70.3**	3,969	293	**35**	10	7
1995	**66.9**	3,200	250	20	11	3
1996	**67.7**	2,410	310	14	6	4

Table 26.2. Jerry Rice: 1993–1996

Year	Receptions	YDS	TDS
1993	98	**1,503**	16
1994	112	**1,499**	15
1995	122	**1,848**	16
1996	**108**	1,254	9

Player of the Year honors for the second time. When Rice made his 127th career TD reception in the first game of the 1994 campaign, he moved into first place on the all-time list. His 1,848 receiving yards in 1995 remain an all-time single-season NFL record. Rice was named First Team All-Pro all four years; he also appeared in the Pro Bowl each season.

Young joined Rice in the Pro Bowl all four years and was named First Team All-Pro in 1993 and 1994. Young's 3,969 passing yards and league-leading 70.3 completion percentage and 35 touchdown passes in 1994 earned him his second NFL MVP Award. Young's numbers fell off somewhat each of the next two seasons because he missed a significant amount of playing time with concussions. But he still remained the league's most accurate passer, leading all NFL quarterbacks in completion percentage for the second and third of four consecutive times.

After finishing the 1993 campaign with a record of 10–6, the 49ers lost the NFC title game to the Cowboys by a final score of 38–21. The 49ers compiled a league-best 13–3 record the following regular season, after which they avenged their earlier loss to the Cowboys by defeating them in the NFC championship game by a score of 38–28. Young threw for two touchdowns and rushed for another during the contest. San Francisco subsequently crushed San Diego in Super Bowl XXIX, defeating the Chargers by a 49–26 margin. Young earned Super Bowl MVP honors by completing six touchdown passes, throwing for 325 yards, and rushing for another 49 yards. Rice caught 10 passes during the contest for 149 yards and three touchdowns, despite playing most of the game with a separated shoulder. The 49ers won their division in each of the next two years as well, but the Packers eliminated them from the playoffs in 1995 and 1996.

Rice missed virtually all of the 1997 campaign with a torn anterior cruciate and medial collateral ligament in his left knee, which he suffered in the season opener. The injury ended a string of 10 consecutive seasons in which he started every game for the 49ers and a streak of 189 total games in which he appeared. Young and the 49ers continued to play exceptionally well in Rice's absence, compiling a record of 13–3 during the regular season, before losing to Green Bay again, this time in the NFC title game. Young completed 67.7 percent of his passes to lead the league in passing accuracy for the fourth straight year. He also threw for more than 3,000 yards for the fifth time in six seasons while tossing 19 touchdown passes and only six interceptions.

Rice returned to the 49ers in 1998 to team up with Young for one final run at the NFC championship. The wide receiver caught 82 passes for a total of 1,157 yards and nine touchdowns. Young established new career highs with 4,170 passing yards and a league-leading 36 touchdown passes. He also completed just over 62 percent of his passes and threw only 12 interceptions to earn Second Team All-Pro honors. The 49ers won their division with a 12–4 record, but they lost the NFC title game to the Atlanta Falcons by a final score of 20–18.

Young and Rice never again played a full season together. Young suffered a severe concussion in the third game of the 1999 campaign, which forced him to the sidelines for the remainder of the year and prompted him to announce his retirement at the end of the season. He ended his career with a 94–49 record as a starter and the highest passer rating (96.8) in NFL history. Along with Washington Redskins Hall of Famer Sammy Baugh, he is the only quarterback to win six NFL passing titles. Young threw for a total of 33,124 yards during his career. He completed 232 touchdown passes, rushed for another 43 touchdowns, and compiled 4,239 rushing yards, the second most by a quarterback in NFL history.

Meanwhile, Rice remained in San Francisco two more years, leaving the 49ers at the conclusion of the 2000 campaign after spending 16 years with them. He had two more big years in Oakland, surpassing 1,000 yards receiving in 2001 and 2002 before his productivity finally began to decline. After spending the entire 2003 season with the Raiders, Rice split his final year between Oakland and Seattle, ending his brilliant 20-year career as the holder of numerous NFL records and with a legacy second to none in the annals of the NFL.

In the eight seasons in which Steve Young and Jerry Rice started in the San Francisco offense, the 49ers won at least 13 games three times, advanced to the playoffs seven times, appeared in four NFC championship games, and won one Super Bowl. Young led the NFL in passing six times, and he topped the league in touchdown passes on four separate occasions. Rice led all NFL receivers in receptions once, receiving yards three times, and receiving touchdowns twice. The two men experienced their greatest success together from 1992 to 1996. During that five-year period, Rice caught a total of 524 passes for 7,305 yards and 67 touchdowns. That averages out to 105 receptions, 1,461 yards, and 13 touchdowns per season. In their eight years together, Young and Rice combined for 14 appearances in the Pro Bowl, eight First Team All-Pro selections, two AP Offensive Player of the Year Awards, two NFL MVP awards, and one Super Bowl MVP award.

Note

Numbers printed in bold indicate that the player led his league in a statistical category.

CHAPTER 26

Merlin Olsen / Deacon Jones

Many outstanding defensive linemen have played alongside one another over the years in the National Football League. Randy White and Harvey Martin manned the defensive front together for the Dallas Cowboys. Reggie White and Clyde Simmons teamed up for the Philadelphia Eagles. Alan Page and Carl Eller lined up on the Minnesota Vikings' defensive line for a decade. And Mean Joe Greene and L. C. Greenwood anchored the left side of the Pittsburgh Steelers' defensive line for 13 seasons. However, no other pair of NFL defensive linemen ever dominated opposing offenses as much as the Los Angeles Rams' tandem of Merlin Olsen and David "Deacon" Jones. The two men formed one half of the Rams' "Fearsome Foursome," which some football experts still consider to be the greatest defensive line in NFL history.

Long before Kurt Warner was threading passes to Torry Holt and Isaac Bruce in the St. Louis Rams' offense otherwise known as the "Greatest Show on Turf," the Rams called the city of Los Angeles home. After spending their first few NFL seasons in Cleveland, the Rams played in LA from 1946 to 1994. With Hall of Fame quarterback Norm Van Brocklin calling signals for the team from 1951 to 1957, the Rams ended up being one of the NFL's most successful franchises for much of the 1950s, even capturing the league championship in 1951. However, the fortunes of the team changed dramatically after the Rams traded away Van Brocklin at the end of the 1957 campaign. After posting a winning record in 1958, the Rams finished each of the next seven seasons with a losing mark, playing particularly poorly in 1959 and 1962, seasons in which they finished 2–10 and 1–12–1, respectively. Not until George Allen took over as head coach of the Rams in 1966 did they once again become contenders. Allen had the foresight to insert Roman Gabriel as his starting quarterback. He also possessed the wisdom to rely heavily on the defensive excellence of his two best players, both of whom joined the team a few years earlier.

The Rams selected Deacon Jones in the 14th round of the 1961 NFL draft, with the 186th overall pick. Defying the odds as a late-round selection, the 6'5", 272-pound defensive end out of Mississippi Valley State earned a starting job on the Rams' defensive line in his rookie season. Jones displayed from the very beginning a rare combination of skills that eventually made him the prototype of the modern defensive end. He possessed not only the strength to push aside opposing offensive linemen but also the speed, agility, and quickness to chase down opposing quarterbacks and running backs. Jones's great quickness and tremendous desire enabled him to become one of the first defensive linemen to pursue plays all over the field. He also played the game with a mean streak and, in his own words, "a deep hatred of quarterbacks." Jones often used the head-slap as a means of freeing himself from his blocker to pursue his quarry. After momentarily stunning the opposing offensive lineman by striking him on the side of his helmet, he used his great quickness to go by him in a blink. Still, Jones frequently had one or two other men waiting to block him, since he often was double- or even triple-teamed.

Playing right alongside Jones on the Rams' defensive front was left tackle Merlin Olsen, whom the team selected with the third overall pick of the 1962 NFL draft. The 6'5", 270-pound all-American out of Utah State made an immediate impact, earning NFL Rookie of the Year honors and being named to the Pro Bowl for the first of a record 14 consecutive times. Like his teammate, Olsen possessed good size and strength, but he also relied heavily on outstanding foot speed, agility, and intelligence to dominate opposing linemen.

Olsen described the training techniques that he used to become one of the most successful defensive linemen in NFL history: "I would lift a minimum of weights. Mine was natural physical strength. I always thought quickness and agility were much more important."[1]

Olsen also discussed the Rams' legendary Fearsome Foursome, which included Jones, Rosey Grier, and Lamar Lundy: "Our whole philosophy was to intimidate the quarterback. We were able to do it. We were pioneers. People still recognize us as, maybe, the best defensive line of all time."[2]

Olsen served as the group's stabilizing leader, enabling his linemates to rush the passer while he anchored the defensive front. Although Olsen did a good job of rushing the passer, he played the run extraordinarily well, often stopping draw plays all by himself or quickly identifying screen passes.

The support that Jones received from Olsen in the middle of the line enabled the defensive end to rush the quarterback with abandon—something that he did better than any other player of his era. Although sacks did not become an official statistic until well after his career ended, closest estimates indicate that Jones averaged a minimum of 15 to 20 sacks during most of his peak seasons. He unofficially became the first player to record a 20-sack season in 1964, when he tackled opposing quarterbacks behind the line of scrimmage a total of 22 times. Later calculations revealed that Jones accumulated as many as 26 sacks in 1967 and that he compiled a total of 173.5 sacks over the course of his career. That figure places him third on the all-time list, behind only Reggie White and Bruce Smith. Deacon's tremendous pass-rushing ability made him the premier defensive end of his time. He is still considered by many football experts to be among the greatest defensive ends of all time, perhaps being surpassed only by Reggie White.

Jones remained with the Rams through 1971, being traded to the San Diego Chargers at the end of that season. He spent two years in San Diego, earning a trip to the Pro Bowl in 1972 before ending his career with Washington in 1974.

At one point during his career, Jones earned unanimous all-NFL honors six straight times, from 1965 to 1970. He was named a First Team All-Pro each year from 1965 to 1969. He appeared in seven straight Pro Bowls at one point, playing in the contest a total of eight times over the course of his career. Jones was selected as the NFL's top defensive player by one major news service in both 1967 and 1968. He was also named the Most Valuable Ram of All-Time by the *Los Angeles Times*, and he was identified as the Defensive End of the Century by *Sports Illustrated*. Jones earned the honor of being named to the NFL's 75 Year Anniversary Team.

Merlin Olsen once marveled at his teammate's skills when he said, "You can't believe Deacon's quickness and speed, even when you're playing next to him."[3] Olsen later noted, "There has never been a better football player than Deacon Jones."[4] The extremely candid Jones agreed: "I came as close to perfection as you can possibly get."[5]

As well as Deacon Jones performed on the outside, Merlin Olsen proved to be equally dominant on the inside. Rivaled only by the Dallas Cowboys' Bob Lilly at defensive tackle throughout most of his career, which lasted until he retired at the end of the 1976 season, Olsen earned First Team All-Pro honors each year from 1966 to 1970. He also earned Second Team All-Pro honors five times. Olsen made All-NFL and All-Western Conference six times each, and he joined Jones on the NFL's 75 Year Anniversary Team.

Merlin Olsen and Deacon Jones played together on the left side of the Los Angeles Rams' defensive line from 1962 to 1971. During their 10 years, they combined for 17 Pro Bowl appearances, 12 All-NFL selections, and 10 First Team All-Pro selections. In addition to performing brilliantly together, Olsen and Jones were durable, missing a total of only seven games between them during that time. Jones played in 191 of a possible 196 contests in his 14 NFL seasons, while Olsen missed only two games in his 15 years in the league, appearing in his team's final 198 contests. The Rams never won an NFL title while Olsen and Jones were members of the team. But they were Coastal Division champions in 1967 and 1969, compiling records of 11–1–2 and 11–3, respectively, and appearing in the Western Conference championship game both times. Los Angeles also finished second in the division to the Baltimore Colts in 1968, posting an outstanding 10–3–1 record during the regular season. The Rams had a solid offense each of those years, but they were most noted for the exceptional play of their defensive line, which Olsen and Jones anchored.

Reflecting on the time the two men spent together, Olsen later said, "I would like to think that, during the 10 years that Deacon and I lined up side-by-side, that we did set a standard that would be hard to equal."[6]

Notes

1. Merlin Olsen, http://www.searchquotes.com/quotes/author/Merlin_Olsen/.
2. Merlin Olsen, http://www.brainyquote.com/quotes/keywords/quarterback.html.
3. Merlin Olsen, http://www.entertainment.howstuffworks.com/deacon-jones-at .html.
4. Merlin Olsen, http://www.articles.latimes.com/2009/apr/21/sports/sp-crowe21.
5. Deacon Jones, http://www.articles.latimes.com/2009/apr/21/sports/sp-crowe21.
6. *Greatest Ever: NFL Dream Team* (Polygram Video, 1996).

CHAPTER 27

Gale Sayers / Dick Butkus

After winning the NFL championship in 1963, the Chicago Bears compiled a disappointing 5–9 record in 1964. The Bears' dismal showing, combined with an earlier trade that netted them a first-round pick in the 1965 NFL draft, enabled them to make consecutive selections with the third and fourth overall picks in that year's draft. Chicago elected to use those picks on University of Illinois linebacker Dick Butkus and Kansas University running back Gale Sayers. Butkus and Sayers combined during the next several seasons to bring a level of respectability to an otherwise mediocre Bears team, establishing themselves in the process as two of the greatest players ever to play in the NFL. Butkus developed into arguably the greatest middle linebacker in league history and, certainly, the most feared and intimidating defensive player of his generation. Meanwhile, Sayers quickly established himself as the period's most exciting and dynamic offensive performer.

One of the National Football League's flagship franchises, the Chicago Bears proved to be the league's most dominant team during its formative years. Chicago captured consecutive NFL titles in 1932 and 1933 before winning another four championships during the 1940s. Legendary players such as Red Grange, Bronco Nagurski, and Sid Luckman donned a Bears uniform at different times, enabling longtime Chicago owner and head coach George Halas to field teams that posted a losing record just once between 1930 and 1951. Often referred to as the "Monsters of the Midway," the Bears remained the league's most talented and physically imposing team throughout much of the period. The 1934 squad even went undefeated during the regular season, compiling a 13–0 record.

Chicago's performance slipped somewhat during the 1950s, with the team posting losing records in both 1952 and 1953. However, the Bears rebounded in 1954, after which they remained competitive the next 10 years, finishing below

.500 just twice between 1954 and 1963. Still, the 1963 squad that compiled a record of 11–1–2 during the regular season and subsequently defeated the New York Giants in the NFL championship game featured an aging group of players that successfully banded together for one last title run. The chinks in the Bears' armor became painfully evident the following season, when they finished just 5–9. In an attempt to rebuild and reenergize his team, George Halas selected Dick Butkus and Gale Sayers with the third and fourth overall picks of the 1965 NFL draft.

Sayers, a former all-American at the University of Kansas, burst on the NFL scene in his rookie season. The 6'0", 198-pound running back electrified fans around the league with his great speed, quickness, and cutback ability. Sayers had the uncanny ability to stop on a dime and accelerate back to full speed in only one or two steps, thereby enabling him to cut back across the field to avoid opposing defenders. Sayers rushed for 867 yards in 1965, averaging 5.2 yards per carry over the course of the season. In addition, he compiled 507 receiving yards, with his great elusiveness also making him the league's most dangerous punt and kickoff returner. Sayers totaled 238 yards on punt returns and another 660 yards returning kickoffs for an NFL-leading 2,272 all-purpose yards. Sayers also led the league with 22 touchdowns and 132 points scored. The "Kansas Comet's" outstanding rookie campaign earned him First Team All-Pro honors for the first of five straight years and his first of four trips to the Pro Bowl.

Sayers won two games almost single-handedly for the Bears that year. He proved to be the difference for the first time in a midseason matchup against the Vikings, scoring four touchdowns, one of which came on a 96-yard game-breaking kickoff return. However, he reserved his finest performance for the next-to-last game of the season, in a contest played against the San Francisco 49ers. Playing on a muddy field with poor traction, Sayers scored a record-tying six touchdowns. Included in the scores were a short swing pass that Sayers converted into an 80-yard touchdown, a 50-yard touchdown run, and a 65-yard punt return for a touchdown. Sayers compiled a total of 336 all-purpose yards on the day, prompting Bears head coach George Halas, who had been in the NFL since its inception in 1920, to say, "It was the greatest performance I have ever seen on the football field."[1]

While Sayers mesmerized opposing defenders, Dick Butkus terrorized opponents who lined up against him on the offensive side of the football. The 6'3", 245-pound two-time unanimous all-American selection out of the University of Illinois made an immediate impact as a rookie, leading the Bears in interceptions and opponents' fumbles recovered. Butkus had good speed, quickness, size, and strength, and he possessed excellent instincts. He made tackles from sideline to sideline, pursuing opposing ball carriers all over the field and manhandling them once he ensnared them in his vise-like grip. He had the speed to cover the best tight ends and running backs in the league on pass plays, as his 22 career interceptions indicate. However, Butkus influenced the game with more than just his agility and ball-hawking skills. He was a tremendous tackler who seemed to engulf his opponents when he hit them. He played the game with a mean streak, unmatched intensity, and a competitive nature that instilled fear in the hearts and minds of opposing players. He also scared his opponents with verbal threats and grunting sounds that often made them think the middle linebacker had animalistic tendencies.

In explaining some of the psychological techniques he employed during games, Butkus said, "When I went out on the field to warm up, I would manufacture things to make me mad. If someone on the other team was laughing, I'd pretend he was laughing at me or the Bears. It always worked for me."[2]

The ferocity with which Butkus played the game was not at all lost on opposing players. Dan Pastorini, Houston Oilers quarterback from 1971 to 1979, still seemed astonished years later when he discussed his first encounter with the Bears middle linebacker: "He is calling me everything in the book. He's threatening to kill me. He's threatening to kill my children. He's threatening to kill my mother and father. He's threatening to kill everybody!"[3]

Rams All-Pro defensive end Deacon Jones said, "He was an animal, and every time he hit you he tried to put you in the cemetery."[4]

Former Cardinals and Packers running back MacArthur Lane described what it was like being tackled by Butkus: "If I had a choice, I'd sooner go one on one with a grizzly bear. I pray that I can get up every time Butkus hits me."[5]

Dan Jenkins once wrote an article in *Sports Illustrated* that claimed, "Dick Butkus is a special kind of brute whose particular talent is mashing runners into curious shapes. . . . Butkus not only hits, he crushes and squeezes opponents with thick arms that are also extremely long."[6]

Butkus established himself as the best middle linebacker in the NFL as a rookie, earning First Team All-Pro honors for the first of five times. He also made the first of eight consecutive appearances in the Pro Bowl. The combined efforts of Butkus and Sayers enabled the Bears to improve their record to 9–5 in 1965, placing them third in the Western Conference, behind only the Green Bay Packers and the Baltimore Colts.

Although Chicago's record slipped to 5–7–2 in 1966, both Butkus and Sayers played exceptionally well. Butkus made Second Team All-Pro for the first of two straight times, while Sayers averaged 5.4 yards per carry in leading the NFL with 1,231 yards rushing. Sayers also led the league with 1,678 yards from scrimmage, 2,440 all-purpose yards, and 31.2 yards per kickoff return. He scored a total of 12 touchdowns.

The Bears finished barely above .500 the following season, compiling a 7–6–1 record in 1967 despite receiving outstanding performances once again from their two great stars. Butkus led the team with an unofficial total of 111 solo tackles, 35 assists, and 18 quarterback sacks. Chicago statisticians later tabulated that the middle linebacker was involved in 867 of 880 total defensive plays for the Bears. Sayers finished third in the league with 880 rushing yards and 12 touchdowns, including three scores on kickoff returns. He led the NFL in total all-purpose yards for the third consecutive year, compiling a total of 1,689 yards over the course of the season.

Sayers got off to another great start in 1968, rushing for 856 yards over the first nine games while averaging a league-best 6.2 yards per carry. However, in a game against the 49ers, he suffered a season-ending injury to his right knee that required immediate surgery, which unfortunately served as a portent of things to come.

Showing no ill effects from his off-season surgery, Sayers returned to the Bears in 1969 to lead the league in rushing for the second time, with a total of 1,032 yards. He also scored eight touchdowns and finished second in the NFL with 1,487 all-purpose yards. But with little talent on the team aside from Sayers and Butkus, Chicago finished 1–13 on the year.

A left knee injury forced Sayers to the sidelines for all but two games in 1970 and 1971. No longer able to run as he once did, Sayers announced his retirement at the conclusion of the 1971 campaign. He ended his career with 4,956 rushing yards, 1,307 receiving yards, and another 3,172 yards on punt and kickoff returns for a total of 9,435 all-purpose yards. At the time of his retirement, Sayers was the NFL's all-time leader in kickoff return yardage. The Kansas Comet averaged 5.0 yards per carry over the course of his career and scored a total of 56 touchdowns. Sayers played in only 68 games in his seven NFL seasons, and none of his statistical achievements place him anywhere near the top in the all-time league rankings. Yet, his legacy remains that of one of the greatest players ever to play the game. In 1969, Sayers was named the top halfback of the NFL's first 50 years. And in 1999, he was ranked number 21 on the *Sporting News* list of the 100 Greatest Football Players.

Despite the brevity of his career, Sayers was elected to the Pro Football Hall of Fame in 1973. In explaining its decision, the selection committee stated, "There never was another to compare with him. What else is there to say!"[7]

While Sayers found it difficult to remain on the field his last few years in the league, Dick Butkus continued to wreak havoc on opposing offenses. The middle linebacker earned First Team All-Pro honors for the third straight year in 1970, leading the Bears with 132 solo tackles and 84 assists while intercepting three passes and recovering two fumbles. A poll taken of NFL coaches that year identified Butkus as the player with whom they would most like to start if they were building a team from scratch.

Nevertheless, the Bears finished 1970 and 1971 with a record of only 6–8. The team fell to 4–9–1 in 1972, a year in which Butkus earned First Team

All-Pro honors for the final time. The linebacker found himself unable to play in five of his team's 14 games the following year, when the pain from a knee injury he first suffered in 1970 became too severe for even him to tolerate. He retired at the end of the year, leaving behind a legacy that has prompted many people to refer to him as the greatest defensive player in NFL history.

Former Rams head coach Tommy Prothro expressed his admiration for Butkus by saying, "He is a legendary football player. I never thought any player could play as well as writers write that he can, but Butkus comes as close as any I've ever seen."[8]

Ted Marchibroda, who spent 35 years coaching in the NFL, said, "I think Dick without question, in my mind, was probably the greatest linebacker that I ever saw."[9]

Gale Sayers and Dick Butkus spent only five full seasons together, from 1965 to 1969. However, they combined for nine Pro Bowl appearances and eight First Team All-Pro selections during that time. Although the Bears never made it to the playoffs during that five-year period, they finished with a respectable record in all but one season, including a 9–5 mark in 1965. Both Sayers and Butkus earned spots on the NFL's 75 Year Anniversary Team in 1994—Butkus at inside linebacker and Sayers at kickoff returner.

Notes

1. George Halas, http://www.profootballresearchers.org/coffin_corner/27-05-1095.pdf.

2. *Greatest Ever: NFL Dream Team* (Polygram Video, 1996).

3. *Greatest Ever: NFL Dream Team.*

4. *Greatest Ever: NFL Dream Team.*

5. MacArthur Lane, http://www.espn.go.com/sportscentury/features/00014131.html.

6. Dan Jenkins, http://www.espn.go.com/sportscentury/features/00014131.html.

7. http://www.oocities.org/disayers40/halloffame.html.

8. Tommy Prothro, http://www.chicagobears.com/tradition/hof-butkus.asp.

9. Ted Marchibroda, http://www.chicagobears.com/tradition/hof-butkus.asp.

An extremely familiar sight—Lou Gehrig congratulating Babe Ruth at home plate after a Babe home run. *Photo © Leslie Jones Collection, courtesy of the Trustees of the Boston Public Library.*

Though members of different teams here, Jimmie Foxx (left) and Al Simmons led the Philadelphia Athletics to 3 straight pennants and 2 world championships earlier in their careers. *Photo © Leslie Jones Collection, courtesy of the Trustees of the Boston Public Library.*

Hank Aaron and Eddie Mathews hit more home runs as teammates than any other tandem in baseball history. *Photo courtesy of CollectAuctions.com.*

Wille Mays (left) and Willie McCovey (right) combined with Felipe Alou to give the San Francisco Giants a formidable threesome in the middle of their lineup during the 1960s. Photo courtesy of the San Francisco Giants. © 2011 S. F. Giants.

Mickey Mantle and Roger Maris set a major league record by combining for 115 home runs in 1961. *Photo courtesy of CollectAuctions.com.*

Detroit's Charlie Gehringer (left) and Hank Greenberg (right) flanking Boston's Jimmie Foxx at the 1937 All-Star Game. Photo courtesy of the Harris & Ewing collection at the Library of Congress.

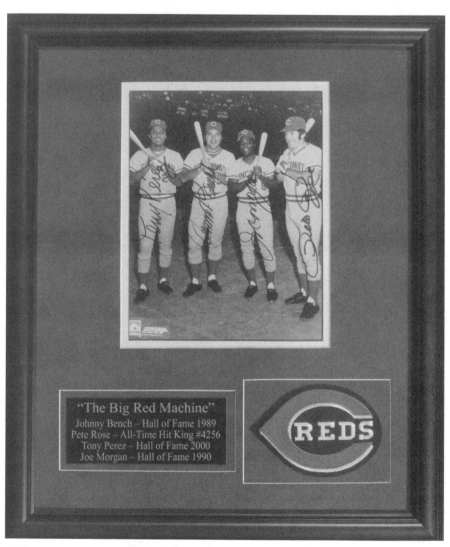

(Left to right) Tony Perez, Johnny Bench, Joe Morgan, and Pete Rose formed the nucleus of Cincinnati's Big Red Machine during the 1970s. Photo courtesy of Collect Auctions.

Don Drysdale (left) and Sandy Koufax (right), seen here flanking Dodger team-mate Greg Goosen.

Ted Williams and Bobby Doerr helped make the Red Sox perennial contenders for the A.L. flag throughout the 1940s. *Photo © Leslie Jones Collection, courtesy of the Trustees of the Boston Public Library.*

Roberto Clemente and Willie Stargell, seen here with teammates Matty Alou and Manny Mota. *Photo courtesy of Richard Albersheim of www.albersheims .com*

Randy Johnson (left) and Curt Schilling (right) shared co-MVP honors at the 2001 World Series. Photo courtesy of Barry Gossage/Arizona Diamondbacks.

The duo of Johnny Sain (left) and Warren Spahn prompted Braves fans to coin the phrase "Spahn and Sain, and pray for rain." *Photo © Leslie Jones Collection, courtesy of the Trustees of the Boston Public Library.*

Bill Terry (left) and Mel Ott proved to be the closest thing the N.L. had to Gehrig and Ruth during their time together. *Photo © Leslie Jones Collection, courtesy of the Trustees of the Boston Public Library.*

Jerry Rice holds virtually every NFL pass receiving record. *Photo courtesy of George A. Kitrinos.*

Joe Montana is considered by many people to be the greatest quarterback in NFL history. *Photo courtesy of George A. Kitrinos.*

After taking over for Montana in San Francisco, Steve Young led the 49ers to another NFL title. *Photo courtesy of George A. Kitrinos.*

Peyton Manning and Marvin Harrison formed the most prolific passing combination in NFL history during their time together in Indianapolis. Photo courtesy of the Indianapolis Colts.

Rookies Dick Butkus (left) and Gale Sayers (right) share a laugh with legendary Chicago Bears head coach George Halas. Photo courtesy of Collect Auctions.

Johnny Unitas set a standard for all future NFL quarterbacks to follow. Photo courtesy of *Richard Albersheim of www. albersheims.com.*

Raymond Berry proved to be Unitas' favorite receiver during their time together in Baltimore. *Photo courtesy of Richard Albersheim of www.albersheims.com.*

Emmitt Smith and Michael Irvin, seen here embracing, combined with Troy Aikman to form Dallas' "Triplets." *Photo courtesy of George A. Kitrinos.*

Troy Aikman calling out the signals as Emmitt Smith (22) awaits the snap from center. *Photo courtesy of George A. Kitrinos.*

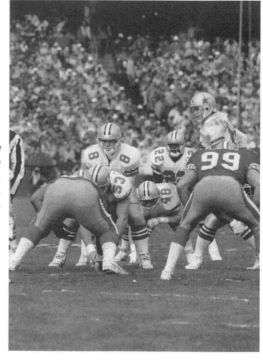

One of the greatest outside linebackers in NFL history, Jack Ham excelled against both the run and the pass. Photo courtesy of the Pittsburgh Steelers.

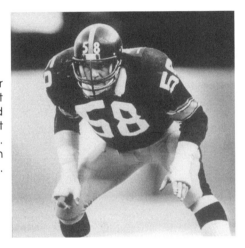

Though somewhat undersized for a middle linebacker, Jack Lambert played with an intensity that helped make him one of the greatest players to ever man the position. Photo courtesy of the Pittsburgh Steelers.

Lynn Swann (left) and John Stallworth (right) formed arguably the greatest pass-receiving tandem in NFL history. Photo courtesy of the Pittsburgh Steelers.

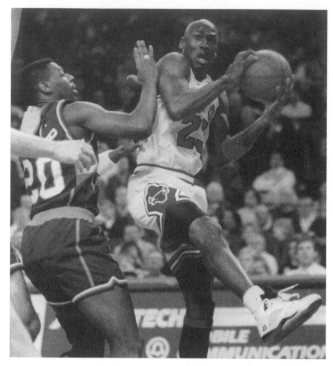

Michael Jordan is widely considered to be the greatest player in the history of pro basketball. *Photo courtesy of Richard Albersheim of www.albersheims .com.*

Scottie Pippen proved to be the perfect complement to Jordan in Chicago. *Photo courtesy of George A. Kitrinos.*

Elgin Baylor and Jerry West, seen here with Wilt Chamberlain, formed the most prolific scoring tandem in NBA history. *Photo courtesy of CollectAuctions.com.*

LeBron James and Dwyane Wade led the Heat to four consecutive NBA Finals appearances and two league championships in their four years together in Miami. *Photo courtesy of Keith Allison.*

Bobby Hull (left) and Stan Mikita (right) proved to be the NHL's top-scoring tandem for much of the 1960s. Photo courtesy of the Chicago Blackhawks.

Bobby Orr (foreground) and Phil Esposito (background) led the Boston Bruins to two Stanley Cups. Photo courtesy of the Boston Bruins.

CHAPTER 28

Johnny Unitas / Raymond Berry

The Baltimore Colts' Johnny Unitas and Raymond Berry were the National Football League's premier players at their respective positions for the better part of a decade. Unitas was the greatest quarterback in the game from 1958 to 1967, while Berry was the sport's finest wide receiver throughout much of the period as well. Together, they formed the most prolific passing combination in the NFL over the league's first 50 seasons. Unitas and Berry made the Colts perennial title contenders, leading the team to back-to-back championships in 1958 and 1959 and to a third appearance in the NFL title game in 1964. The quarterback and wide receiver accomplished all they did together in spite of the fact that they were both considered to be long shots to succeed in the NFL when they first entered in the mid-1950s.

The professional career of Johnny Unitas began inauspiciously in 1955, when the Pittsburgh Steelers—who selected Unitas in the ninth round of that year's NFL draft with the 102nd overall pick—ended his dream of playing for his hometown team by cutting him. The 6'1", 195-pound quarterback out of Louisville University subsequently spent the 1955 campaign playing semipro ball on the Pittsburgh sandlots before being signed by Baltimore head coach Weeb Ewbank at the end of the season for $17,000 on a make-the-team basis. After initially making the Colts' 1956 roster as a backup, Unitas unexpectedly became the team's starting quarterback when an injury shelved the previous starter just four games into the season. Unitas held onto the job for most of the next 15 seasons, establishing himself in the process as the greatest quarterback to play in the NFL up to that point and as arguably the greatest field general in league history.

Unitas began to make a name for himself in 1957 when he earned the first of his eight consecutive Pro Bowl selections. The quarterback became a household name the following season, when he led the Colts to the first of two consecutive NFL titles. Unitas earned First Team All-Pro honors for the first of five times during the regular season by leading Baltimore to an 8–2 record and the Western Conference championship. He subsequently displayed the many qualities that eventually made him an NFL legend during the NFL championship game against the New York Giants.

Played in New York's Yankee Stadium, the contest turned out to be a seesaw affair that featured numerous lead changes and shifts in momentum. Although the Giants once trailed by a score of 14–3, they punted the ball to the Colts with two minutes left in the fourth quarter, clinging to a 17–14 lead. After taking possession on his own 14-yard line, Unitas calmly proceeded to lead his team down the field for a game-tying field goal with only seven seconds left on the clock. Exhibiting tremendous guile, leadership, confidence, play-calling ability, and passing skills, the quarterback completed seven consecutive passes at one point, shredding the vaunted Giants defense in the process. Unitas continued to go through New York's defense as if it were Swiss cheese during the subsequent overtime session (the first in league history), engineering a textbook 80-yard-touchdown drive that gave the Colts their first NFL title.

Giants Hall of Fame middle linebacker Sam Huff later expressed his admiration for the manner in which Unitas drove Baltimore down the field: "There's one man that made the difference, and that was John Unitas. He was the difference in that football game."[1]

Frequently referred to as the "Greatest Game Ever Played," it was that 1958 title tilt between Baltimore and New York that helped put the NFL on the map. Prior to that game, the league ranked a distant second to college football in popularity. But the furor created by that contest dramatically increased the demand for the professional game, prompting the league to sign a huge television deal shortly thereafter.

Unitas deserves much of the credit for helping the NFL grow in popularity and also for bringing a title to the city of Baltimore. Nevertheless, he received a considerable amount of help in that championship game from his favorite wide receiver, Raymond Berry, who was on the receiving end of virtually all of the quarterback's passes as he drove his team inexorably down the field during the game's final moments. Perhaps the two men developed such an affinity for each other because they both experienced a considerable amount of adversity prior to establishing themselves as the premier players in the league at their respective positions.

Selected by the Colts in the 20th round of the 1954 NFL draft, Raymond Berry wasn't given much of a chance of making the Baltimore roster when he appeared at the team's training camp for the first time later that year. At 6'2" and 195 pounds, the Southern Methodist University product had good size, but he possessed only marginal speed, and he needed to wear special shoes since one of his legs was shorter than the other. Although Berry defied the odds by making the Colts' roster, he didn't play at all his first season. However, he worked extremely hard in practice and during the subsequent off-season, concentrating primarily on making difficult catches and perfecting his route-running techniques. By Berry's own count, he eventually developed 88 moves that helped free him from his defender. The wide receiver also had superb hands that enabled him to make extremely difficult catches look relatively easy. Berry's hard work, dedication, and pass-receiving skills earned him a starting spot on Baltimore's offense by 1956.

The receiver made 37 receptions for 601 yards in his first year as a starter. He followed that up by making 47 catches for six touchdowns and a league-leading 800 receiving yards in 1957 en route to earning Second Team All-Pro honors. Berry established himself as the NFL's best wide receiver the following year, beginning a string of extremely successful seasons in which he teamed up with Unitas to form the most prolific passing combination that the league had seen up to that point. These are the numbers that Berry compiled over the next few seasons:

1958: **56** catches, 794 yards, **9** TDs
1959: **66** catches, **959** yards, **14** TDs
1960: **74** catches, **1,298** yards, 10 TDs
1961: 75 catches, 873 yards

Berry earned First Team All-Pro honors in each of the first three seasons. He also earned a spot on the Second Team three other times during his career. After leading the NFL with 56 catches and 9 TD receptions in 1958, Berry caught another 12 passes for 178 yards and one touchdown against the Giants in the NFL title game that made both he and Unitas famous. He caught a career-high 14 touchdown passes the following year, before establishing new career bests with 74 receptions and 1,298 receiving yards in 1960.

Berry spent six more years in the NFL before retiring from the game at the conclusion of the 1967 season, with 631 pass receptions, 9,275 receiving yards, and 68 touchdown receptions. Berry's 631 catches represented an NFL record at the time of his retirement. In addition to being named either First or Second Team All-Pro a total of six times, he was selected to appear in six Pro Bowls over the course of his career.

As Berry continued to compile huge pass-receiving totals, Johnny Unitas joined the great Jim Brown as the league's most recognizable player. The Baltimore quarterback led his team to a 9–3 record during the 1959 regular season. He then passed the Colts to another victory over the Giants in the NFL title game, giving them their second consecutive league championship. Unitas's performance earned him the NFL's Most Valuable Player Award for the first of three times. He earned league MVP honors in 1964 and 1967 as well. In the first of those years, Unitas led the Colts to the Western Conference title and a spot in the NFL Championship Game with a 12–2 regular-season record. The Colts finished 11–1–2 in the quarterback's final MVP season of 1967.

Plagued by an ailing throwing arm, Unitas spent most of the 1968 campaign sitting on the sidelines watching his backup, Earl Morrall, lead Baltimore to a league-best 13–1 record. However, the New York Jets stunned the heavily favored Colts in the Super Bowl, causing something of a rift to develop between Unitas and Baltimore head coach Don Shula. As Unitas observed the manner in which Morrall continued to struggle throughout the contest, he waited for Shula to insert him into the game. The Baltimore coach finally turned to Unitas late in the third quarter, with the Colts trailing New York by a score of 13–0. Unitas eventually led the Colts to their only touchdown of the game, closing the gap to 16–7. Asked after the game if he felt he could have brought his team back had he been inserted at the start of the second half, Unitas stoically replied, "I didn't need that much time."[2]

Unitas reclaimed his starting job the following season, but the Colts suffered through a dismal campaign as they attempted to recover psychologically from the shocking upset they suffered at the hands of the Jets in the Super Bowl. Fully recuperated by 1970, Baltimore compiled a record of 10–2–1 in the 13 starts that Unitas made for the team during the regular season, before capturing the Super Bowl title that eluded them two years earlier.

Unitas spent two more years in Baltimore, before signing on with San Diego for one final season in 1973. He retired at the end of the year having compiled a career record of 118–64–4 as a starter, along with a mark of 6–2 in postseason play. Unitas threw for 40,239 yards and 290 touchdowns over the course of his career—both NFL records at the time of his retirement. He still holds the league record for completing at least one touchdown pass in 47 consecutive games. Unitas led NFL quarterbacks in passes completed three times, passing yardage four times, and touchdown passes four straight years, from 1957 to 1960. He threw a career-high 32 TD passes in his first MVP season of 1959. Unitas was either a First or Second Team All-NFL selection eight times during his career.

In their 12 seasons as teammates, Johnny Unitas and Raymond Berry combined for 16 selections to the Pro Bowl. Between them, they earned eight First Team All-Pro selections and another six nominations to the Second Team.

Noting the special qualities that made his teammate the NFL's greatest quarterback during the time they spent together in Baltimore, Berry commented, "Some of Unitas's greatest strengths were his mental toughness, his competitiveness, and his confidence."[3] Bill Curry, who played with Unitas on the Colts for six years, said of his former teammate, "He just had something that the top quarterbacks have—ice water in his veins. It really spooked the defense. They thought he was Houdini."[4]

Even Unitas's opponents found it difficult not to express their admiration for him. Hall of Fame defensive end Deacon Jones, well known for his hatred of quarterbacks, had this to say about the Baltimore QB: "I always said, in my estimation, he was the greatest quarterback of all time. They didn't call him *The Golden Arm* for nothing. I think, more than just his talent as a thrower, was his field-generalship. You don't get this anymore because coaches control the game from the sidelines. But this man was phenomenal. He was born to call plays. He could diagram them on the ground in the huddle."[5]

The many intangible qualities possessed by Unitas were the things that cause numerous old-timers and football historians to call him the greatest quarterback ever to play the game. Unitas certainly didn't have the size, speed, maneuverability, or throwing arm of most modern-day quarterbacks, but he possessed as much intelligence and leadership ability as anyone who ever played quarterback in the NFL. His unique skill set made him the measuring stick against which all future generations of quarterbacks will continue to be measured.

Notes

Numbers printed in bold indicate that the player led his league in a statistical category.

1. *Greatest Ever: NFL Dream Team* (Polygram Video, 1996).
2. *SportsCentury: Fifty Greatest Athletes—Johnny Unitas*, television program (ESPN, 1999).
3. *Greatest Ever: NFL Dream Team.*
4. *Greatest Ever: NFL Dream Team.*
5. *Greatest Ever: NFL Dream Team.*

CHAPTER 29

Troy Aikman / Emmitt Smith / Michael Irvin

I know . . . I know. This is supposed to be a ranking of dynamic duos, not tremendous trios. I just felt that I would have been somewhat remiss had I mentioned two members of the Dallas Cowboys' "Big Three" of the 1990s without including the third member. Troy Aikman, Emmitt Smith, and Michael Irvin were all essential to the success of a Dallas team that won three Super Bowls over a four-year period at one point during the decade.

The Dallas Cowboys experienced the usual growing pains of any expansion team when they first entered the National Football League in 1960. However, under innovative head coach Tom Landry, they soon became a perennial title contender and one of the league's most successful franchises. The Cowboys recorded 20 consecutive winning seasons under Landry, from 1966 to 1985, winning 13 divisional titles, five NFC titles, and two Super Bowls in the process. But the conservative and aging Landry no longer appeared capable of delivering his message to a younger generation of Dallas players by the mid-1980s. The team finished out of the playoffs three straight years, from 1986 to 1988, prompting new Cowboys owner Jerry Jones to unceremoniously relieve Landry of his duties prior to the start of the 1989 campaign. Jones subsequently replaced Landry with University of Miami head coach Jimmy Johnson, the owner's former teammate at the University of Arkansas.

It should have come as a surprise to no one that Michael Irvin, who Dallas selected with the 11th overall pick of the 1988 NFL draft, became an instant favorite of both Jones and Johnson once they took over the team. The 6'2", 210-pound wide receiver, who played for Johnson at Miami, was blessed with all the physical tools necessary to become an outstanding wideout at the NFL level. Although Irvin did not possess exceptional running speed, he had excellent hands, ran precise routes, and had outstanding size and strength. It was the last quality that enabled him to become one of the league's most physical wide receivers, giving him the ability to catch balls with defenders draped all over him. Drawing Jones and Johnson even more to Irvin was his attitude, which reflected the same brashness, cockiness, and arrogance that both owner and coach displayed at times. Supremely self-confident, Irvin helped give the Cowboys much of the swagger they exhibited during the 1990s. Still, it took the trash-talking Irvin some time before he found himself successfully able to back up his words with his on-field performance in Dallas.

Irvin earned a starting job in the Dallas offense as a rookie, but he caught only 32 passes during the Cowboys' dismal 3–13 campaign. Nevertheless, he averaged a league-leading 20.4 yards per reception in compiling a total of 654 receiving yards. Irvin was joined in the starting lineup the following year by quarterback Troy Aikman, whom the Cowboys selected with the first overall pick of the 1989 draft. The former UCLA all-American started 11 games for Dallas in 1989, but the team struggled with the rookie quarterback calling the signals, finishing the season with a 1–15 record. Aikman completed just under 53 percent of his passes, for nine touchdowns and 18 interceptions.

The Cowboys finally began to show signs of improvement the following year after they selected Florida running back Emmitt Smith with the 17th overall pick of the 1990 draft. Dallas improved its record to 7–9, with Smith rushing for 937 yards and 11 touchdowns en route to earning Offensive Rookie of the Year honors and the first of his eight Pro Bowl selections. With Smith accompanying him in the Dallas backfield, Aikman improved his performance as well, raising his completion percentage to 56.6 percent. However, he continued to struggle at times, completing only 11 touchdown passes while throwing 18 interceptions. Irvin, who missed significant playing time due to injuries in 1989 and 1990, remained basically ineffectual over the course of those two seasons, catching a total of only 46 passes in 18 games.

Everything started to come together for Irvin and the Cowboys in 1991. Dallas concluded the campaign with a record of 11–5, advancing to the playoffs for the first of five consecutive times. The Cowboys won the Super Bowl in three of the next four years, taking home the Lombardi Trophy at the end of 1992, 1993, and 1995. Irvin also began a string of five straight seasons in which he compiled more than 1,000 receiving yards:

1991: 93 receptions, **1,523** YDS, 8 TDS
1992: 78 receptions, 1,396 YDS, 7 TDS
1993: 88 receptions, 1,330 YDS, 7 TDS
1994: 79 receptions, 1,241 YDS, 6 TDS
1995: 111 receptions, 1,603 YDS, 10 TDS

Irvin earned First Team All-Pro honors in 1991 and appeared in the Pro Bowl all five years, establishing himself during that period as one of the NFL's top go-to guys. A tremendous big-game performer, he recorded a total of eight touchdown catches in postseason play over the course of his career. Irvin had seven receptions for 100 yards and two touchdowns in the Cowboys' 38–27 victory over Green Bay in the 1995 NFC championship game. He followed that up by catching five passes for 76 yards during Dallas's 27–17 victory over Pittsburgh in Super Bowl XXX.

Irvin proved to be the perfect target for Aikman, whose performance also took a quantum leap in 1991. The third-year quarterback led the NFC with a 65.3 completion percentage, beginning in the process a string of six consecutive seasons in which he completed better than 63 percent of his passes. He also made the first of six straight appearances in the Pro Bowl after throwing for 2,754 yards, 11 touchdowns, and only 10 interceptions.

Aikman ended up having his two finest seasons in 1992 and 1993, leading the Cowboys to victories in the Super Bowl both years. He threw for a career-high 3,445 yards in the first of those campaigns, helping Dallas compile a 13–3 record during the regular season. He also completed 23 touchdown passes while throwing only 14 interceptions. Aikman then directed the Cowboys' offense to a total of 116 points in their three playoff victories, including a 52–17 drubbing of the Buffalo Bills in Super Bowl XXVII. Aikman earned Super Bowl MVP honors by completing 22 of 30 passes for 273 yards and four touchdowns. He followed up that performance by leading the Cowboys to a 12–4 record and another trip to the Super Bowl in 1993. Aikman completed an NFL-leading 69.1 percent of his passes during the regular season, for 3,100 yards, 15 touchdowns, and only six interceptions. He subsequently led Dallas to another victory over Buffalo in the Super Bowl. The team captured its third NFL title in four years in 1995 by defeating the Pittsburgh Steelers in Super Bowl XXX.

Still, the Cowboys' most outstanding performer during their period of dominance may well have been their superb running back Emmitt Smith:

1991: **1,563** rushing yards, 258 receiving yards, 13 TDS
1992: **1,713** rushing yards, 335 receiving yards, **19** TDS
1993: **1,486** rushing yards, 414 receiving yards, 10 TDS
1994: 1,484 rushing yards, 341 receiving yards, **22** TDS
1995: **1,773** rushing yards, 375 receiving yards, **25** TDS

Smith was selected to appear in the Pro Bowl all five years; he also was named First Team All-Pro each season from 1992 to 1995. In 1993, he became the only running back to win the NFL rushing title, the NFL MVP award, a Super Bowl championship, and the Super Bowl MVP award in the same season. In leading the NFL in rushing from 1991 to 1993, Smith became one of only four running backs in league history to lead the league in that category three or more consecutive seasons (Steve Van Buren, Jim Brown, and Earl Campbell were the others).

The 5'9", 210-pound Smith didn't possess great size or speed. However, he had superb balance, tremendous desire, and an enormous heart. Smith was also among the game's most durable players, missing a total of only seven games in his 13 seasons with the Cowboys and surpassing 1,000 yards on the ground in 11 straight years at one point. A veritable touchdown-scoring machine, Smith scored at least 10 touchdowns in nine different seasons.

Although Dallas failed to make it back to the Super Bowl after 1995, both Smith and Irvin continued to excel for several more seasons. In fact, Smith continued his string of 1,000-yard rushing campaigns through 2001. Meanwhile, Irvin made 64 receptions for 962 yards in 1996 before posting consecutive 1,000-yard receiving years in 1997 and 1998. However, a serious injury early in 1999 limited Irvin to only four games the entire year. He subsequently announced his retirement at the end of the season, ending his 12-year playing career with 750 receptions for 11,904 yards and 65 touchdowns. Irvin caught more than 70 passes in a season seven times, and he surpassed 1,000 yards in seven campaigns. He led the NFL in receiving yards once, and he finished second two other times. Irvin was later named to the NFL's All-Decade Team of the 1990s.

The Cowboys' inability to win another championship during the decade was directly related to the inability of Aikman to remain on the field for an extended period. Although he remained healthy throughout most of 1996 and 1997, the quarterback found himself going in and out of the Dallas starting lineup each of the next three seasons due to a series of concussions that eventually forced him to retire at the end of the 2000 campaign. Aikman left the game with a 61.5 career completion percentage, 32,942 passing yards, 165 touchdown passes, and 141 interceptions. He was named to four All-Pro Teams, and his 90 wins during the 1990s make him the winningest quarterback of any decade in NFL history. Aikman is also one of only four quarterbacks with at least three Super Bowl victories (Terry Bradshaw, Joe Montana, and Tom Brady are the others).

Smith remained with the Cowboys through 2002, a season in which he broke Walter Payton's all-time rushing record. He spent his final two years with the Arizona Cardinals, retiring at the end of 2004 with more rushing attempts (4,409), rushing yards (18,355), and rushing touchdowns (164) than anyone in NFL history. Smith is also second all-time with 175 total touchdowns and 21,579 yards from scrimmage, and he averaged 4.2 yards per carry over the course of his career.

Troy Aikman, Michael Irvin, and Emmitt Smith spent nine full seasons as teammates on the Dallas Cowboys. The three men were most effective from 1991 to 1995, with each player being named to the Pro Bowl in all five of those seasons. During that five-year period, Smith and Irvin combined to score a total of 127 touchdowns for an average of just over 25 per season. In 1995 alone, they scored 35 touchdowns between them. Dallas appeared in four consecutive NFC championship games from 1992 to 1995, winning the Super Bowl in three of those years. During their time together, the Cowboys' Big Three combined for a total of 19 appearances on the Pro Bowl squad and another six First Team All-Pro selections.

Note

Numbers printed in bold indicate that the player led his league in a statistical category.

CHAPTER 30

Lawrence Taylor / Harry Carson

Lawrence Taylor and Harry Carson spent eight years together on the New York Giants' defense, forming what may well have been the greatest linebacker tandem in NFL history. Taylor revolutionized the outside linebacker position, gaining general recognition over the course of his career as arguably the greatest defensive player in league history. Meanwhile, Carson was consistently brilliant on the inside for more than a decade.

After appearing in six NFL title games and winning one league championship between 1956 and 1963, the New York Giants failed to make the playoffs the next 17 years, finishing with more wins than losses only two times between 1964 and 1980. The team had some outstanding individual players during that period. Speedy wide receiver Homer Jones thrilled Yankee Stadium crowds with his spectacular touchdown receptions. Safety Carl "Spider" Lockhart appeared in consecutive Pro Bowls during the late 1960s. Quarterback Fran Tarkenton and running back Ron Johnson almost led New York to a postseason berth in 1970 with a record of 9–5. And outside linebacker Brad Van Pelt earned five straight Pro Bowl selections from 1976 to 1980. However, middle linebacker Harry Carson was unquestionably the best player to suit up in a Giants uniform during that dark period in franchise history.

Originally a defensive end at South Carolina State University, Carson moved to inside linebacker after New York selected him in the fourth round of the 1976 NFL draft. He became a starter midway through his rookie season, quickly developing into one of the league's top players at his position. At 6'2" and 237 pounds, Carson had good size for a middle linebacker, but he also possessed several other outstanding attributes that soon made him one of the most feared and respected defenders in the league. A fierce hitter and ferocious tackler, Carson had the agility and range to track down opposing ball carriers, as well as the intensity, intelligence, and leadership skills needed to provide direction to his teammates, on and off the field.

New York finished with a losing record in each of Carson's first five years in the league, with the linebacking tandem of Carson and Brad Van Pelt proving to be the team's only bright spot during that time. Generally considered to be the NFL's premier run-stopping linebacker during the late 1970s and early 1980s, Carson earned his first two Pro Bowl selections in 1978 and 1979. He was also named the Giants team captain in 1979, a distinction he held the remainder of his career. Carson's fortunes and those of the entire New York Giants organization changed dramatically, though, midway through the 1980 campaign when the linebacker was forced to miss the team's final few games with a season-ending injury. The Giants' defense completely fell apart in Carson's absence, causing New York to finish with one of the league's worst records. The team's poor performance turned out to be a blessing in disguise, however, since it enabled them to select North Carolina outside linebacker Lawrence Taylor with the second overall pick of the NFL draft.

Lawrence Taylor made an immediate impression on his New York Giants teammates. Harry Carson later recalled, "The first play that he went in during his rookie training camp we knew that this guy was something special. You could tell that this guy was like from another planet."[1]

Safety Beasley Reece, Taylor's teammate in New York from 1981 to 1983, offered his recollections from that first training camp: "You saw things that made you go, 'My God, did you just see that?'"[2]

The 6'3", 242-pound Taylor soon began creating a stir around the entire league as well. Before long, opposing teams began devising complicated blocking schemes to prevent LT from destroying their quarterback and demolishing their running backs. Taylor's size, speed, agility, and intensity made him the NFL's most dominant defensive player—one capable of completely disrupting the offenses of opposing teams.

Former Washington Redskins quarterback Joe Theismann revealed, "You walk into an offensive meeting and you sit down, and the first thing that comes out of the coach's mouth is, 'How do we block number 56?'"[3]

Legendary coach and television commentator John Madden believed that any such meetings invariably ended in futility: "I don't care who you bring—guard, tackle, center—you weren't going to block Lawrence Taylor."[4]

Dick Butkus, perhaps the greatest middle linebacker ever to play the game, expressed his admiration for Taylor by mentioning the qualities that LT possessed that made him such a difficult player for opposing offenses to prepare for: "When you get a guy like Lawrence, who's got the size, the speed, the intensity, and everything else, and then you add his heart, then you've got a superman on your hands."[5]

Taylor's immense talent enabled him to make the other players around him better. His ability to rush the passer, run down ball carriers from behind, and confuse and intimidate his opponents inspired confidence in his teammates, raising their level of play as well. Former Giants coach Bill Parcells said of Taylor, "He would inspire me, his teammates, and the rest of the defense. He would do those kinds of things. And it's a rare person that can do that."[6]

Taylor not only inspired his teammates but led New York into the playoffs for the first time in 18 years in his first year in the league. The Giants upset favored Philadelphia in the first round of the 1981 playoffs, before losing to the eventual world-champion 49ers in the next round. For his efforts, Taylor was named both the AP Defensive Rookie of the Year and the AP Defensive Player of the Year. He was also selected to appear in the Pro Bowl for the first of 10 consecutive times and was named First Team All-Pro for the first of eight times.

Former Chicago Bears linebacker Mike Singletary entered the NFL the same year as Taylor. The Bears great later recalled, "There were times when you saw him play that you thought, 'Wait a minute . . . the guy can't be that good!'"[7]

Although changes in the Giants' coaching staff caused them to struggle as a team in 1982 and 1983, Taylor continued to perform at an extremely high level. He earned First Team All-Pro honors each year, as well as AP Defensive Player of the Year honors for the second consecutive time in 1982.

While Taylor continued to pile up all the individual accolades and garner most of the media attention, teammate Carson remained steady as a rock in the middle of the Giants' defense, leading the team in tackles virtually every year. New York's defense allowed opposing ball carriers only 3.59 yards per rushing attempt from 1981 to 1987. Carson was credited with 856 tackles during that seven-year period, including 627 unassisted stops. He saved his greatest individual performance for a 1982 Monday night contest against the Packers, making 20 solo tackles and assisting on five others.

In truth, it was Carson's consistently excellent play on the inside that allowed Taylor to freelance as much as he did on the outside. Carson's ability to stop the run brought stability to the interior of the Giants' defense, thereby enabling LT to line up in any number of spots along the defensive front. While watching New York's defense operate, John Madden commented, "As good as Lawrence Taylor is on the outside, Harry Carson is just as good on the inside."

Carson's peers expressed their respect and admiration for him by naming him to appear in the Pro Bowl a total of nine times during his career, including each year from 1982 to 1988. He was selected First Team All-Pro in 1981 and 1984, was named to the Second Team five times, and was also a two-time All-NFL selection.

After playing poorly in 1982 and 1983, the Giants began to come together as a team in 1984, beginning a stretch during which they advanced to the playoffs in five of the next seven years. Quarterback Phil Simms emerged as the team's leader on offense, and Carl Banks joined Carson and Taylor in 1985, giving New York arguably the finest linebacking trio in NFL history. The Giants were eliminated from the postseason by the eventual world champions in 1984 (San Francisco) and 1985 (Chicago), but they captured the NFL title in 1986 by defeating Denver 39–20 in Super Bowl XXI. Carson finished second on the team to Banks, with 118 tackles during the season. Meanwhile, Taylor led the league with 20.5 sacks en route to winning AP Defensive Player of the Year and NFL MVP honors. In being named league MVP, Taylor became the first defensive player to be so honored in 17 years.

Carson spent two more years captaining New York's defense, before retiring at the conclusion of the 1988 campaign. He led the Giants in tackles in six of his 13 seasons, including each year from 1981 to 1984. In addition to his other honors, Carson was named All-NFC five times during his career.

Taylor remained with the Giants through 1993, leading the team to another NFL title in 1990. Even though he remained an extremely effective player to the end, his skills began to slowly diminish after that second championship season. No longer able to accomplish the things he did earlier in his career by the sheer strength of his will, LT retired after 13 years in the league as the NFL's second all-time leader in sacks, with 132.5 to his credit (he has since slipped to ninth). He compiled more than 15 sacks in a season three times, was named All-NFC 10 times, and was selected as the AP Defensive Player of the Year three times. Taylor earned a spot on the NFL's 75th Anniversary Team in 1994, leaving behind a legacy of being perhaps the greatest defensive player in NFL history. If nothing else, he completely redefined the way that the outside linebacker position was played.

Raiders Hall of Fame defensive end Howie Long said of Taylor, "He was the first of his kind. A 6'4", 245-pound linebacker who could run a 4.5 40 [4.5-second 40-yard dash]."[8]

In their eight years together as teammates on the Giants, Harry Carson and Lawrence Taylor helped lead their team to four playoff appearances and one Super Bowl victory. They combined for 15 appearances in the Pro Bowl during that period, nine First Team All-Pro selections, and five selections to the Second Team.

Notes

1. *SportsCentury: Fifty Greatest Athletes—Lawrence Taylor*, television program (ESPN, 1999).

2. *Fifty Greatest Athletes—Lawrence Taylor.*
3. *Fifty Greatest Athletes—Lawrence Taylor.*
4. *Fifty Greatest Athletes—Lawrence Taylor.*
5. *Fifty Greatest Athletes—Lawrence Taylor.*
6. *Fifty Greatest Athletes—Lawrence Taylor.*
7. *Fifty Greatest Athletes—Lawrence Taylor.*
8. *Fifty Greatest Athletes—Lawrence Taylor.*

CHAPTER 31

Jack Lambert / Jack Ham

If any pair of linebackers played at a level comparable to the one that Lawrence Taylor and Harry Carson reached together with the Giants during the 1980s, that duo was the extraordinary tandem of Jack Lambert and Jack Ham—one that helped lead the Pittsburgh Steelers to four world championships during the 1970s.

The Pittsburgh Steelers of the 1970s may well have been the greatest team in the history of the National Football League. In addition to winning an unprecedented four Super Bowls over a six-year period, they had arguably the greatest assemblage of talent in league history. The Pittsburgh offense featured no fewer than five future Hall of Famers—quarterback Terry Bradshaw, running back Franco Harris, center Mike Webster, and wide receivers Lynn Swann and John Stallworth. Meanwhile, their "Steel Curtain" defense is still considered by many football experts to be the greatest ever. Pittsburgh's front four of Mean Joe Greene, Dwight White, L. C. Greenwood, and Ernie Holmes terrorized opposing quarterbacks, and cornerback Mel Blount was as good as any defensive back in the game. Yet, the heart and soul of Pittsburgh's defense was the exceptional linebacking tandem of Jack Ham and Jack Lambert, who were the unit's two most indispensable players. Still, despite their impressive array of talent, the Steelers' rise to the top was a slow and arduous one.

The Pittsburgh Steelers experienced little in the way of success throughout most of the 1950s and 1960s. One of the NFL's most consistent losers, Pittsburgh regularly finished with one of the league's worst records. The one saving grace for the team ended up being that their poor showings usually enabled them to pick one of the nation's top collegiate players when the league held its annual draft at the conclusion of each season. In 1969, the Steelers began to build the team that eventually came to dominate the league, when they drafted defensive tackle Joe Greene with the fourth overall pick in the first round. They made

Louisiana Tech quarterback Terry Bradshaw the draft's first overall pick the following year, then continued to stockpile talent by selecting all-American Penn State linebacker Jack Ham in the second round of the 1971 draft.

The 6'1", 225-pound Ham became a starter on the Pittsburgh defense in his rookie season, demonstrating almost immediately the many gifts that eventually enabled him to become one of the greatest outside linebackers in NFL history. In addition to possessing a considerable amount of physical talent, Ham soon developed a reputation for being one of the league's most cerebral players. He also became known for his calm nature and for the incredible consistency he displayed throughout his career.

Ham, who played left (strong side) linebacker, did a superb job of containing the opposing team's running game. However, as well as Ham played the run, he may have been even more effective against the pass. Ham demonstrated the degree to which he excelled at that particular aspect of the game in his second year in the league, when he intercepted a career-high seven passes. In one of his finest moments, he came up with two interceptions against the Raiders in the 1974 AFC championship game. Ham's 32 career interceptions place him third all-time among NFL linebackers. He earned the first of his eight consecutive Pro Bowl selections in his third season, making the squad each year from 1973 to 1980. Ham was named First Team All-Pro for the first of six straight times the following year, which happened to coincide with the arrival of Jack Lambert in Pittsburgh.

The 1974 NFL draft turned out to be an exceptional one for the Steelers. After selecting Lynn Swann with their first pick, Pittsburgh chose Jack Lambert, Mike Webster, and John Stallworth in subsequent rounds, thereby forming much of the nucleus of the team that went on to win four of the next six Super Bowls. Lambert, a 6'4", 220-pound linebacker out of Kent State University, was taken by the Steelers in the second round. After winning the starting middle linebacker job on Pittsburgh's defense as a rookie, Lambert soon became the unit's emotional leader and defensive captain. Lambert's intelligence, speed, quickness, and range quickly earned him the respect of all the veterans on the team, and his intensity and aggressiveness gave the unit an edge it previously lacked. In discussing Lambert, Pittsburgh head coach Chuck Noll said, "When you start talking about attitude and focus, Jack is the epitome. He was the most focused individual I've ever had."[1]

Lambert was named the NFL's Defensive Rookie of the Year in 1974, a year in which he helped lead the Steelers to their first world championship. He established himself in subsequent seasons as the premier middle linebacker of his era, appearing in nine straight Pro Bowls from 1975 to 1983, earning six First Team All-Pro selections, and being named the NFL's Defensive Player of the Year in 1976. In spite of his relatively lean frame, Lambert quickly developed into one of the league's most intimidating players, bludgeoning opposing quarterbacks and running backs with his vicious hits and frightening them with his verbal taunts. Yet, Lambert was also an extremely skilled and tactical player. Noted for his ability to drop into pass coverage, Lambert intercepted 28 passes during his career. He had six interceptions in 1979 alone.

Speaking of his former teammate's pass-coverage skills, Jack Ham said, "Of all the middle linebackers—Ray Nitschke, Willie Lanier, Dick Butkus—what set Jack apart was his ability to play the pass."[2]

Another former member of Pittsburgh's linebacking corps, Andy Russell, had this to say: "Lambert may have had the image of a wild man, but he killed you with his precision."[3]

The NFL did not officially record tackles and sacks until the 1980s, making it impossible to know with any degree of certainty the number of tackles Lambert made during his career. However, there is little doubt that he led the Steelers in tackles throughout most of his career and that he also finished among the league leaders in that category virtually every year. There also is no questioning the integral role that Lambert played during Pittsburgh's championship run and the legacy he left behind when he retired at the end of 1984 after suffering a severe toe injury during the season.

Former Cleveland Browns coach Sam Rutigliano once stated emphatically, "Jack Lambert is the Pittsburgh Steelers."[4]

And Jack Ham continued to praise his former teammate when he said, "Jack Lambert was the most complete middle linebacker ever to play."[5]

Lambert returned the favor to Ham, stating, "Jack Ham, in my opinion, is the greatest outside linebacker that ever played the game. Tremendous technique. He did everything right. He played the run the way you were supposed to play it. He played the pass the way you were supposed to play it. Consummate. He was just the best that ever played the game. No question in my mind about it."[6]

Jack Lambert and Jack Ham lined up alongside one another on Pittsburgh's defense for nine straight years, from 1974 to 1982. They appeared in six AFC championship games and four Super Bowls during that period, finishing on top each time they made it to the big game. In those nine seasons, they combined for 13 appearances in the Pro Bowl and 11 First Team All-Pro selections. Ham was named the NFL's Defensive Player of the Year in 1975. Lambert won the honor the following year. Both Lambert and Ham were also extremely durable. Lambert missed only six games due to injury during his first 10 years in the league, while Ham played every game in eight of his 12 NFL seasons, appearing in 178 out of a possible 190 contests. It would be difficult to argue too strenuously with anyone who claimed that Lambert and Ham were the greatest linebacking tandem in NFL history.

Notes

1. *Greatest Ever: NFL Dream Team* (Polygram Video, 1996).
2. *Greatest Ever: NFL Dream Team.*
3. *Greatest Ever: NFL Dream Team.*
4. *Greatest Ever: NFL Dream Team.*
5. *Greatest Ever: NFL Dream Team.*
6. *Greatest Ever: NFL Dream Team.*

CHAPTER 32

Jim Taylor / Paul Hornung

Under the direction of legendary head coach Vince Lombardi, the Packers created an NFL dynasty in the tiny city of Green Bay, Wisconsin, during the 1960s, capturing five league championships and winning two Super Bowls between 1961 and 1967. At the heart of the team's success throughout much of the period was the backfield tandem of Jim Taylor and Paul Hornung—two men who excelled as teammates in spite of their contrasting personalities and diametrically opposed lifestyles.

The Green Bay Packers were one of the National Football League's least successful franchises throughout most of the 1950s, reaching their nadir in 1958 when they finished with a record of only 1–10–1. The team's fortunes began to change at the conclusion of that year, though, when ownership elected to hire former Giants' backfield coach Vince Lombardi as the Packers' new head coach and general manager. Lombardi subsequently made one of his first moves converting Paul Hornung, the team's backup fullback in each of the previous two seasons, into the Packers' starting halfback.

The 6'2", 215-pound Hornung had originally been selected by Green Bay with the first overall pick of the 1957 NFL draft. An all-American quarterback at the University of Notre Dame, Hornung was voted college football's 1956 Heisman Trophy winner at the end of his senior season. However, Hornung had a difficult time transitioning to life in the NFL his first two seasons, rushing for a total of only 629 yards and five touchdowns in a part-time role after being shifted to fullback. Many observers believed that a large part of Hornung's problem lay in his lack of total dedication to his sport caused by his basic inability to properly establish his priorities. Nicknamed the "Golden Boy" for his blond hair, good looks, and seemingly charmed life, everything previously came quite easy to Hornung, who developed a reputation for being a playboy who had as much fun off the field as he did on it. Things began to change, though, under the strict tutelage of the extremely regimented Lombardi, who saw the raw talent in Hornung and used his innate ability to motivate men to bring out the best in his new halfback. Hornung rushed for 681 yards and seven touchdowns in his first season under Lombardi en route to earning his first Pro Bowl selection.

Another significant move that Lombardi made in his first season as head coach was to insert Jim Taylor at starting fullback. The 6'0", 214-pound Taylor had been taken by the Packers out of Louisiana State University in the second round of the 1958 draft. Splitting time with Hornung at the fullback position as a rookie, Taylor rushed for only 247 yards on just 52 carries. He almost doubled that yardage in 1959, rushing for 452 yards from scrimmage and scoring six touchdowns on the ground. Taylor soon became Green Bay's bread-and-butter guy, carrying the ball in most short-yardage situations and rarely failing to deliver. With Taylor and Hornung establishing themselves as the team's starting backfield, Bart Starr maturing into the team's starting quarterback, and Lombardi starting to build the team's offensive line and defense, Green Bay's record improved to 7–5 in 1959.

Although they ended up losing the NFL title game to Philadelphia, the Packers claimed the Western Division title the following year. Taylor and Hornung realized their full potential that season, being named to appear in the Pro Bowl together for the first time. Hornung earned First Team All-Pro honors by rushing for 671 yards and scoring a league-leading 15 touchdowns, 13 of which came on the ground. He also caught 28 passes for another 257 yards and two touchdowns, establishing himself in the process as the league's most versatile running back. In addition to excelling at running the famed "Packer Sweep," Hornung was an outstanding blocker, pass receiver, and kicker. Furthermore, his college experience at quarterback made him extremely adept at running the halfback option.

Meanwhile, Taylor began a string of five consecutive seasons in which he rushed for more than 1,000 yards:

1960: **230** rushes, 1,101 yards, 4.8 yards per carry, 11 TDs
1961: 243 rushes, 1,307 yards, 5.4 yards per carry, **16** TDs
1962: **272** rushes, **1,474** yards, 5.4 yards per carry, **19** TDs
1963: 248 rushes, 1,018 yards, 4.1 yards per carry, 10 TDs
1964: 235 rushes, 1,169 yards, 5.0 yards per carry, 15 TDs

Taylor was named to the Pro Bowl in each of those five years. He also earned consensus First Team All-Pro and NFL MVP honors in 1962, a season in which he broke the great Jim Brown's string of rushing titles by leading the league with 1,474 yards on the ground (Brown won the rushing title his eight other years in the league). More important, the Packers won the NFL championship in 1961 and 1962, defeating the New York Giants in the title game both times.

While Taylor had his greatest season in 1962, Hornung reached the zenith of his career one year earlier, when he helped lead the Packers to their first NFL title under Lombardi. Hornung posted rather modest numbers on the ground over the course of that 1961 campaign, carrying the ball only 127 times for just 597 yards and an average of 4.7 yards per carry. He also made just 15 receptions for 145 yards, scoring a total of 10 touchdowns, eight of which came on the ground. Yet, doubling as the team's placekicker, Hornung earned First Team All-Pro honors for the second straight year by leading the league in scoring for the third consecutive time. After topping the circuit with 94 points in 1959 and 176 points in 1960, Hornung led the NFL with 146 points in 1961 en route to earning NFL MVP honors. Hornung almost missed the 1961 title game against the Giants due to his obligations to the U.S. Army, but President John F. Kennedy granted the league's Most Valuable Player temporary leave after receiving a telephone call from Coach Lombardi. Hornung scored 19 points in his team's 37–0 thrashing of Lombardi's former team, scoring one touchdown and kicking three field goals and four extra points. Although Hornung wasn't nearly as effective the following season, he helped the Packers win their second straight NFL championship by compiling 387 total yards and scoring seven touchdowns.

In spite of the tremendous amount of success that Taylor and Hornung enjoyed together, they could not have been more different in the eyes of the public. Hornung, everybody's all-American, was the fair-haired boy with his blond hair and good looks. Everything seemed to come to him easily. In stark contrast, Taylor, with his crew cut and rugged features, had the face of a football player. He was grizzled and intense; he played the game with a mean streak; and he was renowned for his ability to play through pain and injuries. Generally ranked behind only Jim Brown among NFL running backs of his era, Taylor drew a great deal of respect from both his teammates and his opponents. Hall of Fame New York Giants linebacker Sam Huff had this to say about Taylor: "Jim Brown was the best running back I ever faced, but Jim Taylor was the toughest."[1]

And in comparing the running styles of the period's top two running backs, Vince Lombardi stated, "Jim Brown will give you that leg and then take it away from you. Jim Taylor will give it to you and then ram it through your chest."[2]

Although Taylor rushed for over 1,000 yards in 1963 and 1964, the Packers didn't make it back to the title game in either of those years. Hornung's season-long suspension for associating with gamblers hurt the team's chances in 1963. And although he returned to the Packers the following season, Hornung clearly wasn't the same player that he was earlier in his career. Still, the halfback netted 635 all-purpose yards and scored eight touchdowns during Green Bay's 1965 march to the title. Hornung experienced his finest moment that year in a game that he didn't even expect to start. Filling in for the injured Elijah Pitts, Hornung scored five touchdowns against the Baltimore Colts, the team that Green

Bay eventually defeated 13–10 in a play-off before overpowering Cleveland 23–12 in the championship game.

Hornung served strictly as a backup in his final season with the Packers, retiring at the end of the 1966 campaign. He ended his career with 3,711 yards rushing, 1,480 yards receiving, and 62 touchdowns. He also kicked 66 field goals and 190 extra points, finishing with a total of 760 points. Hornung's ability to cross the opponent's goal line when his team needed a big touchdown was noted by Vince Lombardi. The halfback's former coach often said that Hornung was an ordinary back until his team got inside the opposing team's 10-yard line. But he also stated that he never saw anyone better from that point on.

Although Jim Taylor failed to gain over 1,000 yards in either of Green Bay's championship years of 1965 or 1966, he was a key contributor to the success of his team both years. Taylor rushed for 734 yards and four touchdowns in 1965, then compiled another 705 yards and six touchdowns the following season. Having played out his option with the Packers, Taylor was signed by the Saints, with whom he spent his final season in 1967. He ended his career with 8,597 rushing yards, a rushing average of 4.4 yards per carry, and 93 touchdowns. At the time of his retirement, Taylor ranked second only to Jim Brown on the all-time rushing list.

Jim Taylor and Paul Hornung spent eight years together on the Packers from 1958 to 1966. They were starting backfield mates in five of those seasons. Between 1959 and 1964, they combined for seven Pro Bowl appearances and three First Team All-Pro selections. They each won a Most Valuable Player Award. Between them, Taylor and Hornung led the NFL in touchdowns three straight years, from 1960 to 1962. They scored 26 touchdowns in each of those years, combining for a total of 78 scores over those three seasons. They were at their best in 1960 and 1961, rushing for a total of 1,772 yards in the first of those years and following that up with another 1,904 yards on the ground in 1961. In their eight years together, Taylor and Hornung appeared in five NFL title games and won four league championships.

Notes

Numbers printed in bold indicate that the player led his league in a statistical category.

1. Sam Huff, http://www.sportsillustrated.cnn.com/vault/topic/article/Jim_Taylor_Football/1900-01-01/2100-12-31/mdd/index.html.

2. Vince Lombardi, with W. C. Heinz, *Run to Daylight* (New York: Prentice Hall, 1963).

CHAPTER 33

Lynn Swann / John Stallworth

Several pass-receiving combinations have compiled more impressive numbers than the Pittsburgh Steelers' 1970s tandem of Lynn Swann and John Stallworth. Neither Swann nor Stallworth ranks among the career leaders in any major statistical category for NFL wide receivers. Neither man often placed among the league leaders during his playing days. However, leading the NFL in pass receiving would have been virtually impossible for either Swann or Stallworth since they played for a Steelers team that relied heavily on their "Steel Curtain" defense and the outstanding running abilities of Franco Harris to batter their opponents into submission. Swann and Stallworth also played during an era in which the rules governing the sport didn't favor the passing game nearly as much as they have for the past two decades. Therefore, it has been significantly easier for more recent combinations of wide receivers to compile huge numbers. But all things considered, Swann and Stallworth may well have formed the greatest wide receiver tandem in NFL history. At the very least, they were both among the finest clutch receivers in the history of the sport.

After earning all-American honors at the University of Southern California, Lynn Swann was selected by the Pittsburgh Steelers in the first round of the 1974 draft with the 21st overall pick. Swann was used sparingly as a wide receiver in his rookie season, catching only 11 passes for 208 yards and two touchdowns. However, he excelled as a punt returner, leading the NFL with 577 return yards and scoring a third touchdown on special teams. Although the Steelers captured their first Super Bowl title at the end of the season, defeating Minnesota 16–7 in Super Bowl IX, Swann failed to make a single reception (Pittsburgh quarterback Terry Bradshaw completed only nine passes the entire game).

Swann became a far more integral part of the Pittsburgh offense in his second season, earning a spot on the starting team and catching 49 passes for a total of 781 yards and a league-high 11 TD receptions. At the end of the campaign, Swann was selected to appear in the Pro Bowl for the first of three times. However, the highlight of his season occurred on Super Bowl Sunday, when he caught four passes for one touchdown and a Super Bowl record 161 yards. Swann's outstanding performance helped Pittsburgh defeat the Dallas Cowboys by a final score of 21–17, earning him Super Bowl MVP honors in the process. In being selected as the game's Most Valuable Player, Swann became the first wide receiver to be so honored. During the contest, the 5'11", 185-pound Swann displayed the many natural gifts that helped make him one of football's consummate receivers. Blessed with outstanding speed and leaping ability, Swann also possessed tremendous agility and body control. He used his unique skill set to outjump Dallas defensive backs in making two of the most acrobatic catches in Super Bowl history. He followed up his exceptional performance in the sport's biggest game by catching 50 passes for 789 yards and seven touchdowns in 1977 en route to earning Pro Bowl honors for the second consecutive season.

It was during that 1977 campaign that another 1974 draft selection by Pittsburgh claimed the other starting wide receiver spot in the Steelers' offense. Coming out of tiny Alabama A&M, John Stallworth was much less heralded than his USC counterpart when the Steelers selected him in the fourth round with the 82nd overall pick. The 6'2", 195-pound Stallworth caught only 16 passes for 269 yards and one touchdown as a backup in his rookie season, before spending the next two years battling injuries. By the time that Stallworth became a starter in his fourth year in the league, Pittsburgh had already won two Super Bowls. However, in his first season as a starter, Stallworth showed the Steelers that he was well worth the wait. Demonstrating the excellent hands, exceptional speed, and outstanding leaping ability that prompted Pittsburgh to draft him three years earlier, Stallworth caught 44 passes for 784 yards and seven touchdowns. The Steelers failed to make it back to the Super Bowl that year, but they returned the following season, with Stallworth proving to be a major factor. He made 41 receptions for 798 yards and nine touchdowns during the regular season, then caught another three passes for 115 yards and two touchdowns during Pittsburgh's 35–31 victory over Dallas in Super Bowl XIII. One of those TD receptions went for 75 yards. Not to be outdone, Swann made seven receptions for 124 yards during the contest; he also scored the Steelers' final touchdown. Pittsburgh's Super Bowl win over Dallas capped a banner year for Swann, who was named First Team All-Pro for the only time in his career after making a career-high 61 receptions for 880 yards and 11 touchdowns.

Swann also performed extremely well in 1979, catching 41 passes for 808 yards and five touchdowns while averaging a career-best 19.7 yards per catch during the campaign. Nevertheless, Stallworth supplanted him that year as the team's number-one threat on offense. Stallworth made 70 receptions, finished second in the league with 1,183 receiving yards, scored eight touchdowns, was selected to appear in the Pro Bowl for the first of four times, and was named First Team All-Pro for the only time in his career. He then performed brilliantly during Pittsburgh's 31–19 victory over the Rams in Super Bowl XIV. Stallworth made three receptions for 121 yards, one of which was an extraordinary 73-yard over-the-shoulder TD catch that put the Steelers in the lead for good early in the fourth quarter and completely changed the momentum of the game.

Pittsburgh didn't come close to making it back to the Super Bowl the following year, with Stallworth's absence from the team for much of the year due to injury proving to be a major factor. Meanwhile, Swann's productivity began to drop off considerably, leaving the team without a consistent deep threat on offense. Swann played three more years for the Steelers, retiring at the end of the 1982 season with 336 total receptions for 5,462 yards and 51 touchdowns. Those numbers hardly seem spectacular. Consider, though, that Swann had 364 receiving yards and 398 all-purpose yards in his four Super Bowl appearances. Both those marks were Super Bowl records at the time. And in spite of his somewhat modest career numbers, Swann was named to the 1970s All-Decade Team.

Former Pittsburgh Steelers teammate Mean Joe Greene discussed Swann's legacy, saying, "Lynn Swann didn't have the stats, but he sure as heck made an impact. No one made a bigger impact. It's like Gale Sayers. He didn't play a long time, but he made an impact. Lynn Swann had that impact. He played a lot of big games."[1]

As Swann's career drew to a close, Stallworth's reached its apex. Stallworth returned in 1981 to make 63 receptions for 1,098 yards and five touchdowns. Stallworth subsequently appeared in the Pro Bowl at the end of the 1982, 1983, and 1984 campaigns. He had his greatest season in the last of those years, establishing career highs with 80 receptions, an AFC-leading 1,395 receiving yards, and 11 TD receptions. Stallworth never again approached those figures in his final three years in Pittsburgh. He retired at the end of 1987 with 537 career receptions, 8,723 receiving yards, and 63 touchdowns.

Stallworth holds Super Bowl records for highest career average per reception (24.4 yards) and highest single-game average (40.33 yards per catch in Super Bowl XIX). One of the greatest postseason performers in NFL history at the wide receiver position, Stallworth had 12 TD receptions and a string of 17 straight games with a catch in postseason play. He also scored a touchdown in an NFL record eight straight playoff games at one point, from 1978 to 1983.

Lynn Swann and John Stallworth started for six years at wide receiver for the Pittsburgh Steelers, from 1977 to 1982. During that six-year period, they combined for four Pro Bowl selections and were each named First Team All-Pro once. They had their three best years together from 1977 to 1979, combining for a total of 307 receptions, 5,242 receiving yards, and 47 touchdowns over the course of those three campaigns. The Steelers won the Super Bowl at the end of the 1978 and 1979 seasons. In those two Super Bowls, Swann and Stallworth combined for 18 receptions, 439 receiving yards, and five touchdowns. Those are the figures that made Swann and Stallworth the greatest postseason pass-receiving tandem in NFL history and arguably the most dynamic pair of wide receivers in the history of the sport.

Note

1. Joe Greene, http://www.answers.com/topic/lynn-swann.

Part III

DYNAMIC BASKETBALL DUOS

CHAPTER 34

Michael Jordan / Scottie Pippen

The Chicago Bulls dominated the NBA for most of the 1990s, winning six of a possible eight league championships between 1991 and 1998. Chicago's starting five featured several solid role players at different times during that period, including Horace Grant, Dennis Rodman, Bill Cartwright, John Paxson, Toni Kukoc, and B. J. Armstrong. Those squads also featured two of the NBA's premier players in Michael Jordan and Scottie Pippen. Jordan, the man generally considered to be the greatest player in basketball history, served as the Bulls' central figure throughout the period, dominating his team as much as he dominated the rest of the league. Meanwhile, Pippen's vast array of skills and tremendous versatility made him the perfect complement to Jordan—his Robin to Michael's Batman, if you will. Together, Jordan and Pippen formed arguably the greatest tandem in league history, enabling their team to establish itself as one of the best ever to compete in the NBA.

After remaining extremely competitive throughout the first half of the 1970s, the Chicago Bulls posted a winning record just twice between 1975 and 1984. The Bulls compiled their best single-season mark over the course of that nine-year stretch in 1980–1981, when they concluded the campaign with a record of 45–37. However, they subsequently failed to win more than 34 games in any of the next three seasons, finishing a dismal 27–55 in 1983–1984. The Bulls' poor showing that year enabled them to select University of North Carolina guard Michael Jordan with the third overall pick of the 1984 NBA draft.

Unlike many other first-year players, it didn't take Jordan long to adjust to life in the NBA. The 6'6", 215-pound guard quickly established himself as one of the league's top players, finishing third in the NBA with a scoring average of 28.2 points per game, collecting just under six assists per contest, and placing among the leaders with 2.4 steals per game. In helping the Bulls improve their record to 38–44, Jordan earned NBA Rookie of the Year honors and a spot on the All-NBA Second Team.

With Jordan missing all but 18 games the following season due to a broken bone in his foot, Chicago took a step backward in 1985–1986, finishing the campaign with a record of only 30–52. Jordan returned to the team the next year, though, to post a scoring average of 37.1 points per game, which enabled him to win the first of his seven consecutive scoring titles. In doing so, he became just the second player in league history to score 3,000 points in a season (Wilt Chamberlain was the first). The NBA's most talented player also posted averages of 5.2 rebounds, 4.6 assists, and 2.88 steals per contest, placing second in the league in the last category. Jordan's exceptional all-around performance earned him the first of seven straight selections to the All-NBA First Team and a second-place finish to Magic Johnson in the league MVP voting. The Bulls finished the regular season with a record of 40–42 and advanced to the playoffs, where they faced the defending champion Boston Celtics in the first round. Although Boston ended up sweeping the series from Chicago in three games, Jordan put on a memorable performance in game 2, setting an NBA playoff record by scoring 63 points in Chicago's 135–131 double-overtime loss in Boston. Using his entire repertoire of fadeaway jumpers, running bank shots, and flying dunks, Jordan put on a one-man show during the contest, which prompted Larry Bird to marvel afterward, "I think he's God disguised as Michael Jordan. He's the most awesome player in the NBA."[1]

Jordan was indeed the league's greatest individual player. His extraordinary quickness and leaping ability, as well as his incredible knack of hanging in the air before releasing his shot, made him virtually unstoppable on offense. He was tremendous at penetrating to the basket and scoring either on lay-ins, dunks, or short jump shots. Jordan also possessed exceptional physical strength, enabling him to back his defender down low before using his great leaping ability to jump over him. The only thing that Jordan lacked when he first entered the league was an outstanding jump shot. But he worked hard on that aspect of his game and eventually developed one of the NBA's deadliest jumpers.

Phil Jackson, who later became Jordan's coach with the Bulls, explained, "The thing about Michael is he takes nothing about his game for granted. When he first came into the league in 1984, he was primarily a penetrator. His outside shooting wasn't up to pro standards. So he put in his gym time in the off-season, shooting hundreds of shots each day. Eventually, he became a deadly three-point shooter."[2]

Jordan's hard work, dedication, and immense talent not only enabled him to win seven consecutive scoring titles but also develop into the finest all-around player in the NBA. In addition to being the league's top scorer, MJ was a good rebounder and passer and a superb defender. He annually placed among the league leaders in steals, topping the NBA in that category on three separate occasions. The numbers that Jordan posted from 1986 to 1993 clearly indicate his all-around brilliance:

1986–1987: **37.1** PPG, 5.2 RPG, 4.6 APG, 2.9 SPG
1987–1988: **35.0** PPG, 5.5 RPG, 5.9 APG, **3.2** SPG
1988–1989: **32.5** PPG, 8.0 RPG, 8.0 APG, 2.9 SPG
1989–1990: **33.6** PPG, 6.9 RPG, 6.3 APG, **2.8** SPG
1990–1991: **31.5** PPG, 6.0 RPG, 5.5 APG, 2.7 SPG
1991–1992: **30.1** PPG, 6.4 RPG, 6.1 APG, 2.3 SPG
1992–1993: **32.6** PPG, 6.7 RPG, 5.5 APG, **2.8** SPG

In leading the league in scoring seven straight times, Jordan tied Wilt Chamberlain's previous NBA record. He also joined Chamberlain as only the second player in league history to average better than 30 points per game for seven straight seasons. In 1986–1987, he became the first player in history to record 100 blocks and 200 steals in the same season. He duplicated that feat the following season, when he earned both NBA MVP and Defensive Player of the Year honors. Jordan also made the All-NBA First Defensive Team for the first of six consecutive times that season. He was named league MVP again in 1990–1991 and 1991–1992.

Equally significant is the fact that Jordan turned the Bulls into a winning franchise during that seven-year period. After being eliminated by Boston in the first round of the playoffs in 1986–1987, Chicago posted a record of 50–32 the following year. The Bulls then won their first playoff series in seven years when they defeated Cleveland in five games, before losing to Detroit in the Eastern Conference semifinals. The Bulls finished the 1988–1989 campaign with a record of 47–35, but they defeated the 57–25 Cleveland Cavaliers in the first round of the playoffs again, winning the decisive fifth game on a last second buzzer-beater by Jordan. Chicago then advanced to the Eastern Conference finals by beating the Knicks in six games in the semifinal round. Although they were eliminated from the playoffs by Detroit for the second consecutive year, the Bulls gave the Pistons all they could handle, finally falling to the eventual world champions in six games. After compiling a 55–27 record in 1989–1990, Chicago again faced Detroit in the Eastern Conference finals. The Bulls easily provided the Pistons with their stiffest competition that postseason, forcing Detroit to a decisive seventh game before finally falling to their old nemesis. (Detroit posted an 11–2 record in its other three playoff series.)

Chicago's three straight playoff losses to Detroit helped Jordan mature both as a player and as a man. The Pistons employed a simple philosophy whenever they faced the Bulls: physically punish and intimidate Jordan. Accordingly, the

Chicago guard first needed to increase his mental toughness before he could truly perform at optimum proficiency. He also needed to place more trust in his teammates before he could become a true champion. Although Jordan was generally reputed to be the NBA's greatest individual talent, he had yet to establish himself as either a great team player or a true team leader. Jordan had so much ability that he often seemed unwilling to distribute the ball to his teammates in pressure situations, choosing instead to assume sole responsibility for the fortunes of his team in the closing moments of close contests.

The hiring of Phil Jackson as Chicago's head coach in 1989 went a long way toward helping Jordan overcome that last obstacle. Jackson convinced his star player that he needed to trust his teammates and allow them to become more involved in the team's offensive flow if he had any hopes of ever winning a championship. Jordan bought into his new coach's philosophy, enabling him to gradually evolve into one of the sport's great all-time leaders. In addition to placing more faith in his teammates, the guard passed on to them his tremendous desire to excel, with his extraordinary talent and competitive spirit often allowing him to seemingly will his team to victory.

Certainly, the addition of another extremely talented player to the Bulls' roster in 1987 made Jackson's philosophy much easier for Jordan to accept. Originally selected by the Seattle Supersonics with the fifth overall pick of the 1987 NBA draft, Scottie Pippen found himself traded to Chicago later on draft day, ostensibly for center Olden Polynice. After coming off the bench as a rookie, the 6'8", 230-pound forward became a starter in the Bulls' frontcourt in his second season, averaging just over 14 points and six rebounds per contest in 1988–1989. Pippen began to assume a larger role in the team's offense in his third year, averaging 16.5 points and 5.4 assists per game while taking on much of the responsibility for running the "triangle offense" that Coach Jackson installed in Chicago. Although Pippen lacked an outstanding outside shot, he excelled at driving to the basket and creating off the dribble. He also possessed superior passing skills and wise judgment when it came to distributing the ball to his teammates. Pippen's gradual development into a solid offensive performer lightened to some degree Jordan's burden, giving the team's best player someone else on whom he could rely in pressure situations.

With Jackson's system fully in place by 1990–1991, Jordan and Pippen thrived together in Chicago's new offensive scheme, leading the Bulls to the first of three consecutive NBA championships—consider Jordan's numbers alongside Pippen's during the Bulls' first three championship years:

1990–1991
Michael Jordan: **31.5** PPG, 6.0 RPG, 5.5 APG, 2.7 SPG
Scottie Pippen: 17.8 PPG, 7.3 RPG, 6.2 APG, 2.4 SPG

1991–1992
Michael Jordan: **30.1** PPG, 6.4 RPG, 6.1 APG, 2.3 SPG
Scottie Pippen: 21.0 PPG, 7.7 RPG, 7.0 APG, 1.9 SPG
1992–1993
Michael Jordan: **32.6** PPG, 6.7 RPG, 5.5 APG, **2.8** SPG
Scottie Pippen: 18.6 PPG, 7.7 RPG, 6.3 APG, 2.1 SPG

In addition to leading the NBA in scoring all three years, Jordan finished near the top of the league rankings in steals each season, topping the circuit in that category in 1992–1993. After being named the NBA's Most Valuable Player in 1990–1991 and 1991–1992, he finished third in the voting in 1992–1993. Jordan was named to both the All-NBA First Team and the All-NBA First Defensive Team all three years.

Pippen established himself as Chicago's number-two option on offense by 1990–1991, with his scoring average surpassing 20 points per game for the first time in his career the following season. He also became the Bulls' primary ball distributor during the period, leading the team in assists all three years. Pippen finished among the league leaders in steals in both 1990–1991 and 1992–1993, and after being named to the All-NBA Second Defensive Team in 1990–1991, he joined Jordan on the First Defensive Team the other two years. In fact, the strongest part of Pippen's game may well have been his defense. His long arms and great quickness allowed him to guard bigger, smaller, and quicker players with equal proficiency. As a result, he generally guarded the opposing team's toughest offensive player, allowing Jordan to freelance in the passing lanes looking for steals. Even though MJ generally received more notoriety for his defense, Pippen was actually the better all-around defender. For that reason, it was Pippen, not Jordan, who guarded Magic Johnson when the Bulls defeated the Lakers in the 1991 finals to win their first NBA title.

After finishing the 1990–1991 regular season with a record of 61–21, the Bulls lost only twice during the postseason en route to capturing their first championship. Particularly satisfying was their four-game sweep of the hated Pistons in the Eastern Conference finals. Chicago subsequently disposed of the Lakers in the NBA Finals in five games, with Jordan earning finals MVP honors by averaging 31 points, 11 assists, and six rebounds during the series.

The Bulls finished with an NBA-best 67–15 record in 1991–1992 before winning their second consecutive championship by defeating Portland in the NBA Finals in six games. Jordan was named Finals MVP for the second straight year.

After posting a 57–25 record during the 1992–1993 regular season, Chicago repeated as league champions by defeating the Phoenix Suns in the NBA Finals in six games. Jordan earned his third straight Finals MVP trophy, performing particularly well in game 4, when he scored 55 points.

Following the death of his father shortly after the conclusion of the 1992–1993 playoffs, Jordan elected to retire from basketball. He subsequently chose to pursue a career in baseball, spending the better part of the next two seasons in the minor league system of the Chicago White Sox.

Although the Bulls remained one of the NBA's better teams in Jordan's absence, they failed to advance beyond the Eastern Conference semifinals in either 1994 or 1995. Filling MJ's shoes proved to be virtually impossible. Nevertheless, Pippen did his best, compiling the two best statistical seasons of his career. In leading the Bulls to a 55–27 record in 1993–1994, Pippen averaged a career-high 22 points and 8.7 rebounds per game while finishing second in the league with just under three steals per contest. The versatile forward placed third in the league MVP balloting; he also earned spots on both the All-NBA First Team and the All-NBA First Defensive Team. Pippen was similarly honored the following season, when he posted averages of 21.4 points, 8.1 rebounds, and a league-leading 2.9 steals per game.

After failing to display the same sort of skills on the baseball diamond that he possessed on the basketball court, Michael Jordan decided to return to the Bulls during the latter stages of the 1994–1995 campaign. Showing a bit of rust after his long layoff, Jordan found himself unable to lead Chicago past Orlando in the Eastern Conference semifinals. But he returned to top form the following year, leading the Bulls to the first of another three consecutive NBA titles. These are the numbers Jordan and Pippen posted in those championship seasons:

1995–1996
Michael Jordan: **30.4** PPG, 6.6 RPG, 4.3 APG
Scottie Pippen: 19.4 PPG, 6.4 RPG, 5.9 APG
1996–1997
Michael Jordan: **29.6** PPG, 5.9 RPG, 4.3 APG
Scottie Pippen: 20.2 PPG, 6.5 RPG, 5.7 APG
1997–1998
Michael Jordan: **28.7** PPG, 5.8 RPG, 3.5 APG
Scottie Pippen: 19.1 PPG, 5.2 RPG, 5.8 APG

In addition to winning his unprecedented eighth, ninth, and 10th scoring titles, Jordan earned league MVP honors for the fourth and fifth times in his career, capturing the honor in both 1995–1996 and 1997–1998. He also was named to the All-NBA First Team and the All-NBA First Defensive Team all three years.

Pippen joined his teammate on the First Defensive Team all three years. He also joined Jordan on the All-NBA First Team in 1995–1996, before being picked for the Second and Third Teams the next two years, respectively.

The Bulls finished with the league's best record each of those years, amassing an NBA record 72 victories in Jordan's first full season back. They defeated Seattle in six games in the 1996 NBA Finals before disposing of Utah in six games in each of the next two years. Jordan was named NBA Finals MVP all three times. It was during the 1997 Finals that Jordan gave one of his most heroic performances.

With the series tied at two games apiece, Jordan's status for game 5 in Utah appeared very much in doubt. Suffering from a viral condition that left him bedridden all day with a splitting headache and nausea, Jordan's playing status was listed as a game-time decision. Even though he had to be treated with medication and fluids before and during the game, an exhausted Jordan willed himself to a 38-point effort against the Jazz, leading his team to a 90–88 victory in the process. The Bulls then captured their fifth NBA championship by defeating the Jazz in game 6 back in Chicago by a final score of 90–86.

After the Bulls won their sixth title the following year, Jordan elected to retire from the game a second time. He spent much of the next three years working in the Washington Wizards' front office before returning to the court as a member of the team in 2000–2001. Jordan played two years in Washington, posting scoring averages of 23 and 20 points per game his final two seasons before announcing his retirement from basketball, for good, at the conclusion of the 2002–2003 campaign. He ended his career with 32,292 points scored—the third most in NBA history. Jordan's scoring average of 30.1 points per game is the best in league history. He also averaged more points per game during the playoffs than any other player, compiling a record 33.4 scoring average and 5,987 total points scored in 179 postseason contests. Jordan's 2,514 career steals place him second on the all-time list. In addition to being named the NBA's Most Valuable Player five times, he finished second in the voting on three other occasions. Jordan was a 10-time selection to the All-NBA First Team; he also earned nine selections to the All-NBA First Defensive Team.

Chicago's sixth championship season also marked the end of Scottie Pippen's time with the Bulls. Unhappy with team ownership, the forward demanded to be traded out of the Windy City almost as soon as Jordan announced his retirement at the end of the 1997–1998 campaign. Traded to the Rockets at the start of the following season, Pippen spent one year in Houston before being dealt to the Portland Trailblazers for six players prior to the start of the 1999–2000 season. Pippen remained in Portland four years, never again averaging more than 14.5 points per contest or leading his team beyond the conference finals. Although he was named to the All-NBA First Defensive Team once more, Pippen never again earned All-NBA First, Second, or Third Team honors. He returned to the Bulls as a free agent prior to the start of the 2003–2004 season, appearing in only 23 games before being released by the team at the end of the year. Pippen ended his career with 18,940 points scored, 6,135 assists, and 2,307 steals. The last figure places him sixth on the all-time list. Pippen averaged 16.1 points, 6.4 rebounds, and 5.2 assists per game in his 17 NBA seasons. He was named to the All-NBA First Team three times, and he was picked for the Second and Third Teams two times each. Pippen was also an eight-time selection to the All-NBA First Defensive Team, and he appeared in a total of seven All-Star Games.

Michael Jordan and Scottie Pippen spent nine full seasons together as teammates. During that time, they combined for 10 selections to the All-NBA First Team and two selections to both the Second and Third Teams. One or the other earned a spot on the All-NBA First Defensive Team 14 times, and the two men made 14 appearances in the All-Star Game during their time together. The Bulls advanced to the Eastern Conference finals in eight of those nine seasons, winning the NBA championship on six occasions.

Notes

Numbers printed in bold indicate that the player led his league in a statistical category.

1. Larry Bird, http://www.nba.com/history/jordan63_moments.html.
2. Phil Jackson, http://www.nba.com/jordan/is_philonmj.html.

CHAPTER 35

Kareem Abdul-Jabbar / Magic Johnson

The NBA's most dominant player for virtually all of the 1970s, Kareem Abdul-Jabbar already had five Most Valuable Player Awards in his trophy case by 1979. Jabbar earned NBA Finals MVP honors in 1971, when he led the Milwaukee Bucks to their only league championship. He was a six-time All-NBA First Team selection; he also was named to the Second Team on three other occasions. The 32-year-old Jabbar had earned every individual accolade possible. Yet, the best part of Jabbar's career had yet to come. The center's final 10 years in the league brought him five more NBA championships and a renewed enthusiasm for the game. They also afforded him the opportunity to team up with arguably the greatest point guard in NBA history, Magic Johnson, who first joined him on the Los Angeles Lakers in 1979. Jabbar and Johnson made the Lakers the Western Conference's dominant team during the 1980s, leading Los Angeles to eight NBA Finals appearances and five league championships in their 10 years together.

After finishing an NBA-worst 27–55 in 1968–1969, the Milwaukee Bucks made UCLA all-American center Lew Alcindor the first pick of the 1969 NBA Draft. The 7'2", 250-pound Alcindor, who led the Bruins to three consecutive national championships in college, was touted as the NBA's next great big man—someone who likely would be able to cause the same types of problems for opposing teams during the 1970s that Wilt Chamberlain presented to his opponents the previous decade. Alcindor lived up to his advanced billing his first year in the league, earning 1969–1970 NBA Rookie of the Year honors by averaging 28.8 points and 14.5 rebounds per game. Alcindor's exceptional performance also earned him spots on both the All-NBA Second Team and the All-NBA Second Defensive Team. The Bucks improved their record to 56–26 during the regular season and subsequently defeated Philadelphia in the first round of the playoffs before losing to the Knicks in the Eastern Conference Finals.

After acquiring Oscar Robertson from Cincinnati prior to the start of the ensuing campaign, the Bucks established themselves as the NBA's dominant team in 1970–1971. Milwaukee compiled a league-best 66–16 record during the regular season, then lost only twice during the playoffs en route to capturing their only championship in franchise history. Alcindor won his first Most Valuable Player Award and earned a spot on the All-NBA First Team for the first of four straight times by averaging 16 rebounds and a league-leading 31.7 points per game. He subsequently won NBA Finals MVP honors by averaging 27 points per contest during Milwaukee's four-game sweep of the Baltimore Bullets.

Alcindor continued to perform at a high level in subsequent seasons, posting the following numbers over the next four years:

1971–1972: **34.8** PPG, 16.6 RPG
1972–1973: 30.2 PPG, 16.1 RPG
1973–1974: 27.0 PPG, 14.5 RPG
1974–1975: 30.0 PPG, 14.0 RPG

After initially embracing the Muslim religion while in college, Alcindor officially changed his name to Kareem Abdul-Jabbar prior to the start of the 1971–1972 campaign. In addition to leading the NBA in scoring that year, he finished either second or third in the league in each of the next three seasons. Jabbar also placed in the top five in rebounding all four years. He led the Bucks to the Midwest Division title in each of the first three seasons, to a spot in the Western Conference finals in both 1971–1972 and 1973–1974, and to a spot in the NBA Finals in 1973–1974. Jabbar was named the league's Most Valuable Player in both 1971–1972 and 1973–1974. He finished second in the voting to Boston's Dave Cowens in 1972–1973. Jabbar earned All-NBA First Team honors in each of the first three seasons and a spot on the All-NBA First Defensive Team in 1973–1974 and 1974–1975.

Aside from his great height, what made Jabbar so difficult for opposing centers to contend with was his tremendous versatility. He combined grace and agility with an overpowering offensive game.

Bob Cousy said that Jabbar "pretty much combines what Bill Russell and Wilt Chamberlain have individually specialized in."[1]

And then there was the skyhook, later referred to by Pat Riley as "basketball's ultimate offensive weapon." Virtually impossible to block, the shot made Jabbar the game's most unstoppable offensive force for more than a decade.

Following Milwaukee's last-place finish in the Midwest Division in 1974–1975, Jabbar asked to be traded to New York or Los Angeles. Feeling somewhat out of place in the Midwestern town, Jabbar believed that he would feel more at home in New York, where he grew up, or Los Angeles, where he attended college. The Bucks accommodated their unhappy superstar, trading him to the Lakers for center Elmore Smith, guard Brian Winters, and two rookies taken in the first round of the draft—forward David Meyers of UCLA and swingman Junior Bridgeman of Louisville.

In somewhat of a rebuilding stage following the recent retirements of Jerry West and Wilt Chamberlain, Los Angeles finished just 30–52 in 1974–1975, coming in last in the NBA's Pacific Division in the process. The presence of Jabbar in the Lakers lineup the following season enabled them to improve their record to 40–42. The new Los Angeles center earned his fourth MVP award by averaging 27.7 points and a league-leading 16.9 rebounds per contest during the season. Jabbar won his fifth MVP trophy in 1976–1977, when he led the Lakers to a 53–29 record and the Pacific Division title by posting averages of 26.2 points and 13.3 rebounds per game. Although the Lakers made the playoffs in each of the next two seasons, they finished the 1977–1978 and 1978–1979 campaigns with somewhat disappointing 45–37 and 47–35 records, respectively. They also came up short each postseason, being swept by Portland in the 1977 Western Conference finals, losing to Seattle in the first round of the 1978 play-offs, and being eliminated by Seattle again in 1979, this time in the conference semifinals.

Just when it appeared that Jabbar might never win another NBA champi-onship, he was joined on the Lakers in 1979 by a 20-year-old rookie with an infectious smile, a highly competitive spirit, and a world of talent.

After leading Michigan State University to the 1979 NCAA championship, Earvin "Magic" Johnson felt that he had nothing left to prove at the collegiate level. Therefore, the 20-year-old point guard decided to forsake his final two years of college eligibility and enter the 1979 NBA draft, where the Los Angeles Lakers selected him with the first overall pick.

Johnson demonstrated that he made the right choice his first year in the league, leading a Laker team that failed to make it past the Western Conference finals in any of the previous six seasons to the NBA championship. Los Angeles posted an outstanding 60–22 record during the 1979–1980 regular season, with Johnson averaging 18 points, 7.7 rebounds, and 7.3 assists per contest. Magic increased his output to 18.3 points, 10.5 rebounds, and 9.4 assists per game during the postseason, as the Lakers advanced to the NBA Finals by thrashing both Phoenix and Seattle in five games to capture the Western Conference title. Johnson saved his greatest performance, though, for the championship series.

An extremely talented Philadelphia 76ers team that disposed of the Boston Celtics in five games in the Eastern Conference Finals awaited Los Angeles in the NBA Finals. After splitting the first four contests with Philadelphia, the Lakers took a 3–2 lead in the series with a 108–103 victory in game 5. However, Los

Angeles center Kareem Abdul-Jabbar severely sprained his ankle while scoring 40 points during the Lakers win. With Jabbar unable to play in game 6 in Philadelphia, Johnson volunteered to start in his place at center. Playing forward and guard as well during the contest, Magic finished the game with 42 points, 15 rebounds, and 7 assists in leading the Lakers to a 123–107 series-clinching victory. For his tremendous all-around effort, Johnson was appropriately named NBA Finals MVP.

During his epic game 6 performance, Johnson put on display for all to see his rare combination of skills. His 6'9" frame made him the tallest point guard ever to play in the NBA. As such, he had the ability to do things that no one else in the league could do. Johnson could back his smaller defender down low, all the while surveying the entire court, and shoot over him if he chose to do so. He could grab a defensive rebound, dribble the length of the court, and either drive to the basket himself for a score or dish the ball off to one of his teammates. He could rebound like a forward and pass and handle the ball as well as any other guard in the league. Such was the versatility Johnson brought to the sport.

As much as Johnson affected his new team with his extraordinary all-around ability, he influenced his teammates with his unselfish style of play and his unbridled enthusiasm. Johnson used his tremendous ball-passing skills to make the other players around him better, often creating easy scoring opportunities for them by drawing opposing defenders to himself. The team-first mentality that he brought with him to the court each night became contagious to the other members of the squad, enabling him to quickly establish himself as an outstanding team leader. Johnson also passed on to his teammates his great love of the game and his passion for winning. Even the usually stoical Jabbar began displaying his emotions more on the court than ever before. Rejuvenated by his new teammate, Jabbar had an exceptional year in 1979–1980, averaging 24.8 points and 10.8 rebounds per game, winning his sixth MVP trophy and being named to the All-NBA First Team for the first time in three seasons.

Jabbar also performed extremely well the following year, posting averages of 26.2 points and 10.3 rebounds per contest, earning All-NBA First Team honors again, finishing third in the MVP voting, and helping the Lakers compile a 54–28 record during the regular season. But with Johnson missing more than half the campaign with an injury, Houston upset Los Angeles in the first round of the playoffs.

Johnson returned to the Lakers in 1981–1982 to help lead them to their second championship in three years. In fact, he teamed up with Jabbar the next eight years to make Los Angeles the Western Conference's dominant team. These are the numbers the two men posted in their five best seasons together during that period:

Jabbar
1981–1982: 23.9 PPG, 8.7 RPG
1982–1983: 21.8 PPG, 7.5 RPG
1983–1984: 21.5 PPG, 7.3 RPG
1984–1985: 22.0 PPG, 7.9 RPG
1985–1986: 23.4 PPG, 6.1 RPG
Johnson
1981–1982: 18.6 PPG, 9.5 APG, 9.6 RPG
1982–1983: 16.8 PPG, **10.5** APG, 8.6 RPG
1983–1984: 17.6 PPG, **13.1** APG, 7.3 RPG
1984–1985: 18.3 PPG, 12.6 APG, 6.2 RPG
1985–1986: 18.8 PPG, **12.6** APG, 5.9 RPG

Johnson finished either first or second in the league in assists all five seasons. He came extremely close to becoming just the second player in NBA history to average a triple-double for an entire season in 1981–1982. He also averaged a league-leading 2.67 steals per game that season. Johnson placed second to Larry Bird in the 1984–1985 MVP voting, and he finished third in the balloting three other times during the period. After being named to the All-NBA Second Team in 1981–1982, Johnson earned a spot on the First Team the other four years.

Jabbar finished in the league's top 10 in scoring in 1981–1982 and 1985–1986. He also placed among the league leaders in blocked shots in each of the first four seasons. Jabbar was named to the All-NBA First and Second Teams two times each during the period.

More important, the Lakers won the NBA championship in two of the five seasons. After compiling a 57–25 record during the 1981–1982 regular season, they breezed through the playoffs, posting a record of 12–2 during the postseason and defeating the 76ers in six games in the NBA Finals. Johnson earned Finals MVP honors for the second time in three years. The Lakers advanced to the NBA Finals in each of the next three years as well, being swept by Philadelphia in four games in 1983 and losing to Boston in seven games the following year. However, they captured their third championship in six years in 1985, exacting revenge on the Celtics by defeating their rivals in six games. Jabbar was named Finals MVP for the second time in his career. Los Angeles failed to repeat as NBA champions the following year, though, suffering a five-game defeat at the hands of underdog Houston in the Western Conference Finals.

Jabbar played three more years with the Lakers, failing to average more than 17.5 points or 6.7 assists per game in any of those seasons. But Los Angeles won the NBA championship in both 1987 and 1988, with the center proving to be a major contributor to both playoff victories. Jabbar performed particularly well during the 1987 postseason, averaging 19.2 points and 6.8 rebounds per game. He finally retired at the conclusion of the 1988–1989 campaign with career averages of 24.6 points and 11.2 rebounds per game. His 38,387 career points are the most in NBA history. He is also fourth on the all-time list with 17,440 rebounds, and he is third in blocked shots, with 3,189 to his credit. In addition to his six MVP awards, Jabbar earned 10 All-NBA First Team selections and five Second Team nominations. He also earned a spot on either the All-NBA First or Second Defensive Team a total of 11 times. Jabbar appeared in 19 All-Star games. He led the NBA in scoring twice, finished second three times, and placed in the league's top five on five other occasions. He averaged better than 20 points per game in each of his first 17 seasons, surpassing 25 points per contest 10 times and exceeding 30 points per game on four occasions. Jabbar led the league in blocked shots four times; he also topped the circuit in rebounding once, placing in the top five in the last category eight other times. He averaged better than 10 rebounds per game in each of his first 12 seasons, averaging more than 16 boards per contest four times. A fine passer out of the pivot, Jabbar also averaged more than five assists per game three times during his career. Many people consider him to be the greatest center in NBA history. If not, he certainly ranks among the top two or three big men of all time.

John Wooden, Jabbar's former coach at UCLA, had this to say about his former protégé: "In my opinion, he is the Most Valuable Player in the history of the game. No player of comparable size and ability was ever as quick and maneuverable, but his unselfish team play has been equally impressive."[2]

Referring to Jabbar's grace and fluidity on the court, Magic Johnson called him "the most beautiful athlete in sports."

As Jabbar approached the end of his career during the latter portion of the 1980s, Johnson continued to expand his offensive repertoire. Primarily a penetrator his first few years in the league, Magic developed an effective outside shot and a "baby hook shot" that enabled him to assume more of his team's offensive burden as Jabbar became less of a factor on that end of the floor. Johnson averaged a career-high 23.9 points per game during the Lakers' 1986–1987 championship campaign while leading the league with 12.2 assists per contest. His exceptional performance earned him his first Most Valuable Player Award. He also was named NBA Finals MVP for leading the Lakers past Boston in six games. Johnson averaged just under 20 points and 12 assists per game the following season, when Los Angeles repeated as NBA champions. He finished third in the MVP balloting.

Yet, even though Johnson became more of a scorer later in his career, he continued to make his greatest impact as a ball distributor. Known for his brilliant passing, which was as flamboyant as that of anyone in the league, Johnson had the ability to deliver the ball to his teammates with deadly accuracy in any number of ways. Be it a behind-the-back pass, a no-look pass, or a bounce pass from midcourt between multiple defenders, no one in the NBA delivered the ball more accurately or more imaginatively than Johnson.

Michael Cooper, a teammate of Johnson's on the Lakers for 11 seasons, once said, "There have been times when he has thrown passes and I wasn't sure where he was going. Then one of our guys catches the ball and scores, and I run back up the floor convinced that he must've thrown it through somebody."[3]

Although the Lakers failed to win the NBA title in any of the next three seasons, they made it back to the Finals in 1989 and 1991, losing to Detroit in 1989 and coming up short against Chicago in 1991. Nevertheless, Johnson earned league MVP honors in 1988–1989 and 1989–1990 before finishing second in the voting to Michael Jordan in 1990–1991. The Laker guard posted the following numbers over that three-year period:

1988–1989: 22.5 PPG, 12.8 APG
1989–1990: 22.3 PPG, 11.5 APG
1990–1991: 19.4 PPG, 12.5 APG

Johnson placed second in the league to John Stockton in assists all three years, earning a spot on the All-NBA First Team each season.

While still at the top of his game, Johnson announced his retirement at the conclusion of the 1990–1991 season after discovering that he was HIV positive. He attempted a comeback with the Lakers in 1995–1996, but he retired for good after appearing in only 32 games that season. He ended his career with 17,707 points and 10,141 assists, the fourth most in NBA history. Johnson posted averages of 19.5 points, 11.2 assists, and 7.2 rebounds per game over the course of his 13 NBA seasons. His average of 11.2 assists per contest is the highest in league history. Johnson averaged better than 10 assists per game nine consecutive seasons, leading the league in that category four times and finishing second on six other occasions. He also averaged more than 20 points per game four times, topping 18 points per contest six other times. He averaged more than eight rebounds per game on three separate occasions. In addition to being named league MVP three times, Johnson was named NBA Finals MVP three times. He was selected to the All-NBA First Team nine straight times, between 1983 and 1991. He also was a Second Team selection once. Johnson appeared in 12 All-Star games.

Larry Bird, Johnson's primary adversary throughout much of his career, expressed the great admiration he had for his rival when he said, "Magic is head and shoulders above everybody else. I've never seen anybody as good as him."[4]

The Lakers appeared in the NBA Finals eight times and won five league championships in the 10 years that Kareem Abdul-Jabbar and Magic Johnson played together in Los Angeles. Jabbar and Johnson combined to win three Most Valuable Player Awards, finishing in the top five in the MVP voting a total of nine times between them during that period. One or the other earned NBA Finals MVP honors four times. The two men combined for 10 appearances on the All-NBA First Team and another four appearances on the Second Team. Both men were named to the First Team in 1983–1984 and 1985–1986. In their 10 years together, Jabbar and Johnson made a total of 19 appearances on the All-Star Team. Had Jabbar truly been in his prime for more than just their first one or two seasons together, the tandem might have been able to surpass Michael Jordan and Scottie Pippen as the number-one duo on this list.

Notes

Numbers printed in bold indicate that the player led his league in a statistical category.

1. Bob Cousy, http://www.answers.com/topic/what-are-some-of-kareem-abdul-jabbars-acheivements.
2. John Wooden, http://www.johnwoodenquotes.com/.
3. Michael Cooper, http://www.answers.com/topic/magic-johnson.
4. Larry Bird, http://www.nba.com/history/players/johnsonm_bio.html.

CHAPTER 36

Bill Russell / Bob Cousy

The Boston Celtics dominated the National Basketball Association from 1957 to 1969, winning 11 out of a possible 13 league championships over that span of time. Although longtime Celtics general manager and head coach Red Auerbach played a significant role in the formation of the team, the person most responsible for the incredible success that Boston experienced throughout the period was Bill Russell, who served as Boston's center in every one of those championship campaigns. Russell revolutionized his position with his athleticism, uncanny shot-blocking ability, and extraordinary rebounding skills. The center clearly served as the driving force behind Boston's unprecedented championship run. However, Russell received a considerable amount of help from his teammates along the way, being assisted most notably by guard Bob Cousy on the Celtics' first six championship teams. Cousy, the league's most creative and innovative player during its formative years, combined with Russell to make the Celtics practically unbeatable during their time together.

After starring at Holy Cross University, Bob Cousy joined a Boston Celtics team in 1950, which finished last in the Eastern Division the previous season with a record of 22–46. Cousy made an immediate impact on his new team, leading the Celtics to a record of 39–30 and a second-place finish in the East in his first year in the league. The 6'1", 175-pound guard averaged 15.6 points and just under five assists per game as a rookie. Cousy increased his output to 21.7 points and 6.7 assists per contest in his second season, finishing third in the league in scoring and second in assists. In leading the Celtics to another second-place finish in the NBA's Eastern Division, Cousy earned All-NBA First Team honors for the first of 10 consecutive times.

Cousy didn't merely establish himself as one of the NBA's top players in his first two years in the league; he began to define the term *point guard*. Prior to Cousy's entrance into the league, the offensive roles of guards were not clearly delineated. However, with Cousy's penchant for controlling the ball and distributing it to his teammates for easy baskets, he became the sport's first true "point guard." He also evolved into the league's first showman, thrilling crowds with his fancy behind-the-back and no-look passes and his ability to put the ball either behind his back or between his legs without losing a step. Cousy's showmanship eventually prompted others to refer to him as the "Houdini of the Hardwood."

Contemporary Bob Davies spoke of Cousy's ball-handling ability: "Cousy was the best dribbler I played against. Trying to take the ball away from him was very difficult."[1]

Former teammate Tom Heinsohn spoke of Cousy's passing skills: "Once that ball reached his hands, the rest of us just took off, never bothering to look back. We didn't have to. He'd find us. When you got into a position to score, the ball would be there."[2]

In 1952–1953, Cousy began a string of eight consecutive seasons in which he led the NBA in assists. He averaged 7.7 assists per contest that season; he also finished third in the league in scoring for the second straight year, with an average of just under 20 points per game. Although the Celtics placed third in the Eastern Division, they finished just 1.5 games out of first, compiling an outstanding 46–25 record during the regular season. Cousy continued his exceptional play in each of the next three campaigns, posting the following numbers:

1953–1954: 19.2 PPG, **7.2** APG
1954–1955: 21.2 PPG, **7.9** APG
1955–1956: 18.8 PPG, **8.9** APG

In addition to leading the NBA in assists each year, Cousy finished among the league leaders in scoring all three times. The NBA didn't begin selecting a Most Valuable Player until 1955–1956, when it presented its first award to Bob Pettit. Cousy finished third in the voting.

Yet, in spite of Cousy's outstanding play, Boston failed in the postseason each year. The Celtics made the playoffs in each of Cousy's first six years in the league. However, they advanced beyond the first round only three times, losing in the Eastern Division finals the other three years. It wasn't until Bill Russell joined Cousy in Boston in 1956 that the Celtics became the NBA's dominant team.

Russell donned a Celtics uniform for the first time 24 games into the 1956–1957 season, after spending the first two months of the campaign leading the U.S. men's basketball team to victory in the Olympic Games. Not accustomed to tasting defeat, the 6'9", 225-pound center previously led the University of San Francisco to 55 consecutive victories, including back-to-back NCAA titles in 1955 and 1956. Russell continued his winning ways in the NBA, leading the Celtics to a league-best 44–28 record during the regular season by averaging just under 15 points and 20 rebounds in his 48 games with the team. Nevertheless, fellow Boston first-year man Tom Heinsohn claimed NBA Rookie of the Year honors, even though his numbers weren't nearly as impressive as Russell's. Although Heinsohn played in all 72 regular-season games for Boston, his 16.2 scoring average exceeded Russell's mark by only 1.2 points per contest, and he averaged half as many rebounds per game (9.8). Russell also lost out to teammate Cousy in the MVP voting. The point guard averaged 20.6 points and a league-leading 7.5 assists per game. The Celtics subsequently captured their first league championship by defeating the St. Louis Hawks in seven games in the NBA Finals. Russell averaged 24.4 rebounds and just under 14 points in Boston's 10 playoff games. Cousy posted averages of 20.2 points and 9.3 assists per contest during the postseason.

Led by their two great stars, the Celtics finished with the NBA's best regular-season record again in 1957–1958, compiling 49 victories against only 23 losses. Cousy averaged 18 points and a league-leading 7.1 assists per game. Russell posted averages of 16.6 points and 22.7 rebounds per contest. The center's 22.7 rebounding average exceeded that of league runner-up Bob Pettit by more than five boards per game. Russell's exceptional performance earned him a spot on the All-NBA Second Team and his first league MVP trophy. The Celtics faced St. Louis again in the NBA Finals, suffering the humiliation of being dethroned as league champions when the Hawks defeated them in six games. Russell saw limited action in the final four contests after injuring his ankle in game 3. His absence from the Boston lineup for much of the decisive sixth game enabled Hawks superstar Bob Pettit to shred the Celtics' interior defense for 50 points during his team's 110–109 victory.

Boston posted at least 52 victories in each of the next eight seasons, winning the NBA championship each year. The team proved to be particularly dominant in 1960–1961, 1961–1962, 1963–1964, and 1964–1965. In the first of those campaigns, the Celtics compiled a record of 57–22 during the regular season before losing just twice during the playoffs en route to winning their third straight title. They finished 60–20 the following season before being severely tested by Philadelphia and Los Angeles in the playoffs, winning both series in seven games. After winning 59 games during the 1963–1964 season, the Celtics coasted to their sixth consecutive championship, losing only once to both Cincinnati and San Francisco in the postseason. The 1964–1965 squad finished 62–18 before squeaking by Wilt Chamberlain's Philadelphia 76ers in the Eastern Division finals. Boston had a much less difficult time with the Lakers in the NBA Finals, needing only five games to dispose of their Western Division counterparts.

While Russell served as the anchor of all eight championship teams, Cousy played for only the first five clubs. The two men posted the following numbers in their five remaining years together:

Russell
1958–59: 16.7 PPG, **23.0** RPG
1959–60: 18.2 PPG, 24.0 RPG
1960–61: 16.9 PPG, 23.9 RPG
1961–62: 18.9 PPG, 23.6 RPG
1962–63: 16.8 PPG, 23.6 RPG
Cousy
1958–59: 20.0 PPG, **8.6** APG
1959–60: 19.4 PPG, **9.5** APG
1960–61: 18.1 PPG, 7.7 APG
1961–62: 15.7 PPG, 7.8 APG
1962–63: 13.2 PPG, 6.8 APG

After leading the league in rebounding in 1958–1959, Russell placed second to Wilt Chamberlain the other four years. The Boston center finished second to Bob Pettit in the 1958–1959 MVP voting, then placed second to Chamberlain in the balloting the following year, before being named the league's Most Valuable Player at the end of each of the next three seasons.

Cousy led the league in assists for the seventh and eighth times in succession the first two seasons, then finished third in the rankings the last three years. In a 1959 contest against the Minneapolis Lakers, he compiled an NBA record 19 assists in one half. Cousy finished fourth in the MVP voting in both 1958–1959 and 1959–1960.

The 1962–1963 campaign ended up being the final season that Russell and Cousy spent as teammates. Although he mounted a brief seven-game comeback as a 41-year-old player/coach with the Cincinnati Royals in 1969–1970, Cousy announced his retirement at the conclusion of the 1962–1963 season. He ended his career with 16,060 points scored and 6,955 assists and with averages of 18.4 points and 7.5 assists per game. Cousy finished in the league's top five in assists in each of his 13 NBA seasons. He also finished in the top 10 in the league in scoring eight times, placing in the top five on four occasions. Cousy averaged better than 20 points per game four times during his career, posting a scoring average between 18 and 22 points per game in 10 straight seasons at one point. In addition to his 10 All-NBA First Team selections, Cousy earned a spot on the Second Team twice. He was a 13-time NBA All-Star and a two-time All-Star Game MVP.

Russell played six more years in the league, leading the Celtics to five more championships. He captured his fifth Most Valuable Player Award at the conclusion of the 1964–1965 campaign, a season in which he averaged 14.1 points and a league-leading 24.1 rebounds per contest. Russell retired at the end of the 1968–1969 season, after serving as Boston's player/coach the previous three years. He ended his career with 21,620 rebounds—the second most in league history. He posted averages of 15.1 points and 22.5 rebounds per game over his 13 NBA seasons, increasing his output to 16.2 points and 24.9 rebounds per contest during the postseason.

The centerpiece of the Celtic dynasty, Russell battled Wilt Chamberlain for preeminence among NBA centers for much of his career, establishing himself in the process as the greatest winner in the history of professional team sports. Though not necessarily the most talented player in the game, Russell possessed many intangible qualities that enabled him, perhaps more than anyone else, to influence the outcomes of contests. His unselfishness and willingness to sacrifice his own personal statistics for the success of his team made the other players around him better. And his incredible intensity, which caused him to view each and every game as a battle of wills, rubbed off on his teammates.

Tom Heinsohn, Russell's teammate for nine years, provided insight into the center's persona: "I think Russell was the foxiest, smartest, meanest player, psychologically, that ever played the game. Whatever it took to win, Russell would do."[3]

Forward Chet Walker, who played against Russell as a member of the Philadelphia 76ers, noted, "The whole game for Bill Russell was a psychological event. He was always testing you."[4]

Russell's tremendous desire and determination often seemed to allow him to will his team to victory. He played his best when the stakes were highest, saving many of his greatest performances for must-win situations. Russell faced 11 decisive playoff games during his career, and he never lost one. He averaged just under 30 rebounds in those 11 contests. In game 7 of the 1960 NBA Finals against the St. Louis Hawks and Bob Pettit, Russell scored 22 points and pulled down 35 rebounds. In game 7 of the 1962 Finals against the Lakers, he scored 30 points. In an overtime game 7 of the 1964 Finals, once again against the Lakers, Russell scored 30 points and pulled down 40 rebounds.

Russell's intensity and desire contributed greatly to Boston's winning ways. But the team also benefited greatly from the center's outstanding athleticism, which enabled him to alter the manner in which the pro game was played. Prior to Russell's arrival in Boston, the NBA game was played mostly below the rim. Most centers were not particularly agile, and few of them were shot blockers. But Russell revolutionized the sport with his intimidating defense, and his superb rebounding and outlet passing keyed the famed Celtics fast break. His uncanny ability to block shots allowed him to cover up for the gambling defensive tendencies of teammates K. C. Jones and Tom Heinsohn and for the defensive shortcomings of Bob Cousy.

Cousy described what it was like playing with Russell: "He not only controlled the backboard completely, but he revolutionized the defensive game."[5]

Heinsohn spoke of the impact that Russell made on the defensive end of the court: "He had such great quickness and agility that he could play three or four guys on the same trip up the court . . . switch off, go back to his own man, block the shot; so he would disrupt their entire offense."[6]

In *From Set Shot to Slam Dunk*, forward George Yardley discussed the kind of impact that he felt Russell made on the game: "There's no question that Bill Russell's coming into the league changed the game. You just couldn't take a lay-up against him. He just took that portion of the game away from you. . . . He was certainly the most intimidating, most dominant person that played sports."[7]

Perhaps Russell's biggest supporter was Red Auerbach, who had this to say: "He made shot-blocking an art and proved that quickness, finesse and brains were a match for brawn."[8]

Ed Macauley—who was ironically part of the trade that allowed the Celtics to draft Russell—said in *From Set Shot to Slam Dunk*, "Russell was absolutely perfect for that ball club. . . . They didn't have a great defensive club, but with Russell back there you didn't need one because no one could get closer than 15 feet. We played them a couple of times when Russell wasn't in the lineup, and they were just an ordinary ball club. With him, they were just superb."[9]

Macauley added, "Russell was the most dominant player to ever play the game. There have been a lot of ballplayers who are better, individually—better shooters, dribblers, rebounders. But no one individual who could put it all together was as important to a particular team as Bill Russell was."[10]

In addition to being named the NBA's Most Valuable Player five times, Russell finished in the top three in the balloting on four other occasions. He was named to the All-NBA First Team three times, and he was selected to the Second Team eight times. Russell earned a spot on the All-Star Team in all but his first season. He finished in the top five in the league in rebounding in each of his 13 seasons, leading the league four times and finishing second seven other times. Russell averaged better than 20 rebounds per game in 10 of his 13 seasons, never averaging fewer than 18.6 boards per contest during his career. He averaged at least 22 rebounds per game in nine seasons, posting a career-high 24.7 rebounding average in 1963–1964. Russell's career rebounding average of 22.5 places him second to Wilt Chamberlain, who averaged 22.9 rebounds per contest over the course of his career. Meanwhile, Russell's career playoff average of 24.9 rebounds per game is the best ever. Although not known as a scorer,

Russell averaged better than 15 points per game in seven seasons, with his personal best being the 18.9 scoring average he compiled in his third MVP season, 1961–1962. Generally acknowledged to be the greatest defensive player in the history of the game, Russell was named the Greatest Player in the History of the NBA by the Professional Basketball Writers Association of America in 1980.

In an interview conducted just prior to the turn of the century, Red Auerbach stated, "There is no doubt in my mind that there has never been, even to this day, a better center than Bill Russell."[11]

In their seven seasons as teammates, Bill Russell and Bob Cousy led Boston to seven NBA Finals appearances and six league championships. Cousy was named the league's Most Valuable Player in 1956–1957. Russell won the award in 1960–1961, 1961–1962, and 1962–1963. He also placed second in the voting in 1958–1959 and 1959–1960, with Cousy finishing fourth in the balloting both years. Both men were named to the All-NBA First Team in 1958–1959. Cousy also made the First Team four other times during the period, earning a spot on the Second Team the other two years. Russell was picked for the First Team again in 1962–1963, and he earned a spot on the Second Team in four of the other five years. Russell finished either first or second in the league in rebounding all seven years. Meanwhile, Cousy led the NBA in assists four times, finishing third the other three years. The two men combined for 13 appearances on the All-Star Team in their seven seasons together.

Notes

Numbers printed in bold indicate that the player led his league in a statistical category.

1. Charles Salzberg, *From Set Shot to Slam Dunk* (New York: Dutton, 1987), 57.

2. Tom Heinsohn, http://www.nba.com/history/players/cousy_bio.html.

3. *SportsCentury: Fifty Greatest Athletes—Bill Russell*, television program (ESPN, 1999).

4. *Fifty Greatest Athletes—Bill Russell*.

5. *Fifty Greatest Athletes—Bill Russell*.

6. *Fifty Greatest Athletes—Bill Russell*.

7. Salzberg, *From Set Shot to Slam Dunk*, 176.

8. *Fifty Greatest Athletes—Bill Russell*.

9. Salzberg, *From Set Shot to Slam Dunk*, 101–2.

10. Salzberg, *From Set Shot to Slam Dunk*, 101–2.

11. *Fifty Greatest Athletes—Bill Russell*.

CHAPTER 37

Elgin Baylor / Jerry West

Bill Russell's great Boston Celtics teams repeatedly thwarted Elgin Baylor and Jerry West in their attempts to win an NBA championship together. Nevertheless, the two Los Angeles Laker greats led their team to five Western Division titles and seven NBA Finals appearances between 1961 and 1970, establishing themselves during that time as the most explosive one-two scoring punch in basketball history.

With big George Mikan manning the pivot, the Minneapolis Lakers dominated the NBA during the league's formative years, winning four out of a possible five championships from 1950 to 1954. However, following Mikan's retirement at the conclusion of the 1955–1956 campaign, Minneapolis posted a losing record in each of the next two seasons, finishing with a league-worst 19–53 mark in 1957–1958. The Lakers' record improved to 33–39 the following season, though, after they selected Seattle University forward Elgin Baylor with the first pick of the 1958 NBA draft.

Baylor had a brilliant first year in the NBA, compiling the league's fourth-highest scoring average (24.9 ppg) and third-best rebounding average (15.0 rpg) over the course of the 1958–1959 campaign en route to earning Rookie of the Year honors and a spot on the All-NBA First Team for the first of seven consecutive times. Even though Minneapolis finished 16 games behind Bob Pettit's St. Louis Hawks in the NBA's Western Division during the regular season, Baylor led the Lakers to a six-game victory over the Hawks in the Western Division Finals. However, Boston subsequently swept Minneapolis in the NBA Finals. Baylor averaged 25.5 points and 12 rebounds per game during his first postseason.

Although the Lakers finished a disappointing 25–50 the following year, Baylor continued to establish himself as one of the league's premier players, placing in the top five in scoring and rebounding once again, with averages of 29.6

points and 16.4 rebounds per game. In addition to gaining general recognition as one of the NBA's best players by his second season, Baylor developed a reputation for being the league's most exciting and dynamic performer. His seemingly endless array of moves made him virtually unstoppable on offense. Baylor's arsenal included a good midrange jumper and a wide variety of post-up moves that often left defenders talking to themselves. The 6'5", 225-pound power forward used his great physical strength to establish his position down low. He then utilized a series of head fakes, spin moves, and his incredible ability to hang in the air to get off his shot against even the tallest of defenders. When Baylor made up his mind to score, no one could stop him. He scored 64 points in a game against Boston at Minneapolis on November 8, 1959. Baylor tallied another 71 points against the Knicks in a game played at Madison Square Garden on November 15, 1960. He also pulled down 25 rebounds in that contest. With Baylor's offensive creativity representing something new to the NBA, it ended up greatly influencing future generations of players.

Baylor had perhaps his greatest season after the Lakers moved to Los Angeles prior to the start of the 1960–1961 campaign. In addition to finishing second in the league to Wilt Chamberlain in scoring with an average of 34.8 points per game, he finished fourth in rebounding with a career-high mark of 19.8 boards per contest. Baylor's extraordinary performance helped the Lakers improve their regular-season record to 36–43, earning him a third-place finish in the league MVP voting at the end of the year. The Lakers subsequently took St. Louis to seven games before finally losing to the Hawks in the Western Division Finals. Baylor played magnificently in the team's 12 playoff games, averaging just over 38 points and 15 rebounds per contest.

The Lakers' initial season in Los Angeles also marked the first time that an extremely talented rookie out of West Virginia named Jerry West donned the team's colors. The 6'2½", 185-pound guard made his NBA debut during the 1960–1961 season, averaging 17.6 points, 7.7 rebounds, and 4.2 assists per game as a rookie. Although West's offensive game continued to evolve in future seasons, he immediately demonstrated the tremendous versatility that eventually enabled him to become one of the greatest players ever. Possessing an exceptional jump shot, West scored the majority of his points from the outside. His quick release, long arms, and extraordinary leaping ability made it extremely difficult for defenders to block his shot. But West also had outstanding quickness that enabled him to drive to the basket and either score from the inside or create open-shot opportunities for his teammates.

Former Boston Celtics player and head coach Tom Heinsohn discussed West's offensive versatility: "You couldn't play a small guy against him because he'd shoot over him. You couldn't play a big guy against him to try to take away the jump shot because he'd go around him with his speed."[1]

West blossomed into a star in his second year in the league, joining his teammate Baylor among the NBA's elite. These are the numbers the two men posted over the next four seasons:

1961–1962
Elgin Baylor: 38.3 PPG, 18.6 RPG, 4.6 APG
Jerry West: 30.8 PPG, 7.9 RPG, 5.4 APG
1962–1963
Elgin Baylor: 34.0 PPG, 14.3 RPG, 4.8 APG
Jerry West: 27.1 PPG, 7.0 RPG, 5.6 APG
1963–1964
Elgin Baylor: 25.4 PPG, 12.0 RPG, 4.4 APG
Jerry West: 28.7 PPG, 6.0 RPG, 5.6 APG
1964–1965:
Elgin Baylor: 27.1 PPG, 12.8 RPG, 3.8 APG
Jerry West: 31.0 PPG, 6.0 RPG, 4.9 APG

Both men were named to the All-NBA First Team all four years. Although Baylor appeared in only 48 games in 1961–1962, he posted the second-highest scoring average in the league (behind Wilt Chamberlain's all-time record, 50.4 ppg). West's average of 30.8 points per game placed him fifth in the league in scoring. West's and Baylor's combined scoring average of 69.1 points per game that year is the second-highest single-season average for two teammates in NBA history, trailing the 72.3 combined average that Chamberlain and Paul Arizin posted for the Philadelphia Warriors the same season. Baylor's average of 18.6 rebounds per game represented the fifth-highest mark in the league. The power forward finished fourth in the league MVP voting, while West finished fifth in the balloting.

Baylor placed second in the league in scoring again the following season; he also finished fifth in rebounding for the second consecutive year. West's scoring average of 27.1 points per game placed him sixth in the league rankings. Baylor finished second in the MVP voting, while West came in fifth.

Both men finished in the top 10 in scoring again in 1963–1964. Baylor also finished ninth in rebounding, while West finished fourth in assists. The following season, Baylor finished fourth in the league in scoring and 10th in rebounding. West placed second in the league in scoring and finished sixth in assists en route to earning a third-place finish in the MVP balloting.

In spite of the tremendous individual performances turned in by Baylor and West throughout the period, the two men invariably experienced terrible disappointment and utter futility at the end of each season.

The Lakers captured the Western Division title in 1961–1962, finishing the regular season with a record of 54–26. However, they lost to Boston in seven games in the NBA Finals, dropping the final contest 110–107 in overtime. West averaged 31.5 points in the Lakers' 13 playoff games. Baylor was even better, averaging 38.6 points and 17.7 rebounds per game during the postseason. The forward turned in an epic performance in game 5 against the Celtics, scoring an NBA Finals record 61 points during the Lakers' 126–121 victory at Boston. Reflecting on Baylor's performance that night, legendary Boston head coach and general manager Red Auerbach later said, "Baylor was so good in that game that he fouled out all of our forwards."[2]

After finishing first in the Western Division again in 1962–1963, the Lakers lost to the Celtics in the NBA Finals for the second straight year, this time in six games. West averaged just under 28 points per game for Los Angeles during the postseason. Baylor posted averages of 32.6 points and 13.6 rebounds per contest.

Los Angeles failed to return to the NBA Finals the following year, losing to the St. Louis Hawks in the division semifinals. However, after capturing their third Western Division title in four years in 1964–1965 by compiling a 49–31 regular-season record, the Lakers again advanced to the NBA Finals, where they faced the Celtics once more. The Lakers found themselves compromised, though, when they had to play the series without Baylor, whose broken kneecap kept him out of the playoffs. The Celtics prevailed in five games, defeating Los Angeles for the third of six times during West's and Baylor's playing days. Nevertheless, West began to cultivate his reputation that postseason as one of the greatest playoff performers in NBA history by averaging 40.6 points per game in his team's 11 playoff contests. He later became the only player to be named Finals MVP in a losing effort, earning the honor in 1969 when the Celtics defeated the Lakers in seven games. In the 108–106 game 7 loss, West scored 42 points, pulled down 13 rebounds, and assisted on 12 baskets, despite playing with an injured hamstring. The Laker guard's consistently exceptional performances under pressure eventually earned him the nickname "Mr. Clutch."

In truth, it was the Lakers' lack of a dominant big man that ultimately led to their downfall in most of those seasons. Not until they acquired Wilt Chamberlain during the 1968–1969 campaign did they have anyone to match up against Boston's Bill Russell. Unfortunately, Baylor was no longer at the top of his game by then. He required surgery at the end of the 1964–1965 season to repair his broken kneecap, limiting him somewhat the rest of his career. Although Baylor remained one of the league's top forwards, he lacked much of the explosiveness that he had his first few years in the league. He also lost some of his uncanny ability to hang in the air long after his defender's feet touched the ground. Baylor averaged only 16.6 points and 9.6 rebounds in his 65 games in 1965–1966.

Yet, even at less than 100 percent, Baylor was still an exceptional performer. He mounted a comeback in 1966–1967, combining with West the next four seasons to once again give the Lakers the league's most prolific scoring tandem. These are the figures the two men posted from 1966 to 1970:

1966–1967
Elgin Baylor: 26.6 PPG, 12.8 RPG, 3.1 APG
Jerry West: 28.7 PPG, 5.9 RPG, 6.8 APG
1967–1968
Elgin Baylor: 26.0 PPG, 12.2 RPG, 4.6 APG
Jerry West: 26.3 PPG, 5.8 RPG, 6.1 APG
1968–1969
Elgin Baylor: 24.8 PPG, 10.6 RPG, 5.4 APG
Jerry West: 25.9 PPG, 4.3 RPG, 6.9 APG
1969–1970
Elgin Baylor: 24.0 PPG, 10.4 RPG, 5.4 APG
Jerry West: **31.2** PPG, 4.6 RPG, 7.5 APG

After a sensational 1965–1966 campaign in which he finished second in the league in scoring with an average of 31.3 points per game, placed second in the league MVP voting, and earned All-NBA First Team honors for the fifth straight year, West continued his stellar play the next four years. In addition to leading the league in scoring in 1969–1970, the Laker guard posted one of the top three scoring averages in each of the other three seasons. He also finished fourth in the NBA in assists in both 1966–1967 and 1969–1970. West was named to the All-NBA First Team in 1966–1967 and 1969–1970, and he earned a spot on the Second Team the other two seasons, even though he missed 31 games in 1967–1968 and another 21 contests in 1968–1969. He finished second in the MVP voting in 1969–1970.

Baylor finished among the league leaders in scoring in each of the first three seasons. He was named to the All-NBA First Team all three times, and he placed third in the MVP balloting in 1967–1968.

After being eliminated in the first round of the playoffs in 1967, the Lakers advanced to the NBA Finals in each of the next three seasons, losing to Boston in 1968 and 1969 and falling to New York in 1970. Baylor appeared in only 54 games in 1969–1970, and Chamberlain missed all but 12 games over the course of the regular season, forcing West to carry the team into the playoffs virtually by himself. The Los Angeles guard continued his exceptional play during the postseason, averaging 31.2 points and 8.4 assists in the Lakers' 18 playoff contests.

The Laker defeat at the hands of the Knicks in the 1970 NBA Finals ended up being one of eight finals losses that West endured during his career. Taking into account his tremendous competitive spirit and his overwhelming desire to excel, there is little doubt that those defeats ate away at him from within. Longtime Lakers broadcaster Chick Hearn once told the *National Sports Daily*, "He took a loss harder than any player I've ever known. He would sit by himself and stare into space. A loss just ripped his guts out."[3]

Boston guard Sam Jones, who faced West in several of those finals series, discussed his foe's competitive spirit: "When you talk about coming to play each night, Jerry West was that player. He was the guy I did not want to play."[4]

West finally got the NBA championship he craved in 1972, when the Lakers defeated the Knicks in five games in the Finals. Still, he later said that the victory didn't come close to erasing the memory of all the other losses.

Sadly, Baylor wasn't able to share in his former teammate's joy when the Lakers captured their first championship since moving to Los Angeles more than a decade earlier. Just a shell of his former self by the 1970s, the forward appeared in a total of only 11 games in his final two years with the team before ironically announcing his retirement early during the Lakers' 1971–1972 championship campaign. Yet, in spite of his inability to win an NBA title, the legacy that Baylor left behind is that of one of the greatest players in league history.

Baylor ended his career with 23,149 points and 11,463 rebounds. His scoring average of 27.4 points per game is the fourth highest in NBA history. An exceptional rebounder as well, Baylor averaged 13.5 rebounds per contest over the course of his career. He is one of only 14 players to score 20,000 points and compile 10,000 rebounds. Baylor averaged better than 20 points and 10 rebounds per game in 11 of his first 12 seasons, topping 25 points and 12 rebounds per contest nine times each. He was selected to the All-NBA First Team a total of 10 times, and he appeared in 11 All-Star Games. He finished in the top five in scoring eight times, placing second on four occasions. Baylor also finished in the top five in rebounding five times. In 134 career playoff games, Baylor averaged 27 points and almost 13 rebounds per contest.

People who were fortunate enough to have seen Baylor play still consider him to be one of the most talented players ever to perform in the NBA.

Jerry West told *Hoop* magazine in 1992, "I hear people talking about forwards today and I haven't seen many that can compare with him."[5]

Bill Sharman, who played against Baylor as a member of the Boston Celtics and later coached him with the Lakers, told the *Los Angeles Times* at Baylor's retirement in 1971, "I say, without reservation, that Elgin Baylor is the greatest corner-man who ever played pro basketball."[6]

Tommy Hawkins, a teammate of Baylor for six seasons and an opponent for four, told the *San Francisco Examiner*, "Elgin certainly didn't jump as high as Michael Jordan, but he had the greatest variety of shots of anyone. He would take it in and hang and shoot from all these angles . . . put spin on the ball. Elgin had incredible strength. He could post up Bill Russell. He could pass like Magic Johnson and dribble with the best guards in the league."[7]

Hawkins then added, "Pound for pound, no one was ever as great as Elgin Baylor."[8]

While Baylor left the game in 1971, West remained with the Lakers through the 1973–1974 campaign. He retired at the end of the season with career totals of 25,192 points and 6,238 assists. He averaged 27 points and 6.7 assists per game over the course of his 14 NBA seasons. West averaged more than 20 points per contest in all but his rookie season, posting a scoring average in excess of 25 points per game in 11 straight seasons at one point. He averaged more than 30 points per game four times. In addition to leading the NBA in scoring in 1969–1970, West placed among the league's top five in that category on five other occasions.

More than just a great scorer, West was also a fine passer and playmaker. After averaging 9.5 assists per game in 1970–1971, he averaged a league-leading 9.7 assists per contest during the Lakers' 1971–1972 championship season. West finished in the top five in assists five times during his career, averaging at least six assists per contest in each of his last nine seasons.

Perhaps the most overlooked aspect of West's game, though, was his defense. He was a terrific defensive player who, because of his phenomenal scoring ability, failed to get the credit he deserved for his outstanding play on that end of the court.

Bill Sharman's final year in the league with Boston was West's rookie season with the Lakers. Sharman also later coached West in Los Angeles. In *From Set Shot to Slam Dunk*, he says, "Although they didn't keep track of the stats as they do today, I would say that Jerry West blocked more shots and had more steals than any guard who ever played in the NBA. He had those long arms and great quickness that was very deceptive until he stole the ball from you a few times."[9]

Sharman went on to say, "He is one of the very few players that was a true superstar on offense and defense. There are only a couple of other players in the history of the league that you can say that about at both ends of the court."[10]

West's defense earned him a spot on the NBA All-Defensive First Team four times and a place on the Second Team once. He also earned 10 selections to the All-NBA First Team, two to the Second Team, and a spot on the All-Star Team in each of his 14 NBA seasons. West's career scoring average of 27 points per game places him fifth on the all-time list. One of the greatest postseason performers in league history, West averaged 29.1 points per game in 153 playoff contests. That figure places him second to Michael Jordan all-time. West averaged better than 30 points per game seven years in the playoffs, and he led the Lakers into the Finals nine times over a 13-year period.

In their 10 full seasons as teammates, Elgin Baylor and Jerry West combined for 14 All-NBA First Team selections and another two selections to the Second Team. Both men earned a spot on the First Team in the same season on five occasions. They also combined for 11 top-five finishes in the league MVP voting and a total of 19 All-Star Game appearances as teammates. Both men averaged more than 25 points per game in the same season six times, and they both finished in the league's top five in scoring three times. During their time together, Baylor and West combined for a total of 12 top-five finishes in scoring, leading the league once and finishing second six other times. One or the other compiled a scoring average in excess of 30 points per game a total of seven times. Baylor finished in the top five in rebounding three times as West's teammate, while the Laker guard placed in the league's top five in assists four times while playing alongside Baylor. The two men combined to average more than 60 points per game in two seasons, also totaling more than 50 points per contest between them seven other times. They also combined to average more than 25 rebounds and 12 assists per game two times each. Although they failed to win an NBA title, Baylor and West appeared in the NBA Finals a total of seven times as teammates.

Notes

Numbers printed in bold indicate that the player led his league in a statistical category.

1. *SportsCentury—Jerry West*, television program (ESPN, 2000).
2. *SportsCentury—Elgin Baylor*, television program (ESPN, 2000).
3. Chick Hearn, http://www.nba.com/history/players/west_bio.html.
4. *SportsCentury—Jerry West*.
5. Jerry West, http://www.nba.com/history/players/baylor_bio.html.
6. Bill Sharman, http://www.nba.com/history/players/baylor_bio.html.
7. Tommy Hawkins, http://www.nba.com/history/players/baylor_bio.html.
8. Tommy Hawkins, http://www.nba.com/history/players/baylor_bio.html.
9. Charles Salzberg, *From Set Shot to Slam Dunk* (New York: Dutton, 1987), 154.
10. Salzberg, *From Set Shot to Slam Dunk*, 154.

CHAPTER 38

Karl Malone / John Stockton

Although they never won an NBA championship as teammates, Karl Malone and John Stockton created basketball magic in Utah for almost two decades. Malone and Stockton led the Jazz into the playoffs in each of the 18 seasons they played alongside one another, making their team a viable contender for the league championship throughout virtually the entire decade of the 1990s. During their time together, Malone established himself as arguably the greatest power forward in NBA history, while Stockton clearly demonstrated that he was among the greatest point guards of all time.

After relocating from New Orleans to Utah prior to the start of the 1979–1980 season, the Jazz proved to be one of the NBA's least successful franchises, winning more games than they lost just once between 1979 and 1985, including posting at least 52 losses in four of those six seasons. Utah's fortunes began to change during the mid-1980s, though, when the team made two extraordinary selections in consecutive NBA drafts. After selecting Gonzaga University point guard John Stockton in 1984, the Jazz drafted Louisiana Tech power forward Karl Malone one year later. Utah finished each of the next 18 seasons with a winning record, advancing to the playoffs each year and capturing five Midwest Division titles.

The 6'1", 175-pound Stockton saw limited playing time his first three seasons with the Jazz, never averaging more than 24 minutes, eight points, or eight assists per game between 1984 and 1987. However, after breaking into Utah's starting lineup in 1987–1988, Stockton quickly developed into the NBA's best passer and perhaps its greatest "pure" point guard. Stockton didn't possess the size, strength, and scoring ability of players such as Oscar Robertson, Magic Johnson, and Walt Frazier. He also lacked the great quickness and explosive scoring ability of Isiah Thomas. But Stockton surpassed everyone else in terms of his ability to set up his teammates for scoring opportunities. He turned passing into an art form, distributing the ball to his teammates in perfect shooting position or in full stride as they headed toward the basket. Stockton knew where his teammates liked to receive the ball, and he delivered it to them with precision, thereby making the other players around him much better than they otherwise would have been.

In discussing Stockton's ability to deliver the ball with great accuracy, former NBA opponent Craig Ehlo once said, "My favorite pass of his is not the feed on the fast break. It's when he first catches the outlet and before he takes a dribble. His head is up and looking down court and he's throwing that baseball pass to the guy streaking for the basket. Someone's busting their butt, and he's rewarding them."[1]

High-scoring forward Tom Chambers, who spent some time with Stockton in Utah, suggested, "There's no mustard on the hot dog. He sees you and delivers it. He sees you a lot of times when other people don't, and he knows how to read people and get the ball to them in the right situation."[2]

Jerry Sloan, Stockton's longtime coach in Utah, added, "He has a sixth sense. It's not just seeing the floor, it's recalling the floor—remembering who is where, and anticipating where they'll be."[3]

Meanwhile, former NBA great and current television analyst Charles Barkley called Stockton "the best pure point guard who ever played the game."[4]

Magic Johnson, who is usually ranked ahead of Stockton in the pantheon of great NBA point guards, found no fault in Barkley's assessment: "There is nobody that can distribute the ball, plus lead his team, like John Stockton. He is the best at it."[5]

The numbers tend to bear out the contentions made by Barkley and Johnson. When Stockton averaged 14.7 points and 13.8 assists per game in his first year as a starter, he began a string of 10 consecutive seasons in which he averaged better than 14 points and 10 assists per game. He led the NBA in assists in the first nine of those years, thereby eclipsing Bob Cousy's previous league mark of eight consecutive assists titles. These are Stockton's numbers from his five best seasons during that stretch:

1987–1988: 14.7 PPG, **13.8** APG
1988–1989: 17.1 PPG, **13.6** APG
1989–1990: 17.2 PPG, **14.5** APG
1990–1991: 17.2 PPG, **14.2** APG
1991–1992: 15.8 PPG, **13.7** APG

Stockton earned All-NBA First or Second Team honors in eight of the nine seasons in which he led the league in assists, earning a spot on the First Team on two occasions. His mark of 14.5 assists per game in 1989–1990 is a single-season

NBA record. In addition to leading the league in assists each year, Stockton placed in the NBA's top five in steals eight times, topping the league in that category twice. A solid scorer as well, Stockton was an outstanding perimeter shooter who shot better than 50 percent from the field over the course of his career.

But it was as a passer that Stockton truly excelled. And at the receiving end of so many of his passes was Karl Malone, the powerfully built 6'9", 250-pound power forward with whom Stockton ran the pick-and-roll to perfection.

Karl Malone earned a starting job in Utah's frontcourt in his rookie season of 1985–1986, averaging just under 15 points and nine rebounds per game. Possessing great physical strength and surprising quickness and agility for a man his size, Malone proved to be one of the NBA's most versatile power forwards in subsequent seasons. In addition to being an outstanding rebounder and a strong defender, he quickly developed into one of the league's top scorers, possessing both a soft touch from the outside and a solid post-up game. Malone's wide array of skills enabled him to establish himself as the NBA's prototypical power forward. In his second year in the league, the "Mailman" began a string of nine consecutive seasons in which he averaged better than 20 points and 10 rebounds per contest:

1986–87: 21.7 PPG, 10.4 RPG
1987–88: 27.7 PPG, 12.0 RPG
1988–89: 29.1 PPG, 10.7 RPG
1989–90: 31.0 PPG, 11.1 RPG
1990–91: 29.0 PPG, 11.8 RPG
1991–92: 28.0 PPG, 11.2 RPG
1992–93: 27.0 PPG, 11.2 RPG
1993–94: 25.2 PPG, 11.5 RPG
1994–95: 26.7 PPG, 10.6 RPG

Malone finished in the top five in scoring in all but the first season, placing second to Michael Jordan on four occasions. He also finished in the top five in rebounding four times during that stretch. Malone was named to the All-NBA First Team seven times during that period, and he was picked for the Second Team once. Stockton joined Malone on the First Team in 1993–1994 and 1994–1995.

The Jazz improved dramatically during that period, capturing two Midwest Division titles, making the playoffs each year, and surpassing 50 victories six times. They were particularly outstanding in 1994–1995, posting a 60–22 record during the regular season. However, Utah made it past the Western Conference semifinals just twice, losing to Portland and Houston in the conference finals in 1992 and 1994, respectively.

Utah's lack of a strong low-post presence ended up being the thing that invariably led to the team's downfall each season. The team surrounded its two great stars with decent complementary players throughout much of the period, but the Jazz simply had no one to contend with the likes of Hakeem Olajuwon and David Robinson in the middle. As a result, Malone and Stockton experienced the frustration of watching the NBA Finals from the comfort of their homes each year.

Yet, even though the Jazz never acquired a dominant center, Malone and Stockton eventually led Utah to consecutive appearances in the NBA Finals. After losing to Seattle in seven games in the 1996 Western Conference Finals, the Jazz had their greatest season in 1996–1997. Posting a franchise-best 64–18 record during the regular season, the Jazz then breezed through the first three rounds of the playoffs en route to capturing the Western Conference title. However, the 69–13 Chicago Bulls subsequently defeated them in six games in the NBA Finals. In spite of the loss, Stockton and Malone both acquitted themselves quite well during the playoffs. Stockton, in particular, came up extremely big at the most critical moments. The point guard averaged 16.1 points and 9.6 assists in Utah's 20 playoff games. In the decisive game 6 of the Western Conference Finals against the Rockets, he scored 13 of his 25 points in the fourth quarter to seal the victory. He then averaged 15 points and nine assists against the Bulls in the Finals. Stockton won game 4 of that series with a three-pointer in the final minute, before sealing the victory by stealing the ball from Michael Jordan and hitting Malone with a perfect length-of-the-court pass. Malone also played extremely well, posting averages of 26 points and 11.4 rebounds during the postseason. At the conclusion of the campaign, the power forward was named the NBA's Most Valuable Player for averaging 27.4 points and 9.9 rebounds per game during the regular season. He earned his first of three consecutive All-NBA First Defensive Team selections as well.

Malone led Utah to an outstanding 62–20 record in 1996–1997, compiling averages of 27 points and 10.3 rebounds per contest during the regular season. Although the Jazz again made short work of their opponents during the Western Conference playoffs, they were thwarted once more in the NBA Finals by the Bulls, who captured their sixth NBA championship in eight years.

Stockton's performance began to fall off somewhat the following season, when he failed to average more than 12 points and 10 assists for the first time since he became a starter 10 years earlier. Still, Stockton remained an effective player until he retired at the end of the 2002–2003 campaign, even though his playing time gradually diminished during that period and the Jazz never again came close to returning to the NBA Finals. Stockton left the game with career averages of 13.1 points and 10.5 assists per game. Only Magic Johnson averaged more assists per game during his career (11.2). Stockton's 15,806 career assists are an NBA record, placing him some 4,000 assists ahead of the runner-up (Jason Kidd). He also scored 19,711 points and compiled an NBA-record 3,265 steals.

Upon Stockton's retirement in 2003, Karl Malone said, "There will not be another one like him."[6]

As Stockton began to approach the latter stages of his career in 1998–1999, Malone earned NBA Most Valuable Player honors for the second time and All-NBA First Team honors for the 11th consecutive season. The Mailman averaged 23.8 points and 9.4 rebounds per game during the strike-shortened regular season, placing in the league's top five in scoring for the 12th straight year. Malone finished in the top five in scoring for the final time in 1999–2000, averaging 25.5 points per contest. He also averaged more than 20 points per game in each of his three remaining years with the Jazz, before he elected to leave the team via free agency to sign with the Lakers at the end of the 2002–2003 campaign. Malone spent only one year in Los Angeles, retiring at the conclusion of the 2003–2004 season after failing to win the NBA title he so desperately craved. Malone averaged 25 points and 10.1 assists per game over the course of his career. His 36,928 points place him behind only Kareem Abdul-Jabbar on the all-time scoring list, and his 14,968 rebounds place him in the top 10 all-time.

Karl Malone and John Stockton led the Jazz into the playoffs in each of their 18 seasons as teammates. Utah captured five Midwest Division titles during that time, advanced to the Western Conference Finals five times, and made two appearances in the NBA Finals. The team won at least 50 games in 11 of those seasons, surpassing 60 victories on three occasions. Malone and Stockton combined for 13 appearances on the All-NBA First Team, eight appearances on the Second Team, and four appearances on the Third Team. Between them, they earned three nominations to the All-NBA First Defensive Team, along with six nominations to the Second Defensive Team. They made 24 appearances on the All-Star Team. Malone and Stockton scored a total of 55,627 points as teammates, and they assisted on 20,476 baskets. Both figures represent NBA records for two teammates.

Notes

Numbers printed in bold indicate that the player led his league in a statistical category.

    1. Craig Ehlo, http://www.nba.com/history/players/stockton_bio.html.
    2. Tom Chambers, http://www.ringsurf.com/online/2197-john_stockton_point_guard.html.
    3. Jerry Sloan, http://www.ringsurf.com/online/2197-john_stockton_point_guard.html.
    4. Charles Barkley, http://www.ringsurf.com/online/2197-john_stockton_point_guard.html.
    5. Magic Johnson, http://www.ringsurf.com/online/2197-john_stockton_point_guard.html.
    6. Karl Malone, http://www.nba.com/history/players/stockton_bio.html.

CHAPTER 39

Shaquille O'Neal / Kobe Bryant

A clash of egos caused the relationship between Shaquille O'Neal and Kobe Bryant to gradually disintegrate, bringing to a premature end one of the greatest pairings in NBA history and relegating the tandem to a lower spot in these rankings than what they otherwise would have received. Nevertheless, the extraordinary talents of O'Neal and Bryant enabled them to lead the Los Angeles Lakers to three consecutive league championships at one point, thereby making them one of the most successful combinations in the history of their sport.

Shaquille O'Neal took the NBA by storm when he first entered the league in 1992. After being selected by the Orlando Magic with the first overall pick of that year's NBA draft, the Louisiana State University product captured Rookie of the Year honors by averaging 23.4 points per game and finishing second in the league with 13.9 rebounds and 3.5 blocked shots per contest. The impact that O'Neal made in his first NBA season was such that he led a team that finished just 21–61 the previous season to a record of 41–41 in 1992–1993.

O'Neal and the Magic continued to grow together over the course of the next three seasons, as Shaq established himself as one of the league's dominant big men:

1993–1994: 29.3 PPG, 13.2 RPG
1994–1995: **29.3** PPG, 11.4 RPG
1995–1996: 26.6 PPG, 11.0 RPG

In addition to leading the league in scoring in 1994–1995, Shaq finished second in 1993–1994 and third in 1995–1996. He also placed among the league leaders in rebounding all three years, finishing second in 1993–1994 and third the following season. O'Neal finished second to San Antonio's David Robinson in the MVP voting in 1994–1995, a season in which he earned All-NBA Second Team honors. Shaq was named to the All-NBA Third Team the other two years.

Orlando posted win totals of 50, 57, and 60 those three seasons, making the playoffs each year and capturing the Atlantic Division title in 1994–1995 and 1995–1996. The Magic advanced to the NBA Finals in 1995, but the Houston Rockets swept them in four games. The Chicago Bulls needed only four games to dispose of them in the Eastern Conference Finals the following year.

At 7'1" and well over 300 pounds, O'Neal simply had too much size and strength for opposing centers to contain, establishing himself before long as the most physically dominating player to come along since Wilt Chamberlain. Shaq typically used his considerable bulk to back his defender down low, from where he employed either a short turnaround jump hook or an emphatic slam dunk to devastate and demoralize his opponent. Although opposing teams often assigned two or three defenders to O'Neal once he got close to the basket, their efforts invariably proved to be futile. The best they could do in most cases was to send the big man to the free throw line by fouling him—a strategy they often employed, since O'Neal proved to be one of the league's worst free-throw shooters.

Following the 1995–1996 campaign, O'Neal elected to leave Orlando for the bright lights of Los Angeles when he signed a seven-year, $121 million contract with a Laker team that had failed to advance beyond the first round of the playoffs since Magic Johnson announced his retirement at the conclusion of the 1990–1991 season. Although O'Neal played extremely well whenever he took the court, he missed a significant amount of playing time his first two years with his new team, appearing in only 51 games in 1996–1997 and competing in just 60 contests in 1997–1998. Still, Shaq earned All-NBA Third Team honors in the first of those years, before being named to the First Team for the first time in his career the following season, when he averaged just over 28 points and 11 rebounds per game. The Lakers won 56 games in 1996–1997 before losing to Utah in five games in the Western Conference semifinals. They finished 61–21 the following year, before being swept by Utah in four games in the Western Conference Finals. O'Neal remained healthy throughout the strike-shortened 1998–1999 campaign, placing second in the league with a 26.3 scoring average and finishing among the leaders with a 10.7 rebounding average en route to earning All-NBA Second Team honors. However, the Lakers came up short in the playoffs again, this time being swept by San Antonio in the Western Conference semifinals.

The 1998–1999 campaign marked the first time that a young and extremely talented guard named Kobe Bryant joined O'Neal in the Lakers' starting lineup. The 20-year-old Bryant had signed with the team right out of high school two years earlier, after being personally scouted by Los Angeles general manager Jerry West. Taken with the 13th overall pick of the 1996 NBA draft, Bryant spent most of his first two seasons coming off the Lakers bench, although he saw his playing time gradually increase to 26 minutes per contest during his sophomore campaign. After averaging only 7.6 points per game as a rookie, Bryant increased his scoring output to 15.4 points per contest in his second season. Inserted into the starting five in his third season, Bryant became the team's number-two scoring option behind O'Neal, averaging just under 20 points per game.

Although the continuing development of Bryant gave the Lakers a second primary offensive threat, the team still needed to learn how to win. With that thought in mind, team ownership hired Phil Jackson to coach the squad prior to the start of the 1999–2000 campaign. The fact that Jackson previously coached the Chicago Bulls to six NBA championships during the 1990s gave him a great deal of credibility with the players, who closely heeded his words. After installing the same triangle offense in Los Angeles that he earlier put in place in Chicago, Jackson set about motivating O'Neal to become a better all-around player. The Lakers' new coach convinced the star center that he needed to improve his rebounding and work harder on the defensive end of the floor if he truly wanted to win a championship. Shaq responded by finishing among the league leaders with 13.6 rebounds and just over three blocked shots per game while leading the NBA with a 29.7 scoring average. O'Neal's exceptional performance led the Lakers to an NBA-best 67–15 record during the regular season, enabling him to capture league MVP honors. He also earned spots on the All-NBA First Team and the All-NBA Second Defensive Team. Shaq was ably assisted by Bryant, who thrived in the team's new offensive system, posting a scoring average of 22.5 points per game. The 21-year-old guard also averaged 6.3 rebounds and just under five assists per contest. Bryant was named to the All-NBA Second Team; he was also picked for the All-NBA First Defensive Team.

While O'Neal battered his opponents down low, Bryant frustrated his defenders on the outside with his quickness, athleticism, wide assortment of moves, and long-range jump shot. The Laker guard's combination of basketball skills and physical talent, along with his competitive drive, prompted many experts to anoint him as the heir apparent to Michael Jordan as the game's greatest all-around player. Like Jordan, Bryant was an explosive scorer, a solid rebounder, playmaker, and defender, and an exceptional natural athlete. He also had a wholesome image that the NBA felt it could use to market its product.

O'Neal and Bryant continued their outstanding play during the postseason, leading the Lakers to their first NBA championship in more than a decade. Bryant averaged just over 21 points in the team's 23 playoff contests. Meanwhile, O'Neal posted averages of 30.7 points and 15.4 rebounds per game en route to capturing NBA Finals MVP honors.

The Lakers repeated as NBA champions in each of the next two seasons, with O'Neal and Bryant serving as the driving forces behind each title run:

2000–2001
Shaquille O'Neal: 28.7 PPG, 12.7 RPG, 2.8 BPG
Kobe Bryant: 28.5 PPG, 5.9 RPG, 5.0 APG

2001–2002
Shaquille O'Neal: 27.2 PPG, 10.7 RPG, 2.0 BPG
Kobe Bryant: 25.2 PPG, 5.5 RPG, 5.5 APG

O'Neal finished third in the NBA in both scoring and rebounding in 2000–2001; he also finished fourth in blocked shots. He placed second in the league in scoring the following year while finishing among the leaders in rebounding and blocked shots. Shaq placed third in the MVP voting and earned a spot on the All-NBA First Team both years.

Bryant continued to become a more integral part of the Lakers offense, placing among the league leaders in scoring both years while increasing his number of assists per game each season. He was named to the All-NBA Second Team for the second consecutive time in 2000–2001 before earning First Team honors for the first time the following season. Bryant was selected to the All-NBA Second Defensive Team both years.

After compiling a regular season record of 56–26 in 2000–2001, the Lakers swept through the playoffs, losing only once en route to capturing their second straight NBA championship. Bryant had a tremendous postseason, averaging 29.4 points, 7.3 rebounds, and 6.1 assists in the Lakers' 16 playoff contests. O'Neal was even more dominant, posting averages of 30.4 points and 15.4 rebounds per game. He earned NBA Finals MVP honors for the second consecutive year.

The 2001–2002 campaign ended in similar fashion. The Lakers finished 58–24 during the regular season before compiling a 15–4 record during the playoffs en route to winning their third straight NBA title. Bryant averaged 26.6 points and just under six rebounds per game during the postseason, while O'Neal averaged 28.5 points and 12.6 rebounds per contest. Shaq was named NBA Finals MVP for the third straight year.

In spite of the Lakers' three-year domination of the NBA, they began experiencing a considerable amount of inner turmoil during the period. The troubles actually started to surface during their second championship season, 2000–2001, when Bryant reached a comparable level of stardom to O'Neal for the first time. In averaging 28.5 points per game, the 22-year-old guard felt that he no longer needed to take a backseat to O'Neal as the team's best player. Bryant believed that his basketball skills far exceeded those of Shaq (which they did), that he was a more complete player (which he was), and that he had become more vital to the success of the team (which was highly debatable). Meanwhile, O'Neal considered himself to be the key to the team's success, believing that the Lakers' offense still needed to be run through him and that the team would only go as far as he could take it. Shaq never had a problem accepting his younger teammate as a member of his supporting cast, often referring to him as his "little brother." But he deeply resented the notion that Bryant had replaced him as the team's best player. At the same time, Kobe began to resent O'Neal's references to him as his "little brother," feeling as though they suggested that he had a less prominent role in the success of the team.

The friction between the two men continued to grow the next few seasons, manifesting itself on the court for the first time in 2002–2003, when the Lakers finished just 50–32 during the regular season before losing to the eventual champion San Antonio Spurs in six games in the Western Conference semifinals. Yet, even as the relationship between O'Neal and Bryant continued to deteriorate, they remained two of the league's premier players. Bryant had perhaps his greatest all-around season in 2002–2003, when, playing in every game for Los Angeles, he established new career highs by averaging 30 points, 6.9 rebounds, 5.9 assists, and 2.2 steals per game. He placed second in the NBA in scoring, at one point running off a string of nine straight games in which he scored at least 40 points. By doing so, Bryant tied Michael Jordan for the second-longest such streak in league history, behind only Wilt Chamberlain. After the seventh of those nine games, one in which Bryant scored 40 points against the Jazz, Utah coach Jerry Sloan marveled, "You're talking about one of the greatest players to play this game."[1] Bryant finished third in the league MVP voting, earned a spot on the All-NBA First Team, and also earned All-NBA First Defensive Team honors.

Meanwhile, O'Neal averaged just over 11 rebounds per game and finished fourth in scoring, with an average of 27.5 points per contest, and fifth in the MVP balloting. He also joined Bryant on the All-NBA First Team and was awarded a spot on the All-NBA Second Defensive Team.

Even though the Lakers eventually fell to the Spurs in the conference semifinals, both O'Neal and Bryant performed exceptionally well during the postseason. Shaq posted averages of 27 points and 14.8 rebounds in the Lakers' 12 playoff games, while Bryant outscored his teammate for the first time in the postseason, averaging just over 32 points per contest.

With Bryant having established himself as the NBA's most popular player and as arguably its finest all-around talent, his personal life took a turn for the worse after the conclusion of the 2002–2003 season, when he was charged with a single count of felony sexual assault stemming from an alleged incident at a Colorado resort. Although an out-of-court settlement was reached prior to the completion of the 2004–2005 campaign, Bryant's previously spotless reputation and wholesome image received irreparable damage. Furthermore, his pending trial unquestionably affected Bryant's performance on the basketball court during the 2003–2004 season, one in which his scoring average dropped to 24 points per game. Nevertheless, the Laker guard was named to the All-NBA First Team for the third straight time. O'Neal joined Bryant on the First Team after averaging 21.5 points and 11.5 rebounds per game during the regular season.

It was during that 2003–2004 campaign that the relationship between O'Neal and Bryant hit rock bottom. Tensions between the two men continued to mount as the Lakers geared their offense more toward Bryant, making O'Neal the team's number-two option on that end of the court for the first time. Angered by his reduced role, Shaq often voiced his displeasure to both Coach Jackson and the media. The inner turmoil created a distraction to the Lakers on the court that contributed greatly to their stunning five-game loss to the underdog Detroit Pistons in the NBA Finals.

Despite Bryant's off-court transgressions, the Lakers had clearly become "Kobe's team." At only 26 years of age, he was six years younger than Shaq, whom Los Angeles ownership believed had seen his best days. Forced to make a decision between the two men, the team elected to place its future in Bryant's hands, trading O'Neal to the Miami Heat. The dealing of Shaq, the subsequent resignation of Jackson as head coach, and the pending litigation against Bryant left the Laker guard with a severely tarnished image. The young man once looked on by many basketball experts as being "the next Michael Jordan" came out of the ordeal looking like a spoiled, pampered, immature, and disingenuous egomaniac.

Faced with the daunting task of trying to resurrect his image in 2004–2005, Bryant began a nine-year stretch during which he clearly established himself as one of the greatest players in NBA history. Playing without Shaq throughout the period, Bryant rivaled LeBron James as the league's finest all-around player in most of those seasons. These are the numbers he compiled from 2004–2013:

2004–2005: 27.6 PPG, 5.9 RPG, 6.0 APG
2005–2006: **35.4** PPG, 5.3 RPG, 4.5 APG
2006–2007: **31.6** PPG, 5.7 RPG, 5.4 APG
2007–2008: 28.3 PPG, 6.3 RPG, 5.4 APG
2008–2009: 26.8 PPG, 5.2 RPG, 4.9 APG
2009–2010: 27.0 PPG, 5.4 RPG, 5.0 APG
2010–2011: 25.3 PPG, 5.1 RPG, 4.7 APG
2011–2012: 27.9 PPG, 5.4 RPG, 4.6 APG
2012–2013: 27.3 PPG, 5.6 RPG, 6.0 APG

In addition to leading the NBA in scoring in two of those seasons, Bryant finished second three times and third twice. On January 22, 2006, he scored 81 points against the Toronto Raptors, thereby posting the second-highest single-game scoring total in NBA history. After being named to the All-NBA Third Team in 2004–2005, Bryant earned First Team honors in each of the next eight seasons. He also earned a spot on the All-NBA First Defensive Team in six of those eight seasons. Bryant finished in the top five in the league MVP voting in eight of the nine years, winning the award in 2007–2008, when he led the Lakers into the NBA Finals. He placed second in the balloting in 2008–2009, when he proved he had the ability to win a championship without Shaq. Bryant averaged just over 30 points per game during the playoffs en route to being named NBA Finals MVP. Unfortunately, a torn Achilles tendon suffered during the latter stages of the 2012–2013 season sidelined Bryant for the first 19 games of the ensuing campaign. He subsequently fractured his left knee in just his sixth game back, bringing his 2013–2014 season to a premature end. Although Bryant will enter the upcoming season at 37 years of age, he anticipates a return to full health—one that will be necessary if the Lakers have any hope of advancing to the playoffs.

As of this writing, Bryant has scored 31,700 points during his career—the fourth-highest total in NBA history. He has averaged 25.5 points per game over the course of his 18 years in the league. Bryant has placed in the league's top five in scoring a total of 12 times, averaging better than 27 points per contest on nine occasions. He has been named to the All-NBA First Team 11 times and the All-NBA First Defensive Team nine times. He has appeared in 15 All-Star Games.

Former Lakers' coach Del Harris stated emphatically, "Nobody can guard Kobe one-on-one. Nobody."[2]

Hall of Fame center Kareem Abdul-Jabbar commented, "Kobe's range is unreal, and he does it his way."[3]

All-Star Chris Bosh said of Bryant, "He takes the type of shots where you don't think they're going in, but suddenly he's rolling, so he's kind of hard to stop."[4]

Former Lakers teammate Rick Fox observed the manner in which Bryant has matured on the court, stating, "He doesn't make his game a personal game anymore."[5]

NBA legend Michael Jordan noted, "I see a lot of myself in him. No doubt about it."[6]

Meanwhile, Shaquille O'Neal failed to reach the same dominant level that he attained earlier in his career after he left the Lakers at the conclusion of the 2003–2004 campaign. Nevertheless, he remained one of the NBA's top big men the next few seasons, earning a spot on the All-NBA First Team at the end of both the 2004–2005 and 2005–2006 campaigns, finishing second in the league MVP voting in the first of those years and being selected to four more All-Star Teams. Shaq averaged 22.9 points and 10.4 rebounds per game his first year in Miami, leading a team that finished just 42–40 the previous year to a record of 59–23 and a berth in the Eastern Conference Finals. Even though he managed to average 20 points and 9.2 rebounds per contest the following year, O'Neal assumed more of a complementary role on the team to allow the extremely talented Dwyane Wade to blossom into the Heat's number-one star. For his efforts, O'Neal collected his fourth NBA title when Miami upset the favored Dallas Mavericks in six games in the NBA Finals.

O'Neal remained in Miami through the middle of the 2007–2008 season, spending the next 1.5 years with the Phoenix Suns. He joined the Cleveland

Cavaliers prior to the start of the 2009–2010 campaign, before ending his career the following year as a member of the Boston Celtics.

O'Neal left the game having scored 28,596 points, pulled down 13,099 rebounds, and blocked 2,732 shots over the course of his career. He is eighth on the all-time scoring list, ninth in blocked shots, and 15th in rebounding. O'Neal retired with career averages of 23.7 points and 10.9 rebounds per game. O'Neal led the league in scoring twice, finishing in the top five eight other times. He averaged better than 25 points per game in 10 of his 19 NBA seasons, surpassing 27 points per contest a total of seven times. O'Neal finished in the top five in rebounding five times, averaging better than 10 rebounds per game in each of his first 13 years in the league. O'Neal also placed in the top five in blocked shots four times, and he led the league in field-goal percentage on 10 occasions. O'Neal earned eight selections to the All-NBA First Team, two nominations to the Second Team, and another four selections to the Third Team. He finished in the top five in the league MVP voting on eight occasions and was named to 15 All-Star Teams.

Shaquille O'Neal and Kobe Bryant were teammates on the Lakers for eight seasons. Los Angeles made the playoffs in each of those eight seasons, advancing to the NBA Finals four times and winning three consecutive championships. In their eight years together, O'Neal and Bryant combined for eight top-five finishes in the league MVP voting, nine selections to the All-NBA First Team, three nominations to the Second Team, and two selections to the Third Team. They made three appearances on the All-NBA First Defensive Team, five on the Second Defensive Team, and 13 in the All-Star Game. O'Neal and Bryant placed in the top five in scoring a total of nine times as teammates, with both men finishing in the top five in that category on two occasions. They were most effective together from 2000 to 2003, posting combined scoring averages those three seasons of 57.2, 52.5, and 57.5 points per game. Bryant finished in the top five in the league MVP voting in two of those years, while O'Neal placed in the top five in the balloting all three seasons.

Notes

Numbers printed in bold indicate that the player led his league in a statistical category.

1. Jerry Sloan, http://www.jockbio.com/Bios/Bryant/Bryant_theysay.html.
2. Del Harris, http://www.jockbio.com/Bios/Bryant/Bryant_theysay.html.
3. Kareem Abdul-Jabbar, http://www.jockbio.com/Bios/Bryant/Bryant_theysay.html.
4. Chris Bosh, http://www.jockbio.com/Bios/Bryant/Bryant_theysay.html.
5. Rick Fox, http://www.jockbio.com/Bios/Bryant/Bryant_theysay.html.
6. Michael Jordan, http://www.jockbio.com/Bios/Bryant/Bryant_theysay.html.

CHAPTER 40

Dwyane Wade / LeBron James

Arguably the most talented duo in the world of professional sports in recent years, Dwyane Wade and LeBron James seemed destined to go down as one of the all-time great tandems as soon as they joined forces in Miami prior to the start of the 2010–2011 NBA season. Even before they became teammates more than five years ago, Wade and James had already established themselves as two of the NBA's elite players, with Wade rivaling Kobe Bryant as the league's premier shooting guard and James gaining general recognition as the finest all-around player in the game. Although the two megastars disappointed Miami fans by failing to win an NBA championship their first year together, they ultimately led the Heat to two world championships and four consecutive NBA finals appearances in their four years together as teammates.

After posting a winning record and advancing to the postseason six straight times between 1995 and 2001, the Miami Heat failed to make the playoffs in both 2002 and 2003, compiling a particularly unimpressive mark of 25–57 over the course of the 2002–2003 campaign. The Heat's fortunes began to change the following year, though, after they selected former Marquette University guard Dwyane Wade with the fifth overall pick of the 2003 NBA draft. With Wade earning All-Rookie honors by averaging four rebounds, 4.5 assists, and just over 16 points per game his first year in the league, the Heat improved their record to 42–40 in 2003–2004, earning a spot in the playoffs in the process. Although they eventually lost to Indiana in the Eastern Conference semifinals, the Heat acquitted themselves well against the team with the league's best regular-season record, extending the 61-win Pacers to six games, with Wade leading the way by posting averages of 18 points and 5.6 assists during the postseason tournament.

The Heat developed into one of the NBA's strongest teams in 2004–2005, concluding the campaign with an Eastern Conference–best 59–23 record after acquiring Shaquille O'Neal from Los Angeles during the off-season. In addition to being strengthened by the addition of O'Neal, Miami benefited from the exceptional play of Wade, who placed in the league's top 10 with averages of 24.1 points and 6.8 assists per game en route to earning his first of eight straight All-Star selections, a nomination to the All-NBA Second Team, and a spot on the All-NBA Second Defensive Team. Wade continued his stellar play during the postseason, averaging 27.4 points, 6.6 assists, and 5.7 rebounds in Miami's 14 playoff games, as the Heat took the defending-champion Detroit Pistons to seven games before finally falling to them in the Eastern Conference Finals. Wade performed particularly well against Detroit in games 2 and 3, scoring 42 and 36 points, respectively, despite playing with sinusitis, the flu, and a knee strain.

Wade's outstanding performance over the course of the campaign made a strong impression on O'Neal, who said of his younger teammate, "Wade has the potential to be a better player than anyone I ever played with. I'm talking about being a shooter, a defender and someone with an all-around game. And a good guy along with it."[1]

With Wade accepting the mantle of leadership from O'Neal in 2005–2006, the Heat reached the pinnacle of their sport, capturing their first NBA championship in franchise history. After averaging 27.2 points, 6.7 assists, 5.7 rebounds, and 1.95 steals per game during the regular season en route to leading Miami to a record of 52–30, Wade took his game to the next level in the playoffs. The Heat defeated Chicago, New Jersey, and Detroit, before prevailing over favored Dallas in six games in the NBA Finals, with Wade posting averages of 28.4 points, 5.7 assists, and 5.9 rebounds in Miami's 23 postseason contests. Particularly impressive against the Mavericks, Wade earned Finals MVP honors by averaging 34.7 points in the six games, helping the Heat overcome an early 2–0 deficit in the series by scoring 42, 36, 43, and 36 points in the final four contests. In addition to scoring 36 points in the series clincher, Wade pulled down 10 rebounds, blocked three shots, and collected four steals.

Over the course of that NBA Finals series against Dallas, Wade put on display for all to see his tremendous all-around talents. Although the 6'4", 215-pound Wade plays the shooting guard position, he has the versatility to play point guard as well. His exceptional quickness, court vision, and ball-handling skills enable him to break down the defenses of opposing teams, while his outstanding leaping ability, wide array of inside moves, and solid perimeter game make him a threat to score from virtually anywhere on the court. Best known for his ability to convert difficult layups, even after hard midair collisions with larger defenders, Wade has spent the past few seasons expanding his post-up game. David Thorpe, an athletic trainer who runs a training center for NBA players in the offseason, suggested, "Watching Wade operate on the left block is literally like watching old footage of MJ [Michael Jordan]."[2] Meanwhile, Wade's tremendous athleticism has enabled him to establish himself as one of the league's top defensive guards as well, annually placing among the leaders at his position in steals and blocked shots.

Legendary coach and current Miami GM Pat Riley said of Wade, "He's an intelligent basketball player and a fast learner. His unselfishness and understanding of the team concept are what makes him great."[3]

Former Utah Jazz head coach Jerry Sloan commented, "His continuation when going to the hoop is the best I've ever seen."[4]

As much as it helped him establish himself as one of the NBA's elite players, Wade's high-flying, aggressive style of play began to catch up with him in 2006–2007, the first of two consecutive seasons in which injuries forced him to sit out 31 of his team's games. Although Wade earned All-Star and All-NBA Third Team honors in the first of those campaigns by averaging 27.4 points and a career-high 7.5 assists per game, a dislocated shoulder and injured left knee limited him to only 51 regular-season contests. Wade and the Heat reached their nadir together the following season, with Miami concluding the campaign with an NBA-worst 15–67 record, as the star guard again found himself limited to 51 games by constant pain in his surgically repaired left knee. Nevertheless, Wade played effectively whenever he took the court, posting averages of 24.6 points and 6.9 assists per game.

Wade returned to the Heat healthy in 2008–2009, enabling Miami to advance to the postseason for the fifth time in six years by compiling a regular-season record of 43–39. In arguably his finest all-around season, Wade led the NBA with a scoring average of 30.2 points per game while averaging 7.5 assists, five rebounds, 2.2 steals, and 1.3 blocked shots per contest en route to earning All-NBA First Team honors and a third-place finish in the league MVP voting. Wade's extraordinary campaign included a 50-point performance against the Orlando Magic, 55- and 46-point efforts against the New York Knicks, and a 41-point performance against the Cleveland Cavaliers and his good friend LeBron James. Over the course of the season, Wade became the first player in NBA history to accumulate at least 2,000 points, 500 assists, 100 steals, and 100 blocks in a season. Although the Heat ended up losing their first-round playoff matchup with the Atlanta Hawks, Wade averaged just over 29 points in the seven games.

Wade followed that up with another banner year in 2009–2010, earning a fifth-place finish in the league MVP balloting and his second consecutive selections to the All-NBA First Team and All-NBA Second Defensive Team by placing among the league leaders, with averages of 26.6 points, 6.5 assists, and 1.8 steals per game. However, the Heat again came up short in the playoffs, losing to the Boston Celtics in five games in the first round. Nevertheless, Wade had another exceptional postseason, averaging 33.2 points, 6.8 assists, and 5.6 rebounds per game against Boston.

A free agent at the conclusion of the 2009–2010 campaign, Wade elected to re-sign with the Heat when the team also came to terms with fellow free agent superstars Chris Bosh and LeBron James. The latter, who announced his decision to join the Heat during a well-publicized live ESPN television special, drew a considerable amount of criticism from various quarters for the manner in which he handled the entire ordeal. In addition to alienating Cleveland Cavaliers fans by "deserting" them, James found himself being vilified for failing to notify the Cleveland organization of his decision beforehand, choosing to "take the easy path" to an NBA title by aligning himself with Wade and Bosh and displaying what many perceived to be an arrogant and narcissistic nature throughout the proceedings.

In announcing his decision, James stated, "In this fall . . . this is very tough . . . in this fall, I'm going to take my talents to South Beach and join the Miami Heat. I feel like it's going to give me the best opportunity to win, and to win for multiple years, and not only just to win in the regular season, or just to win five games in a row, or three games in a row—I want to be able to win championships. And I feel like I can compete down there."[5]

Informed of James's decision minutes before the show began, Cleveland Cavaliers majority owner Dan Gilbert subsequently lambasted the superstar in the media, publishing an open letter to fans that referred to James's pronouncement as a "selfish," "heartless," "callous," and "cowardly betrayal" while foolishly guaranteeing that the Cavaliers would win an NBA title before the "self-declared former King."

Meanwhile, NBA legend Michael Jordan also criticized James for his decision not to remain in Cleveland, where he would have been able to continue his quest to win a championship as "the guy." Stating, "I wanted to defeat those guys,"[6] Jordan suggested that he would not have contacted rivals from other teams such as Magic Johnson and Larry Bird in an attempt to combine forces had he been in the same situation as James. Yet, Jordan added, "Things are different [now]. I can't say that's a bad thing. It's an opportunity these kids have today."[7]

Although James left Cleveland a hated man, there can be no doubting that he turned the Cavaliers into contenders almost single-handedly in his eight years with the team. After concluding the 2002–2003 campaign with an NBA-worst 17–65 record, the Cavaliers made James the first overall pick of the 2003 NBA draft. Two months shy of his 19th birthday when he made his NBA debut later that year, James—who became a media sensation while starring at Saint Vincent–Saint Mary High School in Akron, Ohio—took the league by storm, earning NBA Rookie of the Year honors by helping the Cavaliers improve their record to 35–47 with averages of just under 21 points and six assists per game.

James continued his ascension into stardom his second year in the league, earning All-Star and All-NBA honors for the first of eight straight times by placing among the league leaders with averages of 27.2 points, 7.2 assists, and 2.2 steals per game. Although the Cavaliers failed to make the playoffs for the seventh consecutive season, they posted a record of 42–40, which represented their best mark during that stretch.

The performance of James at only 20 years of age left NBA Hall of Famer Rick Barry musing, "I fantasize about LeBron's ability. He is the best player I have ever seen at this age."[8]

James led Cleveland into the postseason tournament the following year, helping the Cavaliers compile a record of 50–32 by averaging a career-high 31.4 points per contest. He also averaged seven rebounds and 6.6 assists per game en route to earning a second-place finish to Steve Nash in the league MVP voting. James's sensational 2005–2006 campaign included a nine-game stretch during which he scored no fewer than 35 points. The feat enabled him to join Michael Jordan and Kobe Bryant as the only players since 1970 to surpass the 35-point mark that many times in succession. James subsequently performed exceptionally well in his first trip to the playoffs, helping the Cavaliers defeat the Washington Wizards in the first round before eventually falling to the defending Eastern Conference champion Detroit Pistons in seven games in the Eastern Conference semifinals. James posted averages of 30.8 points, 8.1 rebounds, and 5.8 assists in Cleveland's 13 playoff games.

The Cavaliers returned to the playoffs in 2006–2007, compiling the same 50–32 mark they posted the previous season. James earned a fifth-place finish in the league MVP balloting by averaging 27.3 points, 6.7 rebounds, and six assists per game. In so doing, he joined Oscar Robertson as the only players in NBA history to average at least 27 points, six rebounds, and six assists per game for three straight years. James then led the Cavaliers to consecutive playoff victories over the Washington Wizards, New Jersey Nets, and Detroit Pistons, putting on a memorable performance against Detroit in the Eastern Conference Finals. After the Cavaliers dug themselves out of a 2–0 hole in the series by winning the next two contests, James refused to let his team lose game 5, recording a franchise-record 48 points, including 29 of the final 30 points his team scored. He also pulled down nine rebounds and assisted on seven baskets during Cleveland's double-overtime victory, a performance that NBA analyst Marv Albert referred to as "one of the greatest moments in postseason history" and one that color commentator Steve Kerr called "Jordan-esque." The Cavaliers subsequently eliminated the Pistons in game 6 before losing to the San Antonio Spurs in four straight games in the NBA Finals, a series during which James averaged 22 points, seven rebounds, and 6.8 assists. James ended up averaging 25.1 points, eight assists, and 8.1 rebounds in Cleveland's 20 postseason games.

The reticence that James often displayed his first two years in Miami to take big shots, coupled with the fearlessness that Wade demonstrated from the time he first entered the league, prompted teammate Chris Bosh to suggest in January 2012 that Wade be the one to take last-second shots for the team in crucial situations. Meanwhile, columnist Harvey Araton pointed out the flaws in James's game in a March 7, 2011, article in the *New York Times*, claiming that he "has not mastered a reliable midrange jumper . . . has not developed a go-to move in the post," and asserting that his options in a half-court set at the end of games "often are a long jump shot or a mad dash to the rim."[10] Nevertheless, James continued to have his fair share of supporters, many of whom sang his praises by claiming that he possessed more all-around ability than any other player in the game. A tremendous physical specimen, the 6'8", 250-pound James has great strength, speed, athleticism, ball-handling ability, and court vision. Michael Jordan admiringly said of James, "He breaks you down because he is such a great player."[11]

James again played exceptionally well for Miami during the 2011–2012 regular season, earning NBA MVP honors for the third time in four years by leading the Heat to a record of 46–20 that enabled them to capture their second straight Southeast Division title. James finished third in the league with averages of 27.1 points and 1.9 steals per game while averaging 7.9 rebounds and 6.2 assists per contest. His outstanding all-around performance earned him his fifth consecutive selection to the All-NBA First Team. Meanwhile, despite being hampered by injuries much of the time, Wade posted solid numbers as well, averaging 22.1 points, 4.6 assists, 1.7 steals, and 1.3 blocks per game en route to earning All-NBA Third Team honors.

James subsequently silenced his critics by performing magnificently during the postseason in leading Miami to the NBA championship. After the Heat defeated New York and Indiana in the first two rounds of the playoffs, James helped them keep their season alive by scoring 45 points and pulling down 15 rebounds in a critical game 6 win over Boston in the Eastern Conference Finals. Miami then defeated Boston in the decisive seventh contest, before disposing of Oklahoma City in five games in the NBA Finals. Capping off a brilliant postseason during which he posted averages of 30.3 points, 9.7 rebounds, and 5.6 assists per game, James earned finals MVP honors by averaging 27.6 points, 10.2 rebounds, and 7.4 assists per contest against the Thunder. Wade also made huge contributions to the Miami effort, averaging 22.8 points, 5.2 rebounds, 4.3 assists, 1.7 steals, and 1.3 blocked shots in his team's 23 playoff games.

James claimed NBA MVP honors for the fourth time in five years in 2012–2013 by leading the Heat to a league-best 66–16 record during the regular season that included a 27-game winning streak—the second longest in NBA history. In one of his finest all-around seasons, James averaged 26.8 points, 8 rebounds, 7.3 assists, and 1.7 steals per contest, also earning in the process his sixth consecutive All-NBA First Team selection and his fifth straight nomination to the All-NBA First Defensive Team. Meanwhile, after undergoing off-season surgery to repair his injured left knee, Wade started the year off slowly. Yet, he ended up contributing significantly to the success Miami experienced during the campaign, posting averages of 21.2 points, 5 rebounds, 5.1 assists, and 1.9 steals per game, en route to earning his ninth consecutive All-Star selection, a spot on the All-NBA Third Team, and a 10th-place finish in the league MVP voting.

Wade subsequently found his performance in the playoffs compromised greatly by a recurrence of his earlier knee problems, which limited him to a scoring average of only 15.9 points per game during the postseason. Nevertheless, he came up big for the Heat in the Finals against San Antonio, averaging 19.6 points per contest over the course of the seven games, including a 32-point effort in Miami's Game 4 win, and a 23-point, 10-rebound performance in the Heat's championship-clinching Game 7 victory. After leading the Heat to easy wins over Milwaukee and Chicago in the first two rounds of the postseason tournament, James proved to be the difference in Miami's seven-game tussle with Indiana in the Eastern Conference Finals, winning Game 1 with a buzzer-beating layup and averaging 29 points per contest over the course of the series. He subsequently earned NBA Finals MVP honors for the second straight time by averaging 25.3 points, 10.9 rebounds, 7 assists, and 2.3 steals during Miami's come-from-behind seven-game win over San Antonio. Particularly brilliant in the final two games of the series, James helped the Heat erase a three-games-to-two deficit by recording a triple-double in Game 6 and tying a Finals record for most points scored in a Game 7 victory by tallying 37 points during Miami's 95–88 win.

Although the Heat failed to repeat as NBA champions in 2013–2014, eventually losing to San Antonio in the Finals in five games, James had another great year, earning a second-place finish in the league MVP balloting and his seventh straight All-NBA First Team selection by averaging 27.1 points, 6.9 rebounds, 6.3 assists, and 1.6 steals per contest. However, he failed to receive sufficient support from Wade, who, despite posting averages of 19 points, 4.5 rebounds, 4.7 assists, and 1.5 steals per contest, found himself limited by injury to only 54 games.

A free agent at season's end, James elected to return to his hometown Cleveland Cavaliers, with whom he hopes to win more championships. Meanwhile, Wade chose to re-sign with the Heat, bringing to an end the four-year union of two of the sport's most talented players. They end their time together having combined to earn eight All-Star selections, seven All-NBA nominations, four top-five finishes in the league MVP voting, two regular-season MVP trophies, and two NBA Finals MVP Awards. Between them, James and Wade finished in the league's top five in scoring a total of five times. They led Miami to four NBA Finals appearances and two league championships. Commenting on the effect each player had on the other, Wade suggested on one occasion, "LeBron brings out the best in me, and I bring out the best in him."[12]

Notes

1. Shaquille O'Neal, http://www.jockbio.com/Bios/Wade/Wade_they-say.html.
2. David Thorpe, http://www.jockbio.com/Bios/Wade/Wade_they-say.html.
3. Pat Riley, http://www.jockbio.com/Bios/Wade/Wade_they-say.html.
4. Jerry Sloan, http://www.jockbio.com/Bios/Wade/Wade_they-say.html.
5. LeBron James, http://www.espn.go.com/blog/truehoop/post//id/17853/lebron james-decision-the-transcript.
6. Michael Jordan, http://www.jockbio.com/Bios/James/James_quotes.html.
7. Michael Jordan, http://www.jockbio.com/Bios/James/James_quotes.html.
8. Rick Barry, http://www.jockbio.com/Bios/James/James_quotes.html.
9. Eric Snow, http://www.jockbio.com/Bios/James/James_quotes.html.
10. Harvey Araton, http://www.nytimes.com/2011/03/07/sports/basketball/08 dribble.html.
11. Michael Jordan, http://www.jockbio.com/Bios/James/James_quotes.html.
12. Dwyane Wade, http://www.jockbio.com/Bios/James/James_quotes.html.

CHAPTER 41

Oscar Robertson / Jerry Lucas

Oscar Robertson and Jerry Lucas had the misfortune of playing for a Cincinnati Royals team that had to compete against Bill Russell's Boston Celtics every year for supremacy in the NBA's Eastern Division. As a result, the two all-time greats never won a championship together. In fact, they never even appeared in an NBA Finals as teammates. Nevertheless, Robertson and Lucas helped turn a losing franchise into one of Boston's most serious challengers for supremacy in the NBA East during their time together.

The Rochester Royals finished either last or next to last in the NBA's Western Division three straight years before relocating to Cincinnati prior to the start of the 1957–1958 campaign. Unfortunately, the change in scenery didn't help the Royals much, since they continued to play poorly in the first three years in their new location. They were particularly bad in 1958–1959 and 1959–1960, posting records of 19–53 and 19–56, respectively. However, the Royals' record improved to 33–46 in 1960–1961, after they selected University of Cincinnati guard Oscar Robertson with the first overall pick of the 1960 NBA draft. The 6'5", 220-pound Robertson took the league by storm, displaying an array of skills not previously possessed by any one player. Robertson was an exceptional outside shooter, a superb passer and ball handler, and an outstanding defender. He also possessed unusual size and strength for a guard, enabling him to back his defender down low to create for himself the best possible scoring opportunity.

Opposing guard Dick Barnett once described Robertson's technique: "If you give him a 12-foot shot, he'll work on you until he's got a 10-foot shot. Give him six, he wants four. Give him two feet, and you know what he wants? That's right, man, a lay-up."[1]

Robertson also used his physical strength and outstanding leaping ability to his advantage under the boards, establishing himself as the league's best rebounding guard. In fact, he even outrebounded the majority of forwards in the league. Robertson's unique skill set enabled him to finish third in the NBA in 1960–1961 with a scoring average of 30.5 points per game, lead the league with 9.7 assists per contest, and average 10.1 rebounds per game. By doing so, he ran away with Rookie of the Year honors and earned a spot on the All-NBA First Team for the first of nine straight years.

The Royals finished last in the NBA's Western Division in Robertson's rookie season, but they jumped to second place the following year, compiling a record of 43–37. Robertson became the only player in NBA history to average a triple-double during that 1961–1962 campaign, posting averages of 30.8 points, 12.5 rebounds, and a league-leading 11.4 assists per game. Oscar finished third in the league MVP voting at season's end. He placed third in the balloting again the following season after leading Cincinnati to a 42–38 record and a third-place finish in the NBA's Eastern Division. The "Big O" averaged 28.3 points, 10.4 rebounds, and 9.5 assists per contest during the regular season, then led the Royals into the Eastern Division Finals, where they took the Celtics to seven games before finally succumbing to the eventual world champions.

Rookie forward Jerry Lucas joined Robertson in Cincinnati in 1963–1964, leading to a successful six-year run together by the two former all-Americans. The Royals compiled a regular-season record of 55–25 in Lucas's first year in the league en route to finishing second in the East, only four games behind first-place Boston. They then lost to the Celtics for the second consecutive year in the Eastern Division Finals, dropping a five-game series. Robertson earned NBA Most Valuable Player honors by averaging 31.4 points, 9.9 rebounds, and a league-leading 11 assists per game over the course of the season. His 11 assists per contest put him well ahead of league runner-up Guy Rodgers, who averaged seven assists per game for the San Francisco Warriors. Robertson's 9.9 rebounding average also left him just short of averaging a triple-double for the second time in three seasons. Meanwhile, Lucas, whom the Royals selected in the first round of the draft out of Ohio State, earned Rookie of the Year honors by averaging 17.7 points per game and finishing third in the league with a rebounding average of 17.4 boards per contest. He also led the NBA with a .527 field-goal percentage. For his efforts, Lucas earned a spot on the All-NBA Second Team.

Although the Royals failed to make it back to the Eastern Division Finals in any of the five remaining seasons that Robertson and Lucas spent as teammates, they remained competitive, with their two best players continuing to excel:

1964–1965
Oscar Robertson: 30.4 PPG, 9.0 RPG, **11.5** APG
Jerry Lucas: 21.4 PPG, 20.0 RPG
1965–1966
Oscar Robertson: 31.3 PPG, 7.7 RPG, **11.1** APG
Jerry Lucas: 21.5 PPG, 21.1 RPG

1966–1967
Oscar Robertson: 30.5 PPG, 6.2 RPG, 10.7 APG
Jerry Lucas: 17.8 PPG, 19.1 RPG
1967–1968
Oscar Robertson: 29.2 PPG, 6.0 RPG, 9.7 APG
Jerry Lucas: 21.5 PPG, 19.0 RPG
1968–1969
Oscar Robertson: 24.7 PPG, 6.4 RPG, **9.8** APG
Jerry Lucas: 18.3 PPG, 18.4 RPG

The Royals played their best ball of the period in the first two years, finishing second in the East with a 48–32 record in 1964–1965 and coming in third the following season with a mark of 45–35, before losing to Boston in five games in the division semifinals.

Robertson finished second in the MVP voting in 1964–1965, before coming in third the following year. In addition to leading the league in assists in three of those seasons, he finished second in scoring once, and he placed third on two other occasions. Robertson was named to the All-NBA First Team all five years.

Lucas joined Robertson on the All-NBA First Team in 1964–1965, 1965–1966, and 1967–1968. The forward also earned a spot on the Second Team in 1966–1967, and he finished fifth in league MVP voting in 1965–1966. Lucas finished third in the NBA in rebounding in each of the first three years, behind Wilt Chamberlain and Bill Russell, before placing second to Chamberlain in 1967–1968. When Lucas surpassed 20 points and 20 rebounds per game in 1964–1965 and 1965–1966, he became one of only three players in NBA history to reach both milestones in the same season (Chamberlain and Nate Thurmond also accomplished the feat). Along with Chamberlain, Thurmond, and Bill Russell, he is also one of only four players to pull down 40 rebounds in one game.

Although Lucas possessed only average strength and leaping ability, the 6'8", 230-pound power forward was one of the greatest rebounding forwards in NBA history. His 15.6 career rebounding average places him fourth on the all-time list, behind Wilt Chamberlain, Bill Russell, and Bob Pettit. In discussing the technique that he used to outrebound bigger and taller opponents, Lucas explained, "I knew everybody's shot in the NBA. I knew where they liked to shoot from, I knew the arc of their shots, I knew who boxed out and who didn't. I just logged that into my basketball computer in my mind."[2]

Lucas also possessed tremendous range on his outside jump shot, which eventually came to be known as the "Lucas Layup." Typically launched in shot-put style from anywhere between 20 and 25 feet out, it was a shot that Lucas hit with amazing regularity, as evidenced by his career .499 field-goal percentage.

An intelligent and cerebral player, Lucas had a remarkable memory and an incredible capacity for retaining numbers and other useful information. His preoccupation with statistics enabled him to keep track of the numbers compiled by every player on the court. Lucas once said, "I knew every play of every team in the league. I had them all memorized."[3]

Unfortunately, Lucas's unique gift sometimes prompted others to label him a selfish player. But nothing could have been further from the truth. Lucas demonstrated that he put his team before himself after he left the Royals only four games into the 1969–1970 season. After spending two years in San Francisco, Lucas was traded to the New York Knicks for Cazzie Russell prior to the start of the 1971–1972 campaign. Expected to be Willis Reed's backup, Lucas assumed a far more prominent role on the Knicks when their captain missed virtually all of the 1971–1972 campaign. Taking over as the team's starting center, Lucas averaged 16.7 points and 13.1 rebounds per game in helping New York advance to the NBA Finals. When Reed returned to the Knicks' starting lineup the following year, Lucas served as a backup for both Reed and starting power forward Dave DeBusschere on New York's 1972–1973 championship team. He retired from the game at the conclusion of the 1973–1974 season with career averages of 17 points and 15.6 rebounds per game.

Robertson remained in Cincinnati through the end of the 1969–1970 season, averaging 25.3 points and 8.1 assists per game in his final year with the team. After experiencing philosophical differences with new head coach Bob Cousy, he was traded to the Milwaukee Bucks at the end of the season. Joining Kareem Abdul-Jabbar (then Lew Alcindor) in Milwaukee, Robertson helped lead the Bucks to their only NBA championship in his first year with the team. He played three more years before retiring at the end of the 1973–1974 campaign. Robertson ended his career with averages of 25.7 points, 7.5 rebounds, and 9.5 assists per game. His scoring average is the eighth highest in NBA history, and he averaged the fourth-most assists per contest. Robertson also ranks 12th all-time in points scored (26,710) and fifth all-time in assists (9,887). The Big O led the NBA in assists six times, finished runner-up twice, and placed in the top five three other times. He finished in the top three in scoring in each of his first seven seasons, making it into the top 10 two other times. Robertson was a 12-time All-Star and a three-time All-Star Game MVP. He not only averaged a triple-double in 1961–1962 but averaged a triple-double over the first five years of his career, posting averages of 30.2 points, 10.4 rebounds, and 10.6 assists per game between 1960 and 1965. Those are the figures that cause many basketball experts to proclaim Robertson as the greatest all-around player who ever played the game.

Jerry Lucas said, "He obviously was unbelievable, way ahead of his time. There is no more complete player than Oscar."[4]

Red Auerbach said of Robertson, "He was the Michael Jordan of his day . . . in a lot of ways."[5]

Chuck Daly said in an interview conducted in the late-1990s: "If Oscar were playing today, against Michael, we might have a huge argument going on."[6]

And Jerry West, who also played against Bill Russell, Wilt Chamberlain, Kareem Abdul-Jabbar, and Bob Pettit during his career, said of Robertson, "Personally, when I look back on my career, he's the greatest player I ever played against—period."[7]

In their six years together, Oscar Robertson and Jerry Lucas combined for nine selections to the All-NBA First Team, one selection to the Second Team, and six top-five finishes in the league MVP balloting. Both players made the All-Star Team every year they were teammates. Robertson led the NBA in assists four times during that period, and he finished in the top three in scoring four times. Lucas placed in the top three in rebounding in five of those years. Robertson surpassed 30 points and 10 assists per game four times each. Lucas averaged at least 20 points per game three times, and he topped 20 rebounds per contest twice. They had their two best seasons together in 1964–1965 and 1965–1966. In the first of those years, they averaged a combined 51.8 points and 29 rebounds per game. They followed that up by averaging 52.8 points and 28.8 rebounds per contest in 1965–1966. The Royals finished second in the NBA's Eastern Division twice during that period, and they made one appearance in the Eastern Division Finals. After the team broke up the tandem of Robertson and Lucas, the Royals posted a losing record and finished out of the playoffs five straight times.

Notes

Numbers printed in bold indicate that the player led his league in a statistical category.

1. Dick Barnett, http://www.nba.com/history/players/robertson_bio.html.

2. Jerry Lucas, http://www.espn.go.com/classic/biography/s/lucas_jerry.html.

3. Jerry Lucas, http://www.espn.go.com/classic/biography/s/lucas_jerry.html.

4. Jerry Lucas, http://www.nba.com/history/players/robertson_bio.html.

5. Red Auerbach, http://www.nba.com/history/players/robertson_bio.html.

6. *SportsCentury: Fifty Greatest Athletes—Oscar Robertson*, television program (ESPN, 1999).

7. *Fifty Greatest Athletes—Oscar Robertson*.

CHAPTER 42

Larry Bird / Kevin McHale

The greatest forward tandem in NBA history, Larry Bird and Kevin McHale teamed up with center Robert Parish to form arguably the greatest frontcourt in the history of the league. The success that Bird and McHale experienced together in Boston enabled them to resuscitate an ailing Celtics team and restore it to prominence during the 1980s.

The Boston Celtics established the greatest dynasty in the history of professional sports from 1957 to 1969, winning 11 NBA championships during that 13-year period. Following Bill Russell's retirement in 1969, Dave Cowens and John Havlicek led Boston to another two titles during the 1970s. However, after winning the second of those championships in 1976, the Celtics saw their record dip to 44–38 in 1976–1977, then to 32–50 in 1977–1978, and finally to an embarrassing 29–53 in 1978–1979. With both Cowens and Havlicek gone, Boston desperately needed a new leader—someone capable of reestablishing Celtic pride and tradition and instilling in the rest of the squad the same selfless approach to the game taken by the many championship teams that reigned supreme in the NBA. Larry Bird brought all those qualities with him when he joined the Celtics in 1979, making the team an instant contender and instilling in his teammates a "team-first" mentality.

After earning all-American honors at Indiana State University, Larry Bird was selected by Boston with the sixth overall pick of the 1978 NBA draft. Although the 6'9", 220-pound forward elected to remain at Indiana State one more year to play his senior season, he eventually joined the Celtics prior to the start of the 1979–1980 campaign. Bird demonstrated to Boston in his first season that he was well worth the wait, leading the team to the NBA's best regular-season record, a 61–21 mark that enabled them to capture the Atlantic Division title. Bird averaged 21.3 points and 10.4 rebounds per game en route to winning Rookie of the Year honors and a spot on the All-NBA First Team for the first of nine consecutive times.

Bird certainly posted impressive numbers in his first year in the league. Even more impressive, though, were the many outstanding qualities that he exhibited as a rookie that earned him the nickname "Larry Legend." Bird wasn't blessed with overwhelming physical gifts; he had neither outstanding foot speed nor exceptional leaping ability. But he was an extremely intelligent and instinctive player who excelled in every aspect of the game. A brilliant outside shooter, Bird was also an adept ball handler and passer, a strong positional rebounder, and a solid team defender. Moreover, he had the innate ability to make the other players around him better. Bird inspired his teammates with his tremendous work ethic, challenged them vocally when he felt he needed to do so, and made them realize that the ultimate goal of winning took precedence over their personal statistics.

With Bird leading the way, Boston finished an NBA-best 62–20 in 1980–1981, then defeated Houston in six games in the NBA Finals to capture the league championship. Bird averaged 21.2 points and 10.9 rebounds per game during the regular season en route to earning a second-place finish in the league MVP balloting for the first of three straight times. Although the Celtics failed to win the NBA title in either of the next two seasons, they posted one of the league's best records both years, advancing to the Eastern Conference Finals in 1981–1982. Bird averaged just under 23 points and 11 rebounds per game in 1981–1982, then increased his output to 23.6 points and 11 rebounds per contest the following season. In addition to finishing runner-up in the MVP voting and earning a place on the All-NBA First Team, Bird was named to the All-NBA Second Defensive Team both years.

In 1983–1984, Bird began a string of three consecutive MVP seasons. These are his numbers from those three campaigns:

1983–1984: 24.2 PPG, 10.1 RPG, 6.6 APG
1984–1985: 28.7 PPG, 10.5 RPG, 6.6 APG
1985–1986: 25.8 PPG, 9.8 RPG, 6.8 APG

The Celtics won the NBA championship in 1983–1984 and 1985–1986, losing to Los Angeles in the NBA Finals the other year. Boston compiled the league's best record in each of those three campaigns, finishing 62–20 in 1983–1984, 63–19 in 1984–1985, and 67–15 in 1985–1986. In being named league MVP three straight times, Bird became only the third player in NBA history to be so honored (Bill Russell and Wilt Chamberlain were the first two). He also was named NBA Finals MVP in 1984 and 1986.

It was during the last of those years that Bird was joined in the Boston starting lineup by Kevin McHale, who served primarily as the Celtics' sixth man his first five years with the team. McHale originally joined the Celtics in 1980–1981, Bird's second season in Boston. The 6'10", 220-pound McHale spent his first three years mostly as a backup, splitting his time between the center and power forward positions. However, his unique skill set continued to earn him significantly more playing time with each passing season. McHale's long arms and variety of low-post moves made him one of the NBA's most difficult individual matchups.

Discussing the problems that McHale presented to opposing teams, former NBA coach and current television analyst Hubie Brown said, "He became the most difficult low-post player to defend—once he made the catch—in the history of the league. He was totally unstoppable because of his quickness, diversification of moves, and the long arms that gave him an angle to release the ball over a taller man or more explosive jumper."[1]

Charles Barkley expressed his admiration for McHale by saying, "He was the best player I ever played against. He was unguardable, defensively."[2]

McHale's long arms also helped make him extremely effective on the defensive end. An outstanding shot blocker, he finished in the league's top 10 in that category five times during his career. McHale was selected to the NBA All-Defensive First Team three times and named to the Second Team on three other occasions.

Although McHale remained Boston's sixth man during the 1983–1984 season, he received as much playing time as most of the starters, averaging 18.4 points and 7.4 rebounds per game in just over 31 minutes of action. McHale's numbers and playing time both increased the following season, when he posted averages of 19.8 points and nine rebounds per contest in winning his second consecutive NBA Sixth Man Award.

While McHale made key contributions to Boston's 1981 and 1984 championship teams, he proved to be the second-most important player on the squad that captured the title in 1986. Inserted into the team's starting lineup at the power forward spot prior to the start of the 1985–1986 campaign, McHale averaged more than 20 points and eight rebounds per game for the first of five consecutive years. He and Bird teamed up during that time to form the greatest forward tandem in NBA history. These are the numbers the two men posted in their three best seasons together:

1985–1986:
Larry Bird: 25.8 PPG, 9.8 RPG, 6.8 APG
Kevin McHale: 21.3 PPG, 8.1 RPG

1986–1987:
Larry Bird: 28.1 PPG, 9.2 RPG, 7.6 APG
Kevin McHale: 26.1 PPG, 9.9 RPG
1987–1988:
Larry Bird: 29.9 PPG, 9.3 RPG, 6.1 APG
Kevin McHale: 22.6 PPG, 8.4 RPG

After being named NBA MVP at the conclusion of the 1985–1986 campaign, Bird finished third in the voting the following year; McHale finished right behind him. Bird also placed second in the 1987–1988 balloting. Larry Legend finished in the top five in scoring in both 1986–1987 and 1987–1988. McHale finished sixth in the league in 1986–1987 with a career-high scoring average of 26.1 points per game. He also topped the NBA that year with a .604 field-goal percentage. Bird was named to the All-NBA First Team for the final three times of his career. McHale joined him on the First Team in 1986–1987. McHale also earned a spot on the All-NBA First Defensive Team all three years.

Foot and lower-back problems limited Bird to only six contests in 1988–1989, temporarily halting the outstanding run of the two Boston forwards. However, Bird returned the following year to average 24.3 points, 9.5 rebounds, and 7.5 assists per game. Meanwhile, after posting averages of 22.5 points and 8.2 rebounds per contest in 1988–1989, McHale averaged 20.9 points and 8.3 rebounds per game in the ensuing campaign. He was named to the All-NBA Second Team each year.

Unfortunately, Bird's back problems grew increasingly worse in subsequent seasons, forcing him to miss huge portions of both the 1990–1991 and 1991–1992 campaigns while playing each of those years in severe pain. He retired at the conclusion of the 1991–1992 season having averaged 24.3 points, 10 rebounds, and 6.3 assists per game over the course of his career. He scored a total of 21,791 points and pulled down 8,974 rebounds. Bird finished in the top 10 in scoring seven times, placing in the top five on four separate occasions. He averaged better than 20 points per game in 11 of his 12 full NBA seasons, topping 25 points per contest four times. He finished in the top 10 in rebounding seven times, averaging better than 10 rebounds per game on six occasions. He also averaged more than seven assists per game three times. In addition to his three MVP awards and nine selections to the All-NBA First Team, Bird was named to the Second Team once and appeared in 12 All-Star Games.

Upon Bird's retirement, NBA commissioner David Stern said, "Larry Bird helped define the way a generation of basketball fans has come to view and appreciate the NBA."[3]

Longtime NBA referee Norm Drucker revealed during a mid-1980s interview in *From Set Shot to Slam Dunk*, "Oscar Robertson was, and is, the greatest guard I ever saw, and, for a long time, I rated him as the greatest ballplayer. I have changed my mind after watching Larry Bird."[4]

And Magic Johnson, Bird's greatest rival, said, "You cannot believe how good Larry Bird is." He then added, "There will never be another Larry Bird."[5]

Kevin McHale remained with the Celtics one year longer than Bird, leaving the game at the end of the 1992–1993 season after seeing his playing time gradually diminish in each of the three previous seasons. He retired with a career scoring average of 17.9 points per game and a rebounding average of 7.3 boards per contest. McHale led the NBA in field-goal percentage twice, with his .554 career shooting percentage placing him ninth in league history. That mark also places him first all-time among forwards. McHale was selected to the All-Star Team seven times in his 13 years in the league.

In their 11 full seasons together, Larry Bird and Kevin McHale led Boston to nine Atlantic Division titles, five NBA Finals appearances, and three NBA championships. They combined for 18 All-Star Game appearances and nine top-five finishes in the league MVP voting. They earned a total of nine selections to the All-NBA First Team as teammates, also earning three nominations to the Second Team. Bird and McHale combined for a total of three selections to the All-NBA First Defensive Team and another four selections to the Second Team. In 1986–1987, their best year together, Bird and McHale averaged a combined 54.2 points and 19.1 rebounds per game between them. They also averaged 52.5 points and 17.7 rebounds per contest the following season.

Notes

1. Hubie Brown, http://www.nba.com/history/players/mchale_bio.html.
2. Charles Barkley, http://www.nba.com/history/players/mchale_bio.html.
3. David Stern, http://www.nba.com/history/players/bird_bio.html.
4. Charles Salzberg, *From Set Shot to Slam Dunk* (New York: Dutton, 1987), 197.
5. Magic Johnson, http://www.nba.com/history/players/bird_bio.html.

CHAPTER 43

Julius Erving / Moses Malone

Although Julius Erving and Moses Malone had already established themselves as two of basketball's most dominant players by the time they joined forces in 1982, neither man had yet won an NBA championship. Both players removed that blemish from their record during the 1982–1983 campaign, when they led the Philadelphia 76ers to one of the greatest single-season performances in NBA history.

Julius Erving first entered professional basketball in 1971 with the ABA's Virginia Squires. In his first season, Erving finished among the league leaders with a 27.3 scoring average and a career-high 15.7 rebounding average. Erving led the ABA in scoring in his second year with Virginia, averaging 31.9 points per contest. He joined the New York Nets the following year, spending his final three ABA seasons with them. In his three years in New York, Erving led his team to two league championships, captured two scoring titles, and won two MVP Awards. He also shared a third MVP trophy with George McGinnis. Over the course of his five ABA seasons, Erving earned All-ABA First Team honors four times, a spot on the Second Team once, and a place on the All-Star Team each year. Perhaps more significant than any of the individual accolades he earned, though, was the fact that Erving became the face of the fledgling league. The ABA's most exciting player, "Dr. J" was one of the sport's great innovators, drawing fans to arenas around the league with his high-flying, midair maneuvers that seemed to defy the laws of gravity. Erving's spectacular dunks and acrobatic lay-ins around the basket became the stuff of legend, elevating the 6'6" forward to icon-like status and bringing credibility to the newly formed league.

However, when the ABA folded at the end of the 1975–1976 campaign, financial difficulties forced the Nets to sell Erving's contract to the Philadelphia 76ers. Erving remained an exceptional player after he joined the more established NBA, although he toned down his game somewhat from the up-tempo, freewheeling style he played in the ABA. In addition to adapting himself to the more conservative style played in his new league, Dr. J accepted a less prominent scoring role in Philadelphia to accommodate several of his offensive-minded teammates. As a result, Erving, who never averaged fewer than 27 points per game in his five ABA seasons, posted a scoring average of "only" 21.6 points per contest in his first year in the NBA. He followed that up with scoring averages of 20.6 and 23.1 points per game the next two seasons, before posting his highest NBA scoring average in 1979–1980, finishing fourth in the league with a mark of 26.9 points per contest. Erving's exceptional performance earned him a second-place finish in the league MVP voting. Dr. J led Philadelphia to a league-best 62–20 record the following year, one in which he averaged 24.6 points and eight rebounds per game. For his efforts, Erving was named the NBA's Most Valuable Player. He finished third in the MVP balloting in 1981–1982 after averaging 24.4 points and just under seven rebounds per game during the regular season.

In spite of the considerable amount of individual recognition that Erving received his first six years in the NBA, each of those campaigns ended in bitter disappointment for the superstar. Erving joined a dysfunctional team when he came to the 76ers in 1976. Teammates such as Lloyd Free, Doug Collins, Darryl Dawkins, and George McGinnis all had a difficult time grasping the team concept. Furthermore, they often withered under the pressure they faced in the playoffs. As a result, the 76ers failed to capture the NBA title in any of Erving's first six years with them, even though they had as much talent as anyone in the league. Particularly disheartening were their NBA Finals losses to Portland in 1977 and Los Angeles in 1980 and 1982.

Erving's luck changed, though, at the conclusion of the 1981–1982 campaign. After ridding themselves of the many selfish players that filled their roster the previous few seasons, the 76ers acquired the league's most dominant low-post player in center Moses Malone. Joining Erving, Maurice Cheeks, Bobby Jones, and the other team-oriented players who remained in Philadelphia, Malone sparked the 76ers to the NBA championship that previously eluded him and Dr. J in his first year with the team. Malone's journey to the 76ers proved to be quite a long one, though, much as Erving's had been a few years earlier.

Beginning his professional career as a 19-year-old with the ABA's Utah Stars in 1974, Moses Malone was one of the first players to enter the pros right out of high school. Malone clearly demonstrated that he wasn't overmatched in his first year in Utah, averaging 18.8 points and 14.6 rebounds per game. After one more year in the ABA, Malone became a member of the NBA's Houston Rockets when the less-established league folded.

After two productive years in Houston, the 23-year-old Malone began to establish himself as an NBA force in 1978–1979. Appearing in all 82 games for the Rockets, Malone averaged 24.8 points and a league-leading 17.6 rebounds per game in helping his team post a 47–35 record, which placed them a close second in the final Central Division standings. For his efforts, Malone was named league MVP for the first of three times.

Malone also performed extremely well in his final three seasons in Houston, averaging at least 25.8 points and 14.5 rebounds per game in each of those campaigns and leading the Rockets to an appearance in the NBA Finals in 1981. He had his finest season for the Rockets in 1981–1982, finishing second in the league with a scoring average of 31.1 points per game and leading the NBA with 14.7 rebounds per contest. Malone's extraordinary performance earned him the second of his three MVP trophies.

In spite of Malone's exceptional campaign, Houston elected to trade him to Philadelphia during the subsequent off-season, giving the 76ers the strong low-post presence they previously lacked. A tenacious rebounder, Malone was particularly effective under the offensive boards, establishing an all-time NBA record by pulling down 6,731 offensive rebounds. He also holds the NBA single-game mark with 21 offensive boards. Malone's size, strength, and attitude made him the NBA's most physically intimidating player. Few players in the league could match the physical strength of the 6'10", 260-pound Malone, which he often used to punish his opponents on both ends of the court. Yet, in addition to the powerful inside game he possessed on offense, he had a surprisingly soft touch on his midrange jump shot.

With Malone joining Erving in the Philadelphia frontcourt, the 76ers dominated the NBA in 1982–1983. After compiling a league-best 65–17 record during the regular season, Philadelphia posted a 12–1 mark in the playoffs, which included a four-game sweep of the defending champion Lakers in the NBA Finals. Malone averaged 26 points and just under 16 rebounds per contest during the playoffs, badly outplaying Kareem Abdul-Jabbar in the finals, out-rebounding the Los Angeles center by a 72–30 margin. Malone's stellar performance earned him Finals MVP honors. The Lakers had eliminated Philadelphia in the Finals in six games the previous year. But following the 76ers' sweep of the Lakers, Philadelphia coach Billy Cunningham said, "Let's not make believe. The difference from last year was Moses."[1]

Erving averaged 21.4 points and 6.8 rebounds per game during Philadelphia's championship campaign, earning a spot on the All-NBA First Team in the process. Meanwhile, Malone posted averages of 24.5 points and a league-leading 15.3 rebounds per contest en route to earning a spot on the First Team as well. He also was named to the All-NBA First Defensive Team and won his third MVP trophy.

Erving and Malone spent three more years together in Philadelphia. Although they never won another NBA championship, they continued to play at a high level. The 76ers finished 52–30 in 1983–1984 but were upset by New

Jersey in the first round of the playoffs. Malone averaged 22.7 points per game and led the league in rebounding for the fifth time, with a mark of 13.4 boards per contest. Erving averaged 22.4 points and just under 7 rebounds per game. Both men were named to the All-NBA Second Team.

Philadelphia posted a record of 58–24 in 1984–1985 before being eliminated by Boston in the Eastern Conference Finals. Erving averaged 20 points per game during the regular season for the final time in his career. Malone averaged 24.6 points per contest and led the NBA in rebounding for the sixth and final time, with an average of just over 13 rebounds per game. He was named to the All-NBA First Team and finished third in the league MVP voting.

Erving and Malone were joined by rookie Charles Barkley in their final year in Philadelphia. The threesome helped lead the 76ers to a 54–28 regular-season record in 1985–1986. Yet, Philadelphia failed to make it past Milwaukee in the conference semifinals, falling to the Bucks in seven games. Erving averaged just over 18 points per game during the regular season, while Malone posted averages of 23.8 points and 11.8 rebounds per contest.

Philadelphia traded Malone to Washington at the end of the season, after which the center had two productive years for the Bullets before moving on to Atlanta for three years. He then spent two years in Milwaukee and another back in Philadelphia before ending his career with San Antonio in 1994–1995. Malone concluded his playing career with a scoring average of 20.3 points per game and an average of 12.3 rebounds per contest. He is sixth on the NBA's all-time scoring list, with 29,580 points to his credit. He also ranks third with 17,834 total rebounds. In addition to his six rebounding titles, Malone finished in the top five another five times. He also finished in the top 10 in scoring eight times, making it into the top five on five occasions. Malone was named to either the All-NBA First or Second Team a total of eight times.

While Malone's playing career lasted another nine years, Erving spent only one more season in Philadelphia before retiring. He called it quits at the end of the 1986–1987 campaign having averaged 24.2 points and 8.5 rebounds per game during his ABA/NBA career. His 30,026 points place him fifth on the all-time scoring list. In addition to the four Most Valuable Player Awards that Erving won during his playing career, he led his team to three league championships. Discounting the five years that Erving spent in the ABA, he led the 76ers into the Finals in four of his first seven NBA seasons. He averaged better than 20 points per game in each of his first nine years in the league. Erving was selected to the All-Star Team in each of his 11 NBA seasons. He was named to the All-NBA First Team five times, and he was selected to the Second Team twice.

Billy Cunningham, Erving's coach on the 76ers during the early 1980s, said, "Julius was the best player I've ever seen in the open court, and that includes Jordan."[2]

Magic Johnson, who grew up watching Dr. J, then played against him for several seasons, said, "Julius Erving did more to popularize basketball than anybody else who's ever played the game. . . . There were other big players, talented players, and great players before him. But it was Dr. J who put the 'WOW!' into the game."[3]

In their four years as teammates, Moses Malone and Julius Erving led Philadelphia to two appearances in the Eastern Conference Finals and one NBA championship. Erving averaged better than 20 points per game in three of those seasons, while Malone topped 22 points per contest each year, led the league in rebounding three times, and earned league MVP and NBA Finals MVP honors once each. Erving and Malone combined for three appearances on the All-NBA First Team, two appearances on the Second Team, and seven All-Star Game nominations. Had they spent more time together, Malone and Erving likely would have received a higher ranking on this list of dynamic basketball duos.

Notes

1. Billy Cunningham, http://www.nba.com/history/legends/moses-malone/index.html.

2. Billy Cunningham, http://www.basketballforum.com/nba-history-aba-too/386765choose-best-supporting-cast-following-trios.html.

3. Magic Johnson, http://www.nba.com/2010/news/features/fran_blinebury/02/24/dr.j/.

CHAPTER 44

Walt Frazier / Earl Monroe

Many people who saw Walt Frazier and Earl Monroe perform together in the New York Knicks' backcourt during the 1970s feel that the tandem formed the greatest backcourt combination in NBA history. The numbers posted by Frazier and Monroe as teammates on the Knicks from 1971 to 1977 were not particularly overwhelming. Both men averaged more than 20 points per game in the same season just once in their six years together. The Lakers' starting backcourt of Jerry West and Gail Goodrich proved to be a more prolific scoring tandem during the early 1970s, but Frazier and Monroe could have posted significantly higher scoring averages had they elected to do so. Instead, they blended their considerable talents into the Knicks' team-oriented system, subjugating themselves for the betterment of their team and making the other players around them better in the process. Yet, ironically, Frazier and Monroe were once the fiercest of rivals, competing against each other in perhaps the greatest team rivalry of their era.

Walt Frazier and Earl Monroe both entered the NBA in 1967. Monroe joined a Baltimore Bullets team still in its infancy that had posted a losing record in each of its four years in the league, including an NBA-worst 20–61 mark the previous season. But with Monroe running the offense, Baltimore's record improved to 36–46 in 1967–1968. Monroe finished third in the league in scoring, with an average of 24.3 points per game en route to winning Rookie of the Year honors.

While Monroe flourished in Baltimore, Frazier struggled in New York. Serving primarily as a backup to starting point guard Butch Komives, Frazier averaged only nine points and 4.1 assists per game as a rookie, frequently turning over the ball on offense. However, Frazier's play improved dramatically when he assumed the starting role some 30 games into the 1968–1969 campaign, after New York traded Komives and starting center Walt Bellamy to Detroit for forward Dave Debusschere. The move not only gave the Knicks one of the league's top power forwards in Debusschere but enabled them to insert Frazier into the starting lineup and move Willis Reed back into his more natural position of center. New York subsequently posted the league's best record over the final 50 games, finishing the year with a mark of 54–28. Meanwhile, Frazier averaged 17.5 points, 7.9 assists, and 6.2 rebounds per contest.

That 1968–1969 campaign also marked the beginning of one of the NBA's greatest rivalries. With Baltimore center Wes Unseld winning both Rookie of the Year and league MVP honors, the Bullets compiled an NBA-best 57–25 regular-season record. Unseld's tremendous outlet passes started Baltimore's fast break, which Monroe led with his superior ball-handling ability and extraordinary open-court skills. The league's best one-on-one player, "Earl the Pearl" dazzled the opposition with his spinning, twisting moves and wide assortment of head fakes and body machinations. Describing what it was like going up against Monroe in those days, Frazier later said, "He didn't know what he was going to do, so how could I? He had the spin move, which was new at the time. . . . When Earl scored on you, it was humiliating."[1]

Although Unseld was named the league's Most Valuable Player, Monroe led the Bullets in scoring and assists, finishing second in the NBA with a 25.8 scoring average. Both players were named to the All-NBA First Team at the end of the year. Yet, despite the presence of Unseld and Monroe, the Knicks swept Baltimore in the first round of the playoffs. Most observers believed that the biggest difference between the two squads was their respective approaches to the game. The Bullets' offense was predicated largely on their fast break and the one-on-one skills of Monroe. Meanwhile, the Knicks employed a "hit the open man" philosophy on offense while placing a great deal of emphasis on team defense. Frazier epitomized the team's style of play, distributing the ball unselfishly to his teammates on the offensive end of the court and playing stellar defense at the other end. Frazier also represented the stylish grace and elegance of the Knicks. Poised and confident, he never seemed flustered by things that transpired around him. On offense, he had smooth, silky moves and an extremely soft touch on his midrange jump shot. He also had superb ball-handling and passing skills and perhaps the fastest hands in the league on defense.

Former Knicks coach Red Holzman once told *Sport* magazine, "The great thing about Clyde [Frazier] is his hands, his anticipation."[2]

Teammate Bill Bradley told that same publication, "It's not only that Clyde steals the ball, but that he makes [the fans] think he's about to steal it, and that he can steal it any time he wants to."[3]

Bradley went on to say, "Frazier is the only player I've ever seen whom I would describe as an artist, who takes an artistic approach to the game."[4]

The Knicks and Bullets renewed their rivalry in each of the next two post-seasons, with each team coming out on top once. The Knicks finished an NBA-best 60–22 in 1969–1970, with Willis Reed being named the league's Most Valuable Player. Frazier finished fourth in the voting after averaging 20.9 points, 8.2 assists, and six rebounds per game during the regular season. Both Reed and Frazier earned spots on the All-NBA First Team at season's end—Frazier, for the first of four times in his career. The guard also earned a spot on the All-NBA First Defensive Team for the first of seven straight times. However, the Bullets, who finished third in the Eastern Division with a record of 50–32, made life difficult for the Knicks in the first round of the playoffs, finally losing to New York in a classic seven-game series. Monroe, who averaged 23.4 points per game during the regular season, improved his scoring average to 28 points against the Knicks in the series. New York went on to capture the NBA championship in 1969–1970, defeating the Lakers in seven games behind a brilliant all-around performance by Frazier in game seven. The Knicks guard scored 36 points and compiled 19 assists, seven rebounds, and five steals in leading his team to a 113–99 victory.

The Bullets, though, turned the tables on the Knicks the following season, defeating New York in seven games in the Eastern Conference Finals. Both Frazier and Monroe had outstanding years for their respective teams. Frazier averaged 21.7 points, 6.7 assists, and 6.8 rebounds per game for the Knicks en route to earning a spot on the All-NBA Second Team. Monroe led Baltimore to a first-place finish in the newly formed Central Division, averaging 21.4 points and 4.4 assists per contest. However, he also began experiencing knee problems that year, something that robbed him of much of his quickness and explosive scoring ability the remainder of his career.

Monroe and the Bullets reached an impasse in their contract negotiations at the end of that 1970–1971 campaign, prompting Baltimore to trade him to—of all teams—the Knicks. While Monroe continued to recover from off-season knee surgery during the early stages of the campaign, the New York media fueled speculation that he and Frazier would be unable to coexist in the same backcourt. Members of the press maintained that the players would need two balls to play together and that Monroe would not be able to adapt his style to fit into New York's team-oriented offense.

Monroe proved everyone wrong after he joined the Knicks some 20 games into the season. Not only did Monroe suppress his natural one-on-one tendencies, sacrificing numerous scoring opportunities to create chances for his teammates, but he worked extremely hard on improving his defense. In fact, Monroe eventually assumed the responsibility of guarding the opposing team's top scoring guard, allowing Frazier to look for steals by freelancing in the passing lanes. Nevertheless, Monroe found his performance compromised somewhat by the lingering effects of his off-season surgery and by his gradual adjustment to life with his new team. Monroe averaged only 20 minutes and 11.4 points per game in his first year in New York. Meanwhile, Frazier had perhaps his finest all-around season, scoring a career-high 23.2 points per game, averaging 5.8 assists and 6.7 rebounds per contest, and being named to the All-NBA First Team for the second time. The Knicks, though, were eliminated by the Lakers in five games in the NBA Finals.

New York returned the favor to the Lakers the following year, defeating them in five games in the NBA Finals. Fully integrating himself into New York's offense over the course of the campaign, Monroe averaged 15.5 points per game during the regular season. Frazier led the Knicks with a scoring average of 21.1 points per contest while averaging 5.9 assists and 7.3 rebounds per game. He was named to the All-NBA Second Team at the end of the year.

Recurring knee problems caused Monroe to miss half of the 1973–1974 season, one in which he averaged only 14 points per game. Frazier, though, continued his stellar play, averaging 20.5 points, 6.9 assists, and 6.7 rebounds per contest in leading the Knicks to a spot in the Eastern Conference Finals, where they lost to Boston in five games. The 1973–1974 campaign proved to be the last highly successful season in New York for quite some time. With their frontcourt decimated by the retirements of Willis Reed, Dave Debusschere, and Jerry Lucas at the end of the previous season, the 1974–1975 Knicks posted a losing record (40–42) for the first time since 1966–1967. Although they advanced to the playoffs, they were quickly eliminated in the first round. The Knicks would not even have made it as far as they did had it not been for the exceptional performances turned in by Frazier and Monroe. Knowing that they needed to score more if the team had any hopes of being successful, the two men had their greatest season together, both averaging more than 20 points per game and being named to the All-Star Team. Monroe posted a scoring average of just under 21 points per contest, while Frazier averaged 21.5 points, six assists, and 6.1 rebounds per game. Frazier also finished second in the NBA with just under 2.5 steals per game en route to earning a spot on the All-NBA First Team for the final time.

Although the Knicks failed to make the playoffs for the first time in a decade the following year, their backcourt continued to perform at any extremely high level. Injuries limited Frazier to only 59 games. Nevertheless, he averaged 19.1 points, 5.9 assists, and 6.8 rebounds per contest. Monroe took over the team scoring lead by averaging 20.7 points per game.

The Knicks compiled the NBA's worst record in 1976–1977, finishing just 22–60 in spite of Monroe's outstanding play. The team's best player that year, Monroe averaged just under 20 points and five assists per game. He was named to the All-Star Team for the second time as a Knick and for the fifth and final time in his career. Meanwhile, Frazier's numbers dropped to 17.4 points and 5.3 assists per contest, amid speculation that he had lost a step and, along with it, much of the quickness that previously made him one of the league's top players. The Knicks traded Frazier to Cleveland at the end of the season for the younger Jim Clemons, who found it impossible to fill Clyde's shoes after he arrived in New York. Failing to find any sort of inspiration away from the big city, Frazier played parts of three years in Cleveland, appearing in a total of only 66 games. He retired at the end of the 1979–1980 season with career averages of 18.9 points, 6.1 assists, and 5.9 rebounds per game. Monroe remained with the Knicks three more years, also retiring at the end of the 1979–1980 campaign. He finished with a career scoring average of 18.8 points per game.

In their six seasons as teammates, Walt Frazier and Earl Monroe helped lead the Knicks to three Eastern Conference Finals, two NBA Finals, and one NBA championship. They combined for seven total appearances on the All-Star Team, three appearances on the All-NBA First Team, and one appearance on the All-NBA Second Team. They had their two best seasons together in 1974–1975 and 1975–1976. In the first of those years, they combined to average 42.4 points per game, both earning a spot on the All-Star Team. The following season, they posted a combined scoring average of just under 40 points per game while totaling just under 10 assists per contest. Over the course of their entire careers, Frazier and Monroe appeared in the All-Star Game 11 times, earned five All-NBA First Team selections, and were nominated to the All-NBA Second Team twice. Monroe placed in the top 10 in scoring three times, and Frazier finished in the top 10 in assists on six occasions.

Looking back at the time that Frazier and Monroe spent together in New York, former teammate Dave Debusschere said, "There's never been two players together that were that good in the same backcourt. They were the best ever."[5]

You will find no argument with either of those statements here.

Notes

1. *New York's Game: History of the Knicks*, video (CBS/FOX, 1989).

2. Red Holzman, http://www.nba.com/history/legends/walt-frazier/index.html (20 August 2010).

3. Bill Bradley, http://www.nba.com/history/legends/walt-frazier/index.html (20 August 2010).

4. Bill Bradley, http://www.nba.com/history/legends/walt-frazier/index.html (20 August 2010).

5. *New York's Game: History of the Knicks*.

CHAPTER 45

Isiah Thomas / Joe Dumars

The Detroit Pistons employed a physically aggressive style of play during the latter portion of the 1980s that eventually earned them the nickname the "Bad Boys." Rugged players such as center Bill Laimbeer and forward Rick Mahorn often antagonized and intimidated the opposition with their objectionable behavior and rough-and-tumble antics. However, the Pistons also possessed a great deal of talent that enabled them to capture two straight NBA championships and advance to the NBA Finals three consecutive years. Unquestionably, Detroit's two most talented players throughout that period were guards Isiah Thomas and Joe Dumars.

The Pistons posted a losing record four straight years between 1977 and 1981, finishing last in the NBA's Central Division in 1979–1980 and 1980–1981 with a combined record of 37–127. Detroit showed marked improvement, though, in 1981–1982 when rookie point guard Isiah Thomas took control of running the team's offense. Thomas averaged 17 points and 7.8 assists per game his first year in the league, helping the Pistons improve their record to 39–43. For his efforts, Thomas was named to the All-Star Team for the first of 12 straight times.

Although Detroit's record slipped slightly the following year to 37–45, Thomas further established himself as the team's leader while laying claim to being one of the NBA's top point guards. Utilizing his speed and great quickness to break down the defenses of opposing teams, Thomas quickly developed into one of the league's most exciting players. An excellent passer and ball handler, he did a superb job of creating off the dribble. Thomas had the ability to penetrate and dish the ball off to a waiting teammate, score himself on a quick drive to the basket, or break free for an outside jump shot. He used his unique skill set to average just under 23 points and 8 assists per game in his sophomore season en route to earning a spot on the All-NBA Second Team.

Thomas led the Pistons to a 49–33 record and a spot in the divisional play-offs for the first time in seven years in 1983–1984 by averaging 21.3 points, 11.1 assists, and 2.5 steals per contest. He placed second in the league in both assists and steals per game over the course of the campaign.

Thomas's exceptional performance earned him his first appearance on the All-NBA First Team. Against New York in the playoffs, Thomas exhibited his ability to take over a game by scoring points in huge bunches. Although the Knicks eventually won game 5 of their opening-round series against the Pistons, Thomas scored 16 points in the final 94 seconds of regulation to send the game into overtime.

Thomas received his second nomination to the All-NBA First Team the following year, as he continued his string of four consecutive seasons in which he averaged better than 20 points and 10 assists per game. These are the numbers he posted those four seasons:

1983–1984: 21.3 PPG, 11.1 APG
1984–1985: 21.2 PPG, **13.9** APG
1985–1986: 20.9 PPG, 10.8 APG
1986–1987: 20.6 PPG, 10.0 APG

The Pistons advanced to the playoffs each of those years, with Thomas being named to the All-NBA First Team the first three seasons. He also earned a spot on the Second Team in the final year.

It was during the 1985–1986 campaign that the Pistons began to form their Bad Boys image. Rick Mahorn was acquired in a trade from Washington, joining Bill Laimbeer in the Detroit frontcourt. Dennis Rodman and John Salley joined the team as rookies the following season, giving the team another two physically aggressive players. It was also during the 1985–1986 season that another key player became a member of the squad. Rookie guard Joe Dumars joined the Pistons that year as well, coming off the bench and posting modest numbers in his first year in the league. Nevertheless, Atlanta eliminated Detroit in the first round of the playoffs, forcing the Pistons to wait another year before becoming a member of the NBA's elite.

The Pistons finished 52–30 in 1986–1987 and subsequently forced the defending NBA champion Boston Celtics to a decisive seventh game before finally losing to them in the Eastern Conference Finals. Thomas continued his exceptional play, being named to the All-NBA Second Team for the second time in his career. Meanwhile, Dumars established himself as an important member of the team, averaging 11.8 points and 4.5 assists per contest after earning a starting spot opposite Thomas in the backcourt. Dumars proved to be the perfect complement to Thomas in the backcourt since he could play without the ball yet score when he was called on to do so. He was also a fine passer and ball

handler, as well as an excellent defender who drew the opposing team's top offensive guard as his defensive assignment every night, thereby allowing Thomas
to focus more on running the team's offense.

Detroit evolved into an NBA powerhouse by 1987–1988, compiling a
regular-season record of 54–28, capturing the Central Division title, and advancing to the NBA Finals against the Lakers. Although the Pistons lost to Los
Angeles in seven games, they demonstrated that they had the ability to compete
against anyone. Meanwhile, Thomas and Dumars showed they were clearly the
NBA's best backcourt. Dumars averaged 14.2 points and 4.7 assists per game
during the regular season, while Thomas posted averages of 19.5 points and 8.4
assists per contest. The latter also revealed his leadership skills and tremendous
mental toughness during Detroit's heartbreaking game 6 loss to Los Angeles.
Playing on a severely sprained ankle, Thomas scored a Finals record 25 points in
the fourth quarter of the contest.

The Pistons reached the pinnacle of their sport in each of the next two
seasons, capturing the NBA title in both 1988–1989 and 1989–1990. Detroit's
level of dominance was such that the team posted playoff records of 15–2 in
1989 and 15–5 in 1990 en route to winning the championship. Thomas and
Dumars played exceptionally well both years, establishing themselves as one of
the greatest backcourt tandems in NBA history. Thomas averaged 18.2 points
and 8.3 assists per game during the 1988–1989 campaign. Meanwhile, Dumars
averaged 17.2 points and 5.7 assists per contest and was named to the All-NBA
First Defensive Team for the first of four times. He also earned Finals MVP honors by averaging 27 points during Detroit's four-game sweep of the Lakers. In
game 3 of the series, Dumars put on one of the most memorable performances
in Finals history, scoring 21 points in the third quarter, including 17 straight
at one point, to lead the Pistons to a come-from-behind victory. The backcourt
duo was equally effective during Detroit's second championship season. Thomas
averaged 18.4 points and 9.4 assists per game in 1989–1990, while Dumars
posted averages of 17.8 points and 4.9 assists per contest. Both men were named
to the All-Star Team, and Dumars was selected to the All-NBA Third Team.

Detroit failed to repeat as NBA champions in 1990–1991, losing to Chicago
in the Eastern Conference Finals. But the Pistons remained a solid team over the
next two seasons, with the heart and soul of the squad being its backcourt combination. Thomas averaged 16.2 points and 9.3 assists per game in 1990–1991.
Dumars posted even better numbers, supplanting Thomas as the team's best
player by averaging 20.4 points and 5.5 assists per contest. Both Thomas and
Dumars were voted onto the All-Star Team for the second consecutive season.
Dumars also received his second straight nomination to the All-NBA Third
Team. Thomas averaged 18.5 points and 7.2 assists per game the following season, while Dumars posted averages of 19.9 points and 4.6 assists per contest en
route to earning a spot on the All-Star Team for the third straight year.

Although Thomas played quite effectively his last two years in the league, he lacked some of the quickness he displayed earlier in his career, preventing him from being able to lead the Pistons into the playoffs either year. After averaging 17.6 points and 8.5 assists per game in 1992–1993, Thomas posted averages of 14.8 points and 6.9 assists per contest in 1993–1994, his final NBA season. He ended his career with averages of 19.2 points and 9.3 assists per game. That last figure places him fifth on the all-time list. Thomas also ranks seventh in career assists, with 9,061 to his credit.

Despite Detroit's inability to advance to the postseason, Dumars had arguably his two finest seasons in 1992–1993 and 1993–1994. He averaged a career-high 23.5 points per game in the first of those campaigns while averaging four assists per contest. Dumars followed that up by posting averages of 20.4 points and 3.8 assists per game in 1993–1994. At the same time, the quiet and dignified Dumars gradually assumed the role of team leader from Thomas. Dumars inspired the other players around him with his tremendous work ethic and willingness to sacrifice his personal statistics for the good of the team. And his self-effacing nature brought stability to a team that included the volatile personalities of players such as Dennis Rodman and Bill Laimbeer.

Dumars remained with the Pistons five more years after Thomas retired, ending his career at the conclusion of the 1998–1999 campaign. He finished with career averages of 16.1 points and 4.5 assists per game.

Isiah Thomas and Joe Dumars spent nine years as teammates. The Pistons made the playoffs in the first seven of those years, advancing to the Eastern Conference Finals five times and the NBA Finals three times, and winning two league championships. In their nine years together, Thomas and Dumars combined for 12 appearances on the All-Star Team. They were both named to the team four years in a row at one point. They also combined for one appearance on the All-NBA First Team, two appearances on the Second Team, and another two on the Third Team. Dumars received four nominations to the All-NBA First Defensive Team, and he was picked for the Second Defensive Team once. Thomas finished in the league's top 10 in assists in seven of those nine seasons, making it into the top five on two occasions. Dumars finished in the top 10 in scoring once. If not the greatest backcourt tandem in NBA history, the combination of Thomas and Dumars would certainly have to be considered one of the two or three best.

Note

Numbers printed in bold indicate that the player led his league in a statistical category.

Part IV

DYNAMIC HOCKEY DUOS

CHAPTER 46

Wayne Gretzky / Mark Messier

The New York Islanders' four-year domination of the National Hockey League ended in 1984 when the Edmonton Oilers defeated them in five games in the Stanley Cup Finals. The Oilers were a young and talented team that featured the league's most potent offense. Right wings Glenn Anderson and Jari Kurri, both only 23 years old, scored 99 and 113 points, respectively. Defenseman Paul Coffey, not yet 23 himself, tallied 126 points, the most by an NHL defenseman to that point, with the exception of Bobby Orr. (Coffey scored 138 points for the Oilers two years later.) Edmonton also received outstanding goaltending from 21-year-old net-minder Grant Fuhr, who led all NHL goalies with 30 victories during the regular season. But the two central figures on Edmonton's Stanley Cup championship team were centers Wayne Gretzky and Mark Messier. Gretzky, who led the league in scoring for the fifth consecutive season with a total of 205 points, was the NHL's most exciting and dynamic player. Messier, who scored 101 points while serving as team captain, had extraordinary leadership skills that made him in many ways the heart and soul of the team. Gretzky, Messier, and the rest of the young Oilers went on to establish the NHL's next great dynasty, winning four out of five Stanley Cups between 1984 and 1988.

An original member of the 12-team World Hockey Association that had its inaugural season in 1972–1973, the Edmonton Oilers were one of four teams absorbed by the National Hockey League when the WHA folded at the conclusion of the 1978–1979 campaign. The fortunes of the Oilers changed forever during that 1978–1979 campaign, when an exceptionally gifted 18-year-old named Wayne Gretzky joined them after his original team, the Indianapolis Racers, folded early in the season. Gretzky first signed with Indianapolis as a 17-year-old underage free agent in 1978. He played just eight games with the Racers before the team went out of business, making him available to Edmonton. Gretzky spent the remainder of the season with the Oilers, scoring 104 points in his 72 games with them and leading his new team to a league-best 48–30–2 record. The Oilers subsequently advanced to the league finals, where they lost to the Winnipeg Jets in six games.

After the WHA folded at the end of the season, the Oilers, Jets, Hartford Whalers, and Quebec Nordiques joined the ranks of the National Hockey League. Although the Oilers finished their first NHL campaign with a record of only 28–39–13, Gretzky earned league MVP honors for the first of eight consecutive times (he ended up winning the award a total of nine times). The 19-year-old center also captured the first of his record eight straight scoring titles, leading the league with 137 points on 51 goals and 86 assists. Gretzky earned Second Team NHL All-Star honors for the first of seven times, and he appeared in the All-Star Game for the first of 18 times.

Although the Oilers improved their record only slightly in 1980–1981, they advanced to the playoffs, where they defeated the Montreal Canadians in three straight games, before losing to the eventual Stanley Cup Champion Islanders in six games in the second round. Gretzky established new single-season records for assists (109) and total points scored (164) in earning First Team NHL All-Star honors for the first of seven consecutive times. The "Great One," as he came to be known, also surpassed Maurice "Rocket" Richard's (1944–1945) and Mike Bossy's (1980–1981) previous record of scoring 50 goals in the season's first 50 games when he tallied his 50th goal in just his 39th contest on December 30, 1981.

Gretzky shattered every mark in the record books the following season when he scored an NHL record 92 goals while establishing new records for assists (120) and points scored (212). The Oilers won the Smythe Division with a record of 48–17–15. However, the Los Angeles Kings upset them in five games in the first round of the playoffs, even though Gretzky scored 12 points during the series.

At only 21 years of age, Gretzky was already being referred to by many hockey experts as the greatest player ever and as one of the premier athletes of all time. Yet, he didn't possess an overwhelming amount of physical talent. At 6'0" and 185 pounds, Gretzky wasn't particularly big, and he certainly wasn't one of the strongest players in the NHL. Nor was he one of the league's fastest skaters. The qualities that truly set Gretzky apart from other players who perhaps possessed superior physical ability were his tremendous anticipation and his incredible feel for the game. The Great One always seemed to be one step ahead of everyone else, possessing an innate ability to anticipate the upcoming moves of every other player on the ice. He seemed to know the direction that the puck would take and the manner in which his teammates and opponents alike would react. As a result, Gretzky had the unique ability to make everyone around him better, establishing himself not only as a great goal scorer but also as the league's top playmaker. In addition to leading the NHL in points scored a record 11 times, he topped the league in assists on 13 occasions, finishing first in that category 12 consecutive times at one point.

Nevertheless, Gretzky found himself unable to lead the Oilers beyond the second round of the playoffs in any of his first three seasons in the NHL. Gretzky gained widespread recognition as the game's greatest player, and his teammates admired and respected him a great deal. But he wasn't a leader in the truest sense of the word. Purely a finesse player who led mostly by example, Gretzky rarely displayed much emotion on the ice. The Oilers needed someone who had the ability to inspire them on and off the ice—someone who had a considerable amount of talent but who played the game with grit, determination, and a mean streak. They also needed someone who wasn't afraid to get in another player's face if he felt that player wasn't carrying his weight. The man who fit that bill perfectly was Mark Messier, who rivaled Bill Russell as the greatest leader in the history of professional team sports.

Messier originally signed with the ill-fated Indianapolis Racers in November of 1978. The 18-year-old appeared in only five games for the team before it folded one month later, making him available to sign as a free agent with the Cincinnati Stingers of the WHA. Messier spent the remainder of the season with Cincinnati, scoring only 11 points in 47 games. When the league folded at the end of the year, Messier joined the Oilers, who subsequently became part of the NHL.

Messier failed to make a huge impact his first two seasons in Edmonton, combining for a total of 96 points from 1979 to 1981. The young center actually amassed far more penalty minutes than he did points during the early stages of his career. Messier often displayed a short temper on the ice, playing the game with an edge that he carried with him the remainder of his playing days. The 6'1", 210-pound center was extremely strong, and he employed an aggressive and physical style of play that made his opponents wary of his presence.

Messier developed into more of a scorer his third year in the league, compiling a total of 88 points in 1981–1982 on 50 goals and 38 assists. He was named a First Team NHL All-Star for the first time at the end of the season. As the young center became more of a factor in the scoring column, he gradually evolved into the Oilers' team leader. Messier possessed an on-ice presence that few players in the league could match, and he displayed a level of intensity and determination that commanded the respect of others. Before long, Messier established himself as the acknowledged leader of the Oilers, developing in the process a reputation that made him one of the most highly regarded players in the NHL.

With Messier leading the way, Gretzky and the rest of the extremely talented young Oilers took their game to the next level in 1982–1983. The Oilers established themselves as an NHL powerhouse that season, beginning a run during which they appeared in the Stanley Cup Finals in five of the next six years. Table 46.1 presents the numbers that Gretzky and Messier posted during that period.

In addition to leading the NHL in assists each season and topping the league in points scored in each of the first five years, Gretzky finished first in goals scored four times. His total of 215 points scored in 1985–1986 broke the record he established four years earlier. Gretzky's 163 assists and 215 points both remain NHL records. The Great One earned league MVP honors at the end of each of the first five seasons. He also earned First Team NHL All-Star honors in each of those five seasons.

Messier appeared in only 55 games during the 1984–1985 campaign, but he was among the league's top players in each of the other five seasons. He placed third in the NHL in assists and scoring in 1986–1987, and he finished fifth in the league in both categories the following year. Messier was named a First Team NHL All-Star in 1982–1983. He was picked for the Second Team the following year.

After capturing their second straight Smythe Division title during the 1982–1983 regular season, the Oilers breezed through the first three rounds of the playoffs, losing only once while eliminating Winnipeg, Calgary, and Chicago. However, they hit a wall when they faced the three-time defending champion New York Islanders in the Stanley Cup Finals, suffering a four-game sweep at the hands of New York while scoring a total of only six goals in the process.

The Oilers compiled a league-best 57–18–5 record the following year, before earning the right to face the Islanders in the Stanley Cup Finals again by defeating Winnipeg, Calgary, and Minnesota in the first three rounds of

Table 46.1. Wayne Gretzky and Mark Messier: 1982–1988

Player	Year	Goals	Assists	Points
Gretzky	1982–1983	**71**	**125**	**196**
	1983–1984	**87**	**118**	**205**
	1984–1985	**73**	**135**	**208**
	1985–1986	52	**163**	**215**
	1986–1987	**62**	**121**	**183**
	1987–1988	40	**109**	149
Messier	1982–1983	48	58	106
	1983–1984	37	64	101
	1985–1986	35	49	84
	1986–1987	37	70	107
	1987–1988	37	74	111

the playoffs. This time, though, a more mature Oilers team turned the tables on New York, defeating the four-time defending champions in five games to capture the first Stanley Cup in franchise history. Gretzky tallied 35 points in Edmonton's 19 playoff contests. Messier scored 26 points on eight goals and 18 assists en route to winning the Conn Smythe Trophy as playoff MVP.

The ensuing 1984–1985 campaign turned out to be a banner year for the Oilers. Gretzky and linemate Jari Kurri finished first and second in the league in goals scored, with 73 and 71, respectively. Gretzky captured his sixth straight scoring title and sixth consecutive Hart Memorial Trophy as the league's Most Valuable Player. Meanwhile, Paul Coffey won his first Norris Trophy as the NHL's top defenseman. The Oilers finished first in the Smythe Division for the fourth straight season, then lost only three times during the entire postseason to capture their second straight Stanley Cup. Messier scored 25 points in Edmonton's 18 playoff games, while Gretzky established new single-season playoff records by tallying 30 goals and 47 points en route to winning the Conn Smythe Trophy.

The Oilers proved to be the NHL's dominant team once again over the course of the 1985–1986 regular season, compiling a league-best 56–17–7 record. Not only did Gretzky establish new single-season records for assists (163) and points (215), but Kurri and Coffey joined him in the league's top four in scoring. However, the Oilers' hopes for a third straight Stanley Cup ended when they faltered in the Smythe Division Finals, suffering a seven-game defeat at the hands of their Alberta neighbors, the Calgary Flames.

The Oilers captured their sixth straight Smythe Division title in 1986–1987, finishing a league-best 50–24–6 during the regular season. Gretzky and Messier finished first and third, respectively, in the league in scoring before continuing their outstanding play during the postseason as the Oilers won their third Stanley Cup in four years. The Great One scored 34 points in Edmonton's 21 playoff contests, while Messier tallied 28 points on 12 goals and 16 assists.

The 1987–1988 campaign proved to be a bit more challenging for the Oilers. Star defenseman Paul Coffey was traded to Pittsburgh at the start of the season following a contract holdout. Edmonton failed to win the Smythe Division for the first time in seven years, placing second to Calgary in the divisional race with a record of 44–25–11. Gretzky also lost his grip on both the scoring title and the MVP award, as Pittsburgh's Mario Lemieux claimed both honors. Nevertheless, the Oilers played magnificently once the playoffs got underway, losing only twice en route to capturing their fourth Stanley Cup in five years. Messier tallied 34 points in Edmonton's 19 postseason contests. Meanwhile, Gretzky challenged his own single-season playoff mark, scoring 43 points to earn his second Conn Smythe Trophy as the Most Valuable Player of the playoffs.

The 1987–1988 season turned out to be the last one that Gretzky and Messier spent together in Edmonton. Citing financial troubles as his motive for making the deal, Oilers owner Peter Pocklington announced a trade on August 9, 1988, that will forever live in infamy as one of the darkest days in the history of Canada. The deal sent Gretzky—the nation's most beloved figure—and two other players to the Los Angeles Kings for two players, three first round draft picks, and an estimated $15–20 million. People closest to the situation in Edmonton believed that Gretzky asked to be sent to Los Angeles to accommodate his young wife, Janet Jones, an aspiring movie actress. Insiders also felt that the sport's greatest player simply had become too big for the city of Edmonton, since he found his every move closely scrutinized by both the media and the general public. They suggested that Gretzky believed a change in scenery had become necessary for him and his wife.

With Gretzky gone, the Oilers finished third in the Smythe Division during the regular season, after which they failed to advance beyond the first round of the playoffs. Meanwhile, the Great One led the Kings to their best regular season record in eight years and a spot in the playoffs, as he continued to make the other players around him better. Gretzky tallied 168 points on 54 goals and a league-leading 114 assists en route to winning the Hart Trophy as the league's Most Valuable Player for the ninth and final time. He also enabled teammate Bernie Nicholls to have the greatest season of his career—one in which he scored 70 goals and 150 points. Gretzky remained in Los Angeles six more years, capturing three more scoring titles, surpassing 90 assists and 120 points four more times each, and helping linemate Luc Robitaille score a career-high 63 goals and 125 points in 1992–1993. After splitting the 1995–1996 season between the Kings and the St. Louis Blues, Gretzky rejoined his former teammate Messier in New York, where he spent his final three years with the Rangers before announcing his retirement at the conclusion of the 1998–1999 campaign.

Gretzky ended his career first on the NHL's all-time scoring list with 894 goals, 1,963 assists, and 2,857 points. His average of 1.92 points per game is the highest ever. Gretzky also holds single-season records for goals scored (92), assists (163), and points (215). He is the only player ever to score as many as 200 points in a season, a feat he accomplished on four separate occasions. The Great One surpassed 70 goals four times, 100 assists 11 times, and 150 points nine times. He led the NHL in scoring a record 11 times, and he was named a First Team NHL All-Star on eight occasions.

As Gretzky proceeded to greatly popularize the sport of hockey in Los Angeles, Messier continued to thrive in Edmonton. After scoring 94 points in his first season without Gretzky, Messier stepped out of the Great One's shadow in 1989–1990, finishing second in the league to his former teammate in scoring, with 129 points, winning the Hart Trophy as the league's Most Valuable Player, earning First Team NHL All-Star honors, and leading the Oilers to the Stanley Cup. During a four-game sweep of Gretzky's Kings in the Smythe Division Finals, the Oilers outscored Los Angeles by a 24–10 margin. They then won their fifth Stanley Cup in seven years—their first without Gretzky—by defeating the Boston Bruins in five games in the Stanley Cup Finals. The win not only substantiated the fact that the Oilers were not merely a one-man team; it legitimized Messier as the leader in Edmonton and as one of the sport's truly great players.

Messier spent one more year with the Oilers before financial concerns prompted team ownership to trade him to the New York Rangers at the conclusion of the 1990–1991 campaign. Messier spent six years in New York, winning his second league MVP award his first year with his new team and leading the Rangers to their first Stanley Cup in 54 years in 1994. He left the Rangers in 1997 after they failed to offer him a new long-term contract. Messier spent his next three seasons with the Vancouver Canucks, before returning to New York in 2000 to finish out his career with the Rangers. He retired at the end of the 2003–2004 season as the second leading scorer in NHL history, behind only Wayne Gretzky, with a total of 1,887 points. His 1,193 career assists place him third on the all-time list, and his 694 goals scored represent the seventh highest total in league history. Messier won six Stanley Cups during his career—five in Edmonton and one in New York—and he played in the second most games (1,756) of any player in NHL history. He was named a First Team NHL All-Star four times, and he was picked for the Second Team one other time. He appeared in a total of 15 All-Star Games.

Wayne Gretzky is generally considered to be the greatest player in NHL history, but Mark Messier is perhaps the most respected player ever to lace on a pair of skates. Gretzky expressed his admiration for his former teammate when he said upon Messier's retirement in 2005, "He was the best player I ever played with."[1]

Glen Sather, Messier's former general manager and coach in Edmonton, attempted to describe Messier's impact on the team: "On the ice, he was a combination of a lot of people. The fire and passion in his eyes, the way he played the game, with determination. He never gave up. Never quit. . . . Off the ice, there's no one like Mark."[2]

Wayne Gretzky and Mark Messier were teammates in Edmonton for nine seasons. They also played together in New York one more year. Over the course of those 10 seasons, Gretzky scored a total of 1,766 points on 608 goals and 1,158 assists. Messier tallied 831 points on 338 goals and 493 assists. That averages out to 65 goals, 165 assists, and 230 points per season between them. Gretzky led the NHL in points scored in eight of those 10 campaigns, topping the circuit in assists each year while finishing first in goals scored five times. Messier placed in the top five in assists and points scored two times each.

Gretzky was named the league's Most Valuable Player in eight of those years, and he was selected as MVP of the playoffs twice. Messier earned playoff MVP honors once. The Oilers won four Stanley Cups during their time together, advancing to the Stanley Cup Finals a total of five times. Gretzky and Messier are considered by most hockey experts to be two of the five greatest players in NHL history, joining Mario Lemieux, Bobby Orr, and Gordie Howe in that extremely select group. That last fact certainly legitimizes their place at the top of these rankings.

Notes

Numbers printed in bold indicate that the player led his league in a statistical category.

1. Wayne Gretzky, http://www.successstories.com/iquote/author/2631/wayne-gretzky-quotes/13.

2. Glen Sather, http://www.nytimes.com/2007/11/12/sports/hockey/12messier.html.

CHAPTER 47

Bobby Orr / Phil Esposito

While the Boston Celtics were winning NBA championships during the 1960s, the Boston Bruins were finishing near the bottom of the National Hockey League standings virtually every season. In a league in which four out of six teams advanced to the postseason each year, the Bruins finished out of the playoffs eight consecutive times between 1960 and 1967. They finished in the NHL cellar in six of those eight seasons. However, Boston's fortunes changed dramatically shortly after a young defenseman named Bobby Orr joined the team in 1966–1967. Orr quickly developed into not only the league's most exciting and dynamic player but also the greatest defenseman ever to lace on a pair of skates. The team received an additional boost when it subsequently traded for an emerging superstar named Phil Esposito. The center evolved into a veritable scoring machine, leading the NHL in goals scored six straight seasons at one point. Orr and Esposito went on to capture seven consecutive scoring titles between them while leading the Bruins to two Stanley Cups during their time together.

The Boston Bruins team that Bobby Orr joined in 1966 was perhaps the least talented squad in the NHL. Boston failed to win more than 21 games in any of the seven previous seasons, compiling the league's worst record in five of those years. Despite the efforts of Orr, the Bruins fared no better in 1966–1967, posting a league-worst 17–43–10 record during the regular season. Nevertheless, the 18-year-old Orr, who signed a developmental deal with Boston four years earlier, won the Calder Trophy as the National Hockey League's Rookie of the Year. The 6'0", 197-pound defenseman also earned Second Team NHL All-Star honors by scoring 41 points on 13 goals and 28 assists.

Orr's immense talent became evident to all NHL observers from the very beginning. He had good size and strength, along with exceptional puck handling, passing, and shooting skills. But the thing that truly set Orr apart from virtually every other player in the league was his tremendous skating ability. Orr's great speed enabled him to rush the puck into the offensive zone and chase down opposing skaters from behind in the defensive end of the rink. His unique skill set allowed Orr to become the sport's first offensive-minded defenseman, changing forever the manner in which the game would be played by future generations of defensemen.

Former Montreal Canadians forward Jacques Lemaire noted, "Bobby Orr had lots of moves and speed. You had to be careful or he would make you look like a fool."[1]

Hockey legend Gordie Howe commented, "Overall I can fairly safely say Bobby Orr impressed me more than anybody with his tremendous talents."[2]

Hall of Fame goaltender Jacques Plante stated, "You can say about each of the great players: He's a good skater, or a good stick-handler, or he has a great shot, but something is always missing. Bobby Orr has it all. He is the best I've seen—ever!"[3]

An injury prevented Orr from playing in 28 of his team's 74 games in the expansion year of 1967–1968. Yet he still earned First Team NHL All-Star honors for the first of eight consecutive times by scoring 31 points and helping the Bruins to a third-place finish in the newly formed Eastern Division, with a record of 37–27–10. Orr also won the Norris Trophy as the league's top defenseman for the first of eight straight seasons.

Boston's efforts were aided immeasurably in the league's first year of the expansion era by a trade that the front office made shortly after the conclusion of the previous campaign. On May 15, 1967, the Bruins traded defenseman Gilles Marotte and forwards Pit Martin and Jack Norris to the Chicago Blackhawks for center Phil Esposito and wingers Ken Hodge and Fred Stanfield. The trio of forwards acquired by Boston in the deal became the team's top scoring line the next several seasons, with Hodge and Stanfield also giving the Bruins size and toughness on the frontline. Meanwhile, Esposito developed into the league's most prolific scorer. After averaging 24 goals and 56 points in his three years in Chicago, the 25-year-old center scored 35 goals and a league-leading 49 assists in his first season in Boston, placing second in the NHL in scoring with a total of 84 points. Yet, despite the efforts of Esposito, Hodge, Stanfield, and Orr, the inexperienced Bruins found themselves eliminated from the playoffs in four straight games by the Montreal Canadiens.

Esposito and a fully healthy Orr led the Bruins into the playoffs again the following year, beginning a string of highly successful seasons together. Table 47.1 presents the numbers that the two men posted over the next seven seasons.

In 1968–1969, Orr became the first defenseman in NHL history to score 20 goals in a season. He became the first defenseman to score 30 goals and 100 points and lead the league in scoring the following year, when he earned NHL

Table 47.1.   Bobby Orr and Phil Esposito: 1968–1975

Player	Year	Goals	Assists	Points
Orr	1968–1969	21	43	64
	1969–1970	33	**87**	**120**
	1970–1971	37	**102**	139
	1971–1972	37	**80**	117
	1972–1973	29	72	101
	1973–1974	32	**90**	122
	1974–1975	46	**89**	**135**
Esposito	1968–1969	49	**77**	**126**
	1969–1970	**43**	56	99
	1970–1971	**76**	76	**152**
	1971–1972	**66**	67	**133**
	1972–1973	**55**	75	**130**
	1973–1974	**68**	77	**145**
	1974–1975	**61**	66	127

MVP honors for the first of three consecutive times. Orr was also named *Sports Illustrated*'s Sportsman of the Year at the conclusion of the 1969–1970 campaign. In leading the NHL in scoring again in 1974–1975 with 135 points, Orr became the first defenseman to surpass 40 goals in a season. In addition to leading the league in scoring twice, Orr finished second three other times and came in third once. Another amazing thing about Orr is that he compiled the best plus/minus ratio in the league (i.e., "goals for" vs. "goals against") in six of those seven seasons. In fact, his +124 rating in 1970–1971 is the best single-season figure ever posted, and his mark of +597 for his career remains the second-best all-time.[4]

In addition to leading the league in goals scored six straight years, Esposito topped the circuit in assists twice and total points five times. His 126 points in 1968–1969 shattered the existing single-season record of 97 points, making him the first player in NHL history to reach the 100-point plateau. Esposito surpassed that figure by 26 points two years later, when he tallied a then mind-boggling 152 points. The center was named the NHL's Most Valuable Player at the end of the 1968–1969 and 1973–1974 campaigns.

Boston became a perennial Stanley Cup contender during the period, winning the cup twice and advancing to the finals a third time. The Bruins finished second in the East in 1968–1969, with a record of 42–18–6. They subsequently lost to the eventual champion Canadiens in six games in the semifinals. Boston posted a regular season record of 40–17–19 in 1969–1970, once again finishing second in the Eastern Division. They subsequently went 12–2 during the playoffs en route to capturing their first Stanley Cup in 29 years. Esposito scored 27 points in Boston's 14 playoff contests on 13 goals and 14 assists. Orr tallied

9 goals and 11 assists for a total of 20 points en route to earning playoff MVP honors. He punctuated his MVP performance by scoring the cup-clinching goal 40 seconds into overtime in game 4 of the Finals versus St. Louis.

The Bruins posted the league's best record for the first time in 30 years in 1970–1971, compiling a franchise-best 121 points by going 57–14–7 during the regular season. However, Montreal defeated them in seven games in the first round of the playoffs, dashing their hopes of winning a second straight Stanley Cup. Undeterred by their early playoff exit the previous year, the Bruins compiled the league's best record again in 1971–1972, finishing the regular season with a total of 119 points. They then went 12–3 during the playoffs, winning their second Stanley Cup in three years by defeating the New York Rangers in six games in the Stanley Cup Finals. Esposito and Orr each scored 24 points in Boston's 15 playoff games, with the latter being named playoff MVP for the second time.

The Bruins remained among the NHL's elite the next three seasons, surpassing 50 victories and 100 points in both 1972–1973 and 1973–1974. Nevertheless, they advanced beyond the first round of the playoffs just once, losing to the Philadelphia Flyers in the Stanley Cup Finals in six games in 1974.

While the Bruins established themselves as perennial contenders for the Stanley Cup during the period, they continued to build on their reputation as the league's most physically intimidating team. With aggressive players such as Hodge, Stanfield, Derek Sanderson, Ted Green, John McKenzie, and Don Marcotte, the Bruins spent almost as much time fighting as they did skating on some nights. Yet, even though Esposito and Orr were not necessarily adverse to dropping the gloves, they usually chose to avoid such skirmishes, preferring instead to exact revenge on the enemy by putting the puck in the opponent's net.

At 6'1" and 210 pounds, Esposito was big, thick, and strong. The center was virtually impossible to move once he established position in front of the opposing team's net. Esposito rarely employed the slap shot, but he had an excellent wrist shot, which he generally released in the direction of the opposing goaltender from close range. He scored the majority of his goals on deflections, rebounds, and tip-ins from just outside the goal crease, prompting some of his detractors to refer to him as a "garbage man." Nevertheless, it would be difficult to find fault with anyone who led the NHL in goals scored six straight years and who topped the league in total points scored on five separate occasions.

While Esposito occasionally drew criticism for his style of play, Orr was widely considered to be the game's greatest player. The defenseman had as good a slap shot as anyone in the league; he possessed tremendous passing and puck-handling skills; and he created numerous scoring opportunities for his teammates by drawing the opposing team's defense to himself. Orr's incredible skating ability made one of his end-to-end rushes truly something to behold.

He typically gathered in the puck from behind his own net, used his skating ability to breeze past the opposing team's forwards, and then employed his puck-handling skills and one final burst of speed to outmaneuver the opposing team's defensemen and goaltender before either putting the puck in the net or setting up one of his teammates for an easy goal.

Opposing goaltender Johnny Bower described the trepidation that he felt every time he saw Orr headed in his direction: "The first thing I would do when I saw Bobby coming down at me was to say a little prayer if I had time. I'm sure I wasn't the only goalie who did that."[5]

Orr's amazing talent enabled him to change the game of hockey forever. Prior to Orr's arrival in Boston, defensemen rarely got involved in the offensive flow of games. Although they occasionally ventured into their opponent's zone during power plays, they spent the majority of their time in their own defensive end, trying to prevent the other team from scoring by protecting their goaltender and clearing the puck out of their zone. Orr's style of play revolutionized the game, altering the thought processes of coaches everywhere and influencing future generations of defensemen.

Phil Esposito expressed his admiration for his former teammate when he said, "He was so dominant. Bobby was the greatest defenseman who ever played the game as far as I'm concerned. I believe in my heart he changed the face of the game."[6]

Goaltender Eddie Johnston, a longtime teammate of Orr, stated, "He could thread a needle with the puck, shoot it like a bullet or float it soft. Orr was the only player who could dictate the tempo of the game, speed it up or slow it down. He could see the whole ice the way a spectator sees it from above. He's the best player I've seen."[7]

Chicago Blackhawks Hall of Fame center Stan Mikita commented, "I never knew a single player who could lift a team as Orr could."[8]

E. M. Swift wrote in an article in *Sports Illustrated* shortly after Orr's retirement, "The great ones all bear a mark of originality, but Bobby Orr's mark on hockey, too brief in the etching, may have been the most distinctive of any player's. . . . He changed the sport by redefining the parameters of his position. A defenseman, as interpreted by Orr, became both a defender and an aggressor, both a protector and a producer."[9]

As Swift noted in his article, the career of Bobby Orr was all too brief. The brilliant defenseman's puck domination and length-of-the-ice rushes made him a marked man, causing opposing players to attempt to extract the puck from him by whatever means necessary. After leading the NHL with 135 points in 1974–1975, Orr appeared in only 10 games for Boston the following season, as he continued to recover from off-season knee surgery. Realizing that the defenseman's best days were behind him, the Bruins declined to offer Orr a new contract the following year. Orr signed on as a free agent with the Chicago Blackhawks in June 1976, but he appeared in only 26 games over the next two seasons. A second surgery on his knee kept Orr off the ice much of the time, and he never regained his incredible skating ability.

After announcing his retirement from hockey in 1979, Orr told Will McDonough of the *Boston Globe*, "When you are young, you think you can lick the world, that you are indestructible. . . . But around 1974–75, I knew it had changed. I was playing, but I wasn't playing like I could before. My knees were gone. They hurt before the game, in the game, after the game. Things that I did easily on the ice I could not do anymore."[10]

More than 30 years after his retirement, Orr still holds NHL single-season records for assists and points scored by a defenseman. He remains the only defenseman ever to lead the league in scoring. In his nine full NHL seasons, Orr was named the league's top defenseman eight times. He was a three-time league MVP, and he earned playoff MVP honors on two separate occasions. Orr led the league in scoring twice, finished second three times, and topped the circuit in assists five times. We are not likely to see his like again.

Former Boston Bruins head coach Don Cherry stated, "The second best thing about being hired by the Boston Bruins was that I'd finally made it as a coach in the NHL. The first best thing was that I was coach of the team for which Bobby Orr was a player. Mind you, I didn't say that I'd coached Bobby Orr because that would be the most presumptuous thing any coach could ever say. He was the greatest hockey player I have ever seen, Gordie Howe and Wayne Gretzky included. The greatest hockey player who ever lived, Bobby Orr, and I love him."[11]

The 1974–1975 campaign was also Esposito's final full season in Boston. The Bruins traded him to the rival New York Rangers just 12 games into the 1975–1976 campaign in a deal that also sent defenseman Carol Vadnais to New York. The Bruins received center Jean Ratelle and defenseman Brad Park in return. Since Esposito loved playing in Boston and hated the Rangers and their fans, he was devastated by the trade. It subsequently took him almost two whole years to adjust to life with his new team. It took the New York fans just as long to accept the center as one of their own. But Esposito finally won them over, and he learned to love New York. Although he was never again a dominant scorer, Esposito spent five productive years with the Rangers, surpassing 78 points each season and helping the team advance to the Stanley Cup Finals in 1978–1979. He retired from the game at the conclusion of the 1980–1981 campaign with 717 goals and 1,590 points. Both figures place Esposito in the top 10 all-time. In addition to winning the NHL's Most Valuable Player Award twice, Espositio earned six First Team NHL All-Star selections and a spot on the Second Team twice. He appeared in 10 All-Star Games during his career.

Bobby Orr and Phil Esposito spent eight full seasons as teammates. Esposito led the NHL in goals scored in six of those campaigns, and he topped the league in assists three times. Orr led the league in assists the other five years. Either Esposito or Orr led the NHL in total points scored in each of their final seven seasons as teammates, finishing first and second in the league in scoring five times. The two men were at their best together in 1970–1971, 1971–1972, 1973–1974, and 1974–1975. In the first of those seasons, they scored 291 points between them. They combined for 250 points the following year, before totaling 267 points and 262 points the final two years. Orr and Esposito won five MVP awards during that time, earned 14 First Team NHL All-Star nominations, and led their team to two Stanley Cups.

Notes

Numbers printed in bold indicate that the player led his league in a statistical category.

1. Jacques Lemaire, http://www.bobbyorr.net/quotes/quotes.php.
2. Gordie Howe, http://www.bobbyorr.net/quotes/quotes.php.
3. Jacques Plante, http://www.bobbyorr.net/quotes/quotes.php.
4. A +597 rating means that Orr's team scored 597 more goals than the opposition when he was on the ice.
5. Johnny Bower, http://www.bobbyorr.net/quotes/quotes.php.
6. Phil Esposito, http://www.bobbyorr.net/quotes/quotes.php.
7. Eddie Johnston, http://www.bobbyorr.net/quotes/quotes.php.
8. Stan Mikita, http://www.bobbyorr.net/quotes/quotes.php.
9. E. M. Swift, http://www.sportsillustrated.cnn.com/vault/article/magazine/.../index.html.
10. Bobby Orr, http://www.bobbyorr.net/quotes/quotes.php.
11. Don Cherry, http://www.bobbyorr.net/quotes/quotes.php.

CHAPTER 48

Bobby Hull / Stan Mikita

Stan Mikita and Bobby Hull of the Chicago Blackhawks proved to be two of the National Hockey League's most dynamic players during the 1960s. Mikita was the league's top center and playmaker for most of the decade, while Hull was the circuit's premier left wing and goal scorer. Along with Detroit's Gordie Howe, the two Chicago stars were the NHL's most dominant players during the era immediately preceding league expansion.

Bobby Hull first joined the Chicago Blackhawks at the tender age of 18 in 1957. Although he totaled only 31 goals and 97 points over the course of his first two seasons, the native of Ontario, Canada, immediately impressed fans around the league with his tremendous physical gifts. The 5'10", 200-pound left wing possessed great physical strength, outstanding skating ability, and the league's hardest slap shot. It appeared to be just a matter of time before Hull joined the NHL's elite.

Hull started to fulfill his great promise his third year in the league, topping the circuit in 1959–1960 with 39 goals and 81 points. Although Hull tallied only 56 points the following year, he helped lead the Blackhawks to the Stanley Cup by scoring four goals and 14 points in Chicago's 12 playoff games. It was also during that 1960–1961 campaign that a young teammate of Hull began to display for the first time the skills that ended up making him one of the league's finest all-around players for the next decade.

Czechoslovakian-born Stan Mikita spent almost as much time in the penalty box as he did on the ice in his rookie season of 1959–1960. Developing a reputation as a hot-tempered roughneck over the course of his first NHL campaign, the 5'9", 175-pound center scored only 26 points while amassing well over 100 minutes in penalties. Although Mikita continued to demonstrate a considerable amount of aggressiveness and determination whenever he hit the ice in his second year in the league, he learned to better control his temper, allowing him to garner more ice time. After scoring 53 points over the course of the regular season, he compiled another 11 points during Chicago's Stanley Cup playoff run.

It wasn't until the following season, though, that Mikita and Hull established themselves as the league's most formidable scoring tandem. Hull became just the second player in NHL history to score 50 goals in a season, joining Montreal's legendary Maurice "Rocket" Richard on an exclusive list. He also tallied 34 assists to lead the league with 84 total points. Mikita added 77 points, placing second in the league with 52 assists. Hull slumped to 31 goals and 62 total points in 1962–1963, but Mikita demonstrated the consistency that eventually became his trademark by scoring 76 points.

During the 1963–1964 campaign, Hull and Mikita began a string of highly successful seasons that placed them among the NHL's elite. Table 48.1 presents the numbers that the two men compiled in some of their best years together.

Some of those numbers might seem relatively modest by modern standards. However, many of them were compiled during the pre-expansion era, when teams played fewer games, talent was more evenly distributed throughout the six team league, and the style of play tended to be more defensive than it later became.

In addition to leading the league in goals scored four consecutive seasons, Hull topped the circuit one other time during that period, also finishing second on two occasions. He led the NHL in that category a total of seven times during his career. When Hull scored 54 goals in 1965–1966, he became the first

Table 48.1. Bobby Hull and Stan Mikita: 1963–1972

Player	Year	Goals	Assists	Points
Hull	1963–1964	**43**	44	87
	1964–1965	39	32	71
	1965–1966	**54**	43	**97**
	1966–1967	**52**	28	80
	1967–1968	**44**	31	75
	1968–1969	**58**	49	107
	1970–1971	44	52	96
	1971–1972	50	43	93
Mikita	1963–1964	39	50	**89**
	1964–1965	28	**59**	**87**
	1965–1966	30	**48**	78
	1966–1967	35	**62**	**97**
	1967–1968	40	47	**87**
	1968–1969	30	67	97
	1969–1970	39	47	86

player in league history to surpass 50 goals more than once. He went on to top the 50-goal mark a total of five times. In addition to leading the NHL in scoring in 1965–1966, Hull finished second three other times during the period. He topped the circuit in points scored a total of three times during his career.

Mikita led the league in scoring four out of five seasons at one point, finishing second the other time. He also topped the circuit in assists three straight years, placing second on three other occasions. Mikita also finished second in goals scored three times.

The two players were particularly dominant in five of those seasons:

1963–1964: Hull led the NHL in goals scored; Mikita finished second. Mikita led the league in total points; Hull finished second.

1965–1966: Hull led the NHL in goals scored and total points; Mikita led the league in assists and finished second in total points.

1966–1967: Hull led the NHL in goals scored; Mikita finished second. Mikita led the league in assists and total points; Hull finished second in points scored.

1967–1968: Hull led the NHL in goals scored; Mikita finished second in goals and led the league in total points.

1968–1969: Hull led the NHL in goals scored and finished second in total points; Mikita finished second in assists and finished fourth in total points.

The two men captured four consecutive NHL MVP awards during that period. Hull earned MVP honors in 1964–1965 and 1965–1966. Mikita won the award in 1966–1967 and 1967–1968.

Yet, in spite of the brilliance of both men, Hull generally received far more recognition than Mikita, who failed to reach the same level of popularity as his teammate with the fans and the media. Nicknamed the "Golden Jet" for his blond hair and exciting skating style, Hull became an icon in Chicago, gradually developing into probably the city's most famous athlete prior to the arrival of Michael Jordan. Hull's colorful style of play and good looks certainly contributed greatly to his popularity, but his tremendous physical talent also made him the city's most recognizable figure.

Mikita himself once noted, "Some athletes are so great they don't have to practice. Bobby Hull is one of them. He is so good, everything comes natural to him. I have to work hard and practice hard. It's not so simple."[1]

Still, there were others who appreciated Mikita's tremendous work ethic and his outstanding all-around ability. Boston Bruins general manager Milt Schmidt once called the center "the most dangerous player in the league."[2]

Toronto Maple Leafs GM Jim Gregory said of Mikita, "He's one of the best all-around hockey players I've seen in my life. It is just his misfortune that two superstars on the same team cannot share the popularity equally. One [Hull] is always the darling of the fans while the other works hard for the slightest applause."[3]

Meanwhile, hockey expert Stan Fischler said in his *Fischler's Hockey Encyclopedia*, "If any single player can be described as the guts of a hockey team, Stan Mikita, the shifty Chicago Blackhawk center, is precisely that man."[4]

Smart, instinctive, tough, and aggressive, the hard-working Mikita spent his entire 22-year career with the Blackhawks, finally retiring from the game at the end of the 1979–1980 campaign. He compiled 1,467 points during his career, the 13th-highest total in NHL history. Mikita was a six-time First Team NHL All-Star, and he was named to the Second Team twice. He appeared in a total of nine All-Star Games.

After scoring 50 goals in his 15th season with the Blackhawks in 1971–1972, Bobby Hull signed with the Winnipeg Jets of the WHA, with whom he spent the next 7.5 seasons before retiring from the game in 1979–1980. He scored a career-high 77 goals and 142 points for the Jets in 1974–1975, ending his WHA career with a total of 303 goals and 638 points. Hull scored 610 goals and 1,170 total points in his 15 years with the Blackhawks. He was a 10-time First Team NHL All-Star, earned a spot on the Second Team twice, and played in 12 All-Star Games.

In addition to winning four consecutive MVP awards and one Stanley Cup during their 13 full seasons together, Bobby Hull and Stan Mikita combined for seven scoring titles. Hull led the league in goals scored seven times as Mikita's teammate. Mikita topped the circuit in assists on three occasions. Hull and Mikita scored 969 goals and 2,109 total points as teammates, combining for 16 First Team NHL All-Star selections, four selections to the Second Team, and 18 All-Star Game appearances.

Notes

Numbers printed in bold indicate that the player led his league in a statistical category.

1. Jim Lynch, "Is Mikita Better Than Hull?" *Hockey* magazine, April 1971.
2. Lynch, "Is Mikita Better Than Hull?"
3. Lynch, "Is Mikita Better Than Hull?"
4. Stan Fischler, *Fischler's Hockey Encyclopedia* (Syracuse, NY: Crowell, 1975).

CHAPTER 49

Bryan Trottier / Mike Bossy

The New York Islanders of the early 1980s were one of the greatest hockey teams ever assembled. While winning four consecutive Stanley Cups, the Islanders demonstrated that they possessed all the ingredients necessary to create a National Hockey League dynasty. New York had an exceptional big-game goaltender in the feisty Billy Smith, whom the team shielded from onrushing puck carriers with an outstanding group of defensemen that included Hall of Famer Denis Potvin. The Islanders also had three solid lines up front that enabled them to play whatever style was needed to win on any given night. Players such as Bob Bourne and John Tonelli supplied speed, grit, and determination, while rugged wingers Clark Gillies and Bob Nystrum not only scored their fair share of goals but also protected their teammates whenever any skirmishes broke out on the ice. And, finally, New York had a pair of tremendous threats on the offensive end of the rink in center Bryan Trottier and right wing Mike Bossy. While the Islanders were a truly great team that featured many key contributors, Trottier and Bossy were, along with Potvin, the most indispensable members of a squad that dominated the NHL from 1979 to 1983.

The Islanders first entered the National Hockey League as an expansion team in 1972. After completing their initial season with the league's worst record, the Islanders selected defenseman Denis Potvin with the first overall pick of the 1973 NHL amateur draft. The team finished near the bottom of the league rankings once again in 1973–1974, giving them the opportunity to make the fourth overall selection of the 1974 draft. After taking powerful left-winger Clark Gillies in the first round, the Islanders selected center Bryan Trottier with the 22nd overall pick in the second round. Though not nearly as big as the 6'3", 210-pound Gillies, Trottier proved to be every bit as aggressive and perhaps even nastier. The 5'11" 195-pound center joined the Islanders as a 19-year-old in 1975 and immediately demonstrated his outstanding leadership abilities by displaying great passion and desire every time he hit the ice. In addition to being strong and tough, Trottier possessed a considerable amount of talent. He was a solid skater, a good shooter, and a superb passer who excelled at setting up his teammates for scoring opportunities. Trottier helped bring a new level of respectability to the Islanders in his first season, scoring 95 points on 32 goals and 63 assists. He was somewhat less successful in his second season, though, scoring only 72 points over the course of the 1976–1977 campaign.

Although the Islanders improved each season, they still appeared to be one or two players away from joining the NHL elite. Trottier and Gillies formed quite a formidable duo on the team's number-one line, but they needed someone to complement them on the right wing—a sniper who could take advantage of Trottier's outstanding playmaking ability. The Islanders got their man when they selected Mike Bossy with the 15th overall pick in the first round of the 1977 amateur draft. Bossy became a star in his first year in the league, displaying as a rookie the quick release and overpowering shot that made him one of the NHL's top goal scorers for the next decade. The right wing finished second in the league with 53 goals in 1977–1978 while collecting 38 assists for a total of 91 points. Meanwhile, the presence of Bossy on his right wing enabled Trottier to flourish as never before. The center scored 46 goals and led the league with 77 assists to finish second to Montreal's Guy LaFleur with a total of 123 points. Trottier earned First Team NHL All-Star honors for the first time at the end of the season.

The Islanders were eliminated from the playoffs in 1977–1978 by the Toronto Maple Leafs before being stunned by the rival New York Rangers in the semifinal round of the postseason tournament the following year. But although that 1978–1979 campaign ended in terrible disappointment for the Islanders, it provided them with much of the impetus for the tremendous run they began the following year. The 1978–1979 campaign also marked the beginning of an incredible run of success that Trottier and Bossy experienced together over the next several seasons. Table 49.1 presents the numbers they posted in some of their best years together.

Trottier was named the league's Most Valuable Player at the conclusion of the 1978–1979 campaign after leading the NHL with a career-high 87 assists and 134 points. He also earned First Team NHL All-Star honors for the second straight time. He earned a spot on the Second Team in 1981–1982 and 1983–1984.

In addition to leading the league in goals scored in two of those seasons, Bossy finished second twice and third another two times. He also placed in the league's top five in points scored in six of those years, finishing second to Wayne Gretzky in 1981–1982 with a career-best 147 points. When Bossy scored 50 goals in the first 50 games of the 1980–1981 season, he became just the second

Table 49.1. Bryan Trottier and Mike Bossy: 1978–1986

Player	Year	Goals	Assists	Points
Trottier	1978–1979	47	**87**	**134**
	1979–1980	42	62	104
	1980–1981	31	72	103
	1981–1982	50	79	129
	1982–1983	34	55	89
	1983–1984	40	71	111
	1985–1986	37	59	96
Bossy	1978–1979	**69**	57	126
	1979–1980	51	41	92
	1980–1981	**68**	51	119
	1981–1982	64	83	147
	1982–1983	60	58	118
	1983–1984	51	67	118
	1984–1985	58	59	117
	1985–1986	61	62	123

player in NHL history to accomplish the feat (Montreal's Maurice "Rocket" Richard was the first). Bossy was named a First Team NHL All-Star in five of those years, earning a spot on the Second Team the other three seasons.

More important, the Islanders won the Stanley Cup in 1980, 1981, 1982, and 1983, with Trottier and Bossy serving as powerful forces during each play-off run. Trottier scored a total of 107 points in 75 playoff contests during that period, while Bossy scored 93 points in 72 games. Trottier was awarded the Conn Smythe Trophy as playoff MVP in 1980. Bossy received the honor two years later.

Although the Islanders failed to win the championship after 1983, they remained in contention for the cup the next few seasons. However, their fortunes took a serious downturn during the 1986–1987 campaign when Bossy suffered a severe injury to his back that ended his playing career. He retired at the end of the season at age 30, with 573 career goals, 553 assists, and 1,126 total points. Bossy's average of 113 points per season over his 10-year NHL career places him second only to Wayne Gretzky all-time. He also averaged 1.5 points per game, a figure that puts him third behind only Gretzky and Mario Lemieux. Bossy finished in the top five in the NHL in goals scored in eight of his 10 seasons, surpassing 50 goals in each of his first nine years in the league and topping 60 goals in five of those seasons. He also compiled more than 100 points seven times.

Trottier remained with the Islanders through the 1989–1990 season, posting solid numbers in 1986–1987 and 1987–1988 before his skills began to diminish. He signed on as a free agent with the Pittsburgh Penguins in 1990, spending his final three years with the team and helping them win consecutive

Stanley Cups in 1991 and 1992. The Islanders haven't come close to winning the cup since Trottier left them. Trottier surpassed 40 goals and 70 assists five times each during his career, also topping 100 points on six occasions. He finished in the league's top five in scoring three times, and he placed in the top five in assists seven times, leading the NHL in that category twice. Although Denis Potvin served as the official captain of the Islanders during their glory years, Trottier was in many ways the heart and soul of the team.

In their 10 full seasons in New York, Bryan Trottier and Mike Bossy combined to score 951 goals and 2,161 points. During that time, they made 12 appearances on either the First or Second NHL All-Star Team, and they were selected to appear in the All-Star Game 15 times. Trottier and Bossy were most effective together in 1977–1978, 1978–1979, and 1981–1982. During the first of those seasons, Bossy finished second in the league in goals, while Trottier led the NHL in assists and placed second in scoring. In 1978–1979, Bossy led the NHL in goals, while Trottier finished first in assists and total points. Both men finished in the top five in scoring in 1981–1982.

Note

Numbers printed in bold indicate that the player led his league in a statistical category.

CHAPTER 50

Mario Lemieux / Jaromir Jagr

Mario Lemieux and Jaromir Jagr were at the top of their games in only three of the five full seasons they spent as teammates on the Pittsburgh Penguins. But they were both among the National Hockey League's premier players in each of those three seasons, leading Pittsburgh to back-to-back Stanley Cups in 1991 and 1992.

Mario Lemieux established himself as an elite player in the NHL almost as soon as he began skating with the Pittsburgh Penguins as a 19-year-old rookie at the start of the 1984–1985 campaign. Drafted by Pittsburgh with the first overall pick of the 1984 NHL entry draft, the 6'4", 235-pound center entered the league with perhaps more physical talent than anyone else who ever played the game. In addition to possessing great size and strength, Lemieux had exceptional skating ability, great hands, a terrific shot, and outstanding passing skills. Quickly joining the league's elite, Lemieux scored 100 points as a rookie, on 43 goals and 57 assists. Over the next five seasons, Lemieux performed so well that he began to inspire debates regarding whether he had surpassed Wayne Gretzky as the sport's greatest player. These are the scoring totals that Lemieux posted over the course of the next five campaigns:

1985–1986: 48 goals, 93 assists, 141 points
1986–1987: 54 goals, 53 assists, 107 points
1987–1988: 70 goals, 98 assists, 168 points
1988–1989: 85 goals, 114 assists, 199 points
1989–1990: 45 goals, 78 assists, 123 points

Lemieux finished second to Gretzky in scoring in 1985–1986 before winning the first of his six scoring titles in 1987–1988 en route to being named the league's Most Valuable Player. His 199 points the following season are the highest total ever posted by any player not named Gretzky.

However, after leading the league in scoring throughout much of the 1989–1990 season, Lemieux found himself sitting out the final two months of the campaign while recovering from a back injury that he suffered during a game against the New York Rangers in February 1990. The injury also forced Lemieux to miss most of the ensuing season, one in which he eventually returned to the Penguins to score 45 points in the team's final 26 games.

While Lemieux continued to recuperate during that 1990–1991 season, another extremely talented player joined the Penguins. Czechoslovakian-born Jaromir Jagr first began skating with the team as an 18-year-old that year, scoring 57 points over the course of his rookie campaign. Like Lemieux, the 6'3", 245-pound Jagr possessed great size and physical strength, excellent hands, and outstanding passing skills. The only thing that the right wing perhaps lacked was Lemieux's fire, which made the latter an outstanding leader and the perfect mentor for Jagr.

After returning from his injury, Lemieux led the Penguins on a successful run in the NHL playoffs that eventually earned them their first Stanley Cup. Lemieux scored 16 goals and 28 assists in 23 playoff games to earn playoff MVP honors. Jagr was somewhat less successful in his first postseason, tallying only three goals and 10 assists.

Completely healthy again in 1991–1992, Lemieux led Pittsburgh back to the Stanley Cup Finals for the second consecutive year. The center scored 44 goals and 87 assists for a league-leading total of 131 points during the regular season. He then captured playoff MVP honors for the second year in a row by scoring 16 goals and 18 assists during the postseason, leading the Penguins to their second consecutive league championship. Jagr, who tallied 32 goals and 37 assists over the course of the regular season, also played well during the playoffs, scoring 11 goals and 13 assists in Pittsburgh's 21 postseason contests.

Jagr's improved play carried over into the 1992–1993 regular season, one in which he scored a total of 94 points on 34 goals and 60 assists. He found himself being overshadowed by Lemieux, though, with the latter scoring 160 points in Pittsburgh's first 60 games en route to earning his fourth scoring title and second Most Valuable Player Award. However, the center's playing career suddenly appeared to be in jeopardy when he was forced to sit out the final six weeks of the campaign after being diagnosed with Hodgkin's disease on January 12, 1993. Lemieux's absence from the Penguins lineup spoiled any chance they may have had of winning their third straight Stanley Cup.

Lemieux's hard work, dedication, and love for the game enabled him to return to the Penguins the following season. However, he ended up appearing in only 22 games after he sustained another injury to his back. In his absence,

Jagr continued to blossom into a true star, reaching a new career high with 99 points on 32 goals and 67 assists.

Struggling with the after-effects of his treatments for Hodgkin's disease, Lemieux sat out the entire strike-shortened 1994–1995 season. Meanwhile, Jagr scored 70 points in Pittsburgh's 48 games to win the first scoring title of his career.

With Lemieux healthy again in 1995–1996, he and Jagr had their greatest season together. Lemieux earned his third MVP trophy by leading the league in scoring for the fifth time with 161 points on 69 goals and 92 assists. Jagr finished second to his teammate in scoring with 149 points on 62 goals and 87 assists. The two men continued their exceptional play together the following season, with Lemieux winning his sixth and final scoring title with a total of 122 points. Jagr also placed among the league leaders with a total of 95 points.

However, that 1996–1997 campaign turned out to be the last full season that Lemieux and Jagr spent together in Pittsburgh. Continuing concerns about his health prompted Lemieux to retire prior to the start of the 1997–1998 campaign. He sat out the next three seasons before coming out of retirement in 2000–2001 to score 76 points in 43 games. Lemieux spent parts of four more years with the team, appearing in more than 26 games just once between 2001 and 2006, before an irregular heartbeat forced him to retire for good during the 2005–2006 campaign. He ended his career with 1,723 points—good enough for seventh on the all-time scoring list. Lemieux's 690 goals and 1,033 assists both place him in the top 10 all-time. In addition to his six scoring titles, three regular season MVP awards, and two playoff MVPs, Lemieux was a five-time First Team NHL All-Star and a four-time Second Team selection. He appeared in 10 All-Star Games during his career.

Legendary Boston Bruins defenseman Bobby Orr once suggested that Lemieux had more talent than any other player he ever saw: "What he can do, I couldn't do. . . . He can do more things than any other player I've ever seen."[1]

Following Lemieux's initial retirement at the end of the 1996–1997 season, Jagr developed into arguably the NHL's greatest player, winning four consecutive scoring titles by posting the following numbers:

1997–1998: 35 goals, 67 assists, 102 points
1998–1999: 44 goals, 83 assists, 127 points
1999–2000: 42 goals, 54 assists, 96 points
2000–2001: 52 goals, 69 assists, 121 points

Jagr's 127 points in 1998–1999, which represented the second-highest total of his career, earned him NHL MVP honors.

Jagr left Pittsburgh after the 2000–2001 season, spending 2.5 years with Washington before joining the New York Rangers for 3.5 seasons. Although he never won another scoring title, Jagr had one more big year in New York, finishing second in the league in scoring in 2005–2006 with a total of 123 points. He signed a huge free agent contract with a team from Russia at the conclusion of the 2007–2008 campaign, apparently ending his career in the NHL. However, after spending three years playing in the KHL, the 39-year-old Jagr returned to North American hockey after signing a one-year, $3.3 million contract with the Philadelphia Flyers prior to the start of the 2011–2012 campaign. After one year in Philadelphia, he moved on to Dallas, Boston, and New Jersey, playing his best hockey for the Devils in 2013–2014, when he scored 67 points, on 24 goals and 43 assists. As of this writing, Jagr has tallied 1,755 points in his 20 years in the league, tying him with Steve Yzerman for sixth place on the all-time scoring list. He has scored 705 goals and collected 1,050 assists. Jagr has earned seven First Team NHL All-Star selections and has been named to the Second Team once. He has appeared in nine All-Star Games.

Mario Lemieux and Jaromir Jagr spent parts of seven seasons together in Pittsburgh, winning the Stanley Cup in their first two years as teammates. Lemieux appeared in more than half of Pittsburgh's games in five of those seasons. Either Lemieux (four times) or Jagr (once) won the NHL scoring title in each of those years. Lemieux also was named the league's Most Valuable Player in two of those five seasons, while Jagr received the honor once. Had Lemieux not missed so much playing time with the Penguins, he and Jagr likely would have finished higher in these rankings.

Note

1. Bobby Orr, http://www.nemesisfl.tripod.com/id31.html.

Part V

OVERALL RANKINGS AND CURRENT DYNAMIC DUOS

Conclusion:
Final Overall Rankings

Now that I have separately listed the most dynamic duos in each of the four major professional team sports—baseball, football, basketball, and hockey—the time has come for me to reveal the overall place in history that each tandem assumes by creating a composite list that encompasses all four sports. As I mentioned earlier, several factors needed to be considered in weighing the level of greatness that the members of one duo reached against that attained by a two-some that competed in a different sport. Although a tandem's level of statistical compilation continued to play an important role, other factors took on greater significance. Longevity, number of championships, personal honors, and legacies all were closely examined. I used all these factors to determine the true level of dominance that the members of each duo attained during their time together.

Having taken into consideration all of the above, I elected to rank the 50 most dynamic duos in sports history in the following order:

1. Babe Ruth / Lou Gehrig
2. Wayne Gretzky / Mark Messier
3. Michael Jordan / Scottie Pippen
4. Joe Montana / Jerry Rice
5. Kareem Abdul-Jabbar / Magic Johnson
6. Bobby Orr / Phil Esposito
7. Bill Russell / Bob Cousy
8. Peyton Manning / Marvin Harrison
9. Steve Young / Jerry Rice
10. Elgin Baylor / Jerry West
11. Jimmie Foxx / Al Simmons
12. Hank Aaron / Eddie Mathews
13. Merlin Olsen / Deacon Jones

14. Gale Sayers / Dick Butkus
15. Karl Malone / John Stockton
16. Willie Mays / Willie McCovey
17. Mickey Mantle / Roger Maris
18. Shaquille O'Neal / Kobe Bryant
19. Johnny Unitas / Raymond Berry
20. Ken Griffey Jr. / Alex Rodriguez
21. Ty Cobb / Sam Crawford
22. Bobby Hull / Stan Mikita
23. Hank Greenberg / Charlie Gehringer
24. Pete Rose / Joe Morgan
25. Greg Maddux / Tom Glavine
26. Sam Thompson / Billy Hamilton
27. Dwyane Wade / LeBron James
28. Oscar Robertson / Jerry Lucas
29. Bryan Trottier / Mike Bossy
30. Sandy Koufax / Don Drysdale
31. Ted Williams / Bobby Doerr
32. Larry Bird / Kevin McHale
33. Troy Aikman / Emmitt Smith / Michael Irvin
34. Lawrence Taylor / Harry Carson
35. Jack Lambert / Jack Ham
36. Mario Lemieux / Jaromir Jagr
37. Roberto Clemente / Willie Stargell
38. Johnny Bench / Tony Perez
39. Jeff Bagwell / Craig Biggio
40. Randy Johnson / Curt Schilling
41. Warren Spahn / Johnny Sain
42. Julius Erving / Moses Malone
43. Bill Terry / Mel Ott
44. Derek Jeter / Bernie Williams
45. Walt Frazier / Earl Monroe
46. Isiah Thomas / Joe Dumars
47. Jim Taylor / Paul Hornung
48. Duke Snider / Roy Campanella
49. Lynn Swann / John Stallworth
50. Ron Santo / Billy Williams

It could be argued that tandems such as Swann and Stallworth, Taylor and Hornung, Jeter and Williams, Lambert and Ham, and Trottier and Bossy deserve a higher ranking since their respective teams won so many championships. Nevertheless, I didn't feel that any of those twosomes reached a level of dominance greater than the ones attained by any of the pairings I placed ahead of them.

It could also be argued that Michael Jordan and Scottie Pippen deserve to be ranked number one since they won more championships together than either Ruth and Gehrig or Gretzky and Messier. However, as good as Pippen was, Jordan was clearly the driving force behind each of Chicago's championship runs. Pippen never demonstrated the ability to lead his team to a championship on his own. He was most effective playing alongside Jordan, using his many skills to complement the game's greatest player. Although Gehrig and Messier generally received far less acclaim than their more famous teammates, they each won multiple championships without them. Furthermore, it would be extremely difficult to rank Pippen even among the 20 or 25 greatest players in the history of his sport. The same thing cannot be said about any of the four men who are included in the top two tandems on this list.

Epilogue:
Current Dynamic
Duos to Watch

Having identified the 50 most dynamic duos in sports history, I now take a look at some currently active tandems that have been performing at a high level the past few seasons. I excluded these pairings from my rankings since none of them have been together long enough to be compared favorably with any of the original 50 combinations. However, it is quite possible that at least one or two of them will eventually surpass several of the twosomes that I included on my list. The following is a summary of what these "current dynamic duos to watch" have accomplished thus far.

Matthew Stafford / Calvin Johnson

Although Matthew Stafford and Calvin Johnson have spent only three full seasons and parts of two others together, they have established themselves as arguably the top quarterback–wide receiver tandem in the National Football League. Stafford laid claim to being perhaps the league's best young signal-caller in 2011, when he became just the fourth quarterback in NFL history to surpass 5,000 passing yards in a season. Even though he failed to perform at the same lofty level in either 2012 or 2013, Stafford remained one of the league's most productive quarterbacks, passing for a total of 49 touchdowns and just over 9,600 yards over the course of those two seasons. Meanwhile, Johnson further established himself as the circuit's most dynamic and unstoppable wide receiver the past three seasons by leading the league in receptions once and pass receiving yardage twice. Together, Stafford and Johnson have helped breathe new life into a dormant franchise that spent the first decade of the twenty-first century losing the majority of its games.

Handicapped by the ineptness of their front office, which manifested itself in a series of highly questionable draft selections, the Detroit Lions posted a losing record each season from 2001 to 2006, compiling a combined mark over that six-year stretch of just 24–72. With Matt Millen serving as president and CEO of the team from 2001 to 2008, the Lions appeared to have no sense of direction, going through three head coaches during that time while failing to improve themselves in the NFL draft each year. Particularly puzzling were the team's three consecutive first-round selections of wide receivers in 2003, 2004, and 2005. After tabbing Michigan State wideout Charles Rogers with the second overall pick of the 2003 draft, the Lions chose Texas receiver Roy Williams with the seventh overall pick the following year. When both Rogers and Williams failed to live up to their advance billing, Detroit stunned everyone by selecting USC wide receiver Mike Williams with the 10th overall pick of the 2005 draft.

With Williams failing to pan out as well and the Lions concluding the 2006 campaign with a record of only 3–13, it appeared to be just a matter of time before team ownership relieved Millen of his duties. Detroit's 0–16 mark in 2008 ended up being the final nail in Millen's coffin, bringing to an end his eight-year run of being the Lions' primary decision maker. Before Millen left, though, he selected another wide receiver in the first round of the draft, tabbing Georgia Tech all-American Calvin Johnson with the second overall pick in 2007.

The Lions finally hit it big with Johnson, who at 6'5" and 240 pounds, has since established himself as the NFL's most physically imposing wide receiver. With his great size and strength, Johnson has the ability to outfight defenders for the ball, and he has the capability of breaking tackles once he makes the reception. More than just a big target, Johnson also has exceptional running speed and great leaping ability. Johnson's tremendous overall skill set has enabled him to rival Larry Fitzgerald as the game's premier wide receiver the past few seasons.

After making 48 receptions for 756 yards and four touchdowns in a part-time role as a rookie in 2007, Johnson became a full-time starter six games into the 2008 campaign when the Lions traded Roy Williams to Dallas for three draft picks. Although Detroit finished the year with an embarrassing 0–16 record, Johnson had an outstanding season, making 78 catches for 1,331 yards and a league-leading 12 TD receptions.

The Lions' poor showing in 2008 enabled them to select quarterback Matthew Stafford with the first overall pick of the following year's draft, after the former University of Georgia all-American chose to forego his final year of collegiate eligibility. Displaying outstanding natural ability and exceptional leadership skills throughout the 2009 preseason, the 6'2", 230-pound Stafford subsequently found himself named Detroit's starting quarterback prior to the team's opening contest by new Lions' head coach Jim Schwartz.

Able to appear in only 10 games as a rookie due to an injured knee, Stafford compiled a record of just 2–8 as a starter in 2009. Nevertheless, he gave the

Lions hope for the future, demonstrating the skills and leadership qualities that prompted Detroit to make him the number one pick in the draft. In week 3, he led the Lions to their first victory since 2007, completing 21 of 36 passes for 241 yards and one touchdown during Detroit's 19–14 win over the Washington Redskins. Stafford led the Lions to their only other win of the campaign on November 22, when he threw five touchdown passes in a 38–37 victory over the Cleveland Browns. In doing so, he became the youngest quarterback ever to toss five TD passes in one game. Making the 21-year-old quarterback's performance even more impressive was the fact that he completed the game-winning touchdown pass as time expired after ignoring team doctors' suggestions to remain on the sidelines after he suffered a separated shoulder on the previous play. In addition to the five touchdown passes, Stafford accumulated 422 yards passing, a record for a rookie at that time. Stafford concluded the year with 2,267 passing yards, 13 touchdowns, 20 interceptions, and a 53.3 completion percentage. Meanwhile, Johnson ended the campaign with 67 receptions for 984 yards and five touchdowns.

The 2010 season turned out to be a lost year for Stafford, who suffered multiple injuries to his throwing shoulder, enabling him to appear in only three games for the Lions. His season ended prematurely when Dr. James Andrews performed surgery on the shoulder to repair an acromioclavicular joint and shave a clavicle. Playing without Stafford, Detroit finished the year 6–10, with Johnson continuing to evolve into the league's most dangerous receiver in Stafford's absence. Johnson caught 77 passes for 1,120 yards and 12 touchdowns en route to earning Pro Bowl honors for the first time in his career.

Everything came together for Stafford, Johnson, and the Lions in 2011, with the team posting its first winning record since 2000. In fact, the Lions' mark of 10–6 earned them their first playoff berth since 1999, when they lost to the Redskins 27–13 in the wild card round. Detroit began the season 5–0 for the first time since 1956, with the undefeated streak featuring consecutive comeback victories in weeks 3 and 4. The Lions trailed the Minnesota Vikings 20–0 at halftime in week 3, before Stafford led them on a second-half comeback that resulted in a 26–23 Detroit win. The Lions again mounted a huge comeback the following week, overcoming a 27–3 third-quarter deficit against the Dallas Cowboys to pull out a 34–30 victory. Stafford and Johnson keyed the comeback by collaborating on two fourth-quarter touchdown passes. Johnson's two touchdown grabs gave him eight TD receptions through the first four games of the season, tying him with Cris Carter for the NFL record for the most consecutive games with multiple touchdown receptions.

Another season highlight occurred on November 20, when Stafford threw for 335 yards and five touchdowns during a 49–35 comeback win over the

Carolina Panthers. In the process, Stafford became the first quarterback since at least 1950 to win three games in a season after trailing by at least 17 points. Stafford joined another select group on January 1, 2012, when he joined Dan Marino, Tom Brady, and Drew Brees as the only quarterbacks in NFL history to surpass 5,000 passing yards in a season by throwing for 520 yards against the Green Bay Packers during a 45–41 week 17 loss. Stafford's performance in the final game of the regular season enabled him to become the only quarterback in NFL history to pass for over 1,500 yards (1,511) and 14 touchdowns over a four-game span. He concluded the campaign with 5,038 passing yards, 41 touchdown passes, 16 interceptions, and a 63.5 completion percentage en route to earning AP Comeback Player of the Year honors and a selection as an alternate to the NFC Pro Bowl squad. Meanwhile, Johnson earned a spot on the Pro Bowl roster for the second straight year and First-Team All-Pro honors for the first time by establishing career highs with 96 receptions, 16 touchdown catches, and a league-leading 1,681 receiving yards.

Stafford and the Lions subsequently suffered through a subpar 2012 season in which the team finished just 4–12 and Stafford threw 20 touchdown passes and 17 interceptions, despite passing for 4,967 yards. Nevertheless, even as the team and its quarterback struggled, Johnson compiled the greatest numbers of his career, again earning Pro Bowl and First-Team All-Pro honors by leading the league with 122 receptions and 1,964 receiving yards, breaking in the process Jerry Rice's previous single-season record for most yards through the air (1,848). Over the course of the campaign, Johnson also established new league marks for most consecutive 100-yard games (8) and most consecutive games with 10 or more receptions (4).

Johnson again performed brilliantly in 2013, making 84 receptions for 1,492 yards and 12 touchdowns, en route to earning his third straight First-Team All-Pro selection. During a 31–30 win over the Dallas Cowboys on October 27, 2013, he caught 14 passes for 329 yards, giving him the highest receiving yardage total in any regulation-length game in NFL history. Meanwhile, Stafford rebounded somewhat from his subpar 2012 campaign, finishing the year with 29 TD passes, 19 interceptions, and 4,650 passing yards. Particularly effective during that October 27 victory over the Cowboys, Stafford passed for a season-high 488 yards against the porous Dallas defense.

Although the Lions finished just 7–9 in 2013, they should be able to contend for the NFL North Division title for many years to come if they can show some improvement on defense since Stafford and Johnson seemingly still having many outstanding years ahead of them. Heading into the 2014 campaign, Stafford is only 26 years old, while Johnson will not turn 29 until shortly after the season gets underway.

Kevin Durant / Russell Westbrook

Rivaling LeBron James and Dwyane Wade as the most dominant twosome in pro basketball the past few seasons, Kevin Durant and Russell Westbrook have transformed the Oklahoma City Thunder into perennial contenders in the NBA's Western Conference during their relatively brief time together. Durant has captured five scoring titles en route to establishing himself as one of the league's elite players, while Westbrook has gradually evolved into one of the NBA's top point guards over the course of his six NBA seasons.

After compiling a losing record in three of the previous four seasons, the Seattle Supersonics posted their worst mark in 21 years in 2006–2007, when they finished the campaign with a record of 31–51. Nevertheless, their poor performance proved to be beneficial to them in the long term, since it enabled them to select University of Texas forward Kevin Durant with the second overall pick of the 2007 NBA draft. Durant, who earned consensus 2007 National College Player of the Year honors at Texas, elected to forego his final three years of collegiate eligibility and enter the NBA draft after just his freshman season. Durant's decision proved to be a wise one since he ended up winning NBA Rookie of the Year honors by averaging 20.3 points per game. Despite the 19-year-old rookie's outstanding performance, the Supersonics concluded the campaign with a Western Conference–worst mark of 20–62, which established a new franchise record for futility, expediting in the process their relocation to Oklahoma City, where they renamed themselves the Thunder.

Although Durant increased his scoring output to 25.3 points per contest his second year in the league (the team's first in Oklahoma City), the Thunder barely improved their record, going 23–59 en route to finishing out of the playoffs for the sixth time in seven seasons. Nevertheless, Oklahoma City fans had to be encouraged by the performance of their new team's outstanding young forward, along with that of rookie guard Russell Westbrook, whom the Supersonics selected with the fourth overall pick of the 2008 NBA draft just six days before they relocated to their new home.

After starring at Leuzinger High School in California, Westbrook spent two years at UCLA before declaring himself eligible for the NBA draft. Westbrook came off the Thunder bench the first few weeks of the season but eventually earned a starting job with his tremendous athleticism and aggressive style of play. Despite being a bit turnover prone and possessing somewhat limited range on his outside jump shot, the 6'3" Westbrook displayed from the very beginning his great quickness, leaping ability, and willingness to challenge taller defenders inside the paint. Considered to be a point guard although he plays more like a shooting guard at times, Westbrook is known for his propensity for attacking the basket. He also has the ability to pull up for a midrange jump shot or pass the ball out to an open teammate. Westbrook earned All-Rookie honors and a fourth-place finish in the 2008–2009 NBA Rookie of the Year balloting by posting averages of 15.3 points, 5.3 assists, and 1.3 steals per game. His outstanding season included a 43-point effort against the Indiana Pacers and a 38-point, nine-assist, 15-rebound performance against the New Jersey Nets.

The combined talents of Durant and Westbrook enabled the Thunder to begin to establish themselves as one of the stronger teams in the extremely competitive Western Conference in 2009–2010. Westbrook posted a scoring average of 16.1 points per game his second year in the league while improving his ball-distribution skills to the point that he averaged eight assists per contest. Meanwhile, Durant led the NBA in scoring for the first of three straight times by averaging 30.1 points per game in helping his team advance to the playoffs with a record of 50–32. Oklahoma City's 27-game improvement from the previous year represented the sixth-biggest turnaround in NBA history. Durant—who at 21 years of age became the youngest player in league history to win the scoring title—earned the first of five consecutive selections to the All-NBA First Team and a second-place finish in the league MVP voting. Although the Thunder ended up losing their first-round playoff matchup with the Los Angeles Lakers in six games, Durant and Westbrook both posted solid numbers against the eventual world champions. Despite shooting only 35 percent from the field, Durant averaged 25 points over the course of the series, including a 29-point, 19-rebound effort during a 101–96 game 3 win at Oklahoma City. Meanwhile, Westbrook averaged 20.5 points, six rebounds, and six assists against Los Angeles.

Durant, Westbrook, and the Thunder continued to grow together in 2010–2011. Oklahoma City finished first in the Northwest Division during the regular season with a record of 55–27. Durant again led the league in scoring, this time with an average of 27.7 points per game. In addition to earning All-Star and All-NBA First Team honors for the second straight year, he placed fifth in the league MVP balloting. Westbrook established new career highs with averages of 21.9 points, 8.2 assists, and 1.9 steals per game en route to earning his first All-Star nomination and his first of three consecutive All-NBA Second Team selections. Durant and Westbrook subsequently excelled together during the postseason, enabling the Thunder to advance to the Western Conference finals, where they eventually lost to the world-champion Dallas Mavericks in five games. Durant led all playoff performers by posting a scoring average of 28.6 in Oklahoma City's 17 postseason contests. Westbrook averaged 23.8 points and 6.4 assists per game, although he shot only 39 percent from the field.

The Thunder posted the fourth-best winning percentage (.712) in franchise history in 2011–2012, concluding the strike-shortened campaign with a mark of 47–19, which enabled them to capture their second straight Northwest Division title. Westbrook ranked among the league leaders with averages of 23.6 points and 1.7 steals per game while averaging 5.5 assists per contest. Durant had arguably his finest all-around season, leading the NBA in scoring for the third consecutive time with a mark of 28 points per contest while expanding his overall game to establish new career highs with eight rebounds, 3.5 assists, and 1.2 blocked shots per contest. Viewed primarily as a scorer earlier in his career due to his exceptional offensive arsenal, which includes a strong post-up game, outstanding quickness driving to the basket, and exceptional range on his outside jumper, Durant developed into more of a complete player and, also, more of a team leader in 2011–2012, earning in the process his third straight All-NBA First Team selection and a second-place finish to LeBron James in the league MVP voting. At their best during a February 19, 2012, home contest against the Denver Nuggets, Durant and Westbrook combined to score a total of 91 points in leading their team to a 124–118 victory. Durant tallied 51 points on the evening, while Westbrook added 40.

Durant and Westbrook continued their outstanding play during the postseason, enabling the Thunder to gain a measure of revenge against the Mavericks by leading their team to a four-game sweep of the defending champions in the first round of the playoffs. The two stars subsequently led Oklahoma City to victories over the Los Angeles Lakers and San Antonio Spurs, before coming up short against LeBron James and the Miami Heat in the NBA Finals. Nevertheless, Durant and Westbrook acquitted themselves quite well against the Heat, concluding the postseason with scoring averages of 28.5 and 23.1, respectively.

The Thunder appeared ready to once again challenge Miami for the NBA title the following year when they captured their third consecutive division title by posting a Western-Conference-best regular season record of 60–22. Durant had another great year, earning a second-place finish to LeBron James in the NBA MVP voting by placing second in the league to New York's Carmelo Anthony with a scoring average of 28.1 points per game, while also averaging 7.9 rebounds, 4.6 assists, and a career-high 1.4 steals and 1.3 blocked shots per contest. Westbrook also performed exceptionally well over the course of the campaign, posting averages of 23.2 points, 7.4 assists, 5.2 rebounds, and 1.8 steals per game. However, after injuring his right knee in the second game of Oklahoma City's first-round playoff matchup against the Houston Rockets, Westbrook found himself unable to compete in any of his team's remaining postseason contests. The Thunder went on to defeat Houston in six games but subsequently lost to Memphis in five games in the next round.

Sidelined for much of the first half of the 2013–2014 campaign after undergoing surgery to repair a slight tear in his right meniscus, Westbrook appeared in only 46 of the Thunder's 81 games. Yet, he still managed to average 21.8

points, 6.9 assists, 1.9 steals, and 5.7 rebounds per contest after he returned to the court. Durant performed magnificently in Westbrook's absence, leading the Thunder to a record of 59–23 by posting a career-high scoring average of 32 points per game that earned him his fourth scoring title in five years. He also posted averages of 7.4 rebounds, 5.5 assists, and 1.3 steals per contest, en route to winning league MVP honors. Particularly dominant during the month of January, Durant averaged 35.9 points per game while scoring at least 30 points 12 straight times, including a career-best 54-point effort against Golden State.

Durant and Westbrook subsequently led Oklahoma City to victories over Memphis and the L.A. Clippers in the first two rounds of the playoffs, before running into a buzz saw known as the San Antonio Spurs in the Conference Finals. Yet, even though San Antonio dispensed of the Thunder in six games, Westbrook turned in an epic performance in Oklahoma City's Game 4 victory, recording 40 points, 10 assists, 5 rebounds, and 5 steals. He finished the postseason with averages of 26.7 points, 8.1 assists, 7.3 rebounds, and 2.2 steals. Durant also played extremely well, averaging 29.6 points, 8.9 rebounds, and 3.9 assists in Oklahoma City's 19 playoff contests.

In their six seasons together, Kevin Durant and Russell Westbrook have combined for eight All-Star appearances, five All-NBA First Team selections, three Second Team nominations, five top-five finishes in the league MVP voting, and one MVP selection. Durant has captured four scoring titles, with Westbrook joining him in the league's top five in that category once. They have led the Thunder to three Western Conference Finals appearances and one trip to the NBA Finals. If this dynamic twosome stays together, it appears to be only a matter of time before they lead their team to an NBA title.

Sidney Crosby / Evgeni Malkin

One of the most dominant twosomes in professional sports in recent years has been the Pittsburgh Penguins' magnificent tandem of Sidney Crosby and Evgeni Malkin. During their relatively brief time together, Crosby and Malkin have given every indication that they will go down as one of the greatest pairings in history. Rivaled only by Washington's Alexander Ovechkin for preeminence among National Hockey League players the past few seasons, Crosby and Malkin have restored the Penguins to prominence since joining forces in 2006, leading the team to the Stanley Cup in just their third season together.

The Pittsburgh Penguins proved to be one of the NHL's strongest teams during the 1990s, winning consecutive Stanley Cups in 1991 and 1992 en route to advancing to the playoffs 11 straight times from 1991 to 2001. However, an unfortunate set of circumstances prevented them from remaining one of the league's top teams the first few years of the 21st century. Health problems severely limited Mario Lemieux's playing time from 2001 to 2006, finally forcing the brilliant center to announce his retirement. Financial considerations also prompted the Penguins to trade away most of their top players to other teams at the beginning of the new millennium. As a result, Pittsburgh failed to make the playoffs three straight times beginning in 2002, compiling the league's worst record over the course of the 2003–2004 campaign.

Following the cancellation of the 2004–2005 season due to a player lockout, the Penguins benefited from their poor performance the previous year by being able to select Sidney Crosby with the first overall pick of the 2005 NHL entry draft. Upon drafting the native of Nova Scotia, Penguins executive Craig Patrick stated, "I've won the Stanley Cup, won gold medals. But getting Sidney Crosby was the happiest day of my life."[1]

One of the most highly regarded draft picks in league history, the 18-year-old center made such a favorable impression on scouts that they gave him the nickname the "Next One," since they believed that he had a skill set comparable to that of Wayne Gretzky. After seeing Crosby play, the Great One himself gushed, "He's dynamite. He's the best player I've seen since Mario [Lemieux]. He's that good."[2]

Lemieux, a part-owner of the Penguins, started out the 2005–2006 campaign as Crosby's teammate before retiring for good during the season. Commenting on the youngster's skills, Lemieux noted, "He said he needs to work on his shot a little bit. But it looks pretty good to me."[3]

Crosby's shot indeed proved to be NHL-ready. The center scored 39 goals and assisted on 63 others to compile a total of 102 points in his rookie season. Crosby's 102 points placed him sixth in the league in scoring and made him the youngest player in NHL history to surpass the century mark. The first-year player quickly earned the respect and admiration of his teammates and opponents alike.

Penguins All-Star forward Mike Modano suggested, "The league hasn't had a guy like this in a long time."[4]

Another of Crosby's teammates, Lyle Odelein, observed, "You can tell he's a big-league player. He wants the puck in big moments."[5]

Former NHL star Gilles Meloche commented, "He keeps you on the edge of your seat. He gets off the ice and you can't wait to see him get back on."[6]

Pittsburgh star forward John LeClair stated, "He's going to be a superstar in this league."[7]

Crosby had all the skills necessary to become a true superstar in the NHL the first time that he stepped onto the ice as a rookie. An exceptional skater, Crosby also excelled as a shooter, passer, and puck handler from the beginning. He also possessed the same innate ability as Wayne Gretzky to make the other players around him better, displaying from the time he first entered the league his tremendous anticipation and special gift of being able to set up his teammates with his extraordinary passing skills.

Longtime NHL coach Mike Keenan noted, "[Crosby] can pass the puck as well as anyone I've seen play the game—maybe with the exception of Wayne [Gretzky] and Mario [Lemieux]."[8]

Another quality that Crosby has demonstrated during his time in the league is a toughness that belies his youthful appearance and that stands in stark contrast to the finesse with which he plays the game. Penguins executive Ed Johnston stated, "You're not going to intimidate this kid. He's not going to back off. There are players like that. When we played against Henri Richard or Frank Mahovlich, the word at our meetings was to leave those guys alone. Ask them how their families are doing, but don't wake them up. If you tick them off, they become even better players."[9]

In spite of the tremendous ability that Crosby displayed his first year in the league, Pittsburgh finished the 2005–2006 campaign in last place in the Eastern Conference, with a record of only 22–46–14. It wasn't until Evgeni Malkin joined "Sid the Kid" in Pittsburgh the following year that the Penguins once again became one of the league's better teams.

Considered to be one of the most talented amateur players to come along in quite some time, the Russian-born Malkin was originally selected by Pittsburgh with the second overall pick of the 2004 NHL entry draft. However, an international transfer dispute delayed Malkin's arrival to the NHL until 2006. The 6'3", 200-pound center made up for lost time his first year in the league, scoring 85 points on 33 goals and 52 assists en route to capturing NHL Rookie of the Year honors.

In his first NHL season, the 20-year-old Malkin displayed a rare skill set that promised to make him one of the league's premier players for a very long time. He entered the professional ranks with outstanding size, strength, and skating ability; exceptional mental and physical toughness; and extraordinary goal-scoring ability. In fact, Malkin has demonstrated during his eight years in the league that he rivals Crosby in terms of his ability to put the puck in the net. As the league's best passer and playmaker, Crosby constantly strives to create scoring opportunities for his teammates. But while Malkin is an adept passer as well, he is viewed first and foremost as a goal scorer.

At one point during Malkin's first NHL season, Crosby commented on his rookie teammate's performance: "He's learning fast, and getting better with every game."[10]

Penguins head coach Michel Therrien indicated that he wanted Malkin to assume more of a leadership role on the team: "I want him to be beside Sid, not following. That's our plan."[11]

Noting Malkin's exceptional ability, Therrien added, "Mario Lemieux is a different player. Jaromir Jagr is a different player. Evgeni has got to understand he's a different player."[12]

The 20-year-old Malkin teamed with Crosby in 2006–2007 to lead the Penguins to a record of 47–35–11, which earned Pittsburgh a spot in the playoffs for the first time in six years. Crosby earned NHL MVP honors in just his second season by leading the league in scoring with 120 points on 36 goals and 84 assists. He also earned First Team NHL All-Star honors. Although the Penguins lost to the Ottawa Senators in five games in the first round of the playoffs, they finally appeared headed in the right direction.

The Penguins continued to improve in 2007–2008, finishing the regular season with a record of 47–27–8 to capture their first division title in 10 years. They subsequently advanced to the Stanley Cup Finals by losing only twice in the first three rounds of the playoffs en route to defeating the Senators, Rangers, and Flyers. However, Pittsburgh came up short against Detroit in the Finals, losing to the Red Wings in six games. Crosby and Malkin proved to be the driving forces behind Pittsburgh's resurgence, compiling the following numbers over the course of the regular season:

Sidney Crosby: 24 goals, 48 assists, 72 points
Evgeni Malkin: 47 goals, 59 assists, 106 points

A high ankle sprain caused Crosby to miss 28 games, thereby reducing his scoring totals considerably. Nevertheless, he managed to score 72 points in only 53 games while providing outstanding leadership to the Penguins as their newly named captain. He also had an exceptional postseason, scoring 27 points in Pittsburgh's 20 playoff contests.

Malkin assumed more of a leadership role on the team in Crosby's absence while also developing into one of the league's top scorers. Malkin tallied 44 points in the 28 games that Crosby missed, ending the season second in the league in scoring with a total of 106 points. He subsequently scored another 22 points during the playoffs. Malkin earned First Team NHL All-Star honors and placed second to Alexander Ovechkin in the league MVP voting.

Crosby and Malkin helped the Penguins reach the pinnacle of their sport in 2008–2009, leading their team to the Stanley Cup. These are the numbers that the two superstars posted during Pittsburgh's championship season:

Sidney Crosby: 33 goals, 70 assists, 103 points
Evgeni Malkin: 35 goals, **78** assists, **113** points

Crosby placed third in the league in scoring; he also finished second in assists. He subsequently tallied 31 points in Pittsburgh's 24 playoff contests, leading his team to victories over Philadelphia, Washington, Carolina, and, finally, the defending champion Detroit Red Wings in the Stanley Cup Finals.

Meanwhile, Malkin led the league in assists and total points scored, earning First Team NHL All-Star honors and a second-place finish in the league MVP balloting for the second straight year. He then led all players in scoring during the postseason, tallying a total of 36 points en route to being named playoff MVP. Malkin's extraordinary performance earned him praise from some of hockey's most prominent figures.

Mario Lemieux said, "We knew he was a great talent, but not to that extent. From what I've seen so far, he's going to be a great player for many years to come."[13]

All-Star forward Marian Hossa stated flatly, "He's the best player in the world."[14]

Sidney Crosby noted, "When things are more desperate, when he knows he's being depended on a little more, he's got that extra jump."[15]

NHL veteran Mark Recchi, a former teammate of both Malkin and Mario Lemieux, suggested, "He's as close to Mario in terms of size and what he can do with the puck as we've seen in a while."[16]

Crosby and Malkin continued to excel together in 2009–2010, compiling the following numbers in their fourth season together:

Sidney Crosby: **51** goals, 58 assists, 109 points
Evgeni Malkin: 28 goals, 49 assists, 77 points

Although an injury forced Malkin to miss more than a month of the campaign, he still managed to score 77 points in the 67 games in which he competed. Meanwhile, Crosby's 51 goals tied him with Tampa Bay Lightning center Steven Stamkos for the league lead, earning him a share of the Maurice Richard Trophy as the league's top goal scorer. He also finished tied for second in the NHL with 109 total points scored en route to earning Second Team NHL All-Star honors. Crosby subsequently received the Mark Messier Leadership Award during the off-season, earning recognition for his superior leadership skills, ability to motivate his teammates, dedication to the community, and the manner in which he set a positive example through his on-ice performance.

Unfortunately, the Penguins' season came to an abrupt end when the Montreal Canadiens defeated them in seven games in the second round of the playoffs. Nevertheless, Crosby and Malkin both played well during the postseason, with Crosby scoring 19 points and Malkin tallying another 11 in Pittsburgh's 13 playoff contests.

The 2010–2011 campaign began well for Crosby, Malkin, and the Penguins, all of whom thrived during the season's first half. From November 5 to

December 28, 2010, Crosby scored at least one point in 25 consecutive games, placing him in a tie for the 11th-longest point-scoring streak in NHL history. He tallied 27 goals and 24 assists for 51 total points during the streak, which included three hat tricks and his 200th NHL goal, which he scored on November 27. Malkin also performed well for the Penguins, scoring 37 points on 15 goals and 22 assists in the team's first 43 games. Both Crosby and Malkin earned starting spots on the Eastern Conference All-Star squad. However, serious injuries prevented both superstars from appearing in the annual All-Star tilt.

Hits to the head in back-to-back games in early January forced Crosby to the sidelines for the remainder of the year with concussion-like symptoms. Meanwhile, Malkin suffered a torn anterior cruciate ligament and medial collateral ligament that knocked him out for the rest of the year as well. Crosby concluded the campaign with a team-leading 66 points in only 41 games, while Malkin found himself unable to add to his total of 37 points in the 43 contests in which he appeared.

Malkin returned to the Penguins fully healthy in 2011–2012 to lead the NHL in scoring for the second time in his career, with a total of 109 points on 50 goals and 59 assists. He finished second in the league in goals scored and placed third in assists en route to earning a spot on the All-Star Team, First Team NHL All-Star honors for the third time in five seasons, and his first league MVP trophy. Crosby proved to be less fortunate, appearing in only 22 games for Pittsburgh after continuing to experience concussion-like symptoms until he finally returned to the team in mid-March. Yet, Sid the Kid demonstrated that he retained his scoring touch during his time away from the game, tallying 37 points on eight goals and 29 assists in the 22 games in which he played. Although the Penguins subsequently lost to the Philadelphia Flyers in the first round of the playoffs, both Crosby and Malkin performed extremely well, with each man tallying eight points in the six games on three goals and five assists.

With the start of the ensuing campaign postponed until January 2013 due to a player lockout as negotiations took place to solidify a new collective bargaining agreement, the NHL season ended up being truncated to only 48 games. Crosby excelled over the course of the first 36 games, tallying a total of 56 points, on 15 goals and 41 assists. However, his regular season ended abruptly on March 30, when a slap-shot off the stick of teammate Brooks Orpik struck him in the mouth, breaking his jaw and necessitating several rounds of reconstructive dental surgery. Forced to sit out the final 12 games of the regular season, Crosby finished third in the scoring race, just 4 points behind Tampa Bay's Martin St. Louis, who led the league with 60 points. Nevertheless, Crosby earned First Team NHL All-Star honors for the second time in his career. Meanwhile, after remaining active during the player lockout by competing in Russia's Kontinental Hockey League (KHL), Malkin returned to the States, where he suffered through an injury-marred season that saw him score 33 points in the 31 games in which he played.

Both Crosby and Malkin returned to the ice full time during the playoffs in the hope of leading their team to its second Stanley Cup in five years. The Penguins fared extremely well in the first two rounds of the postseason tournament, defeating the Islanders in six games, before needing only five games to dispose of the Ottawa Senators. Crosby and Malkin combined to score a total of 31 points in Pittsburgh's first 11 playoff contests, with Crosby notching 15 points, on 7 goals and 8 assists, and Malkin scoring 4 goals and assisting on 12 others, for a total of 16 points. However, they subsequently ran up against a hot goaltender in Boston's Tuukka Rask, who limited the Penguins to just two goals during the Bruins' four-game sweep of Pittsburgh in the Eastern Conference Finals.

Malkin continued to be plagued by injuries in 2013–2014, appearing in just 60 of the Penguins' 82 games. Yet, he managed to score 72 points, on 23 goals and 49 assists. Able to play virtually the entire schedule of games for the first time since 2009–2010, Crosby had a banner year, scoring 36 goals and leading the NHL with 68 assists and 104 points, en route to earning First Team NHL All-Star honors for the third time and league MVP honors for the second time.

Having tallied a total of 109 points during the regular season (second only to the Bruins in the Eastern Conference), the Penguins entered the playoffs as one of the favorites to advance to the Stanley Cup Finals. However, after defeating the Columbus Blue Jackets in six games in the first round, they suffered the indignity of having the New York Rangers overcome a three-games-to-one deficit against them in the Conference Semi-Finals, thereby eliminating them from the postseason tournament. Neither Crosby nor Malkin performed particularly well during the playoffs, with Crosby scoring just 9 points, on 1 goal and 8 assists, and Malkin tallying 14 points, on 6 goals and 8 assists.

The fact that Malkin has remained fully healthy in just one of the past five seasons certainly raises a few red flags about his future. Meanwhile, Crosby's history with concussions remains a huge concern moving forward. However, if both men can remain relatively healthy, they figure to go down as one of the greatest pairings in NHL history. Crosby will not turn 27 until shortly before the 2014–2015 campaign gets underway, while Malkin will celebrate his 28th birthday approximately two months before the season begins. Crosby has scored a total of 769 points as of this writing, while Malkin has tallied 632 points. Crosby has already surpassed 100 points five times. Malkin has topped the century mark in scoring on three occasions. Each man has scored at least 50 goals in a season once and led the league in scoring twice. In their eight seasons together, Crosby and Malkin have combined to win three NHL Most Valuable Player Awards and one playoff MVP award. They have earned a total of six First Team NHL All-Star nominations, one Second Team selection, and four All-Star Game nominations. They have led the Penguins into the Stanley Cup Finals twice, capturing the league championship in just their third season together.

Notes

Numbers printed in bold indicate that the player led his league in a statistical category.

1. Craig Patrick, http://www.jockbio.com/Bios/Crosby/Crosby_they-say.html.
2. Wayne Gretzky, http://www.jockbio.com/Bios/Crosby/Crosby_they-say.html.
3. Mario Lemieux, http://www.jockbio.com/Bios/Crosby/Crosby_they-say.html.
4. Mike Modano, http://www.jockbio.com/Bios/Crosby/Crosby_they-say.html.
5. Lyle Odelein, http://www.jockbio.com/Bios/Crosby/Crosby_they-say.html.
6. Gilles Meloche, http://www.jockbio.com/Bios/Crosby/Crosby_they-say.html.
7. John LeClair, http://www.jockbio.com/Bios/Crosby/Crosby_they-say.html.
8. Mike Keenan, http://www.jockbio.com/Bios/Crosby/Crosby_they-say.html.
9. Ed Johnston, http://www.jockbio.com/Bios/Crosby/Crosby_they-say.html.
10. Sidney Crosby, http://www.jockbio.com/Bios/Malkin/Malkin_they-say.html.
11. Michel Therrien, http://www.jockbio.com/Bios/Malkin/Malkin_they-say.html.
12. Michel Therrien, http://www.jockbio.com/Bios/Malkin/Malkin_they-say.html.
13. Mario Lemieux, http://www.jockbio.com/Bios/Malkin/Malkin_they-say.html.
14. Marian Hossa, http://www.jockbio.com/Bios/Malkin/Malkin_they-say.html.
15. Sidney Crosby, http://www.jockbio.com/Bios/Malkin/Malkin_they-say.html.
16. Mark Recchi, http://www.jockbio.com/Bios/Malkin/Malkin_they-say.html.

Glossary: Abbreviations and Statistical Terms

2B	Two-base hits. Doubles.
3B	Three-base hits. Triples.
AB	At bats. The number of times that a player comes to the plate to try to get on base. It does not include those times when a walk was issued, when the player hit a sacrifice fly to score a runner, or when the player advanced a base runner via a sacrifice bunt.
APG	Assists per game.
AVG	Batting average. The number of hits divided by the number of at bats.
BB	Bases on balls, better known as *walks*. A free trip to first base as a penalty to the pitcher when he fails to get the ball over the plate four times during an at bat.
BLKS	Blocked shots.
BPG	Blocked shots per game.
CG	Complete games pitched.
COMP %	Completion percentage. The number of successfully completed passes divided by the number of passes attempted.
ERA	Earned run average. The number of earned runs that a pitcher gives up per nine innings. This does not include runs that scored as a result of errors made in the field, and it is calculated by dividing the number of runs given up by the number of innings pitched and multiplying the result by nine.
FG %	Field-goal percentage. The number of successful field-goal attempts divided by the total number of shots attempted.

GOALS	Awarded when a hockey player shoots the puck into the net, behind the opposing team's goaltender.
GS	Games started by a pitcher.
HITS	Base hits. Awarded when a runner safely reaches at least first base upon a batted ball, if no error is recorded.
HR	Home runs. Fair ball hit over the fence or one hit to a spot that allows the batter to circle the bases before the ball is returned to home plate.
INTS	Interceptions. Passes thrown by the quarterback that are caught by a member of the opposing team's defense.
IP	Innings pitched.
L	Losses.
OBP	On-base percentage. Hits plus walks plus hit-by-pitches, divided by total number of plate appearances.
PCT	Winning percentage. A pitcher's number of wins divided by his number of total decisions (wins plus losses).
POINTS	Total points scored by a hockey player (goals plus assists).
PPG	Points per game.
RBI	Runs batted in. Awarded to the batter when a runner scores upon a safely batted ball, a sacrifice, or a walk.
REBS	Rebounds.
RPG	Rebounds per game.
RUNS	Runs scored by a player.
SB	Stolen bases.
SLG PCT	Slugging percentage. The number of total bases earned by all singles, doubles, triples, and home runs, divided by the total number of at bats.
SO	Strikeouts.
SPG	Steals per game.
STLS	Steals.
TD PASSES	Touchdown passes.
TD RECS	Touchdown receptions.
TDS	Touchdowns.
W	Wins.

Bibliography

Books

Baseball Digest, April 1951.

Bjarkman, Peter C. *The Biographical History of Basketball*. Chicago: Masters Press, 2000.

DeMarco, Tony. *The Sporting News Selects 50 Greatest Sluggers*. St. Louis, MO: Times Mirror Magazines, 2000.

Dewey, Donald, and Nicholas Acocella. *The Biographical History of Baseball*. New York: Carroll & Graf, 1995.

Ford, Whitey, with Phil Pepe. *Few and Chosen: Defining Yankee Greatness across the Eras*. Chicago: Triumph Books, 2001.

Hareas, John, foreword by John Havlicek. *NBA's Greatest—The NBA's Best Players, Teams, and Games*. New York: DK, 2003.

Koppett, Leonard. *24 Seconds to Shoot—The Birth and Improbable Rise of the NBA*. Kingston, NY: Total/Sports Illustrated, 1968.

Lieb, Fred, and Lawrence Ritter. *Baseball As I Have Known It*. Lincoln: University of Nebraska Press, 1996.

Nemec, David. *Players of Cooperstown—Baseball's Hall of Fame*. Lincolnwood, IL: Publications International, 1994.

Ritter, Lawrence. *The Glory of Their Times*. New York: Random House, 1985.

Salzberg, Charles. *From Set Shot to Slam Dunk*. New York: Dutton, 1987.

Shalin, Mike, and Neil Shalin. *Out by a Step: The 100 Best Players Not in the Baseball Hall of Fame*. South Bend, IN: Diamond Communications, 2002.

Shouler, Ken, Bob Ryan, Sam Smith, Leonard Koppett, and Bob Bellotti. *Total Basketball—The Ultimate Basketball Encyclopedia*. Toronto, ON: Sport Media, 2003.

Sugar, Bert Randolph. *The 100 Greatest Athletes of All Time*. New York: Citadel Press, 1995.

Thorn, John, and Pete Palmer, eds., with Michael Gershman. *Total Baseball*. New York: HarperCollins, 1993.

Williams, Ted, with Jim Prime. *Ted Williams' Hit List*. Indianapolis, IN: Masters Press, 1996.

Videos

Champions—The NBA's Greatest Teams. CBS/FOX, 1992.
Greatest Ever: NFL Dream Team. Polygram Video, 1996.
The Life and Times of Hank Greenberg. Twentieth Century Fox, 2001.
New York Yankees: The Movie. Magic Video, 1987.
New York's Game: History of the Knicks. CBS/FOX, 1989.
Pinstripe Power: The Story of the 1961 New York Yankees. New York: Major League Baseball, 1987.
Roger Maris: Reluctant Hero. ESPN, 1998.
The Sporting News' 100 Greatest Baseball Players. National Broadcasting, 1999.
Sports Century: Fifty Greatest Athletes—Bill Russell. ESPN, 1999.
Sports Century: Fifty Greatest Athletes—Johnny Unitas. ESPN, 1999.
Sports Century: Fifty Greatest Athletes—Lawrence Taylor. ESPN, 1999.
Sports Century: Fifty Greatest Athletes—Oscar Robertson. ESPN, 1999.
Sports Century: Fifty Greatest Athletes—Sandy Koufax. ESPN, 1999.
Sports Century: Fifty Greatest Athletes—Ted Williams. ESPN, 1999.
Sports Century: Fifty Greatest Athletes—Ty Cobb. ESPN, 1999.
Sports Century: Fifty Greatest Athletes—Willie Mays. ESPN, 1999.
Sports Century—Elgin Baylor. ESPN, 2000.
Sports Century—Jerry West. ESPN, 2000.
Sports Century—Roberto Clemente. ESPN, 2003.

Internet Websites

"The Ballplayers," at BaseballLibrary.com, http://www.baseballlibrary.com/baseball-library/ballplayers.
"Biographies," at Hickoksports.com, http://www.hickoksports.com/hickoksports/biograph.
"Greatest Hockey Legends," at GreatestHockeyLegends.com, http://www.greatesthockeylegends.com.
"Hall of Famers," at Hoophall.com, http://www.hoophall.com/hoophall/hall of famers.
"Hall of Famers," at Profootballhof.com, http://www.profootballhof.com/hof/member.
"Historical Stats," at MLB.com, http://www.mlb.com/stats_historical/individual_stats_player.
"History," at BaseballHallofFame.org, http://www.baseballhalloffame.org/about/history.
"The Players," at Baseball-Almanac.com, http://www.baseball-almanac.com/players.
"The Players," at Baseballink.com, http://www.baseballink.com/baseballink/players.
"The Players," at Baseball-Reference.com, http://www.baseball-reference.com/players.

"The Players," at Basketball-Almanac.com, http://www.basketball-almanac.com/players.

"The Players," at Basketballreference.com, http://www.basketballreference.com/basketballreference/players.

"The Players," at Hockey-Almanac.com, http://www.hockey-almanac.com/players.

"The Players," at Hockeyreference.com, http://www.hockey-reference.com/players.

"The Players," at NBA.com, http://www.nba.com/history/players.

"The Players," at Profootballreference.com, http://www.pro-football-reference.com/players.

"The Players," at Wikipedia.org, http://en.wikipedia.org/wki.

Index

About the Author

Robert W. Cohen is a sports historian who grew up in New York City during the 1960s and 1970s rooting for the Yankees, Giants, Knicks, and Rangers. The author of several historical sports books, including *The 50 Greatest Players in New York Yankees History* (2012), *The 50 Greatest Players in St. Louis Cardinals History* (2013), *Pro Basketball's All-Time All-Stars: Across the Eras* (2013), and *The 50 Greatest Players in New York Giants Football History* (2014). Cohen has appeared on numerous sports talk radio programs around the nation to discuss his previously published works. He has also produced a considerable amount of content for an internet website called TheBaseballPage.com. Originally from the Bronx, New York, Cohen now lives in northern New Jersey with his wife, Li, and daughter, Katie.